Travelling the T

Artist: **Charles Church** **AFTER THE RACE** *Courtesy of:* **The Artist**

KENSINGTON WEST PRODUCTIONS

HEXHAM ENGLAND

1

Kensington West Productions Ltd,
5 Cattle Market, Hexham,
Northumberland NE46 1NJ
Tel: (01434) 609933 Fax: (01434) 600066
e-mail: kensingtonwest@btconnect.com

Editor
Julian West

British Racecourse & Around the World Editor
Barry Roxburgh

Design & Production
Diane Ridley

Sub Editors
Peter Killick
Tanya Marshall

Origination & Print
Pre Press, Hong Kong

Front cover
Artist: Graham Isom WINDSOR
Courtesy of: Rosenstiel's

Acknowledgements

The twentieth edition of Travelling the Turf has been as ever a great pleasure to prepare. We are grateful to many people in this compilation particularly to those readers who have written in with their favourite pubs, hotels and general comments. Your time and trouble is much appreciated. As ever we are extremely grateful to many people: Racecourse managers who have supplied us with our information, Tamarisk Doyle, her team at Horse Racing Ireland, not to mention those who work to promote racing furlongs further away. Fine art has always played a key role in our publication and we have introduced a rare collection of old and new work this year. My thanks go to the numerous artists and galleries who have helped us collate this collection. My particular thanks go to David Roe and his colleagues at Rosenstiel's who have for twenty years been invaluable supporters of Travelling the Turf. This company has a great eye for catching tremendous euestiran art, and in this edition the work of Graham Isom is particularly note worthy. In addition we are grateful to the hoteliers who have helped us with the local favourites section. Special thanks also to John Gosden for writing the foreword. He is a highly regarded figure and we wish him well in the following season.

Finally, I would like to thank my friends and family who have supported Travelling the Turf over the years without whose support this twentieth edition would not have been published.

Special Tribute: My grateful thanks to all who have helped me but particularly Graham Rock who was so sadly taken from us way before time. He picked me up when I was down–critical in life just as in racing.

For Mowel, Rory, Izzy, Millie and Honor.

*Artist: **Katy Sodeau** EARLY MORNING NEWMARKET*
*Courtesy of: **The Artist***

Foreword

The list of those who have provided the Foreword for each edition of Travelling the Turf over the past twenty years reads like a veritable Who's Who of Racing. The names of Piggott, Dettori, O'Neill, Francome, McCoy, Scott, O'Sullevan and Stoute, of Lords Wakeham and Zetland, of Saville and Sangster provide an A to Z of the racing world.

In the case of jockeys and trainers, the memory of famous victories keeps their names as resonant today as when they were in their prime. Others, often confined to racing's backroom of administration, will see their legacy carried on through an industry that is as sure-footed for future success as it can be.

Sadly some, like Robert Sangster, whose colours, along with Lord Howard de Walden and Sheikh Mohammed, adorned our first cover, are no longer with us. Yet their spirit will live on in racing for many years to come through the horses they and others have bred.

This year we returned to the famous training establishment at Manton to ask its present master for a few words as Foreword to the 20th Edition. His training career has spanned the continents and continues to flourish in the grand tradition of Flat racing…

Travelling the Turf is an informative and well-researched publication. It celebrates the internationalisation of racing and the beauty and excitement of so many racecourses.

Its detailed analysis of the regions and the particular individual characteristics of the racecourses is second to none. It is only by reading through the book that one realises the uniqueness of British racecourses, and the enjoyment that can be gained from staying in the area for any of the meetings.

John H M Gosden
Manton

Contents

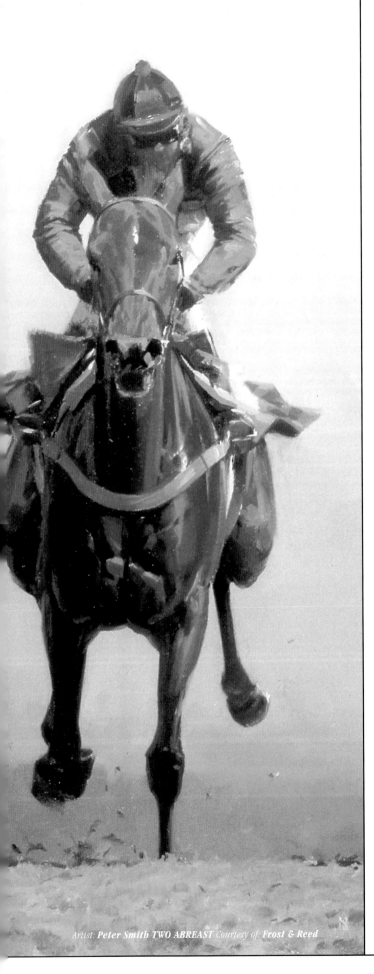

Artist: Peter Smith TWO ABREAST Courtesy of Frost & Reed

Contents

NATIONWIDE RACING HOSPITALITY

"... YOUR ATTENTION TO DETAIL HELPED EVERYTHING
RUN LIKE CLOCKWORK..." - IPC EQUESTRIAN GROUP

GLASS-FRONTED BOXES OR
BALCONIED BOXES ENSURE
UNRIVALLED VIEWS OF
THE ACTION

WHETHER YOU REQUIRE A CORPORATE SUITE TO ENTERTAIN CLIENTS AND COLLEAGUES, OR WISH TO ARRANGE THAT SPECIAL DAY FOR FRIENDS AND FAMILY, ARENA EVENTS OFFERS AN UNBEATABLE PORTFOLIO OF HOSPITALITY PACKAGES AT RACECOURSES THROUGHOUT THE UK.

Arena Events can provide hospitality facilities at nearly every race meeting in the calendar. Our Arena Scene viewing boxes are positioned in prime locations at most of the major race meetings, whilst we source the best possible on-site facilities at the few "Classics" where we do not have our unique viewing structures.

Official hospitality appointments include:

Cheltenham National Hunt Festival since 1985
Aintree Grand National Festival since 1986
Newbury Racecourse since 2003

Creating Spectacular Events

HOSPITALITY FACILITIES AT MOST MAJOR RACE MEETINGS, FROM THE GRAND NATIONAL TO CHELTENHAM, ROYAL ASCOT TO GLORIOUS GOODWOOD

"... YOUR STAFF WERE VERY HELPFUL AND NOTHING WAS TOO MUCH TROUBLE..." - TSL ENGINEERING

YOUR ONE STOP SHOP FOR QUALITY HOSPITALITY AT RACECOURSES NATIONWIDE

We will tailor a day to meet your needs. Services include:

- Venue selection service both in the UK and abroad
- Package choice to suit your budget and audience
- Tipsters to guide guests through the racecard and form
- Overnight accommodation & travel management
- Event management throughout for a trouble free day

arena EVENTS

08707 20 30 10   www.arenaevents.com   info@arenaevents.com

*E*ndless debates will always take place as to whether the horses and jockeys (and even trainers!) are as good today as they were 20 years ago. It is always tempting to downgrade the current crop in favour of misty eyed memories of past heroes of the turf and the sound of the immortal voice of Sir Peter O'Sullevan calling home the Derby or Grand National winner does little to dispel this. We'll leave this debate for others to hash out in their favourite watering holes.

The one thing that we can safely say is that the racecourses of today have improved out of all recognition compared with the often sorry state in which they were found when Travelling the Turf published its first edition. Indifferent ownership and part time management, lack of investment, general neglect and, it has to be said, a near contempt for the paying customer had all conspired over the previous decades to do everything to discourage people from going racing. At the bottom end of the punter pecking order facilities had little changed from your granny's day, while corporate money bought itself some comfort in private boxes at the top end of the scale. While not trying to pat the old back too hard, I would like to think that Travelling the Turf has done more than its bit to encourage, cajole and otherwise convince racecourses that it was in their own best interests, and for the sport in general, that people could go racing in some comfort, find shelter when they needed it and have some decent food and drink at the same time. True there is still some way to go to achieve this basic standard at a few courses, but for the vast majority, facilities have improved out of all recognition during the last two decades.

Competition with other sports for the public's pounds has of course driven this forward as well. But today, there also seems to be a new attitude to running racecourses that puts the emphasis on a welcoming atmosphere and a commitment to deliver on promises that are made in glossy brochures. Keeping long time customers happy and attracting new audiences who have never gone racing before seems to the order of the day, not the exception. Without question Ascot sets a high standard here – mind you it wasn't always like that. Our first correspondence basically told us to sod off! Mind you, at least they wrote back. Today there's a positive, highly regarded team – Douglas Erskine-Crum should take much of the plaudits for this.

Of course any investment in comfort and facilities costs money and we can't blame a racecourse for trying to recoup some of it by raising admission charges. The fact is that most people, customers, punters or whatever they are called, don't mind paying more money if they are more or less guaranteed a good time. Racing luck and the weather notwithstanding. But is the racing product still value for money? Twenty years ago a mid-week fixture at Haydock Park cost £7.50, £5 and £2 to get into the County Stand, Tatts and the Newton Enclosure respectively. Bank Holidays and weekends were a few pence to a couple of pounds more. In 2005 you will have to pay £32 to get into the Premier Enclosure (rising to £40 on 'Premium Days'), £19 for the County Enclosure, £12 for Tatts and £6 for the Newton Enclosure. Haydock is probably a bit unusual as it has four different levels of admission, and the facilities that go with them, while the current trend seems to be reducing the number of enclosures. Still, at the top end of the scale that's quite a hike, while at the bottom level, it still seems pretty cheap. A family can still have a day out at the races for a tenner and some change: those who might otherwise have a round of golf or go to a football match probably don't balk

at paying the price at the top end of the scale. If you plan a bit ahead and claim some of the discounts that are on offer for parties and groups, or join as an annual member there are bargains to be had. One of the great things about racing is that it's a very sociable sport and that's something that many other sports lack. There definitely seems to be a price for everyone at a course like Haydock and most others, and if attendances are anything to go by, Haydock doesn't seem to have any problems pulling in the punters.

Put in the perspective of international racing though and you soon realise that courses in Britain and Ireland are a bit of an exception in charging as much as they do. Go to Longchamp for the Arc weekend and you find you will only have to pay about £7 to get in the one large enclosure that fits all but the horse's owners, trainers and their connections. Go to many North American tracks and the basic admission is free. Some of these places are palaces in terms of their facilities, but if you dig a little deeper you will find that either the costs are paid for by other activities, such as endless rows of slot machines, or the government props them up from going bankrupt by giving them a cut of the relatively larger amount of money that is bet off course. Go to Longchamp and you will hardly find any French people. They don't seem to want to go racing, no matter how cheap it is to get in, so there isn't really any value in that.

Back in old Blighty, while some may lament the increasing demise of the old pecking order of Members, Tattersalls, Silver Ring and the Course, the very names conjuring up a decreasing level of comfort and privilege, there can be little doubt that the reorganisation of enclosures and simplifying of their names can only be a good thing in attracting new racegoers. We would like to point out that giving an enclosure a new name is one thing, but actually making the facilities better is far more important no matter what label is put on it. Renaming the Members' the 'Premier Enclosure' might also lead some people to think that a game with a round ball might be taking place instead of a contest between jockeys and horses! Let's hope that this is not just a marketing ploy or an excuse to jack up the prices of badges but a real attempt to deliver on the promise of a truly excellent facility.

As the immortal bard said, many years before racing became a sport for the masses, "What's in a name! A rose by any other name might smell as sweet." Far more important than renaming an enclosure, has been making racecourses the more welcoming and pleasant places they are today than they were 20 years ago. Simple as it might seem, this has not been an easy, or even straightforward task.

First of all you had to have many people on all kinds of levels to agree that this was both desirable and necessary. Given the opportunity by the powers that be to stage racing on a Sunday when most people, and especially families, could go, many racecourses have responded enthusiastically and now produce a great day out at a reasonable cost. Those that have embraced Sunday racing and put on special entertainments for children, as well as good facilities for their parents, have been rewarded in spades with record attendances. It's hard to believe that many people thought this was not a very good idea just a few years ago, and there are probably a few out there who still don't. But the reality is, as more and more of racing's main events are staged on weekends, not only will the quality of Sunday racing improve, but so will the audiences which it attracts. If sympathy is due, it is for the stable staff and while this is not exactly Travelling The Turf's main subject, no industry that neglects its staff will prosper. I hear through people who know more about this area, that conditions are much improved – the expression 'a business is only as good as its people' is surely as apt of racing as any.

Another interesting, relatively recent development that is no doubt related to this is the fact that there are now a lot more women in senior positions, if not actually running racecourses than ever before. Where once the fairer sex were seemingly confined to the hospitality side of things, now they are Managing Directors, Clerks of the Course and Raceday Managers. As well as being as competent as their male counterparts in all of these roles, there is no doubt that many women bring a bit extra to the job in understanding the needs of racing's new audiences in families, younger people and well, other women. Girls on top, great!

There is no doubt that racing depends on sponsorship these days - to offer the stakes large enough to attract the top horses. This is as true of flat racing as it is of the jumps. Happily today there are few major races (and even most minor ones) that don't attract a sponsor and courses work hard to make sure that they are well taken care of and come back year on year. Sponsorship sometimes produces some race names that are as long as an undergraduate essay, but that's a small price to pay for some valued financial support. With major players and major events, media exposure is a must and there must be some concern in sponsorship circles if persistent rumours of racing being dropped by its major terrestrial commercial carrier, Channel 4, prove unfortunately true. We hope and trust not, but no one should be complacent and believe that major sponsors will carry on if most racing exposure on television is limited to the die-hards who are committed enough to pay for a subscription service on some obscure digital service. Indeed credit must go to all at Channel 4 for their outstanding coverage of an increasing number of race meetings and courses. The Beeb can still produce the goods for some of the meetings they cover and also have a winning package when they choose, but the contribution Channel 4 has made to the whole industry should not be underestimated.

However, contrary to this, a worrying trend seems to be the domination of racing sponsorship by the betting industry. The tote, bookmakers and betting exchanges seem to be falling all over each other to sponsor anything and everything that involves four legs. Still, sponsorship has always followed the money and this is not unhealthy in itself. But as they say, The Lord giveth and taketh away and racing might just be wise if it heeded the advice not to put all its apples in the same basket. Surely a good mix of sponsorship, which doesn't leave racing vulnerable to the whims of one industry or the fickle dictats of government policy, would be a more ideal situation. It was with this in mind that we welcomed the announcement by the good people of Aintree that the Grand National is to be run under the John Smith's banner for at least the next three years. This is one of the oldest names in racing sponsorship, going way back to 1959 when its Magnet Ale became the first commercial sponsor in flat racing. Today the John Smith's name is carried on at York in one of the season's great handicaps, at Newcastle for the Northumberland Plate, as well as at Uttoxeter and Newbury. It's a good mix of flat and jumps races and gives the brewer year-round exposure. Actually, the beer is pretty good too, so even when you blow your wad on any one of these races, you can still drown your sorrows with their product. Sounds like a pretty good fit to us!

However, it would be wrong not to mention Ivan Straker and Seagram who helped to save the National when it hit a fence and looked out of the running – the sponsorship as it then metamorphosed into the Martel Grand National was one of the great sporting / commercial partnerships of a generation.

Speaking of partnerships, a fairly crucial word in this wonderfully hit and miss sport – we owe huge thanks to the many racecourse personnel who have assisted us in our quest to find better racing. We've received some wonderful support from many of the racecourses but we'd also like to thank the many people who have sent in suggestions about how the book can be improved. The twentieth issue has been entirely re-edited but many of these ideas have not as yet been introduced – this will happen in the 21st edition when we hope to extend the information that the racegoer might find to be of interest.

When I first came up with the idea for Travelling The Turf, I was on a beach having just made a mess of my law degree. I came up with a plan – great pubs and hotels near racecourses, racing days out, racing weekends – let's produce a book - it sounded fun. Well it has been great fun which is a fair reflection on many days travelling the turf, watching and enjoying the sport of horseracing which is as colourful and exciting as any.

Artist: **Terence Gilbert EPSOM DERBY** _Courtesy of:_ **The Artist**

20 Years of Excellence in National Hunt Racing

*T*here are moments and places in racing that never fail to get the pulse beating faster. Win or lose, you are glad to say you went, saw and felt something that transcends the ordinary day in, day out world. Year after year, Cheltenham provides a gilded frame to these moments in life, a golden place for the ultimate challenge of jockey and horse over those forbidding and often frightening obstacles.

During a National Hunt season that now never seems to end, ask any jockey, owner, trainer, bookmaker, punter or pundit what they are looking forward to next and the universal refrain will ring around one place and one place alone: Cheltenham. The alpha and omega of jump racing, everything seems to revolve around this shrine in the Cotswolds and the eternal spring that is its annual Festival.

This feeling and sense of place cannot be artificially contrived by some bright marketing department nor possibly replicated elsewhere. Constant nurturing, years of dedication, millions of pounds of investment have kept it thriving, refreshed it, improved it and made it what it is today.

Cheltenham has succeeded perhaps more than any other racecourse in Britain, or even the world, during the past 20 years because of a commitment to the longer term and a patience that realises that some things take time to bring about correctly. As a racecourse it typifies the essence of what national hunt racing is all about. No precocious, untried two year olds here, but solid, stoutly bred animals that come back year after year to win the admiration of their fans and friends.

Cheltenham's position of supremacy has literally been built from the ground up. A few years ago we asked Managing Director Edward Gillespie if he could pinpoint one feature that was most important in building and maintaining the course's success. He highlighted the improvements that had been made to ensure the ground was the best it could be for winter jump racing. By making sure this was right, he could almost guarantee that trainers would send their best horses to race there. With this in place, and a lot of work to make certain the surroundings were as comfortable as possible, the sponsors and fans were sure to follow.

Over the past few years Cheltenham has managed to extend the popularity of the spring Festival meeting to its other fixtures as well and while the crowds are good, there is not the crush of the March meeting and the facilities can be more readily enjoyed. The Open Meeting in November has already taken on a life of its own with packed stands and betting ring now a common sight. Cheltenham is a complete racecourse in virtually every aspect of its operations. For the racegoer there is something to do before, during and after racing as with no other course. As most meetings are spread over more than one day, a visit to Cheltenham becomes a real break away from the normal routine and a chance to get in some serious punting, not to mention the attendant hospitality. We know of no other course where you can take a steam train to the venue, listen to news and commentaries on Cheltenham's own Festival radio, take a tour of the facilities, hear the jockeys and trainers describe their horse's prospects around the parade ring, go shopping on a vast high street of racing paraphernalia, see a parade of local hounds or listen to a Dixieland jazz band or dance an Irish jig. Get there when the gates open at 10:30, stay all day and then relive the experience over a pint in a local pub. Yes, Cheltenham seems to begin where other courses leave off.

Typical of Cheltenham's approach to things is the new Centaur complex. Not only does it provide a sweeping new entrance with a Hall of Fame that suitably honours jumping greats but it provides a greatly needed indoor space when the Cotswold spring fails to arrive on time. You can have a bet, take in some food and drink, watch the racing on a giant screen and listen to some entertainment–all without risking the unkindness of the elements outside.

With its fantastic natural setting and great views of the finest course for jump racing in the world, Cheltenham has much to

Artist: **Graham Isom** *BEST MATE Courtesy of:* **Rosenstiel's**

Artist: **Neil Cawthorne GOLD CUP MORNING** *Courtesy of:* **The Artist**

recommend it even without the man-made improvements. That they work so well and have not dominated the countryside feel and atmosphere is admirable. This is, after all, still a country course that celebrates the horse. The pre-parade ring, stable area and staff accommodation, weighing room and other recently upgraded facilities all attest to this.

Some may have been surprised when Cheltenham put in a bid to host Royal Ascot when that course closed for renovations. Few national hunt courses would have displayed the ambition to hold what is one of the premier flat occasions of the calendar. That Cheltenham did not get it is perhaps immaterial. It tried and had

the ambition to do it. Perhaps equally significant is the move this year to a four day Festival. This will not be some watered down product, but, with some new races such as a two and a half mile championship, the logical extension of something that even more people will be able to enjoy.

No other racecourse but Cheltenham has consistently topped our league tables as often and thoroughly deserved to be awarded our accolade of 15 Years of Excellence in 2000.

Well done Cheltenham and congratulations on being our National Hunt Racecourse of the Past 20 years.

Artist: **Elizabeth Sharp A QUICK REMINDER** *Courtesy of:* **The Artist**

Artist: **Roy Miller SIX OF THE BEST** *Courtesy of:* **The Artist**

20 Years of Excellence in Flat Racing

Perhaps fittingly as it sat happily beside the home of one of the best known names in British confectionery for so many years, York Racecourse is a veritable chocolate box of delights. Although some might squabble over what are truly the best bits to sample, the truth is that there is something for everyone at the Knavesmire.

The Terry's factory next door may now be closed, but racing at York thrives. While the many physical improvements and innovations have gone on over the years, the course has also managed to maintain its unique atmosphere. Anyone who had not been over the intervening years might well marvel at the size and scale of the new stands but they would surely feel right at home and welcome as well. This has not been an easy achievement but the work of many skilful hands and minds, from John Smith, who ran the course for many of the last twenty years, to the present incumbent Chief Executive William Derby, and Lord Halifax who heads up the York Race Committee.

There is something about York that typifies Northern racing. The main meetings might be big, dress-up-in-your-best-gear affairs, yet the atmosphere is relaxed. There is lots of hustle and bustle but also time to sit back and enjoy the scenery, the gleam of a horse's coat in the parade ring, or just people watching and enjoying a leisurely drink in the champagne bar.

While York might exemplify the spirit of flat racing in the North of England, there is nothing provincial about its facilities or hospitality. To take just one example, a bottle of good Champagne can be hard to find at a reasonable price at any restaurant, never mind on a racecourse. Yet York has consistently offered a fine product of that region of France for many years and at a price that has hardly changed over that time. The food is also of a very high quality, whether you are satisfied with a simple basket of fish and chips, an ice cream or a full course lunch in one of the many restaurants. No course should ignore the importance of this area in its operations and York puts in far more attention to quality and service than perhaps any other course.

Artist: **Jacqueline Stanhope YORK** *Courtesy of:* **The Artist**

York has accomplished one difficult feat very well over the past twenty years and that is to blend the new with the old, to update and expand the facilities while not destroying the atmosphere and history that has made the course what it is in the first place.

We well might feel nostalgia for the old winner's enclosure in front of the weighing in room but the new one at the end of the parade ring is a significant improvement and much safer for the spectators, jockeys and horses. Not many courses would knock down a large concrete gallery just a few years after it was erected, but York saw this did little to improve anyone's enjoyment of the facilities or the scenery and rightly pulled it down. On a racecourse as in any business, to admit your mistakes and do something about it is commendable and nothing but positive.

Three new massive stands have been built in the last twenty years at York. They dominate its imposing skyline and yet tucked away between them is the old County stand. It's a fine place of calm and cool, where even the Gents loos sparkle and standards of comfort go back to a bygone era. It has all the history of the Knavesmire built into its walls, something that you can never replace instantly with glass and steel. From its top balcony, with its simple wooden floor and few bits and pieces of seating, you can get what is probably one of the finest views of racing on the planet. Yet right next door, for those who like modern comfort, no other stand in racing can probably match the combined facilities of the new £20 million Ebor Stand and its neighbouring Knavesmire Stand.

The ultimate accolade for many would be if someone asked to have their party at your house. This is exactly what has happened to York as the august officials at Ascot come this year to hold the ultimate garden party in horse racing and possibly in any sphere, the Royal Meeting in June. We are sure they will not be disappointed. While it is true that Ascot itself will be running the show, the York management has provided a magnificent frame in which to place the painting.

The sight of the Royal procession coming down the Knavesmire each day of the meeting will no doubt be provide a memorable moment for the thousands in the stands as well as those who get into the Ascot style with their own picnic in the carparks.

As well as putting York in the world racing spotlight for a year, the Royal Ascot meeting will provide a lasting legacy on the racecourse itself with the building of the course extension to complete the circuit of the main track. This will open up many more possibilities for future racing by extending the range of racing distances on offer. The Group races of the Royal meeting will be just a taste of things to come.

York Racecourse is one of the best in the world of flat racing and we are pleased to have the honour of naming it for our 20 Years of Excellence in Flat Racing award.

Artist: **Neil Cawthorne JOCKEYS GET MOUNTED** *Courtesy of:* **The Artist**

tight track and the Open Course in the centre offers intimate viewing of the action. Innovative developments maximise the available space, the buzz of the crowds make for an unbeatable atmosphere and the location means the racecourse is truly a community track. Racing has taken place at Chester's beloved Roodee since Roman times and a few millennia later the course is still a humming magnet for racing fans from the North West of England and beyond.

At the helm today is Chief Executive Richard Thomas who came to Chester five years ago after a more than successful stint at not-too-far away to Haydock Park where he also won our annual award, not once but twice! He is someone who quite obviously knows his local market and what appeals to the North West audience.

"People in the region place a high value on sports and leisure pursuits. You only have to look at the following inspired by football clubs and the crowds at live sporting events to see that," he points out. "Equally, people have high expectations. You have to give them a very good quality "cxpcricncc" and once they have adopted the event / sport as their own, they will keep coming back."

Chester hosts a mere dozen meetings each year, a seriously abbreviated total compared with many other courses. Still, virtually every one has become a date in the diary, an annual fixture, for one or more groups of racing fans. For them it is an event planned weeks, or even months, in advance.

"We offer something that will appeal to different types of racegoers," says Richard. "Last year our Family Funday in July attracted a crowd of more than 46,000 people. Our Ladies' Evening in June puts the spotlight on fashion and groups of women come to enjoy a night out. Roman Day celebrates the city's Roman heritage, whilst serious punters come to the

*C*hester is no stranger to Travelling the Turf's Racecourse of the Year award, having won the accolade once before in 1994. If this gem on the Dee deserved the award then, it more than deserves a repeat performance this year. Although it is probably best known for its famous early May fixture–a time of spring anticipation, of hope and high expectations–Chester has now spread its success throughout the season, with meeting after meeting packed with crowds averaging 21,000 people.

This does not happen by chance. First impressions are that the course is challenged by the limited room for expansion and its location - situated in the centre of a city with its attendant urban diversions and congestion; the track itself - a flat oval where neither jockey nor horse can take a necessary breather. Clearly, anyone planning a new racecourse here would shudder at the prospect. However, key to Chester's success has been turning these characteristics to its advantage. The course stands, backed up against the City walls, allow a spectacular panorama of the

Saturday fixtures and the corporate market enjoy days off during the week. For each group of people, Chester Racecourse is the place to be and to be seen. Each meeting becomes a major social event that takes place right on the City's doorstep."

Last year the three-day May Festival was moved from a Tuesday to Thursday to a new Wednesday to Friday slot and was extremely successful. High profile television coverage broadcasts the quality of the racing on offer: the MBNA Europe Bank Chester Vase, totesport Chester Cup, and the BETDAQ Ormonde Stakes. Chester now boasts nine Pattern and Listed races, including a new Group 3 race this year in the Huxley Stakes, one of only two new pattern races granted in Europe, and total prize money of £1.35 million during its season.

Successfully accommodating its legions of fans is no mean feat at a course where space is as hard to come by as picking the winner of the Chester Cup.

"We try to have something new, refurbished or updated just about every time someone comes here," says Richard. "Over the last few years we have invested over £3 million on improvements, which has enabled us to refurbish the entire County Stand including the introduction of air conditioning as well as improving and developing the Paddock and hospitality areas. Some are large projects like building a tunnel to the Parade Ring in the centre, but a lot are just smaller, attention to detail things."

In 2005, £1million is being spent on making the County and Tattersalls Stands more spacious with the addition of covered, balconied areas at the back of both the stands. New toilets will also grace the Dee Stand.

But the improvements are not only for the punters, as a new stable block will be built on course to accommodate the main attraction - the horses. Although the quaint spectacle of horses being led to each race through the city streets will come to an end by 2006, the new facility will be much more user friendly to the sometimes fractious thoroughbreds concerned, not to mention their, owners, trainers and handlers!

Things have already improved considerably for those whose job it is to look after the horses. "We have a new 97 bedroom hotel on site, The Express by Holiday Inn," says Richard, "and that is where we put up the stable staff. It's is a far cry from the old dormitory hostel that we used to have and shows how highly we appreciate the involvement of those at the grass roots end of racing."

Typically for ventures associated with Chester, the hotel ran at 70 per cent occupancy during its first year of opening and presumably will be a sell out in years to come.

In another innovative move the course has entered into partnership with a firm of first class caterers, Heathcotes Outside, who will be providing the food and drink this year. Themed champagne bars, seafood, strawberries and cream and Pimms should keep the visitors more than satisfied in the various restaurants, boxes, suites, marquees and chalets available.

Richard Thomas is justly proud of the accomplishments of the course during the past few years and rightly points to his staff who have helped him achieve what has been some astounding success.

Just when you think they might be able to put their feet up a bit and rest on their laurels during the closed winter season, the stark fact looms large that employees at Chester link up with their colleagues at Bangor-on-Dee Racecourse! Although only 25 minutes apart, Chester and Bangor couldn't be much more dissimilar.

"Running Bangor is also an exciting challenge," says Richard. "In a way we have the best of both worlds - great jump racing in the country and superb flat racing in the middle of the city. All our management resources are shared by both courses and we are able to generate a lot of positive benefits for sponsors and customers between what couldn't be two more contrasting places in the racing world."

Far from the tight confines of city bound Chester, perhaps this is where Richard Thomas has finally achieved the one thing high up on his eternal wish list - more space!

Racing Calendar

JANUARY 2005

Date	Racecourse	Race Name
1 Jan	Cheltenham	"Cantor Sport "Dipper" Novice"
	Cheltenham	Junior Standard Open
8 Jan	Sandown Park	Sandown Ladbroke Hurdle Hurdle
	Sandown Park	Gerrard Wealth Management Tolworth Novice Hurdle
15 Jan	Kempton Park	Tote Scoop6 Lanzarote Handicap Hurdle
	Warwick	Leamington Novice Hurdle
	Warwick	Tote Classic Gold Cup Handicap
22 Jan	Ascot (tbc)	Victor Chandler (Handicap)
	Ascot (tbc)	Victor Chandler Lightning Novice
	Haydock Park	Bet Direct Peter Marsh (Limited Handicap)
	Haydock Park	Red Square Reloaded Champion Trial Hurdle
	Haydock Park	Premier Hurdle
29 Jan	Cheltenham	Byrne Bros Cleeve Hurdle
	Cheltenham	Pillar Property
	Cheltenham	Wragge & Co Finesse Juvenile Novice Hurdle
	Cheltenham	Ladbroke Trophy (Handicap)
	Cheltenham	Listed Novice Hurdle
	Doncaster	River Don Novice Hurdle
	Doncaster	Skybet Handicap

Artist: **Roy Miller THE SNOW TUNNEL** *Courtesy of:* **The Artist**

JANUARY

		North	Midlands	South		
1	Saturday	Catterick Bridge	Cheltenham	Fontwell Park	Saturday	1
			SOUTHWELL (AWT)			
2	Sunday		SOUTHWELL (AWT)	Plumpton	Sunday	2
3	Monday	Wetherby	SOUTHWELL (AWT)	Exeter	Monday	3
	(Bank Holiday)			Folkestone	(Bank Holiday)	
4	Tuesday	Ayr	WOLVERHAMPTON (AWT)	LINGFIELD PARK (AWT)	Tuesday	4
5	Wednesday		Hereford	LINGFIELD PARK (AWT)	Wednesday	5
			SOUTHWELL (AWT)			
6	Thursday		Ludlow	Wincanton	Thursday	6
			WOLVERHAMPTON (AWT)			
7	Friday	Musselburgh	Towcester		Friday	7
			WOLVERHAMPTON (AWT)			
8	Saturday	Haydock Park	Uttoxeter	LINGFIELD PARK (AWT)	Saturday	8
				Sandown Park		
10	Monday	Newcastle	WOLVERHAMPTON (AWT)	Taunton	Monday	10
11	Tuesday	Sedgefield	Leicester		Tuesday	11
			SOUTHWELL (AWT)			
12	Wednesday		WOLVERHAMPTON (AWT)	LINGFIELD PARK (AWT)	Wednesday	12
				Newbury		
13	Thursday	Catterick Bridge	SOUTHWELL (AWT)	LINGFIELD PARK (AWT)	Thursday	13
14	Friday	Kelso	Huntingdon		Friday	14
			WOLVERHAMPTON (AWT)			
15	Saturday	Wetherby	Warwick	Kempton Park	Saturday	15
				LINGFIELD PARK (AWT)		
17	Monday	Doncaster	WOLVERHAMPTON (AWT)	Plumpton	Monday	17
18	Tuesday		SOUTHWELL (AWT)	Folkestone	Tuesday	18
			Towcester			
19	Wednesday	Newcastle	Fakenham	LINGFIELD PARK (AWT)	Wednesday	19
20	Thursday		Ludlow	Taunton	Thursday	20
			SOUTHWELL (AWT)			
21	Friday	Musselburgh	WOLVERHAMPTON (AWT)	Chepstow	Friday	21
22	Saturday	Catterick Bridge		Ascot (venue to be confirmed)	Saturday	22
		Haydock Park		LINGFIELD PARK (AWT)		
				Wincanton		
24	Monday		Southwell	Fontwell Park	Monday	24
			WOLVERHAMPTON (AWT)			
25	Tuesday	Sedgefield	Leicester		Tuesday	25
			SOUTHWELL (AWT)			
26	Wednesday	Wetherby	Huntingdon	LINGFIELD PARK (AWT)	Wednesday	26
27	Thursday		SOUTHWELL (AWT)	Plumpton	Thursday	27
			Warwick			
28	Friday	Doncaster	WOLVERHAMPTON (AWT)	Folkestone	Friday	28
29	Saturday	Ayr	Cheltenham	LINGFIELD PARK (AWT)	Saturday	29
		Doncaster				
31	Monday		WOLVERHAMPTON (AWT)	Exeter	Monday	31
				Kempton Park		

CAPITALS: Flat racing Lower Case: National Hunt AWT: (All weather track) †: Evening Meeting

FEBRUARY 2005

Date	Racecourse	Race Name
5 Feb	Sandown Park	Scilly Isles Novice
	Sandown Park	Tote Scoop6 Sandown (Handicap) Hurdle
	Sandown Park	Agfa Diamond (Handicap)
	Wetherby	Gerrard Wealth Management Rossington Main Novice Hurdle
	Wetherby	Towton Novice
12 Feb	Warwick	Michael Page International Kingmaker Novice
	Newbury	Sodexho Prestige Game Spirit
	Newbury	AON
	Newbury	AON Standard Open
	Newbury	Tote Gold Trophy (Handicap) Hurdle
19 Feb	Ascot (Lingfield)	Ritz Club Ascot
	Ascot (Lingfield)	Amlin Reynoldstown Novice
	Haydock Park	De Vere Prestige Novice Hurdle
	Haydock Park	Haydock Park Gold Cup (Handicap)
	Uttoxeter	Singer & Friedlander National Trial (Handicap)
	Wincanton	Axminster Kingwell Hurdle
	Wincanton	Country Gentleman's Association
20 Feb	Fontwell Park	Collins Stewart National Spirit Hurdle
25 Feb	Kempton Park	Rendlesham Hurdle
	Kempton Park	Gerrard Wealth Management Dovecote Novice Hurdle
	Warwick	Michael Page International Standard Open
26 Feb	Kempton Park	Pendil Novice
	Kempton Park	Adonis Juvenile Novice Hurdle
	Kempton Park	Racing Post (Handicap)
	Lingfield Park	Bet Direct from Littlewoods Winter Derby Trial
	Newcastle	Tote Northern National (Handicap)

Artist: **Neil Cawthorne WINTER GALLOPS** *Courtesy of:* **The Artist**

FEBRUARY

		North	Midlands	South		
1	Tuesday		SOUTHWELL (AWT)	LINGFIELD PARK (AWT) Taunton	Tuesday	1
2	Wednesday	Newcastle	Leicester	LINGFIELD PARK (AWT)	Wednesday	2
3	Thursday	Kelso	SOUTHWELL (AWT) Towcester		Thursday	3
4	Friday	Catterick Bridge	WOLVERHAMPTON (AWT)	Fontwell Park	Friday	4
5	Saturday	Wetherby		Chepstow LINGFIELD PARK (AWT) Sandown Park	Saturday	5
6	Sunday	Musselburgh	Hereford SOUTHWELL (AWT)		Sunday	6
7	Monday	Sedgefield	SOUTHWELL (AWT) WOLVERHAMPTON (AWT)		Monday	7
8	Tuesday		Market Rasen SOUTHWELL (AWT)	LINGFIELD PARK (AWT)	Tuesday	8
9	Wednesday	Carlisle	Ludlow	LINGFIELD PARK (AWT)	Wednesday	9
10	Thursday		Huntingdon SOUTHWELL (AWT)	Wincanton	Thursday	10
11	Friday		Bangor-On-Dee WOLVERHAMPTON (AWT)	Kempton Park	Friday	11
12	Saturday	Ayr	Warwick †WOLVERHAMPTON (AWT)	LINGFIELD PARK (AWT) Newbury	Saturday	12
13	Sunday	Ayr	Hereford	Exeter	Sunday	13
14	Monday		WOLVERHAMPTON (AWT)	LINGFIELD PARK (AWT) Plumpton	Monday	14
15	Tuesday	Newcastle	SOUTHWELL (AWT)	Folkestone	Tuesday	15
16	Wednesday	Musselburgh	Leicester	LINGFIELD PARK (AWT)	Wednesday	16
17	Thursday		SOUTHWELL (AWT)	Sandown Park Taunton	Thursday	17
18	Friday		Fakenham WOLVERHAMPTON (AWT)	Sandown Park	Friday	18
19	Saturday	Haydock Park	Uttoxeter WOLVERHAMPTON (AWT)	Lingfield Park Wincanton	Saturday	19
20	Sunday		Towcester	Fontwell Park	Sunday	20
21	Monday	Carlisle	WOLVERHAMPTON (AWT)	LINGFIELD PARK (AWT)	Monday	21
22	Tuesday	Sedgefield	SOUTHWELL (AWT)	LINGFIELD PARK (AWT)	Tuesday	22
23	Wednesday	Doncaster	Ludlow	LINGFIELD PARK (AWT)	Wednesday	23
24	Thursday	Haydock Park	Huntingdon SOUTHWELL (AWT)		Thursday	24
25	Friday		Warwick WOLVERHAMPTON (AWT)	Kempton Park	Friday	25
26	Saturday	Newcastle		Chepstow Kempton Park LINGFIELD PARK (AWT)	Saturday	26
27	Sunday	Musselburgh	SOUTHWELL (AWT)		Sunday	27
28	Monday		WOLVERHAMPTON (AWT)	LINGFIELD PARK (AWT) Plumpton	Monday	28

CAPITALS: Flat racing Lower Case: National Hunt AWT: (All weather track) †: Evening Meeting

MARCH 2005

Date	Racecourse	Race Name
5 Mar	Kelso	Tote Exacta Premier Kelso Novice Hurdle
	Newbury	Vodafone Gold Cup
12 Mar	Sandown Park	EBF/Doncaster Bloodstock Sales Mares Bumper Final Hurdle
	Sandown Park	European Breeders Fund 'NH' Novice Final (Handicap)
	Sandown Park	Sunderlands Imperial Cup (Handicap) Hurdle
	Wolverhampton	Littlewoods Bet Direct Lincoln Trial (Handicap)
15 Mar	Cheltenham	Smurfit Champion Hurdle Challenge Trophy Hurdle
	Cheltenham	Irish Independent Arkle Challenge Trophy Novice
	Cheltenham	Letheby & Christopher Supreme Novice Hurdle
	Cheltenham	William Hill NH (Handicap)
	Cheltenham	Cheltenham Hurdle Juvenile Novices' Handicap Hurdle
16 Mar	Cheltenham	Queen Mother Champion
	Cheltenham	Royal & SunAlliance Novice
	Cheltenham	Royal & SunAlliance Novice Hurdle
	Cheltenham	Weatherbys Champion Bumper Standard Open
	Cheltenham	Coral Eurobet Cup (Handicap) Hurdle
	Cheltenham	Fulke Walwyn Kim Muir Challenge Cup (Handicap)
17 Mar	Cheltenham	Bonusprint Stayers' Hurdle
	Cheltenham	Cathcart Challenge Cup
	Cheltenham	Mildmay of Fleet Challenge Cup (Handicap)
	Cheltenham	Pertemps Final (Handicap) Hurdle
	Cheltenham	Cheltenham Chase Ltd Novice Handicap
	Cheltenham	NH Steeple Chase Challenge Cup (Amateur Riders Novice)
18 Mar	Cheltenham	Tote Cheltenham Gold Cup
	Cheltenham	JCB Triumph Novice Hurdle
	Cheltenham	Cheltenham Novice Hurdle Hurdle
	Cheltenham	Vincent O'Brien County (Handicap) Hurdle
	Cheltenham	Cheltenham Grand Annual Challenge Cup (Handicap)
	Cheltenham	Christie's Foxhunter Challenge Cup
19 Mar	Lingfield Park	Littlewoods Bet Direct Winter Derby
	Lingfield Park	Spring Cup
	Uttoxeter	John Smith's Midlands Grand National (Handicap)
	Uttoxeter	EBF Tattersalls (Ireland) Mares Final Novice (Handicap)
26 Mar	Kempton Park	Blue Square Easter (colts & geldings) Flat
	Kempton Park	Blue Square Masaka (fillies) Flat
	Kempton Park	Snowdrop (fillies) Flat
	Kempton Park	Magnolia Flat
	Kempton Park	Coral Eurobet Rosebery Handicap Flat
31 Mar	Doncaster	Doncaster Mile Flat

Artist: **Stephen Cook AT WORK** *Courtesy of:* **The Artist**

MARCH

		North	Midlands	South		
1	Tuesday	Catterick Bridge	Leicester	LINGFIELD PARK (AWT)	Tuesday	1
2	Wednesday	Wetherby	SOUTHWELL (AWT)	Folkestone	Wednesday	2
3	Thursday		Ludlow	LINGFIELD PARK (AWT) Taunton	Thursday	3
4	Friday	Doncaster	WOLVERHAMPTON (AWT)	Newbury	Friday	4
5	Saturday	Doncaster Kelso	Huntingdon	Newbury	Saturday	5
6	Sunday		Market Rasen	Kempton Park	Sunday	6
7	Monday		Hereford WOLVERHAMPTON (AWT)	LINGFIELD PARK (AWT)	Monday	7
8	Tuesday	Newcastle	SOUTHWELL (AWT)	Exeter	Tuesday	8
9	Wednesday	Catterick Bridge	Bangor-On-Dee	Fontwell Park	Wednesday	9
10	Thursday	Carlisle	Towcester	Wincanton	Thursday	10
11	Friday	Ayr	Leicester	Sandown Park	Friday	11
12	Saturday	Ayr	SOUTHWELL (AWT) (Matinee) WOLVERHAMPTON (AWT)	Chepstow Sandown Park	Saturday	12
13	Sunday		SOUTHWELL (AWT) Warwick		Sunday	13
14	Monday		Stratford-On-Avon	Plumpton Taunton	Monday	14
15	Tuesday	Sedgefield	Cheltenham SOUTHWELL (AWT)		Tuesday	15
16	Wednesday		Cheltenham Huntingdon WOLVERHAMPTON (AWT)		Wednesday	16
17	Thursday	Hexham	Cheltenham SOUTHWELL (AWT)		Thursday	17
18	Friday		Cheltenham Fakenham	LINGFIELD PARK (AWT)	Friday	18
19	Saturday	Newcastle	Bangor-On-Dee Uttoxeter WOLVERHAMPTON (AWT) (Matinee)	LINGFIELD PARK (AWT)	Saturday	19
20	Sunday	Carlisle		Fontwell Park	Sunday	20
21	Monday		Hereford SOUTHWELL (AWT)	LINGFIELD PARK (AWT)	Monday	21
22	Tuesday	Wetherby		Exeter LINGFIELD PARK (AWT)	Tuesday	22
23	Wednesday		Towcester	Chepstow LINGFIELD PARK (AWT)	Wednesday	23
24	Thursday		Ludlow WOLVERHAMPTON (AWT)	Wincanton	Thursday	24
26	Saturday	Carlisle Haydock Park	WOLVERHAMPTON (AWT) (Matinee)	KEMPTON PARK Newton Abbot	Saturday	26
27	Sunday (Easter Sunday)	MUSSELBURGH	Towcester	Plumpton	Sunday (Easter Sunday)	27
28	Monday (Bank Holiday)	REDCAR Sedgefield	Fakenham Huntingdon WARWICK	KEMPTON PARK Plumpton YARMOUTH	Monday (Bank Holiday)	28
29	Tuesday	PONTEFRACT	WARWICK	Chepstow	Tuesday	29
30	Wednesday			Exeter FOLKESTONE Fontwell Park	Wednesday	30
31	Thursday	DONCASTER	Ludlow	LINGFIELD PARK (AWT)	Thursday	31

CAPITALS: Flat racing Lower Case: National Hunt AWT: (All weather track) †: Evening Meeting

23

APRIL 2005

Date	Racecourse	Race Name
1 Apr	Doncaster	Freephone Stanley Spring Mile (Handicap)
2 Apr	Doncaster	Cammidge Trophy Flat
	Doncaster	Freephone Stanley Lincoln (Handicap) Flat
	Newbury	EBF Crandon Park Stud Mares 'NH' Novice Final (Handicap) Hurdle
3 Apr	Kelso	Ashleybank Investments Scottish Borders National (Handicap)
6 Apr	Nottingham	Gordon Lamb Further Flight Flat
7 Apr	Aintree	Martell XO Anniversary 4yo Novice Hurdle
	Aintree	Long Distance Hurdle
	Aintree	Martell Cup
	Aintree	Martell Mersey Novice Hurdle
	Aintree	Martell Red Rum Handicap
	Aintree	Martell Handicap Hurdle
8 Apr	Aintree	Martell Melling
	Aintree	Martell Sefton Novice Hurdle
	Aintree	Martell Mildmay Novice
	Aintree	Martell Top Novice Hurdle
	Aintree	Martell Noblige Handicap Hurdle
	Aintree	John Hughes Trophy (Handicap)
9 Apr	Aintree	Martell Aintree Hurdle
	Aintree	Martell Maghull Novice
	Aintree	Martell Champion Standard Bumper
	Aintree	Martell Grand National (Handicap)
	Aintree	Cordon Bleu Handicap Hurdle
	Lingfield Park	Fosters International Trial
12 Apr	Newmarket	Shadwell Stud Nell Gwyn (fillies) Flat
	Newmarket	NGK Spark Plugs Abernant Flat
13 Apr	Cheltenham	Faucets for Mira Showers Silver Trophy (Limited Handicap)
	Newmarket	Weatherbys Earl of Sefton Flat
	Newmarket	Victor Chandler European Free Handicap Flat
14 Apr	Cheltenham	Lady Rebecca Mares Only Handicap Hurdle
	Newmarket	Macau Jockey Club Craven (colts & geldings) Flat
	Newmarket	Feilden Flat
	Ripon	Silver Bowl (fillies) Flat
16 Apr	Ayr	Ashleybank Investments Future Champion Novice
	Ayr	Samsung Electronics Scottish Champion (Limited Handicap) Hurdle
	Ayr	Gala Casinos Daily Record Scottish Grand National (Handicap)
	Newbury	Lane's End Greenham (colts & geldings) Flat
	Newbury	Dubai Duty Free Fred Darling (fillies) Flat
	Newbury	Dubai Irish Village John Porter Flat
	Thirsk	Stanley Racing Thirsk Classic Trial Flat
22 Apr	Sandown Park	Sandown Park Classic Trial Flat
	Sandown Park	Concept Hurdle
23 Apr	Leicester	Leicestershire Flat
	Sandown Park	Queen Elizabeth the Queen Mother Celebration Handicap
	Sandown Park	Betfred Mile Flat
	Sandown Park	Betfred Gold Cup (Handicap)
	Sandown Park	Betfred Gordon Richards Flat
26 Apr	Bath	European Breeders Fund Lansdown (fillies) Flat
27 Apr	Ascot (Lingfield)	Bovis Homes Sagaro Flat
	Ascot (Lingfield)	Sodexho Pavilion Flat
	Ascot (Lingfield)	Milcars Swinley (fillies) Flat
	Ascot (Lingfield)	Paradise Flat
	Ascot (Lingfield)	Sony Victoria Cup (Handicap) Flat
30 Apr	Newmarket	2000 Guineas (colts & fillies) Flat
	Newmarket	Victor Chandler Palace House Flat
	Newmarket	Newmarket (colts) Flat

APRIL

		North	Midlands	South		
1	Friday	DONCASTER		LINGFIELD PARK (AWT) Newbury	Friday	1
2	Saturday	DONCASTER	Bangor-On-Dee †WOLVERHAMPTON (AWT)	KEMPTON PARK Newbury	Saturday	2
3	Sunday	Kelso	Market Rasen	Wincanton	Sunday	3
4	Monday		SOUTHWELL (AWT) WOLVERHAMPTON (AWT) YARMOUTH		Monday	4
5	Tuesday	Sedgefield	SOUTHWELL (AWT)	FOLKESTONE	Tuesday	5
6	Wednesday	CATTERICK BRIDGE	NOTTINGHAM	LINGFIELD PARK (AWT)	Wednesday	6
7	Thursday	Aintree	LEICESTER	Taunton	Thursday	7
8	Friday	Aintree	SOUTHWELL (AWT)	LINGFIELD PARK (AWT)	Friday	8
9	Saturday	Aintree NEWCASTLE	Hereford	LINGFIELD PARK (AWT)	Saturday	9
10	Sunday	Hexham	Worcester	Newton Abbot	Sunday	10
11	Monday	Kelso	SOUTHWELL	LINGFIELD PARK (AWT)	Monday	11
12	Tuesday	MUSSELBURGH	NEWMARKET	Exeter	Tuesday	12
13	Wednesday	BEVERLEY	Cheltenham NEWMARKET		Wednesday	13
14	Thursday	RIPON	Cheltenham NEWMARKET		Thursday	14
15	Friday	Ayr THIRSK	†WOLVERHAMPTON (AWT)	NEWBURY †Taunton	Friday	15
16	Saturday	Ayr THIRSK	Bangor-On-Dee †NOTTINGHAM †WOLVERHAMPTON (AWT)	NEWBURY	Saturday	16
17	Sunday	Carlisle	Stratford-On-Avon	Wincanton	Sunday	17
18	Monday	Hexham PONTEFRACT	†WOLVERHAMPTON (AWT)	Plumpton †WINDSOR	Monday	18
19	Tuesday	NEWCASTLE	SOUTHWELL †Towcester	†BRIGHTON FOLKESTONE	Tuesday	19
20	Wednesday	CATTERICK BRIDGE Perth	†Worcester	EPSOM DOWNS †LINGFIELD PARK (AWT)	Wednesday	20
21	Thursday	BEVERLEY Perth	†SOUTHWELL (AWT)	†BATH Fontwell Park	Thursday	21
22	Friday	Perth	WOLVERHAMPTON (AWT)	†Chepstow †Newton Abbot SANDOWN PARK (MIXED)	Friday	22
23	Saturday	†HAYDOCK PARK RIPON	LEICESTER Market Rasen †WOLVERHAMPTON (AWT)	SANDOWN PARK (MIXED)	Saturday	23
24	Sunday	Wetherby	Ludlow	BRIGHTON	Sunday	24
25	Monday	HAMILTON PARK	†SOUTHWELL (AWT) Towcester WOLVERHAMPTON (AWT)	†WINDSOR	Monday	25
26	Tuesday		SOUTHWELL (AWT) †WARWICK	BATH Newton Abbot †YARMOUTH	Tuesday	26
27	Wednesday	†Kelso PONTEFRACT	†Cheltenham	Exeter LINGFIELD PARK	Wednesday	27
28	Thursday	†Kelso REDCAR	Hereford SOUTHWELL (AWT)	†LINGFIELD PARK (AWT)	Thursday	28
29	Friday	MUSSELBURGH	†Bangor-On-Dee NOTTINGHAM Southwell	†Fontwell Park	Friday	29
30	Saturday	†Hexham THIRSK	NEWMARKET Uttoxeter †Worcester	GOODWOOD	Saturday	30

CAPITALS: Flat racing Lower Case: National Hunt AWT: (All weather track) †: Evening Meeting

MAY 2005

Date	Racecourse	Race Name
1 May	Newmarket	1000 Guineas (fillies) Flat
	Newmarket	Jockey Club Flat
	Newmarket	Dahlia (fillies) Flat
	Newmarket	R.L. Davison Pretty Polly (fillies) Flat
2 May	Kempton Park	Jubilee Handicap Flat
	Sedgefield	John Smiths Durham National (Handicap) Chase
4 May	Chester	Victor Chandler Chester Vase Flat
5 May	Chester	UPM-Kymmene Cheshire Oaks (fillies) Flat
	Chester	Tote Chester Cup (Handicap) Flat
6 May	Chester	Betfair.com Ormonde Flat
	Chester	Philip Leverhulme Dee Flat
	Chester	Breitling Watches & Waltons of Chester Huxley Flat
7 May	Haydock Park	Merewood Homes Swinton (Handicap) Hurdle
	Haydock Park	Merewood Homes Spring Trophy Flat
	Lingfield Park	Derby Trial (colts & geldings) Flat
	Lingfield Park	Oaks Trial (fillies) Flat
	Lingfield Park	Chartwell (fillies) Flat
	Lingfield Park	Tote Scoop6 Sprint Handicap Flat
9 May	Windsor	Royal Windsor Flat
11 May	York	Duke of York Flat
	York	Tattersalls Musidora (fillies) Flat
12 May	York	Tote Dante Flat
	York	Tote.co.uk Middleton (fillies) Flat
	York	Bank of Scotland Business Banking Hambleton Rated St (Handicap) Flat
13 May	Hamilton Park	Braveheart Rated St Flat
	Newbury	Swettenham Stud Fillies' Trial Flat
	York	Yorkshire Cup Flat
	York	Michael Seely Memorial Glasgow Flat
14 May	Newbury	Juddmonte Lockinge Flat
	Newbury	Aston Park Flat
	Newbury	Carnarvon Flat
	Nottingham	Kilvington (fillies) Flat
18 May	Goodwood	Letheby & Christopher Predominate (colts & geldings) Flat
19 May	Goodwood	Victor Chandler Lupe (fillies) Flat
20 May	Goodwood	Festival Flat
	Goodwood	European Breeders Fund Conqueror (fillies) Flat
21 May	Haydock Park	EBF Pinnacle (fillies and mares) Flat
	Haydock Park	Dunwoody Sports Marketing Sandy Lane (Rated) Flat
	Haydock Park	Tote Credit Club Silver Bowl (Handicap) Flat
	Kempton Park	Heron Flat
	Kempton Park	Achilles Flat
	Newmarket	King Charles II Flat
	Newmarket	Haven and British Holidays Fairway Flat
	Newmarket	Coral Sprint (Handicap) Flat
	Stratford-on-Avon	Intrum Justitia Cup Champion (Hunters) Chase
27 May	Goodwood	On The House Flat
30 May	Redcar	Freephone Stanley Zetland Gold Cup (Handicap) Flat
	Sandown Park	Bonusprint Henry II Flat
	Sandown Park	National Flat
31 May	Sandown Park	Brigadier Gerard Flat

MAY

		North	Midlands	South		
1	Sunday	HAMILTON PARK	NEWMARKET	SALISBURY	Sunday	1
2	Monday	DONCASTER	WARWICK	KEMPTON PARK	Monday	2
	(Bank Holiday)	NEWCASTLE			(Bank Holiday)	
		Sedgefield				
3	Tuesday	†CATTERICK BRIDGE	LEICESTER	BATH	Tuesday	3
			Ludlow	†Exeter		
4	Wednesday		CHESTER	CHEPSTOW	Wednesday	4
			Fakenham			
5	Thursday	†Wetherby	CHESTER	†CHEPSTOW	Thursday	5
				FOLKESTONE		
				Newton Abbot		
6	Friday	†HAMILTON PARK	CHESTER	LINGFIELD PARK	Friday	6
			NOTTINGHAM	†Wincanton		
7	Saturday	BEVERLEY	NEWMARKET	LINGFIELD PARK	Saturday	7
		HAYDOCK PARK (MIXED)	†Warwick			
		Hexham				
		†THIRSK				
8	Sunday		Uttoxeter	Plumpton	Sunday	8
				Worcester		
9	Monday	REDCAR	†Towcester	KEMPTON PARK	Monday	9
			WOLVERHAMPTON (AWT)	†WINDSOR		
10	Tuesday	MUSSELBURGH	Hereford	†Newton Abbot	Tuesday	10
			†Huntingdon			
			YARMOUTH			
11	Wednesday	†NEWCASTLE		BRIGHTON	Wednesday	11
		†Perth		Exeter		
		YORK				
12	Thursday	†CARLISLE	†Ludlow	SALISBURY	Thursday	12
		Perth				
		YORK				
13	Friday	†Aintree	NOTTINGHAM	NEWBURY	Friday	13
		†HAMILTON PARK				
		YORK				
14	Saturday	THIRSK	Bangor-On-Dee	NEWBURY	Saturday	14
			NOTTINGHAM			
			†Uttoxeter			
			†Worcester			
15	Sunday	RIPON	Fakenham		Sunday	15
			Market Rasen			
16	Monday	†MUSSELBURGH	WOLVERHAMPTON (AWT)	BATH	Monday	16
				Newton Abbot		
				†WINDSOR		
17	Tuesday	BEVERLEY	†LEICESTER	LINGFIELD PARK (AWT)	Tuesday	17
		REDCAR	†Towcester			
18	Wednesday	Kelso	SOUTHWELL (AWT)	†Folkestone	Wednesday	18
		†Sedgefield		GOODWOOD		
19	Thursday	†DONCASTER		GOODWOOD	Thursday	19
		†Kelso				
		NEWCASTLE				
		Wetherby				
20	Friday	HAYDOCK PARK	NEWMARKET	†BATH	Friday	20
			†Stratford-On-Avon	GOODWOOD		
21	Saturday	CATTERICK BRIDGE	NEWMARKET	†KEMPTON PARK	Saturday	21
		HAYDOCK PARK	†Stratford-On-Avon	LINGFIELD PARK		
22	Sunday		Hereford	BRIGHTON	Sunday	22
			Southwell			
23	Monday	BEVERLEY	LEICESTER	†WINDSOR	Monday	23
		CARLISLE				
		†THIRSK				
24	Tuesday	RIPON	NOTTINGHAM	LINGFIELD PARK	Tuesday	24
		†Sedgefield	†Worcester			
25	Wednesday	Cartmel		Fontwell Park	Wednesday	25
		†RIPON		†KEMPTON PARK		
				LINGFIELD PARK		
26	Thursday	AYR	†Huntingdon	BATH	Thursday	26
		†Wetherby		Newton Abbot		
27	Friday	CATTERICK BRIDGE	†Towcester	BRIGHTON	Friday	27
		†PONTEFRACT	WOLVERHAMPTON (AWT)			
28	Saturday	†Cartmel		GOODWOOD	Saturday	28
		DONCASTER		†LINGFIELD PARK		
		Hexham				
		MUSSELBURGH				
29	Sunday		NEWMARKET	Fontwell Park	Sunday	29
			Uttoxeter			
30	Monday	Cartmel	LEICESTER	CHEPSTOW	Monday	30
	(Bank Holiday)	REDCAR		SANDOWN PARK	(Bank Holiday)	
31	Tuesday	CARLISLE	LEICESTER	†SANDOWN PARK	Tuesday	31
			†Hexham			
		REDCAR				

CAPITALS: Flat racing Lower Case: National Hunt AWT: (All weather track) †: Evening Meeting

JUNE 2005

Date	Racecourse	Race Name
1 Jun	Beverley	Hilary Needler Trophy (fillies) Flat
3 Jun	Epsom Downs	Vodafone Oaks (fillies) Flat
	Epsom Downs	Vodafone Coronation Cup Flat
	Epsom Downs	Temple Flat
	Epsom Downs	Princess Elizabeth Vodafone (fillies) Flat
	Epsom Downs	Vodafone Surrey Flat
4 Jun	Epsom Downs	Vodafone Derby (colts & fillies) Flat
	Epsom Downs	Vodafone Diomed Flat
	Epsom Downs	Vodafone 'Dash' (Rated) Flat
	Epsom Downs	Vodafone Woodcote Flat
	Haydock Park	Betfair.com John of Gaunt Flat
	Haydock Park	Stanley Racing Cecil Frail (fillies) Flat
5 Jun	Perth	City of Perth Gold Cup (Handicap) Chase
6 Jun	Pontefract	Pipalong (fillies and mares) Flat
11 Jun	Leicester	Leicester Mercury Flat
12 Jun	Salisbury	Axminster Carpets Cathedral Flat
14 Jun	Royal Ascot (York)	St James's Palace (colts) Flat
	Royal Ascot (York)	Queen Anne Flat
	Royal Ascot (York)	King's Stand Flat
	Royal Ascot (York)	Coventry Flat
	Royal Ascot (York)	Windsor Castle Flat
	Royal Ascot (York)	Ascot (Handicap) Flat
15 Jun	Royal Ascot (York)	Prince of Wales's Flat
	Royal Ascot (York)	Queen Mary (fillies) Flat
	Royal Ascot (York)	Windsor Forest (fillies and mares) Flat
	Royal Ascot (York)	Jersey Flat
	Royal Ascot (York)	Sandringham Rated (Handicap) Flat
	Royal Ascot (York)	Royal Hunt Cup (Heritage Handicap) Flat
16 Jun	Newbury	Ballymacoll Stud Flat
	Royal Ascot (York)	Gold Cup Flat
	Royal Ascot (York)	Ribblesdale (fillies) Flat
	Royal Ascot (York)	Norfolk Flat
	Royal Ascot (York)	Hampton Court Flat
	Royal Ascot (York)	King George V (Heritage Handicap) Flat
	Royal Ascot (York)	Britannia (Heritage Handicap) (colts & geldings) Flat
17 Jun	Royal Ascot (York)	Coronation (fillies) Flat
	Royal Ascot (York)	King Edward VII (colts & geldings) Flat
	Royal Ascot (York)	Queen's Vase Flat
	Royal Ascot (York)	Albany Stakes Flat
	Royal Ascot (York)	Wolferton Rated Flat
	Royal Ascot (York)	Buckingham Palace Handicap Flat
18 Jun	Royal Ascot (York)	Golden Jubilee Flat
	Royal Ascot (York)	Hardwicke Flat
	Royal Ascot (York)	Chesham Flat
	Royal Ascot (York)	Duke of Edinburgh (Heritage Handicap) Flat
	Royal Ascot (York)	Wokingham (Heritage Handicap) Flat
	Royal Ascot (York)	Queen Alexandra Flat
	Warwick	Eternal (fillies) Flat
22 Jun	Carlisle	Crowther Homes Carlisle Bell (Handicap) Flat
	Carlisle	Tote Credit Club Cumberland Plate (Handicap) Flat
25 Jun	Newcastle	Kronenbourg 1664 Chipchase Flat
	Newcastle	EBF Hoppings (fillies) Flat
	Newcastle	Foster's Lager Northumberland Plate (Handicap) Flat
	Newmarket	Criterion Flat
	Newmarket	Fred Archer Flat
	Newmarket	Empress (fillies) Flat
	Windsor	Gala Bingo Berkshire Flat
	Windsor	Tote Scoop 6 Leisure Flat
	Windsor	Midsummer Flat
26 Jun	Uttoxeter	Britannia Building Society English Summer National (Handicap) Chase

JUNE

		North	Midlands	South		
1	Wednesday	†BEVERLEY NEWCASTLE	NOTTINGHAM †SOUTHWELL (AWT) YARMOUTH		Wednesday	1
2	Thursday	HAMILTON PARK HAYDOCK PARK	†Uttoxeter	BRIGHTON †SANDOWN PARK	Thursday	2
3	Friday	†HAYDOCK PARK THIRSK	WOLVERHAMPTON (AWT)	EPSOM DOWNS †GOODWOOD	Friday	3
4	Saturday	DONCASTER HAYDOCK PARK	Worcester	†CHEPSTOW EPSOM DOWNS †LINGFIELD PARK	Saturday	4
5	Sunday	Perth	Stratford-On-Avon	BATH	Sunday	5
6	Monday	†PONTEFRACT		FOLKESTONE Newton Abbot †WINDSOR	Monday	6
7	Tuesday	REDCAR	†CHESTER †Huntingdon	SALISBURY	Tuesday	7
8	Wednesday	BEVERLEY †HAMILTON PARK	Hereford Market Rasen	†NEWBURY	Wednesday	8
9	Thursday	RIPON	SOUTHWELL (AWT) †Uttoxeter YARMOUTH	†BRIGHTON	Thursday	9
10	Friday	CATTERICK BRIDGE	WOLVERHAMPTON (AWT)	†CHEPSTOW †GOODWOOD SANDOWN PARK	Friday	10
11	Saturday	Hexham RIPON	†LEICESTER	BATH †LINGFIELD PARK SANDOWN PARK	Saturday	11
12	Sunday	DONCASTER	Stratford-On-Avon	SALISBURY	Sunday	12
13	Monday	THIRSK	†WARWICK	BRIGHTON †WINDSOR	Monday	13
14	Tuesday	CARLISLE ASCOT AT YORK	†Hereford	†Newton Abbot	Tuesday	14
15	Wednesday	HAMILTON PARK ASCOT AT YORK	Worcester	†CHEPSTOW †KEMPTON PARK	Wednesday	15
16	Thursday	†Aintree †BEVERLEY ASCOT AT YORK	SOUTHWELL (AWT)	NEWBURY	Thursday	16
17	Friday	AYR REDCAR ASCOT AT YORK	†NEWMARKET	†GOODWOOD	Friday	17
18	Saturday	AYR REDCAR ASCOT AT YORK	NEWMARKET †WARWICK	†LINGFIELD PARK	Saturday	18
19	Sunday	Hexham PONTEFRACT	WARWICK		Sunday	19
20	Monday	MUSSELBURGH †RIPON	NOTTINGHAM	†WINDSOR	Monday	20
21	Tuesday	BEVERLEY		BRIGHTON †NEWBURY †Newton Abbot	Tuesday	21
22	Wednesday	CARLISLE	Worcester	†BATH †KEMPTON PARK SALISBURY	Wednesday	22
23	Thursday	†HAMILTON PARK NEWCASTLE THIRSK	†LEICESTER	SALISBURY	Thursday	23
24	Friday	†NEWCASTLE	Market Rasen †NEWMARKET	FOLKESTONE WOLVERHAMPTON (AWT)	Friday	24
25	Saturday	†DONCASTER NEWCASTLE	CHESTER NEWMARKET	†LINGFIELD PARK WINDSOR	Saturday	25
26	Sunday		Uttoxeter	WINDSOR	Sunday	26
27	Monday	†MUSSELBURGH PONTEFRACT	WOLVERHAMPTON (AWT)	†WINDSOR	Monday	27
28	Tuesday	HAMILTON PARK		BRIGHTON	Tuesday	28
29	Wednesday	CATTERICK BRIDGE Perth	Worcester	†CHEPSTOW †KEMPTON PARK	Wednesday	29
30	Thursday	HAYDOCK PARK Perth	YARMOUTH	†EPSOM DOWNS †NEWBURY	Thursday	30

CAPITALS: Flat racing Lower Case: National Hunt AWT: (All weather track) †: Evening Meeting

JULY 2005

Date	Racecourse	Race Name
1 Jul	Sandown Park	Gala Flat
	Sandown Park	Dragon Stakes Flat
2 Jul	Haydock Park	Lancashire Oaks (fillies) Flat
	Haydock Park	Old Newton Cup (Handicap) Flat
	Sandown Park	Coral Eclipse Flat
	Sandown Park	Porcelanosa Sprint Flat
	Sandown Park	Distaff (fillies) Flat
	Sandown Park	Esher Flat
	Sandown Park	Tote Scoop6 Handicap Flat
5 Jul	Newmarket	Falmouth (fillies) Flat
	Newmarket	Princess of Wales's UAE Equestrian & Racing Federation Flat
	Newmarket	Cherry Hinton (fillies) Flat
6 Jul	Newmarket	TNT July (colts & geldings) Flat
	Newmarket	Bahrain Trophy Flat
7 Jul	Newmarket	Darley July Cup Flat
	Newmarket	Weatherbys Superlative Flat
	Newmarket	Ladbrokes Bunbury Cup (Handicap) Flat
8 Jul	York	Cuisine de France Summer (fillies) Flat
9 Jul	Ascot (Lingfield)	Michael Page International Silver Trophy Flat
	Chester	City Wall Flat
	York	Webster's Silver Cup Rated St (Handicap) Flat
	York	John Smith's Cup (Handicap) Flat
16 Jul	Haydock Park	Manchester Evening News July Trophy (colts & geldings) Flat
	Market Rasen	Tote Scoop 6 Summer Plate Handicap Chase
	Market Rasen	Tote Exacta Summer Hurdle
	Newbury	Shadwell Stud Rose Bowl Flat
	Newbury	Steventon Flat
	Newbury	David Wilson Homes Hackwood Flat
	Newbury	Weatherbys Super Sprint Flat
	Newmarket	Food Brokers Aphrodite (fillies) Flat
18 Jul	Ayr	Daily Record Scottish Derby Flat
	Ayr	Land O'Burns (fillies) Flat
21 Jul	Sandown Park	Star (fillies) Flat
22 Jul	Ascot (Newbury)	October Club E.B.F. Valiant (fillies) Flat
	Chepstow	Oakgrove Stud Golden Daffodil (fillies) Flat
23 Jul	Ascot (tbc)	King George VI and Queen Elizabeth Diamond Flat
	Ascot (tbc)	Princess Margaret (fillies) Flat
	Ascot (tbc)	Tote International (Handicap) Flat
24 Jul	Ascot (tbc)	Hong Kong Jockey Club Sprint (Handicap) Flat
26 Jul	Goodwood	Richmond (colts & geldings) Flat
	Goodwood	Theo Fennell Lennox Flat
	Goodwood	Peugeot Gordon Flat
27 Jul	Goodwood	Sussex Flat
	Goodwood	Veuve Cliquot Vintage Flat
	Goodwood	Tote Gold Trophy (Handicap) Flat
28 Jul	Goodwood	Lady O Goodwood Cup Flat
	Goodwood	King George Flat
	Goodwood	Betfair Molecomb Flat
29 Jul	Goodwood	Oak Tree (fillies) Flat
	Goodwood	Glorious (Rated) Flat
	Goodwood	William Hill Mile (Handicap) Flat
	Goodwood	Stewards' Sprint (Handicap) Flat
30 Jul	Goodwood	Vodafone Nassau (fillies) Flat
	Goodwood	Vodafone EBF Lily Langtree (fillies and mares) Flat
	Goodwood	Vodafone Thoroughbred Flat
	Goodwood	Vodafone Stewards' Cup (Handicap) Flat
	Newmarket	Stubbs Flat
31 Jul	Chester	Queensferry Flat
	Newbury	EBF Chalice (fillies) Flat

JULY

		North	Midlands	South		
1	Friday	†BEVERLEY †HAYDOCK PARK	SOUTHWELL (AWT) WARWICK	SANDOWN PARK	Friday	1
2	Saturday	BEVERLEY †CARLISLE HAYDOCK PARK	LEICESTER †NOTTINGHAM	SANDOWN PARK	Saturday	2
3	Sunday		Market Rasen	BRIGHTON	Sunday	3
4	Monday	MUSSELBURGH †RIPON		BATH †WINDSOR	Monday	4
5	Tuesday	PONTEFRACT	NEWMARKET JULY †Uttoxeter †WOLVERHAMPTON (AWT)		Tuesday	5
6	Wednesday	CATTERICK BRIDGE	NEWMARKET JULY †Worcester	†KEMPTON PARK LINGFIELD PARK	Wednesday	6
7	Thursday	†DONCASTER	NEWMARKET JULY WARWICK	†EPSOM DOWNS FOLKESTONE	Thursday	7
8	Friday	YORK	†CHESTER WOLVERHAMPTON (AWT)	†CHEPSTOW LINGFIELD PARK	Friday	8
9	Saturday	†HAMILTON PARK YORK	CHESTER NOTTINGHAM	LINGFIELD PARK †SALISBURY	Saturday	9
10	Sunday	HAYDOCK PARK Perth	Stratford-On-Avon		Sunday	10
11	Monday	AYR	†WOLVERHAMPTON (AWT)	Newton Abbot †WINDSOR	Monday	11
12	Tuesday	BEVERLEY		BRIGHTON	Tuesday	12
13	Wednesday	CATTERICK BRIDGE	Uttoxeter †Worcester	†KEMPTON PARK LINGFIELD PARK	Wednesday	13
14	Thursday	Cartmel †DONCASTER HAMILTON PARK	LEICESTER	†EPSOM DOWNS	Thursday	14
15	Friday	CARLISLE †HAMILTON PARK †PONTEFRACT	†NEWMARKET Southwell WARWICK		Friday	15
16	Saturday	†HAYDOCK PARK RIPON	Market Rasen NEWMARKET	†LINGFIELD PARK NEWBURY	Saturday	16
17	Sunday	REDCAR	Stratford-On-Avon	Newton Abbot	Sunday	17
18	Monday	AYR †BEVERLEY		BRIGHTON †WINDSOR	Monday	18
19	Tuesday	AYR	YARMOUTH		Tuesday	19
20	Wednesday	CATTERICK BRIDGE	†LEICESTER Worcester	LINGFIELD PARK †SANDOWN PARK	Wednesday	20
21	Thursday	†DONCASTER	Uttoxeter	BATH †FOLKESTONE SANDOWN PARK	Thursday	21
22	Friday	YORK	†NEWMARKET WOLVERHAMPTON (AWT)	ASCOT (VENUE TO BE CONFIRMED) †CHEPSTOW	Friday	22
23	Saturday	NEWCASTLE YORK	NOTTINGHAM	ASCOT (VENUE TO BE CONFIRMED) †LINGFIELD PARK †SALISBURY	Saturday	23
24	Sunday	PONTEFRACT	NEWMARKET	ASCOT (VENUE TO BE CONFIRMED)	Sunday	24
25	Monday	Sedgefield	SOUTHWELL (AWT) †YARMOUTH	†WINDSOR	Monday	25
26	Tuesday	BEVERLEY		GOODWOOD	Tuesday	26
27	Wednesday	MUSSELBURGH	†LEICESTER	GOODWOOD †KEMPTON PARK Newton Abbot	Wednesday	27
28	Thursday	CARLISLE †MUSSELBURGH	Stratford-On-Avon	†EPSOM DOWNS GOODWOOD	Thursday	28
29	Friday	THIRSK	Bangor-On-Dee †NEWMARKET †NOTTINGHAM	GOODWOOD	Friday	29
30	Saturday	DONCASTER †HAMILTON PARK THIRSK	NEWMARKET	GOODWOOD †LINGFIELD PARK	Saturday	30
31	Sunday		CHESTER Market Rasen	NEWBURY	Sunday	31

CAPITALS: Flat racing Lower Case: National Hunt AWT: (All weather track) †: Evening Meeting

AUGUST 2005

Date	Racecourse	Race Name
6 Aug	Haydock Park	Petros Rose of Lancaster Flat
	Newmarket	Sweet Solera (fillies) Flat
10 Aug	Salisbury	European Breeders Fund Upavon (fillies) Flat
	Salisbury	Stonehenge Flat
11 Aug	Salisbury	Sovereign (colts & geldings) Flat
12 Aug	Newbury	Newbury Racecourse Washington Singer Flat
13 Aug	Newbury	Stan James Geoffrey Freer Flat
	Newbury	Stan James Hungerford Flat
	Newbury	Stan James St Hugh's (fillies) Flat
	Ripon	William Hill Great St Wilfrid (Handicap) Flat
14 Aug	Bath	EBF Dick Hern Flat
	Pontefract	Slatch Farm Stud Flying Fillies' Flat
16 Aug	York	Juddmonte International Flat
	York	Great Voltigeur (colts & geldings) Flat
	York	Lonsdale Cup Flat
	York	Acomb Flat
17 Aug	York	Aston Upthorpe Yorkshire Oaks (fillies) Flat
	York	Scottish Equitable Gimcrack (colts & geldings) Flat
	York	Costcutter Roses (colts & geldings) Flat
	York	Tote Ebor (Handicap) Flat
18 Aug	York	Victor Chandler Nunthorpe Flat
	York	Peugeot Lowther (fillies) Flat
	York	European Breeders Fund Galtres (fillies) Flat
	York	City of York Flat
20 Aug	Beverley	Beverley Bullet Sprint Flat
	Chester	Bet Direct Chester (Rated) Flat
	Sandown Park	Iveco Daily Solario Flat
	Sandown Park	Sunley Atalanta (fillies) Flat
22 Aug	Hamilton Park	Flower of Scotland (fillies and mares) Flat
	Windsor	Winter Hill Flat
24 Aug	Brighton	Tote Exacta Virginia (Rated) (fillies) Flat
27 Aug	Goodwood	Celebration Mile Flat
	Goodwood	San Miguel March Flat
	Newmarket	Hopeful Flat
	Windsor	August Flat
28 Aug	Goodwood	Touchdown in Malaysia Prestige (fillies) Flat
29 Aug	Ripon	Berfair.com Ripon Champion Two Yrs Old Trophy Flat
31 Aug	York	Strensall Flat

AUGUST

		North	Midlands	South		
1	Monday	†CARLISLE RIPON		Newton Abbot †WINDSOR	Monday	1
2	Tuesday	CATTERICK BRIDGE		BRIGHTON	Tuesday	2
3	Wednesday	NEWCASTLE PONTEFRACT	†YARMOUTH	BRIGHTON †KEMPTON PARK	Wednesday	3
4	Thursday	HAYDOCK PARK	YARMOUTH	†BRIGHTON CHEPSTOW †FOLKESTONE	Thursday	4
5	Friday	†HAYDOCK PARK Sedgefield	†NEWMARKET Worcester	LINGFIELD PARK	Friday	5
6	Saturday	†AYR HAYDOCK PARK REDCAR	NEWMARKET	†LINGFIELD PARK WINDSOR	Saturday	6
7	Sunday	REDCAR	LEICESTER	LINGFIELD PARK	Sunday	7
8	Monday	†THIRSK	Southwell WOLVERHAMPTON (AWT)	†WINDSOR	Monday	8
9	Tuesday			BATH Newton Abbot	Tuesday	9
10	Wednesday	BEVERLEY †HAMILTON PARK	YARMOUTH	SALISBURY †SANDOWN PARK	Wednesday	10
11	Thursday	BEVERLEY †HAYDOCK PARK		†CHEPSTOW SALISBURY SANDOWN PARK	Thursday	11
12	Friday	†CATTERICK BRIDGE NEWCASTLE	†NEWMARKET	FOLKESTONE NEWBURY	Friday	12
13	Saturday	RIPON	Bangor-On-Dee †Market Rasen NEWMARKET	†GOODWOOD NEWBURY	Saturday	13
14	Sunday	PONTEFRACT	Stratford-On-Avon	BATH	Sunday	14
15	Monday		NOTTINGHAM †YARMOUTH	BRIGHTON †WINDSOR	Monday	15
16	Tuesday	HAMILTON PARK YORK			Tuesday	16
17	Wednesday	CARLISLE YORK	†NOTTINGHAM Worcester	†KEMPTON PARK	Wednesday	17
18	Thursday	YORK	CHESTER WOLVERHAMPTON (AWT)	†CHEPSTOW †Fontwell Park	Thursday	18
19	Friday	AYR	CHESTER †WOLVERHAMPTON (AWT)	†SALISBURY SANDOWN PARK	Friday	19
20	Saturday	BEVERLEY †REDCAR	CHESTER	†LINGFIELD PARK Newton Abbot SANDOWN PARK	Saturday	20
21	Sunday		Southwell	FOLKESTONE Newton Abbot	Sunday	21
22	Monday	HAMILTON PARK	LEICESTER †WOLVERHAMPTON (AWT)	†WINDSOR	Monday	22
23	Tuesday	†Perth	†Worcester YARMOUTH	BRIGHTON	Tuesday	23
24	Wednesday	CATTERICK BRIDGE Perth		BRIGHTON	Wednesday	24
25	Thursday	MUSSELBURGH	Bangor-On-Dee	LINGFIELD PARK	Thursday	25
26	Friday	†NEWCASTLE THIRSK	NEWMARKET	†BATH SALISBURY	Friday	26
27	Saturday	Cartmel YORK	†Market Rasen NEWMARKET	GOODWOOD †WINDSOR	Saturday	27
28	Sunday	BEVERLEY	YARMOUTH	GOODWOOD	Sunday	28
29	Monday (Bank Holiday)	Cartmel NEWCASTLE RIPON	Huntingdon WARWICK	CHEPSTOW EPSOM DOWNS	Monday (Bank Holiday)	29
30	Tuesday	RIPON Sedgefield	LEICESTER		Tuesday	30
31	Wednesday	YORK		LINGFIELD PARK Newton Abbot	Wednesday	31

CAPITALS: Flat racing Lower Case: National Hunt AWT: (All weather track) †: Evening Meeting

SEPTEMBER 2005

Date	Racecourse	Race Name
1 Sep	Salisbury	EBF Dick Poole (fillies) Flat
3 Sep	Haydock Park	Stanley Leisure Sprint Cup Flat
	Haydock Park	Superior Mile Flat
	Haydock Park	Stanleybet.co.uk Old Borough Cup Flat
	Kempton Park	Milcars September Flat
	Kempton Park	Sirenia Flat
7 Sep	Doncaster	Park Hill (fillies) Flat
	Doncaster	"£200,000 St Leger Yearling" Flat
	Doncaster	Tote Trifecta Portland (Handicap) Flat
8 Sep	Doncaster	GNER Doncaster Cup Flat
	Doncaster	GNER Park Flat
	Doncaster	May Hill (fillies) Flat
	Doncaster	JRA London Office's Kyoto Sceptre (fillies) Flat
	Doncaster	Scarbrough Flat
	Epsom Downs	Fortune Flat
9 Sep	Doncaster	Champagne (colts & geldings) Flat
	Doncaster	Amco Corporation Troy Flat
	Doncaster	DBS St Leger Yearling Flat
10 Sep	Chester	Henry Gee (fillies and mares) Flat
	Doncaster	St Leger (colts & fillies) Flat
	Doncaster	Polypipe Flying Childers Flat
	Goodwood	Stardom Flat
11 Sep	Goodwood	Select Flat
	Goodwood	Starlit Flat
14 Sep	Yarmouth	John Musker (fillies) Flat
15 Sep	Ayr	Harry Rosebery Flat
16 Sep	Newbury	Dubai Duty Free Mill Reef Flat
	Newbury	Dubai Duty Free Cup Flat
17 Sep	Ayr	Faucets First for Faucets Firth of Clyde (fillies) Flat
	Ayr	Doonside Cup Flat
	Ayr	Tote Ayr Gold Cup (Handicap) Flat
	Newbury	Dubai Duty Free Arc Trial Flat
	Newbury	Dubai International Airport World Trophy Flat
	Newbury	John Smith's Handicap Flat
23 Sep	Ascot (Lingfield)	Princess Royal Willmott Dixon (fillies) Flat
	Ascot (Lingfield)	EBF Harvest (fillies) Flat
	Ascot (Lingfield)	Watership Down Stud Sales (fillies) Flat
24 Sep	Ascot (tbc)	Queen Elizabeth II Flat
	Ascot (tbc)	Meon Valley Stud Fillies' Mile (fillies) Flat
	Ascot (tbc)	Hackney Empire Royal Lodge (colts & geldings) Flat
	Ascot (tbc)	Diadem Flat
	Ascot (tbc)	Rosemary Rated (fillies) Flat
25 Sep	Ascot (tbc)	Young Vic Theatre Cumberland Lodge Flat
	Ascot (tbc)	Miles & Morrison October (fillies) Flat
	Ascot (tbc)	Fenwolf Flat
	Ascot (tbc)	Mail On Sunday Mile Final (Handicap) Flat
26 Sep	Hamilton Park	Hamilton Park 2yo Series Final Flat
27 Sep	Goodwood	Charlton Hunt Supreme Flat
	Goodwood	Foundation Flat
29 Sep	Newmarket	"£100,000 Tattersalls Autumn Auction" Flat
	Newmarket	Cheveley Park (fillies) Flat
	Newmarket	Somerville Tattersall (colts & geldings) Flat
	Newmarket	UAE Equestrian & Racing Federation Rous
	Newmarket	Unicoin Homes Noel Murless Flat
30 Sep	Newmarket	Shadwell Stud Middle Park (colts) Flat
	Newmarket	Shadwell Stud Joel Flat
	Newmarket	Fishpools Godolphin Flat

SEPTEMBER

		North	Midlands	South		
1	Thursday	CARLISLE		SALISBURY	Thursday	1
		REDCAR				
2	Friday	HAYDOCK PARK		CHEPSTOW	Friday	2
				KEMPTON PARK		
3	Saturday	HAYDOCK PARK	Stratford-On-Avon	FOLKESTONE (Matinee)	Saturday	3
		THIRSK	†WOLVERHAMPTON (AWT)	KEMPTON PARK		
4	Sunday	YORK	Worcester	Fontwell Park	Sunday	4
5	Monday	NEWCASTLE	WARWICK	BATH	Monday	5
6	Tuesday	CATTERICK BRIDGE	LEICESTER	LINGFIELD PARK	Tuesday	6
7	Wednesday	DONCASTER	Uttoxeter	EPSOM DOWNS	Wednesday	7
8	Thursday	DONCASTER		CHEPSTOW	Thursday	8
				EPSOM DOWNS		
9	Friday	DONCASTER	Bangor-On-Dee	SANDOWN PARK	Friday	9
10	Saturday	DONCASTER	CHESTER	GOODWOOD	Saturday	10
		MUSSELBURGH	WOLVERHAMPTON (AWT) (Matinee)			
11	Sunday	CARLISLE	Stratford-On-Avon	GOODWOOD	Sunday	11
12	Monday	MUSSELBURGH		FOLKESTONE	Monday	12
		REDCAR				
13	Tuesday	THIRSK	YARMOUTH	SALISBURY	Tuesday	13
14	Wednesday	BEVERLEY	YARMOUTH	SANDOWN PARK	Wednesday	14
15	Thursday	AYR	YARMOUTH		Thursday	15
		PONTEFRACT				
16	Friday	AYR	NOTTINGHAM	NEWBURY	Friday	16
17	Saturday	AYR	WARWICK	LINGFIELD PARK (AWT) (Matinee)	Saturday	17
		CATTERICK BRIDGE	†WOLVERHAMPTON (AWT)	NEWBURY		
18	Sunday	HAMILTON PARK	Uttoxeter	Plumpton	Sunday	18
19	Monday		LEICESTER	CHEPSTOW	Monday	19
				KEMPTON PARK		
20	Tuesday	BEVERLEY	NEWMARKET	BRIGHTON	Tuesday	20
21	Wednesday	Perth		GOODWOOD	Wednesday	21
		REDCAR				
22	Thursday	Perth		Fontwell Park	Thursday	22
		PONTEFRACT				
23	Friday	HAYDOCK PARK	Worcester	LINGFIELD PARK	Friday	23
24	Saturday	HAYDOCK PARK	Market Rasen	ASCOT (VENUE TO BE CONFIRMED)	Saturday	24
		RIPON		KEMPTON PARK (Matinee)		
25	Sunday	MUSSELBURGH	Huntingdon	ASCOT (VENUE TO BE CONFIRMED)	Sunday	25
26	Monday	HAMILTON PARK	WOLVERHAMPTON (AWT)	BATH	Monday	26
27	Tuesday	Sedgefield	NOTTINGHAM	GOODWOOD	Tuesday	27
28	Wednesday	NEWCASTLE		LINGFIELD PARK (AWT)	Wednesday	28
				SALISBURY		
29	Thursday	AYR	Hereford		Thursday	29
			NEWMARKET			
30	Friday	Hexham	NEWMARKET	LINGFIELD PARK	Friday	30

CAPITALS: Flat racing Lower Case: National Hunt AWT: (All weather track) †: Evening Meeting

OCTOBER 2005

Date	Racecourse	Race Name
1 Oct	Newmarket	Peugeot Sun Chariot (fillies) Flat
	Newmarket	Oh So Sharp (fillies) Flat
	Newmarket	Tote Cambridgeshire (Handicap) Flat
	Redcar	Two-Year-Old Trophy Flat
	Redcar	Guisborough Flat
5 Oct	Wincanton	Tote Rising Stars Novice Chase
8 Oct	Salisbury	Willmott Dixon Cornwallis Flat
	Salisbury	Tom McGee Autumn Flat
	York	Newton Fund Managers Rockingham Flat
	York	Coral Eurobet Sprint Trophy (Handicap) Flat
13 Oct	Newmarket	EBF Boadicea (fillies and mares) Flat
	Newmarket	Lanwades Stud Severals (fillies) Flat
14 Oct	Newmarket	Bentinck Flat
15 Oct	Kempton Park	Listed Novice Hurdle Flat
	Kempton Park	Charisma Gold Cup (Handicap) Chase
	Newmarket	Emirates Airline Champion Flat
	Newmarket	Darley Dewhurst (colts & fillies) Flat
	Newmarket	Victor Chandler Challenge Flat
	Newmarket	Owen Brown Rockfel (fillies) Flat
	Newmarket	Newmarket Darley Flat
	Newmarket	Jockey Club Cup Flat
	Newmarket	Tote Cesarewitch (Handicap) Flat
17 Oct	Pontefract	Tote Bookmakers Silver Tankard Flat
21 Oct	Doncaster	DBS October Yearling Flat
	Newbury	Vodafone Horris Hill (colts & geldings) Flat
22 Oct	Aintree	Molyneux Novice Chase
	Chepstow	Persian War Novice Hurdle
	Doncaster	Racing Post Trophy (colts & fillies) Flat
	Doncaster	Doncaster Flat
	Newbury	St Simon Flat
	Newbury	Swettenham Stud Radley (fillies) Flat
23 Oct	Aintree	Fieldspring Old Roan (Limited Handicap) Chase
25 Oct	Yarmouth	Lady Godiva (fillies and mares) Flat
28 Oct	Newmarket	Egerton Stud James Seymour Flat
	Newmarket	EBF Bosra Sham (fillies) Flat
29 Oct	Lingfield Park	United House Handicap Chase
	Newmarket	Ben Marshall Flat
	Newmarket	Zetland Flat
	Newmarket	European Breeders Fund Montrose (fillies) Flat
	Wetherby	Peterhouse Group Charlie Hall Chase
	Wetherby	John Smith's West Yorkshire Hurdle
	Wetherby	Stanley Racing Wensleydale Juvenile Novice Hurdle
30 Oct	Lingfield Park	EBF Fleur de Lys Flat

OCTOBER

		North	Midlands	South		
1	Saturday	REDCAR	NEWMARKET SOUTHWELL (AWT) (Matinee) †WOLVERHAMPTON (AWT)	EPSOM DOWNS Fontwell Park	Saturday	1
2	Sunday	Kelso	Market Rasen Uttoxeter		Sunday	2
3	Monday	PONTEFRACT		BRIGHTON WINDSOR	Monday	3
4	Tuesday	CATTERICK BRIDGE	Huntingdon LEICESTER		Tuesday	4
5	Wednesday		NOTTINGHAM Towcester	Exeter	Wednesday	5
6	Thursday		SOUTHWELL (AWT) Worcester	Wincanton	Thursday	6
7	Friday	Carlisle YORK		NEWBURY	Friday	7
8	Saturday	Hexham YORK	Bangor-On-Dee WARWICK (Matinee)	Chepstow SALISBURY	Saturday	8
9	Sunday	NEWCASTLE		BATH GOODWOOD	Sunday	9
10	Monday	AYR	WOLVERHAMPTON (AWT)	WINDSOR	Monday	10
11	Tuesday	AYR	LEICESTER SOUTHWELL (AWT)		Tuesday	11
12	Wednesday	Wetherby	Uttoxeter	LINGFIELD PARK (AWT)	Wednesday	12
13	Thursday		Ludlow NEWMARKET SOUTHWELL (AWT)		Thursday	13
14	Friday	REDCAR	NEWMARKET	BRIGHTON	Friday	14
15	Saturday	CATTERICK BRIDGE	NEWMARKET Stratford-On-Avon	Kempton Park LINGFIELD PARK (AWT) (Matinee)	Saturday	15
16	Sunday	MUSSELBURGH	Hereford Market Rasen		Sunday	16
17	Monday	PONTEFRACT		Plumpton WINDSOR	Monday	17
18	Tuesday		SOUTHWELL (AWT) YARMOUTH	Exeter	Tuesday	18
19	Wednesday	NEWCASTLE	NOTTINGHAM	BATH	Wednesday	19
20	Thursday	Haydock Park	Ludlow	BRIGHTON	Thursday	20
21	Friday	DONCASTER	Fakenham	NEWBURY	Friday	21
22	Saturday	Aintree DONCASTER Kelso	WOLVERHAMPTON (AWT) (Matinee)	Chepstow NEWBURY	Saturday	22
23	Sunday	Aintree	Towcester	Wincanton	Sunday	23
24	Monday		LEICESTER WOLVERHAMPTON (AWT)	LINGFIELD PARK (AWT)	Monday	24
25	Tuesday	CATTERICK BRIDGE	Cheltenham YARMOUTH		Tuesday	25
26	Wednesday	Sedgefield	Cheltenham NOTTINGHAM		Wednesday	26
27	Thursday		Stratford-On-Avon	LINGFIELD PARK (AWT) Taunton	Thursday	27
28	Friday	Wetherby	NEWMARKET Uttoxeter		Friday	28
29	Saturday	AYR Wetherby	NEWMARKET SOUTHWELL (AWT) (Matinee) †WOLVERHAMPTON (AWT)	Lingfield Park	Saturday	29
30	Sunday	AYR Carlisle		LINGFIELD PARK (AWT)	Sunday	30
31	Monday		Warwick WOLVERHAMPTON (AWT)	Plumpton	Monday	31

CAPITALS: Flat racing Lower Case: National Hunt AWT: (All weather track) †: Evening Meeting

NOVEMBER 2005

Date	Racecourse	Race Name
01 Nov	Exeter	Williamhill.co.uk Haldon Gold Cup (Limited Handicap) Chase
03 Nov	Musselburgh	Willie Park Trophy Flat
05 Nov	Doncaster	EBF Gillies (fillies and mares) Flat
	Doncaster	CIU Serlby Flat
	Doncaster	Charles Sidney Mercedes Benz Wentworth Flat
	Doncaster	Tote Scoop6 November (Handicap) Flat
	Wincanton	K J Pike & Sons Elite (Limited Handicap) Hurdle
	Wincanton	Badger Brewery Handicap Chase
11 Nov	Cheltenham	Gerrard Wealth Management Sharp Novice Hurdle
12 Nov	Cheltenham	Open Juvenile Novice Hurdle
	Cheltenham	Paddy Power Gold Cup (Handicap) Chase
	Cheltenham	Open Trophy (Handicap) Chase
	Cheltenham	Tote Bookmakers Handicap Hurdle
13 Nov	Cheltenham	Independent November Novice Chase
	Cheltenham	Greatwood (Handicap) Hurdle
	Cheltenham	Betfair Open Bumper
18 Nov	Windsor	PricewaterhouseCoopers Ascot Hurdle
19 Nov	Haydock Park	Edward Hanmer Memorial (Limited Handicap) Chase
	Huntingdon	BBA Peterborough Chase
	Lingfield Park	Littlewoods Bet Direct Churchill
	Windsor	First National Gold Cup (Limited Intermediate Handicap) Chase
20 Nov	Aintree	Tote Becher (Handicap) Chase
	Plumpton	Sussex National (Handicap) Chase
26 Nov	Newbury	RBI Promotions Newbury Novice Chase
	Newbury	RBI Promotions Long Distance Hurdle
	Newbury	Systems by Design Fulke Walwyn Novice Chase
	Newbury	Hennessy Cognac Gold Cup (Handicap) Chase
	Newbury	Stan James Gerry Feilden (Limited Intermediate Handicap) Hurdle
	Newcastle	Pertemps 'Fighting Fifth' Hurdle

Artist: **Heather St Clair Davis COMING OFF THE HEATH** *Courtesy of:* **Frost & Reed**

NOVEMBER

		North	Midlands	South		
1	Tuesday	CATTERICK BRIDGE	Worcester	Exeter	Tuesday	1
2	Wednesday		NOTTINGHAM	Chepstow Kempton Park	Wednesday	2
3	Thursday	Haydock Park MUSSELBURGH	Towcester		Thursday	3
4	Friday	Hexham	YARMOUTH	Fontwell Park	Friday	4
5	Saturday	DONCASTER Kelso	SOUTHWELL (AWT) (Matinee) †WOLVERHAMPTON (AWT)	Sandown Park Wincanton	Saturday	5
6	Sunday	Ayr	Hereford Market Rasen		Sunday	6
7	Monday	Carlisle	Stratford-On-Avon WOLVERHAMPTON (AWT)		Monday	7
8	Tuesday	Sedgefield	Huntingdon SOUTHWELL (AWT)		Tuesday	8
9	Wednesday		Bangor-On-Dee WOLVERHAMPTON (AWT)	Lingfield Park	Wednesday	9
10	Thursday		Ludlow	LINGFIELD PARK (AWT) Taunton	Thursday	10
11	Friday	Newcastle	Cheltenham WOLVERHAMPTON (AWT)		Friday	11
12	Saturday	Wetherby	Cheltenham SOUTHWELL (AWT) (Matinee) Uttoxeter †WOLVERHAMPTON (AWT)	LINGFIELD PARK (AWT)	Saturday	12
13	Sunday	Carlisle	Cheltenham	Fontwell Park	Sunday	13
14	Monday		Leicester WOLVERHAMPTON (AWT)	Folkestone	Monday	14
15	Tuesday		Fakenham SOUTHWELL (AWT)	LINGFIELD PARK (AWT)	Tuesday	15
16	Wednesday	Hexham	SOUTHWELL (AWT)	Kempton Park	Wednesday	16
17	Thursday		Hereford Market Rasen	Wincanton	Thursday	17
18	Friday	Kelso		Exeter Windsor	Friday	18
19	Saturday	Haydock Park	Huntingdon SOUTHWELL (AWT) (Matinee) †WOLVERHAMPTON (AWT)	LINGFIELD PARK (AWT) Windsor	Saturday	19
20	Sunday	Aintree	Towcester	Plumpton	Sunday	20
21	Monday		Ludlow SOUTHWELL (AWT)	LINGFIELD PARK (AWT)	Monday	21
22	Tuesday	Sedgefield	SOUTHWELL (AWT) Warwick		Tuesday	22
23	Wednesday	Wetherby		Chepstow Lingfield Park	Wednesday	23
24	Thursday	Carlisle	Uttoxeter	Taunton	Thursday	24
25	Friday	Musselburgh	WOLVERHAMPTON (AWT)	Newbury	Friday	25
26	Saturday	Newcastle	Towcester †WOLVERHAMPTON (AWT)	LINGFIELD PARK (AWT) Newbury	Saturday	26
27	Sunday	Doncaster	Leicester	Newbury	Sunday	27
28	Monday		SOUTHWELL (AWT) WOLVERHAMPTON (AWT)	Folkestone	Monday	28
29	Tuesday		Hereford SOUTHWELL (AWT)	LINGFIELD PARK (AWT)	Tuesday	29
30	Wednesday	Catterick Bridge	WOLVERHAMPTON (AWT)	Plumpton	Wednesday	30

CAPITALS: Flat racing Lower Case: National Hunt AWT: (All weather track) †: Evening Meeting

DECEMBER 2005

Date	Racecourse	Race Name
2 Dec	Sandown Park	Winter Novice Hurdle
3 Dec	Chepstow	John Hughes Rehearsal (Limited Handicap) Chase
	Haydock Park	Listed Novice Hurdle
	Sandown Park	Mitsubishi Shogun Tingle Creek Trophy Chase
	Sandown Park	Extraman Trophy Henry VIII Novice Chase
	Sandown Park	William Hill (Handicap) Hurdle
	Sandown Park	"Sun ""King of the Punters"" Mildmay Cazalet Memorial Handicap Chase"
10 Dec	Cheltenham	Victor Chandler Bula Hurdle
	Cheltenham	Tripleprint Bristol Novice Hurdle
	Cheltenham	Tripleprint Gold Cup (Handicap) Chase
	Lingfield Park	Arena Racing December Novice Chase
	Lingfield Park	Summit Novice
16 Dec	Windsor	Cantor Sport Long Walk Hurdle
	Windsor	Kennel Gate Novice Hurdle
17 Dec	Haydock Park	Tommy Whittle Chase
	Windsor	Cantor Sport Noel Novice Chase
	Windsor	Silver Cup (Handicap) Chase
26 Dec	Wetherby	Rowland Meyrick (Handicap) Chase
	Kempton Park	Pertemps King George VI Chase
	Kempton Park	Pertemps Christmas Hurdle
	Kempton Park	Pertemps Feltham Novice
27 Dec	Wetherby	Castleford
	Chepstow	Finale Juvenile
	Chepstow	Coral Eurobet Welsh National (Handicap)
	Kempton Park	Wayward Lad Novice
29 Dec	Newbury	TFM Cyntergy Challow
	Newbury	"Championship" Stakes Standard Open"

Artist: **David Dent WINTER MORNING** *Courtesy of:* **The Artist**

DECEMBER

		North	Midlands	South		
1	Thursday		Leicester Market Rasen	Wincanton	Thursday	1
2	Friday		WOLVERHAMPTON (AWT)	Exeter Sandown Park	Friday	2
3	Saturday	Haydock Park Wetherby	†WOLVERHAMPTON (AWT)	Chepstow Sandown Park	Saturday	3
4	Sunday	Kelso	SOUTHWELL (AWT) Warwick		Sunday	4
5	Monday	Newcastle	WOLVERHAMPTON (AWT)	LINGFIELD PARK (AWT)	Monday	5
6	Tuesday	Sedgefield	SOUTHWELL (AWT)	Fontwell Park	Tuesday	6
7	Wednesday	Hexham	Leicester	LINGFIELD PARK (AWT)	Wednesday	7
8	Thursday		Huntingdon Ludlow	Taunton	Thursday	8
9	Friday	Doncaster	Cheltenham WOLVERHAMPTON (AWT)		Friday	9
10	Saturday	Doncaster	Cheltenham SOUTHWELL (AWT) †WOLVERHAMPTON (AWT)	Lingfield Park	Saturday	10
12	Monday		SOUTHWELL (AWT) WOLVERHAMPTON (AWT)	Plumpton	Monday	12
13	Tuesday		SOUTHWELL (AWT) Warwick	Folkestone	Tuesday	13
14	Wednesday		Bangor-On-Dee	LINGFIELD PARK (AWT) Newbury	Wednesday	14
15	Thursday	Catterick Bridge	SOUTHWELL (AWT)	Exeter	Thursday	15
16	Friday		Uttoxeter WOLVERHAMPTON (AWT)	Windsor	Friday	16
17	Saturday	Haydock Park Newcastle		LINGFIELD PARK (AWT) Windsor	Saturday	17
18	Sunday	Musselburgh	SOUTHWELL (AWT)		Sunday	18
19	Monday	Doncaster	WOLVERHAMPTON (AWT)	LINGFIELD PARK (AWT)	Monday	19
20	Tuesday		SOUTHWELL (AWT)	Fontwell Park LINGFIELD PARK (AWT)	Tuesday	20
21	Wednesday		Ludlow WOLVERHAMPTON (AWT)	LINGFIELD PARK (AWT)	Wednesday	21
22	Thursday	Ayr	Fakenham SOUTHWELL (AWT)		Thursday	22
26	Monday (Bank Holiday)	Sedgefield Wetherby	Huntingdon Market Rasen Towcester WOLVERHAMPTON (AWT)	Kempton Park Wincanton	Monday (Bank Holiday)	26
27	Tuesday (Bank Holiday)	Wetherby	Leicester SOUTHWELL (AWT)	Chepstow Kempton Park	Tuesday (Bank Holiday)	27
28	Wednesday	Catterick Bridge	WOLVERHAMPTON (AWT)	Newbury	Wednesday	28
29	Thursday	Musselburgh		LINGFIELD PARK (AWT) Newbury	Thursday	29
30	Friday	Haydock Park		LINGFIELD PARK (AWT) Taunton	Friday	30
31	Saturday		Uttoxeter Warwick WOLVERHAMPTON (AWT)	Lingfield Park	Saturday	31

CAPITALS: Flat racing Lower Case: National Hunt AWT: (All weather track) †: Evening Meeting

Scotland

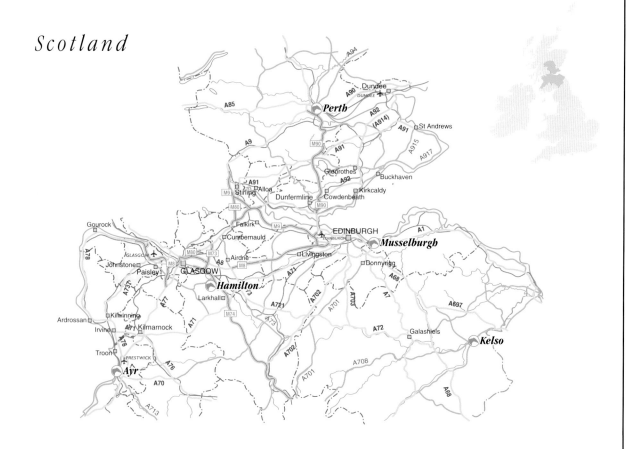

The North

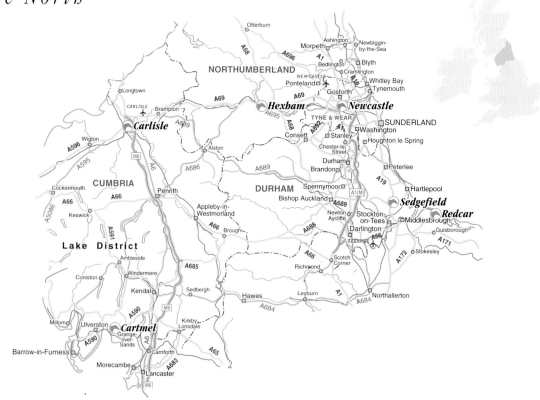

Yorkshire

The North West

East Midlands & East Anglia

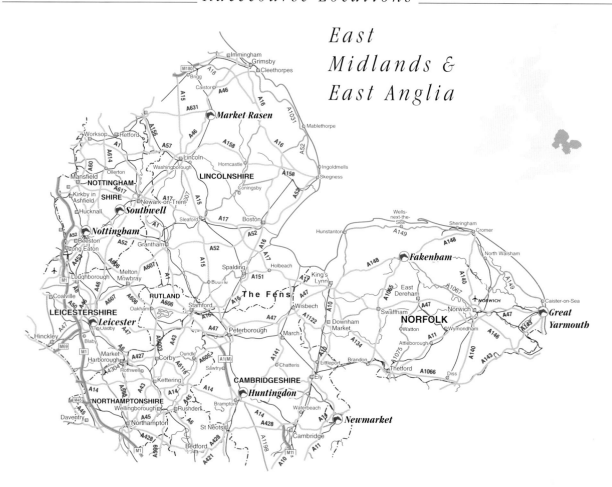

The Midlands & South Wales

London & The South

The South West

British Racecourses

Artist: **John King GLORIOUS GOODWOOD** *Courtesy of:* **The Artist**

47

*Artist: **Graham Isom** AINTREE GRAND NATIONAL*
*Courtesy of: **Rosenstiel's***

Aintree is in the capable and safe hands of **Charles Barnett**, who acts as the **Managing Director**. **AJA Tulloch** is the **Clerk of the Course** with **Dickon White** as **Marketing Manager** and **Karan White** as **Sales Manager**. If you wish to make enquiries with reference to the Grand National Festival, please write to: **Aintree Racecourse Co Ltd, Aintree, Liverpool L9 5AS, tel: 0151 523 2600, fax: 0151 522 2920.** *Website: www.aintree.co.uk*

The racecourse itself lies five miles from the centre of Liverpool in the suburb of Aintree and approximately one mile from the end of the M58 and M57. Travellers coming up from London should expect a journey of some 213 miles. The M1/M6 double is the answer for these southerners, while visitors from north of Merseyside might care to use another motorway double—the M6 followed by the M58. Northbound travellers from Birmingham should use the M5 before joining the M6/M57. If you are a train traveller then the Euston line is the one to be on to Liverpool Lime Street station. From Liverpool Central take the Merseyrail to Aintree. The station is opposite the course entrance. Car drivers should note that there is a convenient 'park and ride' system located off the M57. On the racecourse all cars and coaches must be pre-booked with the racecourse before they arrive at the course. Coach parking is no longer allowed in the central enclosure, giving much improved viewing on the Mildmay course. The Steeplechase enclosure has seated viewing for 600 and a total capacity of 25,000. If you prefer to fly, (helicopters only please), do contact the course in advance. You will need written permission from Philip Pickford. Contact him on 0161 7996967.

Aintree has some of the best and most unique jumping action in the country. Nothing can compare with the sight of large fields tackling the National fences. Although many might say the Grand National is not the test it once was, the close finishes of recent years stamp the fact that this is racing of the highest quality. The Aintree Festival in April lasts three days and features pattern races each day. Champions and old favourites reappear every year, particularly in the National with many horses seeming to love the big day and being kept in reserve just for the occasion. During the meeting, racing takes place over three different courses—the Grand National course, the Mildmay course and the Hurdle course. Friday features the Topham Trophy over the National fences, whetting the appetite for the big day. You also have a sight of the Grand National fences on the Thursday during the Aintree Foxhunters Chase, and prospective star hurdlers

appear in the Aintree Novices Hurdle. Aintree has a new sponsor for the Grand National in John Smith's, a name long familiar to punters and those who enjoy a pint. The famous brand is one of racing's oldest sponsors, on the flat and over the jumps, and we are sure that this new relationship will flourish in the coming years.

For the Festival, admission charges for 2005 are £34 for the County enclosure on Thursday, rising to £72 for a place in the Princess Royal, Queen Mother or County stands on Grand National Day. Three day badges were also available and if you buy them before December 22 the price drops from £156 to £135 for the Princess Royal and Queen Mother stands with similar discounts for the County and Aldanati stands and Tattersalls. But you don't have to spend this much to enjoy the wonders of Aintree on National Day as a mere £10 will get you into the Steeplechase enclosure and children are admitted free of charge; excellent value considering you will be closer to the action than many others attending. The Steeplechase and Tattersalls Enclosures have bookmaking and Tote facilities, and an arcade of shops. Entry to these enclosures costs between £10 and £30, depending on the day. Transfer badges may be purchased daily subject to availability. Various discounts are available for parties of 20 or more if you contact the course well in advance. For all other meetings a one admission price policy of £15 has been introduced (with discounts for early booking), allowing access to all public areas, with accompanied children aged 16 and under admitted free.

A sensible addition to Aintree's facilities is the starvision screens, of which there are six on National Day, giving you a life-size view of the action—essential for some if they are to see the racing, given the large crowds that attend. The November two-day Becher's meeting is also a first-class event, and the May evening meeting has also become a regular fixture, which is a pleasure to report.

The Princess Royal Stand holds a large ground floor Irish Bar, incorporating a betting shop and food and drink outlets for Tattersalls racegoers. There is seating for 1,000 people within West Tip, plus standing room for a further 2,000, with access to the Champagne Bar. There are also 16 private rooms, 10 of which overlook the racecourse, and triple-

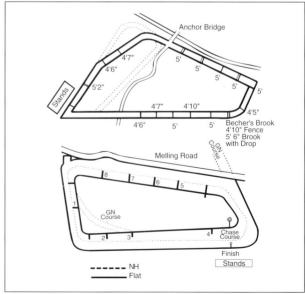

decker corporate hospitality units. On the top floor is the magnificent Princess Royal Suite restaurant seating 350 with its own private viewing balcony for patrons and unrivalled views of the course. Other facilities in Tattersalls include the Chair Pavilion which overlooks the Chair fence, bringing extra facilities to Tatts patrons. The radically enlarged Aintree Pavilion has covered seating in Tatts. The West Tip seats are also available which along with the triple decker corporate hospitality units have greatly improved viewing at the course.

There are a variety of restaurants at Aintree, and patrons should call the racecourse for details. Catering at all on-course eateries is by racecourse specialists Letheby & Christopher.

Commendably, Aintree has announced plans for a three year £30-million redesign and redevelopment of the racecourse with work to start right after the 2005 Grand National meeting and to be completed in 2007. Two new grandstands, next to the Queen Mother Stand, will be linked by a central walkway and two–tiered bar areas. Each grandstand will provide five tiers of premium viewing as well as terracing for 1,400 at ground level. On the first level will be a large restaurant overlooking the racecourse. Other levels will have new seating as well as spaces for disabled people and their helpers and six private suites with racecourse views.

Other improvements include re-location of the Parade Ring, Winner's and Unsaddling Enclosures, plus construction of a new Weighing Room and Stables. This project will also incorporate the building of a Pre-parade Ring, accessible to the general public. The Parade Ring, with an enlarged horse walk, will ensure that all 40 entrants for the Grand National can continue to be safely managed. This new facility will also allow for elevated viewing for up to 4,000 spectators. A new Winner's Enclosure will be sited within the Parade Ring complex, providing far greater capacity for viewing to racegoers.

A new glass fronted Weighing Room will be sited at the south end of the Parade Ring and give vastly improved facilities for jockeys as well as letting spectators see the weighing in and weighing out for each race. A relocated and improved entrance to the racecourse will be created through Grand National Avenue, providing panoramic views of all of the grandstand areas and the new Parade Ring. The existing Parade Ring will become an entrance garden, available to all racegoers, and will incorporate the existing statues of Red Rum and Sir Peter O'Sullevan CBE.

A new Aintree Pavilion for Tattersalls customers will include full public bar, catering and betting facilities and will cater for up to 10,000 racegoers.

Aintree's management is very sensitive to the needs of its racing fans and is keen to preserve the historic atmosphere of the course. With a new sponsor for its world famous Grand National in John Smiths, things look set for many seasons of great jumping action here.

Artist: **Peter Smith ONLY THE BOLD** *Courtesy of:* **Frost & Reed**

_I_f you're planning a visit to Liverpool and Merseyside, call the Accommodation Hotline: 0845 601 1125 or visit _www.visitliverpool.com_. But Travelling the Turf has already scoured the area for the best watering holes, eateries and places to lay your weary head. This is what we recommend:

In Liverpool, the more luxurious hotels include the **Thistle Liverpool** 0151 227 4444, which boasts two especially remarkable sights: the docklands of the river Mersey and a giant statue of one of Liverpool's best known sons, John Lennon. **The Crowne Plaza** 0151 243 8000 and **The Liverpool Marriott** 0151 476 8000 are also two good bets. The **Liverpool Moat House** 0151 471 9988 is also a good runner in this national field. A perfect restaurant for visiting racegoers is the well thought of **Hope Street Restaurant** 0151 707 6060 whose growing reputation is built on its stylish, innovative menu.

Finally, a marvellous pub to visit is the celebrated **Philharmonic** 0151 709 1163—a great place to assess the form on Grand National Eve.

The Lancashire coast yields some excellent golf courses: Royal Liverpool, Royal Birkdale and Royal Lytham St Annes. In Lytham, the **Clifton Arms** (01253) 739898 is a thoughtfully modernised Edwardian hotel. In Lytham St Anne's, the **Chadwick Hall Hotel** (01253) 720061 is well turned out and the restaurant is well thought of. The **Bedford** (01253) 724636 and the **Glendower** (01253) 723241 are also worthy candidates. Further south in Southport, with its gorgeous sands where Red Rum used to gallop, there are a number of good pubs and a hotel of note is the **Scarisbrick** (01704) 543000. The Royal Clifton (01704) 533771 also merits a pre-race inspection and for a budget break, the **Bold Hotel** (01704) 532578 will almost certainly lead to a return visit. A

restaurant to consider is the **Warehouse Brasserie** (01704) 544662 for unpretentious food and great atmosphere. Heading south, **Tree Tops Country House Hotel** 0870 381 8950 is a safe bet for an overnight stay or an excellent dinner. Pubs to head for in this area are the **Ship** at Lathom and the **Scotch Piper** at Lydiate, totally unspoilt, loads of character but no food – a real drinker's pub. If you are envisaging a particularly good day and don't mind a trip, **Paul Heathcote's Restaurant** (01772) 784969 is outstanding and can be found in Longridge near Preston.

At Hoylake you might be tempted to stay at the **Bowler Hat Hotel**, Birkenhead (0151) 6524931. The **De Vere Daresbury Park** (01925) 267331, handily situated near to Warrington, is also one to consider. Also near Warrington the **Hanover International Hotel** (01925) 730706 does special racing breaks including racing papers and transport to and from the racecourse.

For those who want to make a weekend of it, there are many places to visit slightly further afield. The **Inn at Whitewell**, (01200) 448222 in Whitewell to the north of Aintree, is a splendid ancient inn, whilst at Knutsford the **Cottons Hotel**, (01565) 650333 is well worth a look. In Cheshire, the **Hartford Hall Hotel**, (01606) 75711 at Northwich offers 16th Century charm along with 20th Century comfort. **Nunsmere Hall** (01606) 889100 is an excellent stayer where the Garden Room Restaurant is first class. What's more, the hotel is almost entirely surrounded by a lake—ideal for throwing oneself in if the big ante-post bet on the National falls at the first and brings down the wife's selection! At Woolton, The **Woolton Redbourne** 0151 421 1500 is a top-notch hotel to start and end a great sporting weekend. Finally, if any more suggestions are needed, then turn to the Haydock Park section for inspiration.

Artist: **Graham Isom THE GRAND NATIONAL** _Courtesy of:_ **Rosenstiel's**

Ascot's management team includes **Douglas Erskine Crum**, the **Chief Executive**; **Nicholas Cheyne**, the **Racing Director**; **Janet Walker**, **Commercial & Finance Director**; **Ronnie Wilkie**, **Operations Director** and **Nick Smith, Head of Public Relations.** Her Majesty's Representative is the **Duke of Devonshire**. The authorities can be contacted at **Ascot Racecourse, Ascot, Berkshire SL5 7JX, tel: (01344) 622211, fax: (08704) 581778**. There is a credit card hotline for all bookings on **(01344) 876876,** e-mail: *enquiries@ascot.co.uk* website: *www.ascot.co.uk/ www.royalascot.co.uk*

Anyone planning a visit to Ascot in 2005 will unfortunately be disappointed as the course is in the midst of the largest redevelopment of any racing facility in Europe, if not the world. But, wait a year, and if all things go to plan, you will be able to experience and enjoy the fruits of what £180 million can buy in the most up to date racing convenience and comfort.

While other courses update their facilities in stages, Ascot has gone all out to do the job in one big go. This has meant a complete repositioning and rebuild of the straight course to provide more space for the new stand and its surrounds and the necessary dispersal of the entire year's fixtures to other courses while the work is going on. Prime among these of course is the Royal meeting in June, which, until things are completed at the Berkshire HQ, has been moved to York's Knavesmire. Officials at Ascot will still be running the Royal show at the new, temporary venue and we are sure the local Yorkshire folk will make them feel very welcome.

Officials at the Berkshire course hope that Ascot racegoers will join northern racing fans to experience what is sure to be a memorable week of spectacular pageantry, stylish fashion, great hospitality and, of course, horseracing of the highest order. Royal Ascot at York will be run along similar lines to the way in which the Breeders' Cup organisers stage their event with a host racecourse in the United States every year. Ascot will run the event with both organisations working together to make this unique Royal Meeting a success.

Capacity has been set at 50,000 each day and there will be a Royal Enclosure at York as well as the daily parade of carriages to deliver the Royal party and their guests. The traditional dress code will also be carried north.

For the latest information in booking arrangements for Royal Ascot at York in 2005, check with their website at *www.royalascot.co.uk*

Hospitality and ticket sales for 2006 are likely to commence in the autumn of this year, although an exact date has not yet been set. Ascot will be writing to everyone who has booked tickets or hospitality at Royal Ascot in recent years, but those wishing to be added to their database to receive information when it becomes available, should send an e-mail to *enquiries@ascot.co.uk* with contact details including a postal address.

The other meeting on the move is the Diamond meeting at the end of July which will be stage managed by the Ascot team at not-too-far away Newbury, while the Shergar Cup meeting in August is going to Windsor, which will also host a number of jumps fixtures in November and December, the first time National Hunt racing has been held there in some years. Leafy

*Artist: **Alexandra Churchill GALILEO***
*Courtesy of: **The Artist***

Lingfield will also host several Ascot jumps fixtures from December to February, including a New Year's eve card, as well as flat racing in May and July.

With the show moving north and to other points in the compass for a year, what will the new Ascot look like when building work is complete? The focal point of the new designs is the new stand itself, with an internal naturally lit galleria, bringing daylight into a covered public concourse. Above the galleria will be a lightweight parasol roof structure that is designed to replicate in architecture the trees that surround the racecourse. Under the stands will be a new covered access road running the length of the stands to hold all the necessary operational services.

Maximum capacity will remain at 80,000 but on really busy days such as the Royal meeting there should be lots more room to move around in. Relocating the track to the north will allow a new 9,000 capacity Parade Ring to be located behind the stands. The pre-parade ring and saddling boxes will be moved in and around the historic Tote building overlooking the current paddock lawns. Interestingly, this area once used to house the pre-parade ring so Ascot is reverting to the original design! Much of the outer red brick walls and the Grade II Listed buildings on the perimeter of the site will be retained to form a backdrop to the lawns with which Ascot is synonymous.

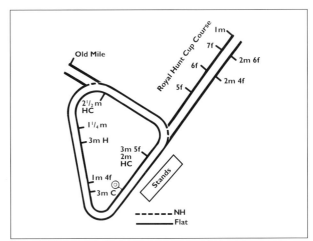

Artist: **David Trundley** *FLAMING JUNE ROYAL ASCOT*
Courtesy of: **The Artist**

Artist: **David Trundley** *CATCHING THE EYE ASCOT*
Courtesy of: **The Artist**

*T*here are numerous excellent hostelries in Berkshire's leafy countryside, making ideal ports of call for a pre or post-race chat. We start our Ascot recommendations with a hotel and restaurant double, the aptly named **Cottage Inn** (01344) 882242 at Winkfield–warmly welcoming nd serving simple but delicious food. Another good eating establishment located in Ascot is the **Thatched Tavern** (01344) 620874—a great atmosphere here as well with first rate beer. The **Rose and Crown** (01344) 882051 has some rooms and good food, and it's very handy for the racecourse. Another pub with a restaurant is the **White Hart** (01344) 882415—the bar snacks here are good. Further west, and in Waltham St Lawrence, the **Bell** 0118 934 1788 is a pub restaurant with a beautifully relaxed atmosphere, ideal for explaining the disastrous losses of the afternoon's racing to one's better half! (but don't take the children). Heading north, the **Horn** 0118 940 1416 at Crazies Hill near Warren Row is a real foody's pub, so much that it would be wise to book at weekends.

Binfield has more than its fair share of good boozers—the **Stag and Hounds** (01344) 483553 and the **Bullfinch** are two of several that should be sampled.

The **Bell** (01635) 578272 at Aldworth is a refreshingly unspoilt pub serving very good simple bar food. No so good for keeping in touch with your bookie though–mobile phones are banned (no credit cards either).

At Bray, the **Monkey Island Hotel** (01628) 623400, securely anchored on its own private island, is an idyllic retreat from the bustle of Ascot. The **Fat Duck** restaurant (01628) 580333 is also one that comes highly recommended. The **Hinds Head** here is a popular pub to shortlist, another jewel is the **Brickmakers Arms** (01276) 472267 - very good fare here. For a more sophisticated experieince, or to celebrate a win in style, **L'Ortolan** 0118 988 3783 will not disappoint if you enjoy classic French cuisine with a twist.

There are many people who will dash straight home after racing but for those wishing to stay locally there are numerous possibilities: the **Berystede Hotel** (01344) 623311 on the Bagshot Road in Ascot, or in Bagshot itself, the **Pennyhill Park Hotel** (01276) 471774, a grand country mansion which also has a commendable restaurant. An alternative which is less pricey is the **Cricketers**, also in Bagshot (01276) 473196. A little further south one arrives in Camberley. Here, the **Frimley Hall Hotel** (0870) 4008224 is not cheap but is most comfortable. Other places that are well worth considering include a brace of hotels in Egham, in neighbouring Surrey. Neither is particularly cheap, but both are extremely comfortable. They are **Great Fosters** (01784) 433822, an outstandingly elegant former hunting lodge with good facilities, and the **Runnymede** (01784) 436171 where a Thames-side setting adds scenic splendour—a warm favourite for racegoers. A jolly restaurant in Egham should also be noted when visiting the races or bloodstock sales— The **Olive Grove** (01784) 439494, where Mediterranean cuisine is the order of the day. Maidenhead is also handy for the course and **Fredrick's Hotel** (01628) 581000 is well worth a visit (a superb restaurant here as well). The **Holiday**

Inn Maidenhead (01628) 506000 is another worthy option. In Sonning, **The Great House** (01734) 692277 comes particularly well recommended for both service and value, as does **French Horn** (01189) 692204 which commands a great view over the Thames and exceptional food and acommodation. Further out in Pingewood, the **Hannover International Hotel** (0118) 9500885, offers a spectacular lakeside situation, but is modern by comparison. Another modern hotel is the Swiss-styled **Coppid Beech** (01344) 303333—a good restaurant here as well.

In Ascot itself, the **Royal Berkshire Hotel** (01344) 623322, is a superb Queen Anne mansion with excellent restaurants and worth noting when visiting this esteemed course. Ascot is synonymous with style and if one wishes to experience the real glamour of days gone by, then a visit to the singularly magnificent **Cliveden** (01628) 668561 is in order. Former home of the Astor family, the house is now an hotel of unrivalled elegance. Another handy local favourite is the **Stirrups Hotel** (01344) 882284 at Maidens Green near Bracknell, a hotel and restaurant combination with prominent racing themes. A night spent in Ascot does not have to be extravagantly expensive. For affordable comfort try the **Highclere Hotel** (01344) 625220 at Sunninghill. The **Jade Fountain** (01344) 627070, in the High Street is also a

Artist: **Susie Whitcombe STRAIGHT MILE START**
Courtesy of: **Osborne Studio Gallery**

good choice for those who enjoy Chinese cooking. Other ideas for the Ascot racegoer can be found in the Windsor, Sandown and Kempton sections of this book. Whatever happens at the racetrack there are numerous fine hostelries at which to celebrate or commiserate in and around Ascot—a thoroughbred racecourse.

Artist: **Graham Isom ASCOT** *Courtesy of:* **Rosenstiel's**

*T*he **General Manager** at Ayr is **William Gorol** while **Clerk of the Course** is **Anthea Morshead** and **Lindsay Smith** is the **Marketing Manager**. They can be contacted at **2 Whitletts Road, Ayr, KA8 0JE, tel: (01292) 264179, fax: (01292) 610140, website:** *www.ayr-racecourse.co.uk* **e-mail:** *info@ayr-racecourse.co.uk* On racedays there is an on-course office at the main Eglinton Stand entrance. The course was acquired recently by **Chairman Alan Macdonald** and **Managing Director Richard Johnstone** and they have wasted little time in announcing some ambitious plans to revitalise what has always been considered Scotland's premier course.

The track is situated just outside Ayr and is easily accessible via the dual carriageway which bypasses the town centre. The course is about 400 miles from London but the motorway network should see you through smoothly and the A713, the A70 and the A77 will carry you to Ayr from Glasgow on the latter stages of your journey to the large, free car parks. If the car journey sounds too much like hard work, then Prestwick Airport is located only 15 minutes away from the racecourse while Glasgow International Airport is only 45 minutes from Ayr. The airstrip in the centre of the course is suitable only for helicopters but please notify the racecourse of your intended arrival. Trains depart from London Euston and the station at Ayr is a mile from the course where a bus trip will complete your journey.

There are several races to look out for, including the Scottish National in April, the Scottish Classic in July and the popular Western Meeting in September which features the Tote Ayr Gold Cup. This three-day meeting provides excellent racing and the ideal excuse for a jaunt to the superb Ayrshire coast. Please note that there will be no racing here in May 2005 due to the redevelopment of the course.

The daily admission rates vary from meeting to meeting. Daily entrance to the Club Enclosure is priced from £18 - £37, while entrance to the Grandstand costs between £13 and £18. OAPs and students with the appropriate identification are welcomed to the racecourse at £5 and £8 for big race days such as the Scottish National and Ayr Gold Cup. Children aged 16 and under admitted free. Groups of over 10 people qualify for a 20 per cent discount if booked seven days in advance. For parties of ten or more there is a special offer of £18 to include admission to the Grandstand and lunch in the Eglinton Suite. If you wish to become an Annual Member, a badge together with a complimentary parking pass in the Western House Car Park will cost £195. This will allow you to attend Ayr's annual fixtures as well as reciprocal meetings at other racecourses.

The on-course catering facilities are comprehensive, ranging from a full tented village to the Western House which caters for parties of 60 to 200, and the Eglinton Rooms which can hold up to 400 guests. The Princess Royal Stand offers nine private boxes for groups from 10 to 100 people with private balconies overlooking the course, and two large sponsors' rooms which can hold up to 90 guests. Private rooms and private boxes are also available for daily hire in the recently refurbished Craigie Stand accommodating from 20 to 60 guests. Corporate hospitality packages run from £75 per person.

There are various restaurants and snack bars at Ayr. Western House is being refurbished and in 2005 will have new dining facilities for 150 people. The Princess Royal Stand has the Roman Warrior restaurant which seats 160 and can also be used for private functions and conferences on non race days. Members can enjoy the facilities of the Seafield Bar, while the Champagne & Seafood Bar is also a new addition to the course.

Artist: **Barrie Linklater A CHALLENGE AT THE LAST FURLONG** *Courtesy of:* **Patterson Gallery**

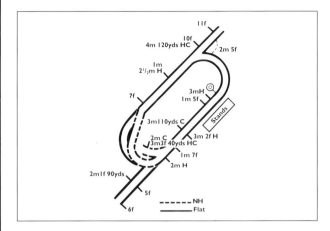

Several million pounds and a few years will see some dramatic changes to Ayr with the addition of a multiplex cinema, hotel and conference centre, and casino. The entrance, parade ring and winner's enclosure are all being redesigned for the benefit of the racegoer and the centre of the course developed to hold a family enclosure.

Ayr is a fine racecourse boasting competitive racing and some spectacular betting events. When the new owners' plans have been completed, Ayr should be in a fine position to celebrate its centenary in 2007.

Local favourites

There are all manner of guesthouses in and around Ayr and the local tourist board will help with any enquiries. People wishing for hotel accommodation also have a good choice when visiting West Scotland and Ayr racecourse.

The **Westin Turnberry Hotel** (01655) 331000 is an extremely stylish place to stay with an array of leisure facilities, including two world-famous golf courses, the Ailsa and the Kintyre. **Culzean Castle** (01655) 884455, perched on its clifftop at Maybole, provides a uniquely different 5 star experience for jaded travellers. Ayr itself is a busy market

town which overlooks the Firth of Clyde. The coastline reveals some charming sandy beaches and attractive fishing villages. The town has many restaurants, bars and hotels, but two hotels which stand out particularly are **Fairfield House** (01292) 267461 and **Enterkine House** (01292) 521608, offering excellent cuisine. At Alloway, the **The Ivy House** (01292) 442336–a restaurant with rooms–and the **Malin Court** (01655) 331457 at Turnberry merit consideration. **Ladyburn** (01655) 740585 at Maybole lies within easy reach of Ayr and also many of the renowned local golf courses and is family run, welcoming and offers excellent food. Good fare can also be found in Ayr at **Fouters Bistro** (01292) 261391 and **Braidwoods** (01294) 835544–a popular restaurant in a lovely setting. **The Sorn Inn** (01290) 551305 at Sorn is a village pub with a serious restaurant.

More golf is available in Prestwick and, as you might imagine, the town is also well placed for the nearby airport of the same name. **Parkstone** (01292) 477286 is a convenient guesthouse. But if it's racing you are after, an ideal place to stay near the racecourse is the **Savoy Park** (01292) 266112 on Racecourse road. The bedrooms are comfortable and the bars and restaurant should also be visited. Further north still, one arrives at yet another golfing delight, Troon. Three more hotels to note are the **Marine** Hotel (01292) 314444 which overlooks the golf course and the Isle of Arran. This is a well equipped and comfortable hotel with a superb bistro. Secondly, visit **Piersland House** (01292) 314747 and **Lochgreen House** (01292) 313343 is also first-class. A short way from Irvine in the Montgreenan Estate, near Kilwinning, lies the **Montgreenan Mansion House** (01294) 557733, former home of Lord Glasgow. Four miles from Kilmarnock, the **Fenwick** (01560) 600478, in the little village of the same name, is both stylish and comfortable—quite tremendous. Our final thoughts are situated some way south of Ayr. **Knockinaam Lodge** (01776) 810471, **Portpatrick**, is an outstanding hotel with a first-class restaurant—a real favourite. Alternatively, for those on their way south, **Farlam Hall** (016977) 46234 near Brampton is another good tip. A very warm welcome, outstanding food and comfortable bedrooms—a winning treble.

Artist: **Malcolm Coward** **ALL TO PLAY FOR** Courtesy of: **The Artist**

*T*he **Manager** here is **Jeannie Chantler** and the **Clerk of the Course** is **Ed Gretton**, both of whom can be contacted at **The Racecourse, Overton Road, Bangor-on-Dee, Wrexham LL13 0DA, tel: (01978) 780323 fax: (01978) 780985**. e-mail: *mail@BangorOnDeeRaces.co.uk* website: *www.BangorOnDeeRaces.co.uk*

The course is located in the Bryn y Pys estate near Bangor-on-Dee on the Welsh border. Chester is some 15 miles to the north and Shrewsbury some 25 miles south. London is a full 180 miles away. The major routes to the course are the A525 from Stoke and the M6. The A41 to Wolverhampton, and the M54 and A41 north towards Chester, can be used to link with the M56 network of the northwest. The course itself lies on the A525, but to reach the course it is necessary to turn off the bypass, drive through the village, and on to the B5069 for Overton-on-Dee. There are also a number of minor routes, the B5130 for instance, which can be taken in preference to the A roads to enjoy the border countryside. There is plenty of free parking at the course. The A5 from Llangollen will assist people travelling from inland Wales. Wrexham and its rail network is four miles away and is part of the Euston line, as are nearby Chester and Shrewsbury. A free bus service is provided by the racecourse, leaving Wrexham Station one and a half hours before the first race and returning after racing. If you wish to make a speedy entry/departure then your helicopter is welcomed, though please contact the Clerk of the Course.

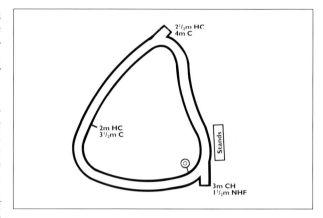

Among the racing highlights are the Wynnstay Hunt evening, the North Western Area point-to-point championship final in May, Ladies Day in July and the Countryside Day in August. As befits a country course, admission prices are a modest £13 for the Paddock and £6 for the Course Enclosure. Book in advance and you can get a £1 discount and a racecard voucher worth the same amount. If you are intent on making regular visits to the track then you ought to consider an Annual Members badge: £130 is the asking price and it is worth noting that the members' car park has one of the best vantage points from which to view the racing. In addition to the days at Bangor, there are 16 reciprocal meetings at some exceptional racecourses.

Artist: **Klaus Philipp NOTHING TO CHOOSE** *Courtesy of:* **The Artist**

Owners and Trainers are well looked after here with a buffet and bar adjacent to the saddling boxes and parade ring with free tea and coffee served all day. The Paddock Restaurant offers views over the racecourse and a three course lunch is priced from £45 per head. A range of hot and cold food is also on offer in the Wynnstay Carvery Restaurant and there are a number of fast food outlets and bars dotted around the course. Private boxes and rooms are available to accommodate from 20 to 80 people, while marquees can be arranged for larger groups.

There is no grandstand at Bangor but the grass banks, offering a head on view of the course, are an excellent substitute. Children and wheelchair-bound racegoers are admitted free and the latter have the benefit of a wheelchair viewing stand. There is ample car parking overlooking the course. There are public telephones and betting shops in the Paddock enclosure and a 'walk in' Tote betting office. The whole course delights with its country setting and splendid atmosphere. If you are seeking a fun day out in 2005 at one of Britain's idyllic national hunt courses, make sure that Bangor is on the shortlist.

Local favourites

This is an area rife with hotels and hostelries. A favourite establishment with the racing fraternity is the **Cross Foxes Inn** (01978) 780380. The **Pen-y-Dyffryn Hall Hotel** (01691) 653700 near Oswestry also comes highly recommended and is ideal for combining a day at the races with a spot of golf. A favourite local pub is the **Union Tavern** (01248) 362462 in Bangor.

Some of the best places to stay are in Llangollen, home of the Eisteddfod festival of song and dance for those who appreciate a fiesta as well as a flutter. The **Wild Pheasant Hotel** (01978) 860629 affords an extremely comfortable stay,

while in the **Chain Bridge Hotel** (01978) 861841 enjoys a fine setting over the River Dee. The restaurant here is good and the bar's ideal for a leisurely chat before racing. At Glyn Ceiriog, the **Golden Pheasant** is modestly priced. Three miles east, the **Bryn Howel Hotel** (01978) 860331 is another cosy place. One of the most strikingly pretty spots is the Horseshoe Pass where the **Britannia Inn** (01978) 860144 is a pleasant place to relax. If you are merely looking for a restaurant **Bodidris Hall** (01978) 790434, a lakeside manor house near Offa's Dyke, where an imaginative menu makes good use of fresh local produce, is an excellent idea. In Llandrillo, **Tyddyn Llan** (01490) 440264 is well thought of and ideal for an early lunch, and it has a few bedrooms too. Another good performer is the **Cross Lanes** (01978) 780555—extremely convenient and increasingly popular with the racing fraternity, it offers special racing breaks. A real gem can be found at **The Cornmill** (01978) 869555—well worth a post-race visit.

In Llanarmon Dyffryn Ceiriog, the **West Arms** (01691) 600665 is over 400 years old and remains a charming place to stay. Renowned for its service, **Glasfryn** (01352) 750500 in Mold is well known for imaginative food in its relaxed bistro-styled restaurant. In nearby Ruthin, the **Ruthin Castle** (01824) 702664 is a classic country house restaurant complete with peacocks. Also close at hand is the **Buck House Hotel** (01978) 780336, extremely handy for the racecourse for those of you who prefer not to travel too far to the races.

Further south in the quiet town of Oswestry, the **Wynnstay** (01691) 655261 is an appealing Georgian inn. Also in this area, **Soulton Hall** (01939) 232786 near Wem guarantees a warm welcome and traditional English cooking in its beautiful tranquil park and walled gardens. One final thought a little further afield is the excellent **Burlton Inn** at Burlton—first class rooms and some very good food—an ideal double after racing at Bangor-on-Dee.

Artist: **Margaret Barrett** OVER THE WATER Courtesy of: **The Artist**

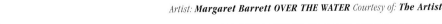

Jon Williams is the **General Manager** and **Tim Long** is **Clerk of the Course** at this delightful course and they can be contacted at **Bath Racecourse, Lansdown, Bath BA1 9BU, tel: (01225) 424609, fax: (01225) 444415** e-mail: *info@bath-racecourse.co.uk* **website:** *www.bath-racecourse.co.uk*

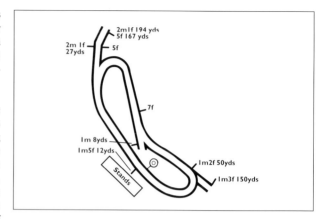

London is approximately 100 miles away, Bath three miles away and Bristol 10 miles yonder. The M4 route is quick but rather boring while the A4 is more interesting but can be fairly congested. Junction 18 off the M4 is the appropriate exit point. The course is well signposted from there, nestling amidst the villages of Kelston, Charlcombe, Swainswick and North Stoke. For travellers from the north and west the M5/M4 is the better route, while the A46 is an alternative if time is not so pressing. If, however, time is of the essence and you decide to take a helicopter, then please land at the north end of the coach park. Car parking areas abound and are free, including the centre of the course. While parking here is free, an entrance fee of £5 per person is levied. Members are entitled to reserved parking. The railway station in Bath is on the main Paddington-South Wales line and buses from the station go to the racecourse. Borderline run special raceday bus services from the centre of Bath at regular intervals, starting two hours before the first race and continuing for up to two hours after the last race upon demand. For details, telephone Badgerline (01225) 464446

Although crowds are always fairly good at Bath, the course is, not surprisingly, at its busiest during its weekend fixtures. The charge for a day's racing is £15 for the Premier Enclosure, which rises to £17 on Premium Meetings, while the Grandstand and Paddock will set you back £10 (£12 Premium Meetings) and the Family Enclosure where you can enjoy a picnic is a modest £5 per head (£7 for Premium days). The Annual Badgeholder scheme, which gives the holder 19 days racing here and several reciprocal days elsewhere is priced at £135 single and a double badge can be ordered for £250. Junior Members (21 and under) are asked to part with £70. For those wishing to organise a larger gathering in advance, a 20 per cent saving can be made on parties of 15 or more in the Premier Enclosure, while a 10 per cent discount applies in the Grandstand & Paddock.

Viewing is good at Bath and the Premier grandstand overlooks the winning post and has rooftop viewing. If you do go up to the roof, please note that you will have reached the highest viewing point of any racecourse in Britain. Although others such as Goodwood and Hexham have superb situations, Bath is actually the highest racecourse of all!

There are nine private boxes available for hire and betting vouchers in units of two or five can be pre-arranged in advance for guests. Should you wish to take a larger party, there are two rooms available for entertaining. Hospitality packages start at £65 + VAT per person and these facilities are well used, so you are advised to book well in advance (01225 424609). If you would prefer a marquee then these can be erected—please contact the racecourse office for further details.

Artist: **Brian Halton FOUR HORSES** *Courtesy of:* **The Artist**

Local Favourites

Bath is a beautiful city with many good hotels and restaurants among its attractions. An excellent hotel is the **Priory** (01225) 331922, where the French cuisine is superb and the Georgian mansion exudes luxury. The **Lansdown Grove** (01225) 483888 is also charming and slightly less expensive! A third sound choice is the **Francis Hotel** (01225) 424105. Bargain seekers will also find solace at the **Dorian House** (01225) 444699, **Oldfield's** (01225) 317984 and **Paradise House Hotel** (01225) 317723. If money is no object, two for the shortlist are the **Bath Spa** (01225) 444424 and the majestic **Royal Crescent** (01225) 823333. Heading south out of town quickly brings you to the excellent **Combe Grove Manor** (01225) 834644 at Monkton Combe. There are some excellent leisure facilities here as well.

The hotel and fine restaurant of **Ston Easton Park** (01761) 241631 is one for the notebook—an outstanding pedigree well worth a detour if your funds are in plentiful supply. In Hinton Charterhouse, **Homewood Park** (01225) 723731 and The **Queensberry** (01225) 447928 are both good. The former is extremely grand, the latter far less so but most pleasant. In Hunstrete, the **Hunstrete House Hotel** (01761) 490490 boasts an outstanding restaurant in a distinguished Georgian manor house set in rolling parkland. **Lucknam Park** (01225) 742777 at Colerne near Bath is another Georgian manor house, quite unsurpassed in luxury and cuisine. There are all manner of restaurants to sample in Bath; among the best are the **Moody Goose** (01225) 466688, **Woods** Restaurant (01225) 314812 or the **Olive Tree** (01225) 447928 at the Queensberry Hotel – smart but less formal than the hotel.

Less pricey, but extremely comfortable accommodation can be discovered in Holcombe, at the **Ring O'Roses** (01761) 232478 which has a tremendous restaurant. In Axford, the **Red Lion** (01672) 520271 is worth the drive for a really special meal. A similar summary could be applied to the **Old Bell** (01666) 822344 in Malmesbury which is a rapidly improving type and well worth considering. In Winterbourne, the **Jarvis Grange Hotel** at Northwoods (01454) 777333 is an elegant place to stay with good leisure facilities. But people who are content with a bar snack or just a post-race pint may care to try any of the following gems. Stanton Wick offers the **Carpenter's Arms** (01761) 490202 a tremendous all rounder, good ales, excellent food, bar meals and restaurant, even some cosy bedrooms if required. The **George** (01373) 834224 at Norton St Philip is charming. For the more adventurous, the **Windsor** Hotel (01225) 422100 has a smart Japanese restaurant where guests can cook their own meals at the table whilst enjoying a cup of Sake. **The Inn** (01225) 722250 at Freshford is appealing, and returning to Hinton Charterhouse, the **Stag** has style. The **Royal Oak**, Winsford, has a delightful country setting, and nearby in Ford, the **White Hart** (01249) 782213 is a welcoming pub with a pleasant restaurant and some bedrooms. Our final selection is the **Manor House** (01249) 782206 also at Castle Combe. Romance is in the air here and racegoers with a conscience should consider it a firm favourite for their less enthusiastic partners, particularly if they also enjoy golf!

Artist: **Klaus Philipp** *THE FAVOURITE OBLIGES Courtesy of:* **The Artist**

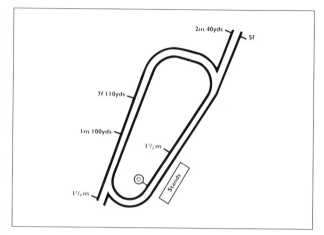

_T_he people to contact at this excellent track are headed by **Sally Iggulden**, who is **Manager and Clerk of the Course**. **Raceday Clerk of the Course** is **James Hutchinson**, while **Assistant Manager** is **Fiona Clancy**. **Jane Johnson** is in charge of **Hospitality, Admissions and Membership** are handled by **Carole Southwick**. They can all be contacted at: **The Racecourse, York Road, Beverley, East Yorkshire HU17 8QZ**, tel: **(01482) 867488/882645**, fax: **(01482) 863892**, e-mail: _info@beverleyracecourse.co.uk_ website: _www.beverley-racecourse.co.uk_

Beverley is situated on the A1035 to the south east of York and north west of the Humber estuary. The southbound traveller should make use of the A1, the A19 and the A1079. If one is travelling from the south or east make your way via the A1(M) to the M62 and then take the A164 Junction. From Lincolnshire, the A15 Humber Bridge followed by the A164 is probably a good each-way bet. There are a number of routes east of Beverley. Should one be venturing from that part of the country, the A1035 looks to be the obvious choice. No matter which direction you come from there are brown tourist signs indicating the way to the course. Parking is free except in the course enclosure where it costs £4. When it comes to a train journey the best idea is to go to Beverley itself, which is on the Hull to Scarborough line. An intermittent bus service runs from Beverley station. For more speedy journeys, helicopters will come in handy. If you happen to have one available you

are welcome to land it in the centre of the course with prior permission from the racecourse.

Beverley stages quite a busy flat schedule each year and its long uphill straight produces some tight finishes. They have been racing around here since 1690 and it was in 1767 that the first races were held on the present site.

Badges in the Club enclosure will set you back £16 but this will get you a seat in the grandstand and fine view of

Artist: **Graham Isom** BEVERLEY _Courtesy of:_ **Rosenstiel's**

the racing. Admission to the Grandstand & Paddock is £10, while the new Minster Enclosure next to the running rail is a mere £5. Picnickers are invited to join the fun in the Course Enclosure for a modest £3 per person and £4 per car. There certainly seems to be a price everyone can afford here! Not only that, but there is an extensive group booking scheme that offers discounts for parties of 20 or more in the Club and 10 or more in all other enclosures. OAPs also receive concessions on the day in all but the Club. Under 16s are admitted free of charge provided they are accompanied. Prospective Annual Members are advised to contact the racecourse office to be put on the waiting list. If your number comes up, a single badge will cost you only £120, or £200 double (Juniors under 21 £70), a real bargain. If you really can't wait, another popular scheme worth considering is an annual Yorkshire Racing season ticket. A single ticket at £260 entitles you to admission to all nine Yorkshire courses (173 fixtures in 2004), or £420 double. Contact Go Racing in Yorkshire on (01937) 580051 for details.

No one need venture too far to slake their thirst or satisfy their appetite at Beverley. In the Club enclosure the Lawn Bar has a garden area overlooking the winning post and offers a choice of seafood sandwiches, while the new Member's Terrace bar has hot sandwiches. The restaurant has views of the course and offers an a la carte luncheon or afternoon tea. Book a table by calling (0113) 2876387. In addition to a range of fast food outlets, the Grandstand and Paddock's Rapid Lad bar offers a full range of hot and cold snacks. The Jockeys Loft is a self-service restaurant on the first floor, while the Paddock Bar has great views of racing as well as some hot snacks. The Minster also has a variety of bars and fast food outlets, as does the Course Enclosure in the centre of the track.

Set on common land high above the market town of the same name, Beverley is well worth a visit by any keen punter, although the competitive racing makes it a real challenge to find a winner!

Local favourites

Beverley is a flourishing market town surrounded by outstanding countryside. To the north, the Wolds and the Yorkshire Moors. To the west, the Pennines and to the east, ragged coastline. The 17th century **Beverley Arms Hotel** (01482) 869241 is an extremely comfortable inn in which to stay and a good place from which to explore.

Aside from the Beverley Arms, the **White Horse** (01482) 868103, better known as Nellies, has a traditional pub atmosphere. The **Corner House,** serving excellent breakfasts at the weekend, is also a good pub to put the racegoer in the right spirit before racing—or equally after the racing is over. **Lairgate** (01482) 882141 is also a worthy contender. **No 1** (01482) 629911 at Hessle is a restaurant with good form. Nearby, a number of welcoming hotels include the **Tickton Grange Hotel** (01964) 543666, a superb Georgian country house two miles from Beverley. Slightly further afield in Driffield one finds the **Bell Hotel** (01377) 256661, a pleasant inn in the market place—ideal for a post-race bar snack or restaurant dinner.

Alternatives to the south of Beverley include **Rowley Manor** (01482) 848248 at Little Weighton—a splendid parkland setting with a particularly relaxing bar, ideal for

studying overnight declarations in style. There is further comfort to be found with another manor, this time in Willerby, the **Willerby Manor** (01482) 652616; a mention here also for the **Grange Park Hotel** (01482) 656488, just to the south of Beverley—well-equipped and comfortable. If you are lured into Hull then **Minerva** (01482) 326909 is the pub to head for with its well kept ales, simple food and relaxing riverside setting.

In Brandesburton, the **Dacre Arms** (01964) 542392 appeals—note the Wensleydale Ploughmans, and **Burton Lodge** (01964) 542847 is worth a visit, while in Bishop Burton, the **Altisidora** is a friendly pub with a delightful setting. The pub takes its name from the 1813 St Leger winner. In South Dalton, the **Pipe and Glass** (01430) 810246 has great character and serves good food while in Market Weighton, the **Londesborough Arms** (01430) 872214 also has bedrooms and is a very friendly place to stay. The **Triton** in Sledmere (01377) 236644 is very popular and ideally situated for **Sledmere House**—well worth a post-race inspection. Yorkshire Pudding lovers should note the **Half Moon** (01482) 843403 at Skidby. The **Manor House** (01482) 881645 at Walkington is very relaxing and the restaurant is first class. Our final recommendation for all 'foodies' is the **Winteringham Fields** (01724) 733096. Here the food is fantastic and there are some delightful bedrooms as well—one for the notebook for those of you considering a trip to Beverley races in 2005.

*Artist: **Charles Church** GOING OUT Courtesy of: **The Artist***

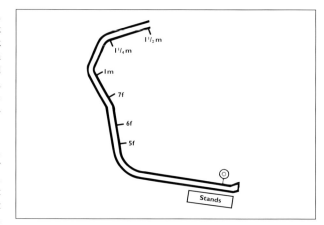

*P*art of the group of courses managed by Northern Racing, the team at Brighton includes **Geoff Stickels** as **Clerk of the Course**, **Phil Bell** as **General Manager** and **Mark Powell** as **Commercial Manager**. They can be contacted on **tel: (01273) 603580** or by **fax: (01273) 673267**. Should you wish to write, the address is: **Brighton Racecourse, Freshfield Road, Brighton, East Sussex, BN2 9XZ e-mail:** *info@brighton-racecourse.co.uk* **website:** *www.brighton-racecourse.co.uk*

The course is situated in one of Brighton's eastern suburbs, high up on White Hawk Hill and about a 60 mile journey from the capital. If you are coming from outside Brighton, head towards Sussex University on the A27 and take the exit for Woodingdean. In the centre of Woodingdean, turn right at the traffic lights and a mile down the road lies the racecourse. Alternatively, you can take the A23 and follow the signs to the racecourse through the town centre, which may take a little longer. The London-Brighton Victoria rail line is most efficient and there is a courtesy bus service from the station to the racecourse on racedays with two trips back after the last. The Brighton/Hove buses all stop near the course too.

Although prices might rise slightly in 2005, admission to the Premier Enclosure is priced at £16, with the Grandstand and Paddock Enclosure at £11. OAPs and students gain admission for £7 and accompanied children under 16 free. If you book online five days before your visit you can save £2 off each badge. Trackside parking in the West Picnic Car Park is priced at £5 per car and £10 per adult. Other parking is free. Annual Membership is priced at £160. This includes free car parking and reciprocal meetings at other courses including Lingfield, Sandown Park, Salisbury, Folkestone and several others.

Parties of between 12 and 150 can be entertained in various places around the racecourse and private boxes can cater for up to 200 guests. Seven new corporate hospitality boxes have recently been added with views of the track, downs and marina. There are also sites for a marquee which can hold 500 guests comfortably. All-inclusive hospitality packages are available per head at £65 - £95 plus VAT. There are numerous bars throughout the course as well as a more formal restaurant, bookings for which can be made by telephoning the racecourse. It is worth noting that all of these facilities are also available for use on non-racedays for exhibitions, weddings, trade fairs and conferences.

There is a cash machine on site, located near the betting shop situated in the Grandstand; there is also an on course betting shop in the Premier Enclosure. Facilities for children

Artist: **Katy Sodeau UP HILL BRIGHTON** *Courtesy of:* **The Artist**

are provided although only at summer meetings. We are pleased to say that for disabled racegoers, there is access to all floors of the Grandstand by lift and ramped access to both Grandstand and Premier Enclosure Bars. Disabled car parking is also available next to the main gate.

Northern Racing has invested almost £5 million since it took over the racecourse and it's starting to pay dividends in terms of the number of people who enjoy a day out there. Last year saw the reinstatement of a high-summer three-day festival in early August. Back in the 'good old days' this festival used to bring Brighton to a standstill with special trains bringing in the punters from London for a day out. There was lots of entertainment on offer with steel bands, parachutists and street theatre, not to mention some really competitive racing including the featured John Smith's Brighton Mile. With a new champagne bar on the Parade Ring lawn and music and dancing until late, we're sure that the final Ladies Evening meeting will prove a massive hit with locals and visitors alike.

Local favourites

Perhaps it's the sea air that makes so many organisations choose Brighton for their annual conference. The best seafront hotels in Brighton are the De Vere **Grand** (01273) 224300 which is quite grand, the **Hilton Brighton Metropole** (01273) 775432, headquarters to many a political conference, the startlingly modern **Thistle Brighton** (01273) 206700 and the **Hilton Brighton West Pier** (formerly the Stakis) (01273) 329744. Hotel du Vin (01273) 718588 is a tastefully converted and well equiped hotel. Highly recommended by the racecourse management are several restaurants in Brighton itself including **Al Duomo** (01273) 326741 and **Al Forno** (01273) 324905 for fans of Italian cuisine, and **Gars** for Chinese near the Town Hall (01273) 321321. Two restaurants also to note are **Sevendials** (01273) 885555 and the unpretentious but good **Black Chapati** (01273) 699011. The **Gingerman** Restaurant

(01273) 326688 and **One Paston Place** (01273) 606933 are also well worth considering. Lovers of Chinese food should shortlist **Choys** (01273) 325305.

The waters of Brighton stretch round the coast and meet with Hove. Here a number of good hotels can be found. One of the best is **Alias Hotel Seattle** (01273) 679799 overlooking the marina. The **Hungry Monk** (01323) 482178, Jevington, is a restaurant to delight you with a wonderful atmosphere and first rate food. Local recommendations also include **Circa** (01273) 471777, and for Indian, **Ganges Brasserie** (01273) 728292. Also not far away from Brighton in Kingston near Lewes you are encouraged to try **Juggs** (01273) 472523—a great 15th Century pub with good real ales and excellent homemade food. **Shelleys** (01273) 472361 is a noted hotel in the High Street.

If you are not content with the seaside offerings in Brighton, then Eastbourne is an elegant and slightly more tranquil alternative. Good value accommodation is plentiful. Examples include the **Lansdowne** (01323) 725174 and the **Chatsworth** (01323) 411016. However, the star of the show is the impressive **Grand** (01323) 412345—great for families, expensive, but very good. A busy pub to note for its tremendous views is the **Devil's Dyke** at Devil's Dyke on the downs above the town. For some really good food, the **York House** Hotel (01323) 412918 is also worth a visit, as is the extremely comfortable **Hilton Avisford Park Hotel** (01243) 551215 at Walberton—well worth the extra journey for those who enjoy excellent food and sporting facilities.

A final selection that should not be overlooked includes **Amberley Castle** (01798) 831992—medieval style with 20th Century comfort. We would also strongly recommend an hotel of real character, **Ockenden Manor** (01444) 416111—a _Travelling the Turf_ favourite. Further north at the delightfully named Pease Pottage, the **Cottesmore Golf & Country Club** (01293) 528256 comes highly recommended.

Artist: **Graham Isom BRIGHTON** Courtesy of: **Rosenstiel's**

At Carlisle, **John Baker** is Course Manager, **Karen Sharpe** is the **Operations Manager**, **Debra Wicks** is in charge of **Sales and Marketing** and **Sue Ellis** handles customer liaison. Their address is **Carlisle Racecourse, Durdar Road, Carlisle, Cumbria, CA2 4TS, tel: (01228) 554700, fax: (01228) 554747, e-mail:** *info@carlisle-races.co.uk* **website:** *www.carlisle-races.co.uk*

Carlisle is a good 300 miles from the capital. However, it is easy to reach for racegoers from all areas of the country. The M6 is the motorway to follow, exiting at junction 42 and then following the signs two miles to the course. The A69 Carlisle-Newcastle road is the best route from the North East, whilst people from areas west of Carlisle should travel on the A595 or the A596. The racecourse is two miles south of the town and the No. 66 bus from Carlisle will deposit you at the course. From London, Carlisle bound trains depart from Euston station or alternatively you can jump on at Kings Cross and change at Newcastle upon Tyne. If you are making the trip by car you will find some 20 acres of grass on which to park your motor. Trackside parking is also available next to the home straight at a cost of £5. Aviators please note that Carlisle airport is some eight miles away. Helicopters can land on the racecourse provided prior arrangements have been made.

The Cumberland Plate and the Carlisle Bell, two of the course's major flat races, are steeped in tradition and are now run on the same day at the end of June meeting. Racing at Carlisle takes place every month of the year and Carlisle's National Hunt course, with its long uphill finish can be notoriously demanding when the ground is testing. The weekday admission charge to the County enclosure is £15, with entry to Tattersalls set at £10. If you make a booking in advance you can gain a £1 discount on both enclosures. Further group discounts are also available. Annual Race Club Membership includes about 22 Carlisle fixtures, as well as a further 26 reciprocal days at other courses and costs £145 single and £220 for a double badge. This drops to £125 and £200 if you are an OAP.

In the new Jubilee Grandstand, Tattersalls ticket holders can enjoy the three food kiosks and two bars on the ground floor of the building as well as viewing the races from the lower terraces. Those race-goers wishing to purchase County badges can view the racing from the upper terracing, the Patterson Bar, or enjoy a meal in The Swifts restaurant also overlooking the finishing post. On the second floor, the Jubilee Grandstand also has seven corporate hospitality boxes available for both companies and individuals wishing to make their visit to Carlisle Racecourse both enjoyable and exclusive. Prices start from £55 per person. Two of the boxes are made available for annual or seasonal lets.

Children are admitted free of charge to the racecourse if accompanied by an adult. Facilities for disabled racegoers are most considerate at Carlisle with free designated parking, a viewing platform on the first floor of the grandstand and specially equipped toilets and easily accessible bars. There is a betting shop in the Paddock area but no banks are in operation on the course. This friendly racecourse is well positioned between Lakeland and the Borders and those of you seeking a day's racing while touring beautiful countryside will find Carlisle a welcoming port of call.

Local favourites

In Carlisle itself, one finds a number of possible candidates for a quiet and comfortable night. Firstly, **Cumbria Park** (01228) 522887 is a distinct posibility. **Lakes Court** (01228) 531951 is a small, stylish Edwardian townhouse worthy of note. Two pubs to consider in nearby Armathwaite are the **Fox and Pheasant** (01697) 472400 overlooking the River Eden and a good bet for real ales and simple bar meals, or the **Dukes Head**–perfect for an overnight stay followed by a hearty breakfast.

South of Carlisle at Tirril, an excellent pub for lovers of real ale, the **Queens Head** (01768) 863219 is well known especially for its own local brew, good food and cosy rooms in case of over indulgence. North of Carlisle lies Rockcliffe where a good pub for a snack is the **Crown and Thistle**. The village guards the mouth of the River Eden and is particularly convenient for the A74. Another riverside setting is provided by the extremely pleasant and welcoming **Crosby Lodge Country House** (01228) 573618 at High Crosby. This hotel enjoys a pastoral setting and also has a good restaurant. Returning to Warwick-on-Eden, the **Queen's Arms** (01228) 560699 is another inn of character. Here you will find a restaurant and some comfortable bedrooms. In Talkin, as well as a good golf course, one finds the **Blacksmiths Arms**—great for bar snacks with some rooms as well.

In Penruddock, the **Hardwick** (01768) 483007 is a pretty, cottagey 18th century pub with a galleried dining room. Best to book, especially in the evenings. North of the A69 at Lanercost, the **Abbey Bridge Inn** (016977) 2224 is an unusual pub with a most appealing hostelry in which to savour a winner in the last. However, **Farlam Hall Hotel** (016977) 46234 is definitely the pick of the paddock, a splendid 17th Century manor house in gorgeous grounds and a grand restaurant as well—a really classical performer in every way. A nearby hotel to note is the **Crown** (01228) 561888 at Wetheral, a coaching inn with first-rate facilities. The Royal Oak, Welton is also thought to be a good type. Last, but certainly not least, for the younger punter planning a racing honeymoon to Carlisle (of which there are surely hundreds!) the **Gretna Chase (01461) 337517** and the **Welcome Lodge (01461) 337566** at Gretna Green will provide the required accommodation. The surrounding hostelries and friendly people, coupled with a well-balanced calendar of sporting fixtures, make a visit to Carlisle racecourse a priority for those of you who have not enjoyed the pleasure.

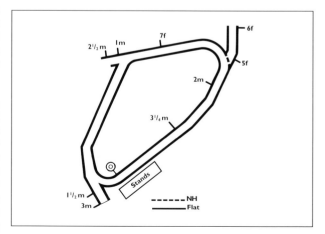

Farlam Hall was opened in June 1975 by the Quinion and Stevenson families, who over the years have both achieved and maintained consistently high standards of food, service and comfort. These high standards have been recognised by all the leading guides with 3 Red Stars and 2 Rosettes from the AA, The Cesar Award from The Good Hotel Guide for Country House Hotel of the Year and also since 1984 membership of Relais and Chateaux.

The old border house, in parts dating back to the seventeenth century was extended to its present size in Victorian times and is now set in acres of mature landscaped gardens which can be seen from the elegant lounges and dining room.

The fine silver, crystal and starched white linen, all combine to create the feeling of a more elegant era and complement the quality of the excellent English country house style cooking produced by Barry Quinion and his team of experienced chefs. Attentive service from the family and their local staff add the finishing touch.

There are only twelve bedrooms in this large house which allows some of the rooms to be on rather a grand scale, while the rooms designed originally for lesser family members are of a more conventional size. This variation in room size permits a wide price range in the tariff. No matter what size or shape, the same care and quality has been applied and, as with the whole house, antique and fine furniture has been used wherever possible.

This area offers a wealth of different attractions - miles of unspoilt country for walking, three golf courses within ten minutes of the hotel, and close by are Hadrian's Wall, Lanercost Priory and Carlisle with the castle, cathedral and museum. The Lake District, Scottish Borders and Yorkshire Dales provide an interesting day's touring. The hotel's proximity to the M6 also makes it an ideal overnight stop when travelling to or from Scotland. Ideally placed for Carlilse and Hexham races and is only one hours scenic drive from Newcastle racecourse. Farlam Hall is located two and a half miles south east of Brampton on the A689, not in Farlam Village.

Farlam Hall Country House Hotel
Brampton, Cumbria
CA8 2NG
Tel: (016977) 46234 Fax: (016977) 46683
e mail: farmlamhall@dial.pipex.com
website: www.farlamhall.co.uk

Cartmel offers festival racing with a fun 'shirtsleeve' atmosphere which makes a welcome contrast to some of the country's more 'stiff upper lip' racecourses. It is immensely popular and a thoroughly successful part of Britain's racing scene. The **Clerk of the Course** is **Andrew Tulloch**, and **Racecourse Manager** is **Charles Barnett**; they can be contacted at **Cartmel Steeplechases Ltd, c/o Aintree Racecourse Co Ltd, Ormskirk Road, Aintree Liverpool L9 5AS, tel: 0151 523 2600, fax: 0151 522 2920.** On racedays contact them at the racecourse itself on **tel: (01539) 536340, fax: (01539) 536004.**

The road to the course meanders through the hills of the Lake District. The most direct routes into the area from the north and south are via the M6, exiting at junction 36 for the A590. From the north east, the A69 is a good bet, whereas the A590 will assist eastbound racegoers. A word of warning, leave plenty of time if travelling by car, especially on bank holidays when traffic can be heavy. By train, the Euston line which stops at Cark in Cartmel (from where a link bus runs to the racecourse throughout the day) and Grange-over-Sands are your best bet. Parking in the Paddock Park is £5 while the Course Area is free. Helicopters can land here too, but only by prior arrangement with the Clerk.

Until the early 1960s racing was held at Cartmel only once a year, on Spring Bank Holiday Monday. Since then it has grown considerably. The Mondays of the Spring Bank Holiday and the August Bank Holiday provide the main and most popular meetings. There is also a meeting in July where just about everyone brings their barbecues for a picnic. Racegoers come from all over the country to enjoy the racing here. After all, what could be better than to spend a week at Cartmel in May with the non-racedays being spent in the surrounding countryside of the Lake District?

There is no daily admission for Members here but the course offers several options for those wishing to take out an annual membership in different packages: Premier Club Member, Hill & Stream Club and Annual Badge Holder. Anyone wishing to become a member should contact the racecourse direct on 015395 36340. The Paddock Enclosure is priced at £15 and the Course, £7. Accompanied children under 16 are admitted free. There are discounted entrance charges to the Paddock (£10) and the Course (£5) for senior citizens. A discount on all admission prices is available for badges purchased 30 days before race meetings. The management, headed by Lord Cavendish who own most of the surrounding scenery as well, continually strive to improve facilities while keeping the spirit of Cartmel intact. In 2004 a new £1.5 million grandstand was completed and opened to the public following a suitable blessing by the local Bishop. No doubt jockeys and stewards will be pleased with their new digs, but even punters will be able to enjoy the new 120 seat restaurant and balcony with its fine view of the parade ring. More people will also be able to see the racing from the grandstand terracing – at least those bits and pieces of the course that actually are visible!

The race meeting, however, brings more than horses to this rural setting. A traditional funfair is in attendance and marquees can be provided for parties on request. There is a marquee layout for corporate hospitality as well as a giant screen on all six days of racing. Picnickers are positively encouraged here although there is a catering marquee in the Paddock. A new addition is the seafood and champagne

Artist: **Elizabeth Sharp** GRASS TRACK *Courtesy of:* **The Artist**

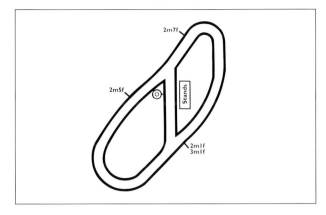

tent which has proved quite popular. There are also a number of additional fast-food outlets around the course, with full facilities in the increasingly popular Grammarfield overflow carpark from the Paddock. Disabled racegoers have their own viewing area at Cartmel. Other public facilities include telephones (for those all-important bets) and a betting shop in both the Paddock and Course enclosures. Cartmel racecourse is a huge success with large crowds attending any race meeting held there, a real testimonial to good old-fashioned country fair fun. Other racecourses are not so fortunate. A visit in 2005 could be a hot favourite.

Local favourites

There is no shortage of hotels in this part of the world and a little guidance cannot go amiss. In Cartmel itself, **Aynsome Manor** (015395) 36653 is a super old manor house which makes a good base. The **King's Arms** holds an imposing position in the square and the **Cavendish Arms** (015395) 36240 is thoroughly recommended. **Uplands** (015395) 36248 is a really pleasing restaurant with rooms if you wish to push the boat out. In Cartmel Fell, one finds the absolutely terrific **Mason's Arms** (015395) 68486, always a friendly crowd and some excellent cooking—watch the foreign beers though, they bring on nasty hangovers when mixed with our own

brews—just as well it also has bedrooms! In Heversham, the **Blue Bell** (015395) 62018 offers excellent value bar lunches and some accommodation. Newby Bridge also offers the larger establishment of **Lakeside** (015395)31207. A little further west in Lowick Green, the **Farmer's Arms** is a pub with similar facilities and an excellent dining room. A newcomer to Cartmel is the very stylish **L'Enclume** (015395) 36362, a restaurant with rooms, specialising in wonderful fish dishes.

Two packs of **Hounds** and a couple of **Hares,** one at Bowland Bridge (015395) 68333 and another at Levens, both have good value bar food. The **Swan** (015395) 31681 at Newby Bridge comes with an enviable reputation and is less than five miles from the racecourse. Two other pleasant establishments with accommodation are the outstanding **Queen's Head** (015394) 32174, Troutbeck, north of Windermere, which also yields the **Mortal Man** (015394) 33193 with its particularly friendly welcome and first-class cooking. Bowness-on-Windermere offers two appealing restaurants: the **Gilpin Lodge** (015394) 88818 which has a beautiful situation two miles out of the town—bedrooms here are first class; and **Linthwaite House** (015394) 88600 is an hotel with fine cooking. In Windermere, there are some spectacular establishments: **Jerichos** (015394) 47111 is a relaxing French restaurant, well worth trying. At the **Miller Howe** (015394) 42536 there is first-class cuisine, breathtaking views and some really special accommodation making this a favourite in the most challenging of fields. Another good runner is **Holbeck Ghyll** (015394) 32375—outstanding menus can be enjoyed here. Further good hotels can be found in and around Underbarrow overlooking the Lyth Valley. In Hawkshead the **Drunken Duck** (015394) 36347 is rightly famous for sophisticated food, stunning views and fishing in its own private tarn–a lovely place to stay. Grasmere offers the **White Moss House Hotel** (015394) 35295—another gem. A similarly favourable critique can be made of the **Wordsworth Hotel** (015394) 35592. Cumbria has a whole host of outstanding hotels and what better excuse could one have for visiting than Cartmel Races?

*Artist: **Elizabeth Sharp** SLIPPING THE REINS Courtesy of: **The Artist***

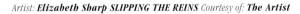

*T*he **General Manager** and **Clerk of the Course** for flat racing at Catterick is **Jonjo Sanderson**. International Racecourse Management is responsible for the overall management of the racecourse and administer the jump racing programme for which **Christopher Tetley** is the raceday **Clerk of the Course**. All general correspondence should be addressed to **Jonjo Sanderson at Catterick Racecourse, Catterick Bridge, Richmond, North Yorkshire, DL10 7PE, tel: (01748) 811478, fax: (01748) 811082, e-mail:** *info@catterickbridge.co.uk* **website:** *www .catterickbridge.co.uk*

Catterick is very convenient for the north and southbound traveller. The A1 is the route to follow and Catterick lies a short distance from the junction of the A66 (Scotch Corner) on the east side of the Great North Road. Travellers from York should take the A59 west until they reach the A1 and then drive north. From another nearby racecourse town — Thirsk (south east), the A170 and the A61 lead to the A1. By rail, the nearest station is at Darlington which is on the speedy line from London's Kings Cross. With regard to parking there are two options: the reserved car park costs £2 a car (or £32 for an annual pass) though on ground adjacent to the racecourse there is free parking for both cars and coaches.

Racing has been taking place at Catterick since 1783 and the course has a full calendar of 28 race days from January to December. A number of distinguished trainers have yards nearby and consequently many a fair nag has been sent to run here in the past. Smaller country courses like Catterick offer a great day out to the average punter, as well as some real value to local sponsors who wish to entertain their clients. Catterick is well situated to attract both people and commercial support, with Leeds, Bradford, York, Newcastle and Teesside an easy drive away. The course offers a good mixture of jump and flat racing, with Wednesdays and Saturdays being the most popular.

A joint husband-and-wife Annual Members badge is good value at £170, while a single badge was £90. You can also get a Member and Guest Badge (transferable) for £180. Annual Membership also includes 12 reciprocal racedays, as well as Yorkshire CCC matches. A price of £15 was asked for joining the Members for a single meeting. Tattersalls were slightly better value at £10, while the Course Enclosure was priced at £3. All children under 16 are admitted free when accompanied by an adult. If you want to organise parties then Catterick is definitely the place to do it. There is a £2 reduction for Tattersalls if as few as 10 people get together, and there is also one free pass for every tenth person.

Catterick has benefited from an extensive face-lift, including refurbishment of the Parade Ring Bar, the Owners and Trainers Bar, God's Solution Bar, and Dining Room. Many of the facilities for jockeys have been improved as well. The old 1926 Grandstand has been extended to provide three private hospitality suites, all with a magnificent view of the course. There are two private luncheon rooms, both of which are extremely comfortable, with space for between 20 and 60 guests to sit down or 80 people to enjoy a buffet; these can be hired at very reasonable rates.

If you enjoy your racing in either the height of summer or the depths of winter, don't forget that, in racing parlance, Catterick is an improving type. Catterick has fondly christened itself 'the course with character'—I have no doubt that in this instance the character will show through extremely well. A visit in 2005 is a must.

Local favourites

With the North Yorkshire moors so close by, Catterick is an ideal place to escape to when a major gamble has gone astray. Alternatively, the dales and fells offer an outstanding number of small hotels and pubs in which to celebrate.

In this area, Middleham stands out as prime racing country with some excellent local establishments. Note **Waterford House** (01969) 622090 — small but most appealing. The **White Swan** (01969) 622093 is a relaxed pub in the Market Square. The **Foresters Arms** at Carlton (01969) 640272 is a restaurant of note. The **Black Swan** (01969) 622221 in Middleham is another must for all racegoers. Another training area is Richmond and here the **Holy Hill Inn**, a pub with restaurant overlooking the castle and the River Swale stands out with its fine ales and some good home cooking, while the **King's Head** (01748) 850220 is another worthy favourite. In Constable Burton the **Wyrill Arms** (01677) 450581 is noted for its generous bar meals complemented by a good wine list. The **Sandpiper** at Leyburn is a good pub with outstanding food, as is the convenient **Farmers Arms,** but you must remember these are only a small selection of some 400 public houses to be found in North Yorkshire. Moulton also reveals some excellent ports of call. The **Black Bull Inn** (01325) 377289 has particularly good fish. **Solberge Hall** Hotel (01609) 779191–a Georgian country house specialising in modern British cooking and the **Three Tuns** (01609) 883301, another pretty restaurant with rooms. A short journey south reveals Northallerton and yet more good accommodation in the form of **Porch House** (01609) 779831.

Scotch Corner also provides a convenient hotel which is handy for a number of courses: the **Quality Hotel** (01748) 850900 only minutes away from the A1. Much of this area is somewhat remote but that is part of its charm. What could be better than a day in the country of North Yorkshire and an evening beside the fire in one of its many friendly hostelries? Thirsk and Ripon may offer alternative suggestions. The **Blue Lion** at East Witton (01969) 624273 is a fine example with good ale and pleasant bedrooms.

Finally, people who enjoy a decent pint and some good pub grub as well as a good restaurant should try The **Green Tree** at Patrick Brompton which is handy for Catterick and Thirsk. As mentioned previously Middleham is a centre of racing excellence nearby. There are a number of pleasant small hotels here the **King Richard III**–is another great suggestion for a relaxed stay and good food.

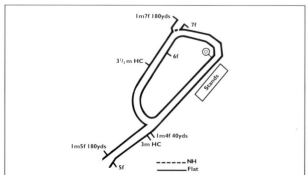

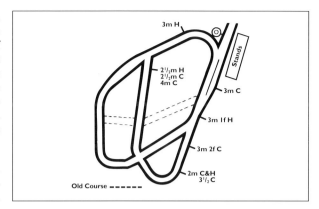

*S*ince Travelling the Turf began, Cheltenham has gone from strength to strength and that's why we have named it the National Hunt Racecourse of the last 20 years. The home of National Hunt racing, Cheltenham has seen constant additions to the facilities to take care of the thousands who trek here each year to take in the highlight of the jumping season, the four day Cheltenham Festival. It is a difficult balancing act to expand, update and improve a course while maintaining a unique atmosphere, but Cheltenham has managed to pull it off every year.

Edward Gillespie is **Managing Director** and **Simon Claisse** is **Clerk of the Course**. They can both be contacted at **Cheltenham Racecourse, Prestbury Park, Cheltenham GL50 4SH, tel: (01242) 513014, fax: (01242) 224227.** For advance bookings for the Festival, ring **(01242) 226226.** Credit cards are welcome. **Website:** *www.cheltenham.co.uk* **e-mail:** *cheltenham@rht.net*

If you are planning to visit these gorgeous Gloucestershire gallops then you are advised to take the train. The main line service leaves Paddington and arrives at Cheltenham Lansdown where a bus is available to take you to the racecourse. A bus also runs from Cheltenham Spa Station for 2 hours before the first race at all meetings. You could also arrive in style on the special raceday steam trains which bring punters right into the racecourse's own station. For information and booking call on (01749) 841591. By car, London is 95 miles away and the course is a mile from Cheltenham's busy town centre. Traffic from the A40 is advised to turn right at the lights near Andoversford which is signposted for Stow on the Wold and aim for Winchcombe. People who prefer the motorway will use the M4 and the M5—the former should be exited at junction 15 and the latter at junction 4 to make the best ground towards Prestbury Park. Whichever direction you approach from, you will find AA signs

to guide you to the racecourse. There is parking for 14,000 cars—all free except during the Festival, when a parking voucher will cost you £10. For Members and coaches parking is free at all times.

Rates of admission vary quite substantially depending on the day and the enclosure, but for the 2004/2005 season prices will vary from £16 to £65 for the Club and £16 to £37 for Tattersalls. For the Best Mate (formerly Courage) Enclosure, entrance ranges from £6 to £22. Naturally prices are higher for the National Hunt Festival but you can save money by booking in advance. Advance booking also ensures your admission, which is wise in view of the capacity crowds that always attend the Festival. There are also group discounts and special packages available for most of the meetings during the year and it's best to inquire from the racecourse about details. Prices vary from meeting to meeting and must be booked in advance but offer really good value including admission, a racecard, totepool betting vouchers, food and refreshment vouchers, and gifts. Advance booking for the Festival and other meetings can be made on the course hotline (01242) 226226.

Artist: **Graham Isom ISTABRAQ AT CHELTENHAM** *Courtesy of:* **Rosenstiel's**

The National Hunt Festival with its massive crowds reflects the interest in this superb sporting meeting. In 2005 this will be spread over four days for the first time and total prize money will exceed £2.5 million. Gems in the crown include the Tote Cheltenham Gold Cup, the Queen Mother Champion Chase and the Smurfit Champion Hurdle. Cheltenham offers a feast of racing in an excellent atmosphere and amidst a perfect setting. Other meetings to note include the three day Open meeting in November featuring the Paddy Power Gold Cup, and in December the Tripleprint Gold Cup and Bula Hurdle.

Membership should definitely be considered and is available to include or exclude the NH Festival. For a full membership including the Festival, £250 is the asking price plus a £100 enrolment fee for new Members. Membership excluding the Festival is £75 for enrolment and £100 for membership. Seniors (over 65 years) are charged an enrolment fee of £25 and membership at £85 while Juniors in the Club 16-24 are charged a membership fee of £150. Membership lasts for the season from October to April.

The facilities at Cheltenham are vast and the course is always well turned out no matter how busy proceedings get. Except for the Festival, boxes are available for daily hire at each meeting for parties of 12 or more from £275 + VAT plus the cost of admission. You can also get a package that includes lunch and tea for £40 + VAT for each guest. Call (01242) 537653 for details. Larger parties of up to 150 can be accommodated in the Grandstand in rooms with reserved viewing areas. Prices, inclusive of admission and lunch, start at £55 plus VAT. There is a huge choice of places to eat and drink here, from full service restaurants to seafood and hamburger stalls. The Mandarin Restaurant serves dishes at about £10, while the Gold Cup Restaurant offers an excellent lunch from about £26. The Panoramic Restaurant on the top floor of the new grandstand offers spectacular views of the course from your table and accommodates 300 diners. Prices for tables of four or 12 range from £72 + VAT per person to £505 for the Festival and can be booked on (01242) 537601.

Children are admitted free (except for the Festival) and disabled racegoers are well looked after with special areas overlooking the parade ring and on the lawn in the Club enclosure. There is also an area reserved for car parking for Members who have applied for a Disabled Driver label. One of the latest additions to the course is the Centaur complex that holds the National Hunt Hall of Fame, a giant screen with 1,000 gallery seats, betting outlets and bars. It holds thousands of people and when it gets very busy the noise can be a bit deafening, but if you need to get under shelter it's probably one of the best places to be. Cheltenham also offers Raceday Tours of the course at all meetings bar the Festival, a great way to find out more about the course and a bit of an inside look at what it means for horses and riders. These last about 20 minutes and leave from the Arkle statue near the Paddock.

We are sure that with Cheltenham's consistent attention to detail and planning, the new four day Festival will add to an already great occasion and allow many more fans from both sides of the Irish sea to enjoy it. If you've never been to Cheltenham for the Festival before, we urge you to do so now. This is one of the sport's great occasions and not to be missed. Book your tickets early, find a place to stay and just go out and enjoy its four days.

The Cottage In The Wood

The Cottage in the Wood Hotel and Restaurant nestles in one of the finest settings of any hotel in England, high on the Malvern Hills, with views stretching below for 30 miles.

Yet it's only just 10 miles off the M5/M50 and half and hour to Cheltenham Racecourse. Add to that Worcester, Hereford, Stratford and Warwick all within an hour, this is truly jump racing country.

The heart of the hotel is a Georgian Dower House with restaurant, bar and eight bedrooms, a few yards away is Beech Cottage with just four bedrooms, once a scumpy house and a little further on you'll find The Pinnacles with 19 sumptuous bedrooms, opened in 2003.

Family owned and run since 1987, son Dominic operates as head chef with 2 AA Rosettes to his name and many other awards, whilst John his father, presides over an award winning wine list of around 600 bins.

Malvern makes a fine touring base giving access to Herefordshire, England's least spoilt county, three cathedral cities, The Three Counties Showground and Worcestershire Golf Course just below.

The Cottage in the Wood Hotel and Restaurant
Holywell Road, Malvern Wells, Worcestershire WR14 4LG
Tel: (01684) 575859 Fax: (01684) 560662
e mail: reception@cottageinthewood.co.uk
website: www.cottageinthewood.co.uk

Cheltenham has set a standard of sport that escalates above the theatre of racing into the realms of racing into the returns of dreams... exaggeration some might think but those who make their annual pilgrimage to The National Hunt Festival each March will confide it has a magic all of its own. The main event may be acted on Prestbury Park's celebrated turf but it's in the pubs and hotels of Cheltenham, the Cotswolds and way beyond that, a different stage is set for some truly exceptional partying. In 2005 when the first 4 day festival is staged; it will be interesting to see how the hotels and bars, not to mention the livers, cope.

Cheltenham itself owes its growth to the discovery of a mineral spring in 1715. Today, the Pittville Pump Room dispenses the only drinkable alkaline water in Britain which may make a pleasant change from the numerous bottles of whisky, champagne and of course Guinness. The best known hotels in town are the **Queen's** 0870 400 8107, scene of many a fine Irish celebration after racing (check out the Gold Cup Bar), and the **Cheltenham Park Hotel** (01242) 222021 which is actually two miles out of Cheltenham, set in nine acres of gorgeous grounds. **On The Park** (01242) 518898 is a very civilised town house hotel which also houses a tremendous restaurant (01242) 227713. There are numerous other small hotels and guesthouses too—a quick phone call

to the local tourist authority is always a good idea. A charming Georgian hotel is **Prestbury House** (01242) 529533. It is particularly handy for the racecourse. An idea for dinner after racing is **81 Restaurant** (01242) 222466 a good restaurant and also bistro of some distinction. **The Hotel Kandinsky** (01242) 527788 is one to note from an excellent small stable - a stylish hotel and some great food. **Le Champignon Sauvage** (01242) 573449 is excellent too; Gold Cup class cuisine is to be enjoyed here. Neither establishment is cheap but both provide excellent excuses for a post-race celebration of major proportions. Less expensive dining and an appealing Chinese restaurant can be found at the **Mayflower** (01242) 522426. While **Indus** is a popular Indian (01242) 516676 that is well thought of. **Le Petit Blanc** (01242) 266800 is a pleasant brasserie in which to spend a few hours studying the form, as is **The Daffodil** (01242) 700055. Another that has been brought to our attention of late includes **Lumiere** (01242) 222200 - it's an absolute gem serving some seriously good food. Also in the town itself, the **Thistle Hotel** (01242) 232691 is modern but most comfortable. For the Festival you must book well in advance. Some people stay as far away as Bath, Stratford or Hereford while others commute daily to the Festival. Naturally, it is easier to find accommodation outside the March extravaganza but plans should not be made at the last minute if you can possibly avoid it.

*Artist: **Philip Toon** CHAMPION TO THE LAST Courtesy of: **The Artist***

*Artist: **Graham Isom** CHELTENHAM Courtesy of: **Rosenstiel's***

It should also be emphasised that although opulence and extravagance are not an uncommon feature of this neck of the woods, cost-conscious visitors are by no means forgotten and some excellent establishments are **Lypiatt House** (01242) 224994, **Prestbury House** (01242) 529533, **Charlton Kings** (01242) 231061 and **Butts Farm** (01242) 524982.

There are also some super restaurants in the better hotels clustered around Cheltenham. In Shurdington, the **Greenway** (01242) 862352 has a lovely rural setting and is a really first class hotel in which to stay (tremendous food here as well). Elsewhere. in nearby Southam, the **Hotel de la Bere** (01242) 237771 is convenient for the racecourse

and there are good leisure facilities here. Upton St Leonards brings us **Hatton Court** (01452) 617412, an elegant hotel in Cotswold stone with good views over the Severn Valley.

One option when racing at Cheltenham is to head off into the nearby Cotswolds. The Cotswolds are an ideal dumping ground in which to discard one's non-racing partners—a wealth of country houses, galleries and antique shops should keep them quiet. **Wesley House** (01242) 602366 is a delightful place to stay in Winchcombe - some rooms and a well thought of restaurant, and historic **Sudeley Castle** is also particularly good. Some places to catch an hour or two's kip are any one of three hotels located in Broadway. The **Lygon Arms** (01386) 852255 exudes charm and style and the Great Hall which acts as the restaurant is superb—expect a fairly large bill though. The **Dormy House** (01386) 852711 is another excellent hotel/restaurant. The **Broadway Hotel** (01386) 852401 is a beautiful Tudor hotel, complete with minstrels gallery—a good each way selection without a doubt. If you are looking for a superbly run pub with an excellent atmosphere try the **Crown and Trumpet** (01386) 853202—it's tremendous. **Goblets** (01386) 854418 is a restaurant for the shortlist. Along with so many small towns, there are a number of restaurants many of which have special menus on, from the local Indian to a more sophisticated bistro - Broadway has its fair share of such places. There's also a number of smaller establishments including **Barn House** (01386) 858633, **Windrush House** (01386) 853577 and **The Old Rectory** at Willersey (01386) 853729–no restaurants but excellent accommodation. A perfect example of a Cotswold manor is the **Buckland**

Corse Lawn House Hotel

Recently elevated to being one of the Top 200 AA Hotels in the country and also named winner of the Good Hotel Guide Cesar Award (the Oscars of the hotel industry,) Country Hotel of the Year 2005, Corse Lawn House is on a roll!

This 3 star luxury country house hotel has belonged to the racing-mad Hine family (of Cognac fame) for 26 years and during that time has undergone a careful programme of restoration to create 19 luxury bedrooms together with two superb eateries; the Restaurant and Bistro.

The hotel is less than half an hour away from both Worcester and Cheltenham racecourses and promises stunning Cotswolds scenery as you drive door to door.

On arrival you will find your larger-than-average bedroom, filled with Hine family antiques as well as thoughtful details such as bathrobes, a bowl of fresh fruit, tea, freshly ground coffee and home-made biscuits.

The Restaurant is the heart of the hotel and Baba Hine (one of Britain's leading lady chefs for the past 26 years) and her talented young team, preside over the kitchen, earning much acclaim for the Dining Room as well as the more casually styled Bistro.

As the Cheltenham entry in this book says "The outstanding Corse Lawn House Hotel is tremendously well run but inevitably packed for Cheltenham; its Restaurant is also excellent and well worth booking months in advance".

Corse Lawn House Hotel
Course Lawn, Nr Tewesbury, Gloucestershire GL19 4LZ
Tel: (01452) 780771 Fax: (01452) 780840
e mail: enquiries@corselawn.com
website: www.corselawn.com

Artist: **Graham Isom** TURNING FOR HOME Courtesy of: **Rosenstiel's**

Although many are able to take in all four days of the Festival, some have to make do with a quick visit. Places to stop afterwards include a number of quaint villages which inevitably yield a selection of boozers. In Colesbourne, the **Colesbourne Inn** (01242)870376 is a good stop-off point for a pre-race breakfast or dinner post racing–there's also some good value acommodation. The **Green Dragon** near Cowley is a super place for bar food. Filling bar snacks and some accommodation are also good at the popular **Mill Inn** (01242) 890204 in Withington. A pleasant Whitbread house in Painswick is the **Royal Oak**, a good idea if you're heading for Tetbury. There are a number of worthy hotels to consider in this area. In Tetbury itself one finds the **Snooty Fox Hotel** (01666) 502436 which is a welcoming coaching inn and the **Close** (01666) 502272 in Tetbury is also extremely promising and one for any shortlist. A little way outside the town one finds one of the area's most outstanding hotels and restaurant, **Calcot Manor** (01666) 890391—tremendous.

Further afield in Malvern Wells, the **Cottage in the Wood** (01684) 575859 offers luxurious accommodation and excellent food and wines. For pub lovers the **Hare and Hounds** in Westonbirt (01666) 880233 is popular with Cheltenham racegoers. People bolting up the M5 may pause for thought as well as a swift one at Twyning where the **Village Inn** is a pleasant village pub. Travellers on the A46 should note the **Mount** at Stanton (01386) 584316—more good value food. For another place to enjoy good food and pub accommodation try the **Kings Head**, Bledington (01608) 658365, a first class stayer.

There's a number of other very fine hotels to consider. Some of the best include the outstanding **Corse Lawn House Hotel**, Corse Lawn (01452) 780479. This is tremendously well run but inevitably packed for Cheltenham—its restaurant is also excellent and well worth booking months in advance. Further away in Blockley, near Moreton-in-Marsh, **Lower Brook House** (01386) 700286 is a delightful Cotswold inn. Cirencester offers two inns of note; the **Fleece Hotel** (01285) 658507 and the 14th century **King's Head**

Artist: **David Dent** STORMING HOME Courtesy of: **The Artist**

(01285) 653322. **Stratton House Hotel** (01285) 651761 on the Gloucester Road also has pre-race appeal. Crossing the county to the Forest of Dean and Coleford, try the **Speech House** (01594) 822607–intimately pleasing. In Ewen, one finds the **Wild Duck Inn** (01285) 770310, a fine inn. Another roost in a welcoming marketplace hotel, the **Bull**, (01285) 712535 can be found in Fairford. In Bibury, **The Swan House Hotel** (01285) 740695 is a sophisticated choice–good food here. **The New Inn at Coln** (01285) 750651 is a great Cotswold inn–perfect for food and accommodation.

Returning to the Cotswolds, that lovely part of England—various ideas for a recommended Cheltenham stayer include: the **Old Farmhouse Hotel** (01451) 830232 in Lower Swell and in Moreton-in-Marsh, the **Redesdale Arms** (01608) 650308. **The Manor House** (01608) 650501 is another great find in this pleasant Cotswold town. In Stonehouse, the **Stonehouse Court Hotel** (01453) 825155 is a fine manor house with an excellent reputation, while **Wyck Hill House Hotel** (01451) 831936 in busy Stow on the Wold also fits into the manorial category and the restaurant here is very good. The **Royalist** (01451) 830670 has a wealth of character and the restaurant is superb–The **Eagle and Child** provides a less formal atmosphere but is still highly regarded. A compliment should also be paid to the popular **Dial House** (01451) 822244, a most pleasant hotel in Bourton on the Water. Continuing our Cotswold tour, the Chipping Campden area is well worth a visit—preferably a long one. The superb **Cotswold House Hotel** (01386) 840330 is a beautiful Regency building where your stay will be both comfortable and relaxing. The restaurant, the **Garden Room** is also good. Two inns to note here include the **Kings Arms** (01386) 840256 and the pleasant **Noel Arms** (01386) 840317. **The Three Ways House** (01386) 438429 is another for the shortlist. For the lover of Italian food, **Caminetto** (01386) 840330 is a local favourite, whilst just outside Chipping Campden, **Charingworth Manor** (01386) 593555 at Charingworth is an hotel where no expense is spared in

making the guests' stay a memorable one. The **Malt House** (01386) 840295 at Broad Campden is also first class.

Less vaunted, but more reasonably priced post-race stabling can be secured in a number of the pubs that riddle the villages of Gloucestershire. In North Nibley, the **Black Horse** (01453) 546841 is recommended—a friendly, beamed pub with some bedrooms available if you want to make a weekend of it. Blockley offers the **Crown** (01386) 700245 with an excellent array of real ales, bedrooms and good bar food. Some fair bar snacks can be tried in the **Slug and Lettuce** in Cirencester. The **New Inn** (01453) 543659 in Waterley Bottom is also highly recommended. In North Cerney, the **Bathurst Arms** (01285) 831281 offers good bed and breakfast besides being a welcoming and popular pub. In Naunton, the **Black Horse** (01451) 850378 is also charming:—excellent bar food and some accommodation here. The Wheatsheaf (01451) 860244 is an inn of character and there is good food here. The same can be said of the **George** in Winchcombe—a converted Whitbread establishment–and also the **Bakers Arms** at Broad Campden (01386) 840515. People returning to London have a plethora of places to discover. If you wish to break the journey consider Eynsham—here one finds a whole clutch of boozers, the best of which is **Newlands** (01865) 881486 which also boasts a first class restaurant. Yet more pleasant village pubs abound: in Fossebridge, the **Fossebridge** (01285) 720721 is popular and in Ford the **Plough** (01249) 782215 has two bedrooms and is a lively local in which to celebrate. In Moreton, **The Old Bailey** (01386) 700408 is a delightfully converted and well turned out Victorian cottage. There are literally hundreds of hostelries in which to reflect on the outcome of the race, and those not to be missed include the **Fox** at Lower Oddington and the **Apple Tree** (01242) 673277 in Woodmancote. Finally, for a really great tip try a pub with rooms and good food: the aptly named **Horse and Groom** (01386) 700413 is an ideal venue before or after racing at Cheltenham.

Artist: **Graham Isom** CHELTENHAM Courtesy of: **Rosenstiel's**

TIBRAQ
Champion Hurdle 1998

TRUNDLEY

*Artist: **David Trundley CHAMPION HURDLER** Courtesy of: **The Artist***

Artist: **Graham Isom AT THE START** *Courtesy of:* **Rosenstiel's**

The management at Chepstow is part of the Northern Racing Group with **General Manager Simon Lee** and **Tim Long** as **Clerk of the Course**. All enquiries should be made to **Chepstow Racecourse, Chepstow, Monmouthshire NP16 6BE. Tel: (01291) 622260, fax: (01291) 627061, e-mail:** *info@chepstow-racecourse.co.uk* **website:** *www.chepstow-racecourse.co.uk*

Superbly located between Bristol and Cardiff, with excellent motorway links to many parts of the UK, the picturesque Wye Valley provides a striking backdrop to the setting in 440 acres of historic parkland. The racecourse is on the A466 Chepstow to Monmouth road, not far from the Severn bridge. From the M4 take the M48 and exit at junction 2. Once at the course you will be delighted to hear that all parking is free. If you make your journey by rail or bus, you can get a connecting raceday bus from the town's stations. The fare is £2 each way and takes 12 minutes from the train station and only seven minutes from the bus station. If a helicopter is more your style, then you may land in the middle of the track, opposite the stands. As yet, light aircraft are not allowed. Bristol airport is approximately 30 miles and Cardiff airport just over 40 miles away,

Chepstow will hold 29 days racing in 2005. Although it stages flat racing as well, Chepstow is perhaps best know for some of National Hunt racing's premier events, including the Coral Welsh National in December. It is a demanding course with an eternal up-hill home straight and never fails to produce some exciting finishes. When the going gets soft, as it usually does, the wise punter can gain a reward by choosing something with a low weight and an abundance of stamina.

Chepstow has two enclosures, the Premier and the Grandstand and Paddock, with. Admission to the Premier Enclosure will cost you £16 for a daily badge, rising to £25 for the Welsh National, while the Grandstand and Paddock's charges are £11 and £18. The course offers generous discounts for groups and for 15 or more people you can get a 20 per cent discount in both enclosures. OAP's and Students gain admission for a £5 discount in both enclosures. There are several other promotional packages

on offer that must be booked in advance. Should you wish to become a regular visitor here, a Premier Annual Badge is well worth considering. For £200 single you can attend all 27 fixtures at Chepstow as well as some 30 other days racing at some of the UK's top courses.

Chepstow is a charming course in an equally charming setting and is definitely one for the notebook. There are a variety of private boxes and hospitality suites that can be hired on racedays. A few years ago the racecourse embarked upon a major £10 million redevelopment project which included a new parade ring and winner's enclosure situated in front of the stands, improvements to the Grandstand entrance and the provision of first-class facilities for jockeys, owners and trainers including a champagne and seafood bar. The building of a brand new Members Stand, racecourse restaurant seating 280 diners and additional hospitality facilities are further examples of change under the new course management. All this has taken much time and money but Chepstow is a course in a glorious natural setting that deserves the very best of attention.

Local favourites

There is a variety of accomodation choice in the local area. In Chepstow itself, the **George Hotel** (01291) 625363 adjoins the 16th Century gate and town walls and is also a good spot for a pint and a snack. You may also consider the **Beaufort Hotel** (01291) 622497, **Castle View Hotel** (01291) 620349, or the **Chepstow Hotel** (01291) 626261, which is close to the racecourse. For those of you seeking a little sustenance the well named **Wye Knot** (01291) 622929 is well worth a visit. In Abergavenny there are a number of suggestions: The **Foxhunter** (01873) 881101 has reallywell produced food. while the **Llansantffraed Court** (01873) 840678 is a hotel to consider. The **Walnut Tree Inn** (01873) 852797 is another favourite for lovers of adventurous cuisine. The **Hilton Newport** (01633) 413737 is a short drive away. If you are a golfer as well as a racing enthusiast, try the **Marriott St Pierre Hotel** (01291) 625261 or the **Celtic Manor Resort** (01633) 413000 near Newport.

Further afield, **Glen-yr-Afon House** (01291) 672302 in Usk provides a peaceful setting. Also in Usk, the **Three**

Artist: **Graham Isom CHEPSTOW** *Courtesy of:* **Rosenstiel's**

Salmons (01291) 672133 is a popular restaurant in a scenic setting. The Welsh border country is well known for its beauty. Some particularly good ideas include a visit to Crickhowell for a night at **Gliffaes** (01874) 730371, a friendly hotel, or a visit to the **Bear Hotel** (01873) 810408. Other thoughts include the **Crown** at Whitebrook (01600) 860254—a popular place to stay, with an excellent restaurant. Be sure to consider the **Bell** at Skenfrith (01600) 750235 on your way to Monmouth—there are some good value rooms available here. The **Carpenter's Arms** in Shirenewton is a pub of note. In Clearwell, a country inn with bedrooms, restaurant and friendly bars is the **Wyndham Arms** (01594) 833666. The **Newbridge** (01633) 451000 at Tredunnock is a firm favourite for food with a Mediterranean flavour and views of the River Usk. Remote but very welcoming **Lough Pool** (01989) 730236 in Sellack serves imaginatove food, beautifully cooked and has recently added bedrooms. Whilst finally, a well located inn for the Forest of Dean is **Speech House**, Coleford (01594) 822607, with some more four posters for the romantic racegoer. Nearby Tintern also offers a

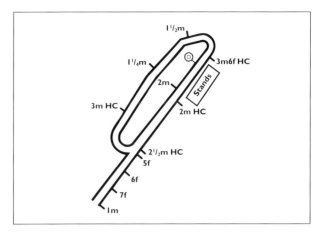

few gems: **Parva Farmhouse** (01291) 68941, a restaurant with rooms, is worthy of a pre-race inspection and The **Nags Head** (01291) 6725820 is ideal for a pre or post-race tipple.

*Artist: **Philip Toon COOL MORN** Courtesy of: **The Artist***

Artist: **Charles Church** *BAY HORSE AND JOCKEY* Courtesy of: **The Artist**

Chester is one of the most unique and historic racecourses in Britain. Spectators hang from the city walls to watch their nap negotiate the tracks around sometimes impossibly tight bends. A length lead coming into the short straight is sometimes hard to overcome, but it's not unusual for some brave jockey to come off the pace and win. Chester remains as popular as ever with Cheshire folk and their guests alike and we are pleased to name it Travelling the Turf racecourse of the year for 2005.

The course is managed by **Richard Thomas** who is **Chief Executive** and **Ed Gretton** who is **Clerk of the Course**. **Katie Hughes** handles the hospitality and **Melanie Simm** the **Sponsorship & Marketing**. They can be contacted at: **The Racecourse, Chester, Cheshire, CH1 2LY, tel: (01244) 304600, fax: (01244) 304649, e-mail:** *enquiries@chester-races.com* **website:** *www.chester-races.co.uk*

The racecourse lies to the south east of the town. The M6/M56 motorways serve racegoers from the north and south of the country, exiting at junction 14. Eastbound travellers will find the M62/M6/M56 the clearest route into Chester while A roads abound in the area. Temporary traffic signs are erected on racedays and traffic is routed around the busy city centre. Cars can be parked in the centre of the course for £5, while coaches go to the Little Roodee just a few minutes away at a £10 charge. The Euston line goes directly to Chester Central and there is a bus service from the station to the course on racedays. For those travelling by helicopter or light aircraft, landing facilities can be arranged at nearby Hawarden Airport (01244 522012/3). Either way you travel to Chester for the races, you are best advised to set off and arrive early as possible as every meeting is very busy.

The principal event of the racing season here is the May Festival meeting and the feature races include the Chester Vase, the Ormonde Stakes, and the Chester Cup. This three day festival is a true delight for racing enthusiasts and you are advised to book badges early in advance. Chester continually sets new attendance records and many meetings are sold out

well in advance. Annual Membership at Chester is £300 and includes car parking and Members entrance for all racing at Chester as well as reciprocal fixtures at nine other courses. A day's membership in the County Stand varies from £26 to £39, depending on which ticket you buy and the meeting concerned. The Stand is split into County Concourse (ground floor only) and County Long Room, the latter being the more expensive option as it provides access to seating and other facilities. Please note that the course has a strict dress code in this area with Gents required to wear a suit or suit jacket, collar and tie. Ladies likewise are asked to wear a 'smart' dress – we'll leave that up to you! Tattersalls & Paddock will set you back from £21, whereas the Dee Stand tickets are reasonably priced at £8. If you wish to attend in the centre of the Course, the charge is £6. No discounts are available for the May meeting but at other times groups of 30 or more can receive a 20 per cent discount in Tattersalls and the Dee Stand. There are concessions to OAP's on the day, but this is subject to availability. Accompanied children under 16 are admitted free to all but the County Stand for which there is a £5 levy. Disabled people and their companions are admitted free to certain areas and there is a viewing platform in the Paddock.

Visitors to the County Stand can view the magnificent panorama of the Roodee, the wide sweep of the River Dee and the Welsh Hills beyond. Chester has private boxes but unfortunately they are all sold out this year – another testimonial to the success of the course. There are betting shops in Tattersalls and the Dee Stands. There have been many improvements here recently, including a refurbished County Stand and a new race winner's entertainment suite. Six trackside chalets will be available at each meeting in a new tented facility. In the County Stand the Turf Restaurant will provide you with full dining facilities, while there are various bars and food outlets in the Concourse and Long Rooms. Tattersalls holds the Champagne, Seafood and Pavilion bar, as well as various other food outlets. Catering is now in done in partnership with the celebrated chef Paul Heathcote's company which promises to bring some new innovations to dining. Owners and Trainers are well looked after here, with their own room on the ground floor of the Leverhulme Stand and another adjacent to the Winning Post in the Paddock. Both offer complimentary food, tea and coffee, champagne or Pimms. It's well worth running your horse here just to sample it!

Some major developments are planned for Chester, including a leisure centre, conference centre, a new grandstand and a new restaurant. In addition, the historic stables that are currently set away from the racecourse are being relocated to the course itself. Chester is an outstanding racecourse in every way and attracts over 200,000 people each year. A visit here is a must for 2005.

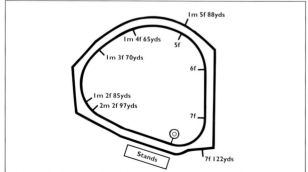

Local favourites

Chester racecourse's on site hotel **The Express by Holiday** 0870 990 4065 is now open, it has 97 bedrooms and overlooks the racecourse. A splendid place to stay is the **Chester Grosvenor and Grosvenor Spa** (01244) 324024—the restaurant, **Arkle**, is particularly well thought of. Further afield, **Broxton Hall** (01829) 782321, and **Thornton Hall** 0151 336 3938 also come highly recommended. Back in Chester, there is an abundance of guesthouses and small hotels so the racegoer on a more limited budget should not worry. Names worth mentioning here are the **Chester Court** (01244) 320779, the **Curzon** (01244) 678581, the **Dene Hotel** (01244) 321165 and the **Eaton** (01244) 320840. Not the cheapest, but still an outstanding favourite, is **Crabwall Manor** (01244) 851666 two miles outside Chester. For good dining in a pub atmosphere, try the **Mill** (01244) 350035 or the **Old Harkers Arms** (01244) 344525—they both have much to commend them. People who enjoy smaller, intimate hotels will surely appreciate the **Green Bough Hotel** (01244) 326241 - it's really excellent. Similarly, albeit further afield, **The White House**, Prestbury (01625) 829376 is an elegant Georgian house with an excellent restaurant, as well as rooms.

Venturing some way north of Chester to the South Wirral and Puddington, one finds the **Craxton Wood Hotel** 0151 339 4717, with a small but selective and very stylish restaurant. People looking for a little luxury when visiting the city should consider one of several hotels. In St Johns Street, **Blossoms** (01244) 323186 is close to the city centre and its many amenities include a good restaurant and two friendly bars. The **Boot** and the **Falcon** are both well worth

considering. A little farther afield, but still convenient for the city is a splendid country house hotel, the **Mollington Banastre Hotel** (01244) 851471. There are excellent facilities available here—together with two restaurants—and its own village pub. In Rowton lies another fine country house—the **Rowton Hall Hotel** (01244) 335262—the service here is good and if you don't want to be in the middle of Chester this may well be the answer. South of the city lies the excellent value and secluded **Pheasant Inn** (01829) 70434. A relative newcomer to the Chester field, the **The Dysart Arms** (01829) 260183 is well worth a pre-race visit. Meanwhile, the **Wild Boar Inn** (01829) 260309 at Beeston has modern facilities and a pleasing setting. The **Hanover International Hotel & Club** (01925) 730706 does special racing breaks including transport to the racecourse. Those who enjoy a little pampering should consider **The Grosvenor** (above) or alternatively the **Grosvenor Pulford** (01244) 570560 which is a really well thought of 'stayer'.

In the countryside, there are some fine pubs to note. The **Bickerton Poacher** in Bickerton is an exceptionally busy pub but is good fun too. The **Cock O'Barton** at Barton is quieter. Further south in Whitchurch is **Dodington Lodge** (01948) 662539, providing top class accommodation. In Tarporley, the **Swan** (01829) 733838 is a worthy pub with a restaurant and some bedrooms if you require them. The **Rising Sun** is also a pub to note here. More of the same can be found in Mold at **Glasfryn** (01352) 750500. Fi nally, a very special hotel can be found at Mold, some twelve miles from Chester. Here, a warm welcome awaits you at **Soughton Hall** (01352) 840811, a stunning hotel in Italianate style with a fine à la carte restaurant. With outstanding hotels and a first class racecourse, a visit to Chester in 2005 simply must be organised.

*Artist: **Norman Hoad TIGHT FINISH** Courtesy of: **The Artist***

Artist: **Philip Toon STRIDING OUT** Courtesy of: **The Artist**

The racecourse, owned by Doncaster Metropolitan Borough Council, is managed by International Racecourse Management Ltd. **Chief Executive John Sanderson is Clerk of the Course, General Manager is Steven Clarke with Chris Oliver as the Operations Manager.** Doncaster's exhibition and conference centre is open all year round and information can be obtained by writing to **Doncaster Racecourse, Leger Way, Doncaster, DN2 6BB, tel: (01302) 304200, fax: (01302) 323271, e-mail:** _info@doncaster-racecourse.com_ **website:** _www.doncaster-racecourse.com_

Doncaster racecourse is in South Yorkshire, one mile from the centre of the town itself. The course is within easy reach of motorways and there is a dual carriageway to the course car parks. The A1 and the M1/M18 are good routes from the south and signs now direct racegoers from all motorway approaches. If you are coming from the west then use the A57 and M18 and from the east the M18 and M180. Let the train take the strain from King's Cross and your journey time will be 85 minutes with a bus from the town to complete the final leg of the journey. Buses from Doncaster (Nos 55, 170 and 171) will drop you 300 metres from the gates—perfect! Helicopters are permitted to land at Doncaster but only by special arrangement, so if this is your desired mode of transport then please check with the Operations Manager first. Car parking is easy here with space for 3,000 cars—all free. There is also a reserved area for Members.

Artist: **Barry Linklater NICE ACTION** Courtesy of: **Patterson Gallery**

The season at Doncaster consists of 29 days' racing, 20 flat and nine over the sticks. Principal meetings are the St Leger Festival in September and the Lincoln Handicap in March, the Racing Post Trophy in October and the Tote November Handicap. Doncaster has the honour of opening and closing the flat season—a worthy privilege for an excellent racecourse.

Rates of admission vary from meeting to meeting. In the Member's Enclosure badges are priced between £16 and £30 for prestigious racedays such as the St Leger festival. In the Grandstand tickets are from £10 to £18 and in the Family Enclosure you will pay from £4 to £6 per head. Group discounts and those for OAP's are also available for the Grandstand. Annual Membership at Doncaster costs £215. Included in this are 25 reciprocal meetings around the country as well as entrance to Yorkshire Cricket Club matches. This has to be good value. Dual Membership is available for £320 and Junior Badges are £80. When you are inviting guests, don't forget to tell them that the course runs a strict dress code of "jacket and tie, and no jeans allowed" in the Members Enclosure. There's nothing more embarrassing than having a guest turned away because of their attire! Boxes, and there are a total of 70 now, are let on an annual basis. A tented village exists for the St Leger meeting.

Artist: **Graham Isom DONCASTER** Courtesy of: **Rosenstiel's**

There are numerous bars together with corporate facilities. The Lincoln Restaurant is situated in the Yorkshire Stand and tables are allocated on a first come, first served basis. The Hospitality Club in the St Leger Banqueting Suite is designed to give racegoers a full day at the races in corporate hospitality style without the need for large numbers (a minimum of two people). The caterers are Metro and they can be contacted on (01302) 304721.

Doncaster has taken a positive lead in promoting racing as family entertainment and raceday activities include a professionally staffed crèche, children's rides, craft stalls and a selection of raceday music. The Giant Screen is present on major racedays and the course has developed its own corporate entertainment department as well as catering for party bookings. Doncaster is a really friendly, well-run racecourse and one which in recent years has dramatically improved.

Of all the racecourses in Britain, Doncaster is one of the most historic and now fast becoming one of the best with a £45 million transformation, incorporating the racecourse and exhibition centre, stabling, bloodstock sales, golf clubhouse and hotel.

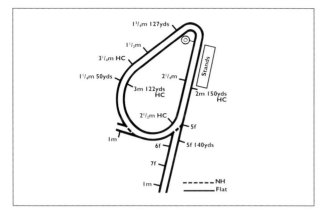

Local favourites

Perhaps not the most attractive of towns, nonetheless Doncaster boasts a number of hotels and hostelries as well as its excellent historic racecourse. In Doncaster, the **Grand St Leger** (01302) 364111 is extremely comfortable and its restaurant has an imaginative menu. A little south of the town, in Bawtry, stands the **Crown Hotel** (01302) 710341, a pleasant inn in a quiet market square. The **Mount Pleasant** (01302) 868219 is shortlisted by people in the know (it's busy but very dependable), and the **Corner Pin** (01302) 323159 also has a good reputation. Two other hotels to consider are the **Danum Hotel** (01302) 342261 in the town centre, and the **Earl of Doncaster** (01302) 361371, a mere half mile from the racecourse. Even closer to the racecourse, the **Grand St. Leger** (01302) 329865 is an excellent each way bet.

For people who may want a little more comfort and style there are three hotels that are warmly recommended north of Doncaster. In Wentbridge, the **Wentbridge House Hotel** (01977) 620444 has a pleasant location in the parkland scenery of the Went Valley. **Monk Fryston Hall Hotel** (01977) 682369 is found in the West Riding village of the same name. South of Doncaster, **The Hellaby Hall Hotel**, Rotheram (01709) 702701 is another good find - some good health and leisure facilities here as well. Pubs to note nearby include the excellent **Inn at Cadeby** and the **Green Tree** at Hatfield Woodhouse (01302) 840305—a few bedrooms here and good value bar food. An inside tip is the **Old Bell** at Barnby Moor (01717) 705212—very old world. Finally, a 300 year-old coaching inn with strong racing connections, the **Salutation** (01302) 340705 is the perfect place for post-race celebrations.

Artist: **Barry Linklater NECK & NECK** Courtesy of: **Patterson Gallery**

Artist: **Sue Wingate SPIRIT OF THE ST LEGER** Courtesy of: **The Artist**

Andrew Cooper is the **Clerk of the Course** and **Director of Racing**, **Stephen Wallis** is the **Managing Director** and **Kerry Mallen** is **Marketing Manager**. They can be contacted at **Epsom Downs Racecourse, Epsom Downs, Surrey KT18 5LQ tel: (01372) 726311, fax: (01372) 748253, e-mail:** *epsom@rht.net* **website:** *www.epsomderby.co.uk*

Epsom stands magnificently on the Surrey Downs of the same name. The mode of transportation depends significantly on the meeting. Derby Day is enormously busy—even helicopters hover in line. However, on other days traffic is less congested. The racecourse is only 15 miles from the centre of London and people heading from that direction should pursue the A3 south, exiting at the Tolworth junction. Traffic from the west is advised to join the M25 and exit at junction 8 or 9 for the course. The M25, if it is flowing freely, also serves people from the east and the south of the country. The A217 is the best route to observe in order to complete your northbound journey. An excellent idea is to take the train. Lines from the London stations of Waterloo, Charing Cross and Victoria stretch to Epsom. The Downs can be reached from Victoria alone, while Tattenham Corner visitors should take trains from either London Bridge or Charing Cross. If you travel to Epsom by train, buses will take you to the course from Morden Station. However, passengers to Tattenham Corner station can enjoy a pleasant walk across the Downs before racing. Many people have picnics here and this seems

as ideal a place as any to indulge in your nosebag. Other places in which to have a pre-race snack are the car parks, of which there are many. Charges vary according to your particular setting. Finally, if you are lucky enough to travel by helicopter, you can land here—it's quite a sight I assure you. Notify the course in advance on (07803) 831211.

There is a range of charges for the various enclosures. Admission to the Queens Stand on Derby Day is restricted to Annual Members and two day ticket holders for which the charge in 2004 was £100 per person. Annual Membership was priced at £150 and only £50 for a Junior Membership badge, and is quite a bargain considering that it covers all racedays at Epsom as well as reciprocal days at other courses and Surrey County Cricket Club. An annual drinks party, newsletters and discounts are also part of the package. Regular prices for tickets to the Queens Stand range from £17 to £22, but cost £50 on Oaks Day. The Grandstand will cost you from £11 to £18 (£27 Oaks Day, £33 Derby Day) and you can reserve seats at an extra charge of £5 for the Oaks and £40 for the Derby. Tickets for the Lonsdale Enclosure are £10 for the Derby meeting but only £5 in July and August and free the rest of the year. If you want to picnic on the Hill, this will cost £10 and £15 on the August Bank Holiday. Booking in advance for the big days will save you some money, as will bringing your own crowd – parties of more than 20 for the Derby meeting receive a £3 per head discount in the Grandstand, rising to a £7 discount on

Artist: **David Dent THE DERBY** *Courtesy of:* **The Artist**

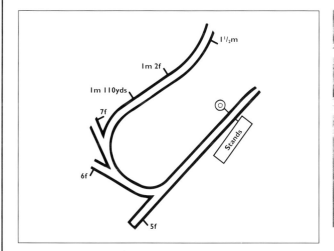

Artist: **Klaus Philipp ON THE NOD** *Courtesy of:* **The Artist**

Derby Day. Students with appropriate identification are offered a 50 per cent discount in the Grandstand on days other than the Derby meeting. There is also the Diamond Club for those over 60 which costs a fiver to join and you can receive a £5 discount on Grandstand tickets (except the Derby meeting). Ring (01372) 470047if you would like an application form. For those at the other end of the age scale, children under 16 are admitted free to all but the Derby meeting if accompanied by an adult. For those who need to entertain their clients or friends, there are over 50 boxes and suites of varying sizes to choose from. Call (01372) 461235 for details. The disabled are also catered for with appropriate ramps, lifts and toilets.

Once installed in the enclosure of your choice there are numerous opportunities to satisfy your appetite or slake your thirst. The Queen's Stand offers many bars and outlets for cold snacks or seafood. The Blue Riband Restaurant is always busy on racedays and advance booking is strongly advised on (01372) 720330. The Grandstand also has many bars and catering facilities as well as the Café Normandie which offers more substantial fare. The Lonsdale Enclosure has lots of fast food outlets, as does the Hill if you require a top-up for your picnic. A bank can be found behind the Grandstand during Derby week should you blow all your cash early on in the Tote or betting shops.

Artist: **Peter Smith TATTENHAM CORNER** *Courtesy of:* **Frost & Reed**

Artist: **_Sue Wingate A CLASSIC FINISH_** _Courtesy of:_ **_The Artist_**

Artist: **_Jacqueline Stanhope K FALLON & J SPENCER_** _Courtesy of:_ **_The Artist_**

While during the rest of the season things are relaxed on the attire front, the Derby meeting is very much a dress-up affair, at least in the Queen's Stand, if not so much elsewhere. Here Gentlemen are required to wear Morning Dress on Derby Day while the Ladies are requested to pull out their best daytime dresses. As befitting a special event for the fillies, the Ladies take the forefront on Oaks Day and you will see as many hats around as at Royal Ascot.

It has taken some pretty solid management and marketing for Epsom to win back the crowds that used to flock here in droves for the Derby meeting. Moving the meeting to a weekend has helped but the premier event of the flat season has so much more competition for attention than ever before and it has taken a lot of work to regain its position in the sporting calendar.

For jockeys, trainers and owners there is no better prize and we are sure just about all of them would trade in a clutch of other group race wins for just one Derby winner. The small fields of some of the Derby trials at Chester, York and Lingfield certainly hasn't helped in the build up to the main event, and seldom now does a Guineas victor seemed destined for Epsom glory, much less the triple crown. It will take something bold for The Derby to reclaim its status as the three year old championship of the season. It is a chance worth taking.

Local favourites

People who are staying in this area (rather than in the capital) should note the **Burford Bridge Hotel** 0870 400 8283 at Box Hill, near Dorking—a welcoming hotel beside the A24 and well sited for Epsom Downs. The **White Horse Hotel**, (0870) 4008282 also has great character, though less class. Both of these are ideal for the tourist as they date back centuries. **Le Petit Pierrot** (01372) 465105 is a popular restaurant to sample. **Chase Lodge** 0870 381 8419 is also convenient for both the races and central London. Epsom itself contains the **Epsom Downs Hotel** (01372) 740643, a good value and relaxing hotel. **Chalk Lane** (01372) 371371 is also well worthy of consideration. In Peaselake a convenient yet unpretentious stayer is the **Hurtwood** Inn Hotel (01306) 730851. Further south in Horley, an hotel for people who enjoy a little peace and quiet, **Langshot Manor** (01293) 786680 is a comfortable old manor house.

Turning back towards the racecourse again, the busy town of Reigate is home to the **Reigate Manor** Hotel (01737) 223883 and the **Bridge House** (01737) 246801, both unpretentious and good value. The **Prince Albert** in Bletchingly is a good place to pop in for a pint, as is the **White Hart** in Godstone—ideal for a steak and a beer.

There are numerous pubs to be found in the area—some near, some far. The **Fox on the River** in Thames Ditton is most obliging as is the **Badgers Rest** in Weybridge. Here **Oatlands Park** (01932) 847242 is an inspired overnight choice. In Kenley one finds the **Wattenden Arms**, an extremely popular pub with some distinguished bar food available. The **Plough** at Blackbrook is also very civilised and the **Plough** (01306) 711793 at Coldharbour offers good

Artist: **_Anne Farrall A CLASSIC_** _Courtesy of:_ **_The Artist_**

food, beer and some accommodation. In Abinger Hammer, **Drakes on the Pond** (01306) 731174 is a super little village restaurant with a growing reputation.

An alternative nearby is to be found in Chipstead—the **Ramblers Rest** (01737) 552661 is not cheap but offers a really first class menu, friendly service and a distinguished wine list. Finally, in Hersham the **Bricklayers Arms** (01932) 220936 is reported to be excellent, where a friendly atmosphere accompanies bold English cooking

The **Old School House** (01306) 711224 in Ockley should be noted—the well priced menu is extremely appealing. Another pleasant pub to inspect near here is the **Punch Bowl** which has a lovely setting and serves some simple bar snacks as well as having a good dining room. Still in Ockley, **Bryce's** (01306) 627430 is a good pub for decent grub and another to note while in this area of Surrey is the **Kings Head,** to be found in Holmbury St Mary, a really good atmosphere here. In Shere, the **White Horse** is also popular—rightly so—it is charming and offers some excellent

home-made food. People who are fond of eating and enjoy the ambience of a good restaurant should try the **Onslow Arms** (01483) 222447 in West Clandon—a classic of its type. The **Bulls Head** is also good here as is the **Jarvis Thatchers Hotel** (01483) 284291, both comfortable and convenient.

The Derby attracts all sorts of people. Gypsies promise you luck but you will still lose your shirt. The Derby is one of the most colourful events of the year and if you want to end it in style visit the village of Nutfield. The hotel here is situated in the former local priory, **Nutfield Priory** (01737) 822066, the perfect place to count your winnings or lick your wounds after a day at the Derby.

Finally, if your appetite has not been whetted by any of these suggestions, then turn to the Kempton Park and Sandown recommendations where you will see more places to satisfy the Surrey racegoer. Certainly if last year's crowds were anything to go by, advance planning in 2005 appears essential.

Artist: **Hubert de Watrigant THE JOCKEYS** *Courtesy of:* **Osborne Studio Gallery**

*I*f you are planning a visit to England's delightful West Country then stop off at Exeter racecourse. This jumping track is in the capable hands of **Geoffrey Billson, Managing Director. Barry Johnson** is **Clerk of the Course** and **Vicki Robinson** is **Assistant Manager.** Their address is **Exeter Racecourse, Kennford, Exeter, Devon EX6 7XS, tel: (01392) 832599, fax: (01392) 833454, e-mail:** *info@exeter-races.co.uk* **website:** *exeter-racecourse.co.uk*

When travelling to the course it may be as well to stick to the motorways to ensure a speedy route — the M5 feeds from the M4 and the M6. The course is some 190 miles from London and seven miles south west of Exeter. Only three miles further down from the end of the M5 motorway the A38 Plymouth road takes you right past the racecourse. On arrival at the racecourse there is ample free parking to be found. The nearest train station is at Exeter, St Davids, which can be comfortably reached from Paddington. On racedays there is a free bus service to the course from the central bus station in Exeter City Centre.

With its splendid views from the top of the Haldon Hills, racing has been taking place here for over 300 years since the time of Charles II. A demanding jumps course, Exeter has seen many top class chasers in the past including the likes of Best Mate, Desert Orchid and Viking Flagship, all of whom went on to be champions. Prime in the fixture list is the early November meeting which features the Haldon Gold Cup. Annual Membership is charged at £160 for a single badge. This also includes many reciprocal days at other courses, although Devon members certainly have to do some travelling to enjoy them! Daily rates are £12 for the Grandstand and Paddock and £17 for the new Haldon enclosed stand. Party discounts are available for groups of 10 or more at £10 per person in the Grandstand and Paddock. Accompanied children under 16 are admitted free of charge.

The course has hospitality rooms in the Anstey and Brockman buildings to suit all sizes of parties from 10 to 100. Private box packages range from £45 to £60 per head, depending on choice of menu. The Brockman Stand features a new betting hall and owners and trainers bar as well as three new hospitality rooms with spectacular views of the course. The Paddock now incorporates the winner's enclosure and provides much improved views of the pre-saddling enclosure. The new Haldon Stand offers excellent viewing from 175 enclosed tiered seats. The Desert Orchid Restaurant can seat up to 200 people and has views over

Artist: **Brooksby STORMY DAY, EXETER** *Courtesy of:* **The Artist**

the course. Bookings may be made on (01392) 832599. The Romany King and William Hill bars provide a range of snacks, as does the Waterloo Boy.

There is an under-5s play area in the old Tote building and accompanied children under 16 are admitted free to the Racecourse. Telephones at the racecourse are located in The Brockman Stand where there is also a betting shop. For the disabled, there is a special viewing platform and toilet facilities. With a racing programme that attracts some of the best national hunt horses around, Exeter's future looks bright indeed.

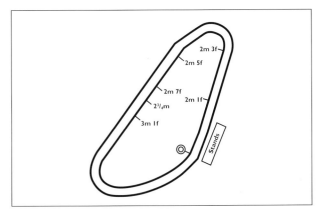

Local favourites

At Dunchideock, three miles from the racecourse is the **Lord Haldon** (01392) 832483, a highly commended country house hotel which organises special racing breaks for visitors to Exeter as well as to Newton Abbot. East of the course lies Exeter and here the **Royal Clarence** (01392) 319955 is the pick of the paddock. **Buckerell Lodge** (01392) 221111 and **St Olaves** (01392) 217736 also have considerable appeal—both have good restaurants. The **White Hart** (01392) 79897 wins approval from those seeking a characterful inn, **Southgate** (01392) 412812 is also a well thought of establishment. New recommendations are the **Hotel Barcelona** (01392) 281000 and, further outside but still handily placed, the really promis-

ing **Barton Cross** (01392) 841245 at Stoke Canon, part 17th Century cottages with plenty of character and good food.

One thought for golfers and holidaymakers alike is the **Thurlestone Hotel** (01548) 560382 in Thurlestone. Many of these hotels are much quieter in the off season and are therefore that much more appealing, so book up now and take a well earned break. A similar drive but well worth it for those who like pleasant pubs with good food and acommodation can be found at Hope Cove - the **Hope and Anchor**.

A good hotel is the **Manor House** (01647) 440355 at Moretonhampstead. The **New Fountain Inn** (01404) 822350 in Whimple is a real favourite. Both the restaurant and accommodation here are first class. In Doddiscombsleigh, one pub that really should be noted is the welcoming (but oddly named) **Nobody Inn** (01647) 52394, with good value bedrooms if you like pub accommodation. The bar food and wine here are really good. Close by, the **Huntsman** is a grand alternative. A tremendous pub for a visit after racing is the **Old Coaching House** (01626) 853270, Chudleigh, with great character and food, whilst on the coast the **Bay Hotel** (01626) 774123 is a comfortable place to stay. Another place to eat is the **Rock Inn** (01364) 661305 at Haytor Vale. In North Bovey, the **Ring of Bells** (01647) 40375 is a well-known real ale pub with accommodation which is also good value. For those spreading their sightseeing net slightly wider, the **Cridford Inn** (01626) 853694 is most appealing — an historic inn, offering good food and accommodation. **Combe House** (01404) 42756, Gittisham, is another outstanding hotel and restaurant, while **Bel Alp House** (01364) 661217 is an excellent hotel.

Heading further into Dartmoor there are some really first class hotels. In Chagford, the **Gidleigh Park Hotel** (01647) 432367 is isolated but beautiful and has a first-class restaurant. The **Great Tree Hotel** (01647) 432491 is also extremely tranquil while the **Mill End** (01647) 432282 has yet another delightfully quiet setting in the Teign Valley. Finally, some 20 miles from Exeter is Ashburton, which houses the **Holne Chase Hotel** (01364) 631471, a lovely country house hotel where fishing is available and a warm welcome assured.

Artist: **Brian Halton** _WHERE DID YOU COME FROM Courtesy of:_ **The Artist**

Artist: **Brooksby** _IN THE PADDOCK, EXETER Courtesy of:_ **The Artist**

Now this is a racecourse which is well worth a visit. It has a tremendous atmosphere and is great fun. **David Hunter** is **Clerk of the Course** and **Racecourse Manager**, and **Vivien Pope** is the **Company Secretary**. All enquiries should be addressed to: **The Racecourse, Fakenham, Norfolk, NR21 7NY, tel: (01328) 862388, fax: (01328) 855908. E-mail:** *info@fakenhamracecourse.co.uk* **website:** *www.fakenham racecourse.co.uk*

Fakenham is a great advertisement for racing on a local level. By and large it offers good value for money and, like several similar courses, it often provides a more enjoyable day's racing than its more illustrious competitors.

Fakenham is situated just off the A148 and the town is bypassed to the north, making your journey somewhat less tricky. Although the course is well signposted from all directions, London is 125 miles away, King's Lynn 22 miles and Norwich 26 miles. From the north, the A1 and A17 combine to make the most direct route. From the south, use the A1065, from the west the A148 and from the east the A1067. Parking facilities at the course are thankfully very good. The main railway station is some 22 miles away at King's Lynn (departing Liverpool Street and King's Cross). Some local bus services do run from the station and the X98 is an express. However, what the area lacks in the way of public transport it makes up for in terms of private facilities. Helicopters may land in the centre of the course.

Fakenham has some fairly worthwhile prizes and is well sponsored by local and national firms. Racing highlights are the Prince of Wales Cup, Queen's Cup, David Keith Memorial Chase, plus a point-to-point and Arab racing. Easter Monday is the major raceday and much recommended.

Badges for the Members' Enclosure cost £16 for the day. Entrance to the Grandstand & Paddock is £11 and admission to the Course Enclosure costs £6. If you're local or just keen on Fakenham then you should buy a £135 annual double badge—a worthwhile saving. Annual single badges can be ordered for £95 and a year's membership includes a staggering 110 reciprocal days at other courses, which is pretty hard to beat. Daily badge holders must pay £8 to park in the Members' while public car parking is free. If you're thinking of organising a party to go to Fakenham, a 15 per cent discount is available for groups of 20 or more, booked in advance.

A Members' Prince of Wales stand has panoramic views of the entire course and holds the Firth Restaurant where you can get a three course meal. It's probably wise to book in advance, which you can do on (01328) 862388. You can get lighter fare in the Members bar and at other food outlets. Drinks can also be obtained in the Long Bar in the Grandstand & Paddock, as well as a choice of nibbles and snacks. For those wishing to entertain in style there are boxes for hire in the Prince of Wales stand, the larger Parade Ring Room that can cater up to 50 people and private marquees by arrangement.

*Artist: **Klaus Philipp BLINKERS** Courtesy of: **The Artist***

Facilities for the disabled are good here and include their own viewing stand and reserved parking. Children are welcome at Fakenham and are admitted free if under 16 and accompanied by an adult. There is a Tote betting shop close to the paddock but no bank to replenish your wallet should you be unsuccessful. Fakenham also operates an upmarket caravan/camping site ideally situated for sampling Norfolk's delights, with the added benefit of free entry to race meetings. All in all, Fakenham is a small, rural and friendly racecourse, well run, well supported and recommended to all those who relish travelling the turf.

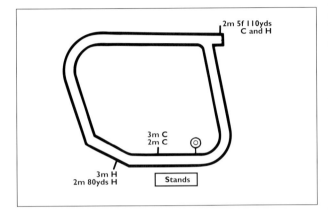

Local favourites

Where better to dream of tomorrow's winners than in the serenely peaceful village of Great Snoring? Here, the secluded and personal **Manor House** (01328) 820597 is an impressive manor house dating back to 1500. Another outstanding place to stay and eat is to be found at Grimston where **Congham Hall** (01485) 600250 is a delightful country house. The **George** (01760) 721238 is in nearby Swaffham. And now for a few inspired selections: **Yetmans Restaurant** in Holt (01263) 713320 is reputed to be very good and we are also informed that the **Lord Nelson** is a highly recommended village pub with food in Burnham Thorpe. Last, but most definitely not least, the quaintly named Barney houses the highly recommended **Old Brick Kilns** (01328) 878305.

If you decide that a little sea air is in order then the **Jolly Sailors** (01485) 210314 at Brancaster Staithe may be somewhere good to visit after racing, boasting a pleasant bar and a fine English menu in the restaurant, as does **The White Horse** (01485) 210262. A little way from the coast, two locations should be considered. Firstly, in Burnham Market, **Fishes** (01328) 738588 where some superb fish can be enjoyed in an informal atmosphere, and secondly, in Burnham Thorpe, the **Lord Nelson**—an original pub with an excellent drop of Greene King.

In Fakenham, there is **Sculthorpe Mill** (01328) 856161, a converted late 18th Century watermill handy for the racecourse, **Blakeney Manor**, as well as the **Crown** (01328) 710209, a pleasant inn with a restaurant and some accommodation. Moving into Blakeney, you find the **Blakeney Hotel** (01263) 740797 a comfortable family run hotel, while the **Manor Hotel** (01263) 740376 has a marvellous quayside setting. Two pubs to note are the **Kings Arms** and the **White Horse** where excellent bar food is available—ideal for a weekend visit after racing. Just west of here, **Morston Hall**, (01263) 741041 has a good racing name and an excellent reputation. Some way off one finds the **Rose and Crown** (01482) 541382 at Snettisham–a stylish, relaxed pub with a surprisingly good wine list and imaginative food. Similarly try the **Hoste Arms** in Burnham Market (01328) 738777, it's a superb inn and makes a fantastic location for a weekend away. Four final places to consider are the **Bull Inn** (01328) 820333 in Little Walsingham which offers accommodation, food and a characterful bar. The **White Horse** (01328) 820645 is an inn to note, as is The **Crown** at Colkirk (01328) 862172. The **Buckinghamshire Arms** (01263) 732133 in Blickling is also well worth a visit. I am looking forward to my next visit already—one for the diary in 2005.

Artist: **Peter Smith SADDLES OFF, BLANKETS ON** *Courtesy of:* **Frost & Reed**

Chris Stickels is **Clerk of the Course** at Folkestone while **Sales and Marketing** are handled by **Emma Santer**. They can both be contacted at **Folkestone Racecourse, Stone Street, Westenhanger Nr Hythe, Kent CT21 4HX. Tel: 0870 2200023. Racedays Tel: (01303) 266407 Fax: (01303) 260185. E-mail:** *emma_folkestoneraces@hotmail.com* **Website:** *www.folkestone-racecourse.co.uk*

Located four miles west of Folkestone, Kent's only track is a mere 65 miles from London. Road users from London should leave the M20 at junction 11 (where there is a sign directing you to the racecourse) and take the A20 towards Lympne, Newingreen and Sellinge. The racecourse is only about one mile from the motorway. From Canterbury the best route is the B2068, the historic Roman 'Stone Street', picking up the AA signs as you go over junction 11. Train users are well catered for—special raceday services depart Charing Cross and Waterloo East (three minutes later) to Westenhanger. The station adjoins the course and is about 100 metres from the main entrance (telephone 0870 603 0405 for details). There is no bus service. Those with helicopters should call the racecourse the day before the meeting to make landing arrangements. Whatever your mode of transport, you will find ample free parking, and for those who like to pack a hamper, you can picnic from a car park and watch the racing.

The racecourse has a mixed calendar with about 20 fixtures, the most popular invariably being the aptly named Garden of England Day which takes place in early September and is well worth a visit, as is the United Hunts, the May jumps meeting.

Annual Membership is priced at £160. One of the particular benefits of your membership is that it includes reciprocal meetings at other tracks. This means that punters can enjoy a taste of flat racing and chasing and hurdling as well as show jumping—ideal for lovers of all manner of equestrian pursuits. Daily rates are £13 for a combined Club and Grandstand admission and £5 per car and £5 per occupant in the Picnic Park. People wishing to organise a party of 15 or more will receive a discount of £2 per person. This should be organised through the racecourse management in advance of the meeting. OAP's also benefit from discounted admission at £9, available only on the day. Children under 16 are admitted free to all areas if accompanied by an adult and there is special entertainment laid on for them during the summer holidays.

If a picnic sounds like hard work then it may be an idea to sample the Lookout Restaurant which overlooks the course. Bookings should be made through Lingfield Park (01342) 834800. The course has twelve splendid boxes that can seat up to 16 guests and are available for hire on a daily basis. Corporate hospitality rates are from £35 per head. The Paddock Brasserie also has a wide choice of meals and snacks as well as tea and coffee. For those inclined to go al fresco, the Spitfire Pavilion is a lawn bar with tables under the trees.

If you wish to place an off-track punt there are Tote and betting shop facilities scattered around the course. If you are disabled, there is a lift in the Grandstand and a disabled toilet on the ground floor.

There are numerous plans afoot for the continued improvement of Folkestone racecourse. It's interesting to note that the course has only one basic admission charge that allows the punter to enter all areas. This is the new trend in British racecourses and does much to break down the mystery for the new racegoer of having to decide between something called the Silver Ring and Tattersalls!

Local favourites

A hotel with a watery view is the **Clifton** (01303) 851231 in Folkestone. Reasonably priced accommodation can also be found at the **Travel Inn** (08701) 977103. There are a number of restaurants to consider; **La Tavernetta** (01303) 254955 is a long-standing favourite—Italian cuisine on this occasion. If you are in Hythe and are searching for a good place to stay then the **Hythe Imperial** (01303) 267441 should be the answer. This hotel is particularly comfortable and offers excellent leisure facilities including special golf packages, ideal for those of you who enjoy following the fairways as much as travelling the turf. **Stade Court Best Western** (01303) 268263 is less elaborate than its near neighbour but most accommodating and friendly. Sandgate, a little west of Folkestone, offers The **Sandgate Hotel** (01303) 220444, a fine hotel with a restaurant of quality, a great place to head for!

Dover obviously contains a host of more modest guesthouses where the welcome is guaranteed to be greater than the bill. A good hotel on the waterfront is **The Churchill** (01304) 203633. Potential gems include **Number One** (01304) 202007 and **Walletts Court** (01304) 852424 which is really outstanding. This is definitely one for those who enjoy good service and some style. An excellent restaurant as well. You'll find it at St Margaret's at Cliffe. In Wingham, the **Red Lion** (01227) 720217 offers a good restaurant and some satisfactory, well priced bedrooms. Deal not only offers some great golf but also Dunkerleys Hotel (01304) 375016 where the seafood and views are reported to be tip top.

One of the most appealing things about Kent is the many pubs one can find. In the delightfully named Petts Bottom, the **Duck** (01227) 830354 is a welcoming pub. The aptly named **Flying Horse** in Boughton Aluph (01233) 620914 is a pub to note—some accommodation here. Chilham, a most attractive little village, offers the **White Horse** (01227) 730355, an old coaching inn, and the **Woolpack** (01227) 730208 where some good accommodation is offered, making it an ideal base for preparing one's excursion to the racecourse. If you can't relax in this village you may as well call it a day! Another pub well worth a visit is the **Five Bells** at Brabourne (01303) 813334 - first class food. The star of the show, in terms of intimate dining, is to be found in Wye, the **Wife of Bath** (01233) 812232. Finally, **Eastwell Manor** (01233) 213000, situated in the gorgeous Eastwell Park, Ashford, is a delightful place with a first class dining room, a front runner in any field. Ideal if you've won a packet on the last at Folkestone. Good luck in 2005.

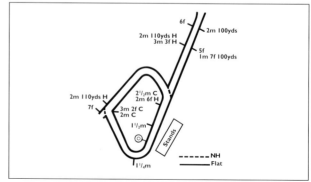

Eastwell Manor is stunningly located in the heart of the Kent countryside within a 3000 acre estate but only a few minutes from junction 9 of the M20, and is the nearest AA✶✶✶✶ hotel to Folkestone racecourse. The exquisite gardens and manicured lawns are a special feature of the hotel which nestles at the foot of the North Downs. There are 62 en suite bedrooms either in the Manor itself or in one of the 19 luxury Mews cottages.

The Pavilion Leisure Spa is one of the finest in England and boasts two 20 metre heated swimming pools, indoor and outdoor. There is a large hydro therapy pool, steam room, sauna, jacuzzi and Technogym gymnasium. 'Dream' Beauty Salon offers an extensive range of Pamper Days, treatments, products and gift vouchers and is open to non-residents.

Eastwell Manor
Eastwell Park, Boughton Lees, Ashford, Kent TN25 4HR
Tel: (01233) 213000 Fax: (01233) 635530
e mail: enquiries@eastwellmanor.co.uk
website: www.eastwellmanor.co.uk

Fontwell Park

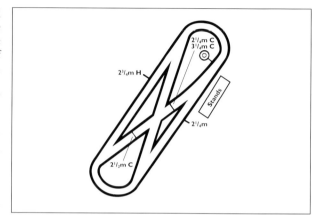

*T*here is no more pleasant a course for a day's National Hunt racing than Fontwell Park where **Phil Bell** is the **General Manager**, **Geoff Stickels** is the **Clerk of the Course** and **Karen Sumner** handles the commercial side of things. They can be contacted at **Fontwell Park Racecourse, Fontwell, Arundel nr Hythe, West Sussex, BN18 0SX. Tel: (01243) 543335, Fax: (01243) 543904. E-mail:** *enquiries @fontwellpark.co.uk* **Website:** *www.fontwellpark.co.uk*

The racecourse is conveniently situated adjacent to the A27 and the A29 roundabout, midway between Arundel and Chichester. London is 60 miles using the M23 and the A29. The M23 adjoins the M25—that frustratingly one-paced track. The A3 is the best selection to make if one is keen to pursue a trunk road. The trains into this county run from Victoria and the nearest station is at Barnham. There are buses from the station to the course on racedays so this may be an alternative mode of transport. There is ample car parking available which is provided free. Helicopters may be landed close to the track if you call ahead to make arrangements.

The racecourse stages about 19 National Hunt fixtures each year. Bank Holiday meetings in May and August are amongst the best attended in the season and offer a perfect opportunity for friends and family to meet, enjoy a picnic and have a fun day out. The best quality action takes place at meetings in November, December and February. Southern National is the feature race on New Year's Eve and helps to create an electric atmosphere. A day of Festival trails in February is perhaps the pinnacle of the season featuring the National Spirit Hurdle and the Fontwell Foxhunters Chase.

Entrance to the racecourse is priced at £16 for daily admission to the Premier Enclosure and £11 for the Grandstand & Paddock. You can save £2 off both of these prices if you book in advance. OAP's can gain entry at £7 to the Grandstand & Paddock on the day. The course also has several package deals on offer that include admission, parking, racecards, a drink, tour of the course and afternoon tea – great value. All accompanied children under 16 enter free and the course lays on funfair rides and entertainers at weekend and holiday fixtures. If you wish to park in the centre of the course and have a picnic go to the Trackside Picnic Area where it costs £5 per car and £11 per head. The Annual Premier badge, which includes reciprocal meetings at other courses, other sports events and organised trips can be yours for £160.

There are 13 private boxes and each can cater for up to 20 guests. Hospitality packages start at £65 per person. There are also larger rooms for hire that can accommodate up to 120 people. The Fontwell House restaurant in the Premier Enclosure offers three course meals and bookings can be made through the racecourse office. For those who enjoy

Artist: **Peter Smith GOING EASY** *Courtesy of:* **Frost & Reed**

fresh air, you should try the Garden Bar overlooking the lawn. In the Grandstand & Paddock there are lots of bars to choose from, all named after some of the great horses that have raced here in the past, including Game Spirit, Salmon Spray, Comedy of Errors and Nickel Coin. There are lavatories for disabled people located here too and in the Premier Enclosure and those with disabled car stickers are entitled to special parking arrangements. If you are blessed with a clear crisp windless day's racing at Fontwell and a couple of fancied flutters oblige you will be pretty close to heaven. A visit to this charming Sussex racecourse is always recommended.

Local favourites

Where better to begin our gastronomic wander around this most pleasant of English counties than in Storrington where we find **Sawyards** (01903) 742331—a distinguished French restaurant. It is extremely popular and bookings for both lunch and dinner are strongly advised. The **Spur** at Slindon is a local pub that is well thought of by the racecourse executive.

Another extremely peaceful and relaxing hotel and restaurant double is the **Roundabout Hotel** (01798) 813838 in West Chiltington—mock Tudor in style, but with plenty of character. If one chooses to visit Arundel, perhaps to view the castle or to browse through some of the delightful antique shops, a particularly relaxing establishment is the **Norfolk Arms Hotel** (01903) 882101—a coaching inn for over 200 years and still welcoming today with the **Butlers Restaurant and Bar** (01903) 882222 providing a fine place to dine. There are numerous pubs in Arundel but one to note is the **Arundel Swan Hotel** (01903) 882314—a

pleasant restaurant here and friendly bars. In addition to bar snacks and a pleasant welcome there is some accommodation here too. A really excellent choice found in Climping is **Bailiffscourt** (01903) 723511—this is the form choice in a truly excellent field. Findon is a pleasing racing village where you will find **Findon Manor** (01903) 872733, a welcoming hotel, and the **Village House** (01903) 873350 where good food can be expected. In the alarmingly named Burpham, The **George and Dragon** (01903) 883131 offers fine fayre to keep the wind up as does the **Burpham Country House** (01903) 882160 - lovely views as well as first class English cuisine. The aptly named **Black Horse** pub (01243) 551213 in Binstead is ideal to whet the racing appetite. The **Royal Oak** at Walberton (01243) 552865 also offers good food and the **Holly Tree** (01243) 554023 is a pub not to overlook. In Barnham the **Barnham Hotel** (01243) 552272 is also worth a visit.

Not everyone will be able to slumber in Sussex, but any visit should certainly be combined with one of the many splendid pubs that adorn the county. The **Fox** at Charlton is a convenient diversion and the **White Hart** at South Harting is especially handy for Goodwood and Fontwell visitors. Farther afield, the **Black Horse** (01798) 342424 in Byworth is also worth a visit—a comprehensive range of bar snacks and a really cosy restaurant, ideal for a quiet evening after racing. In Petworth, there's a number of places to note. **Soanes** (01798) 343659 is a charming restaurant at which to have a spot of dinner and **Horse Guards Inn** (01798) 342332 is a pub which serves fine meals. In Pulborough, the **Chequers Hotel** (01798) 872486 is a small Queen Anne building where lunch and dinner are both well priced. More expensive, but quite superb, is nearby **Amberley Castle** (01798) 831992 near Arundel. Its outer walls predate racing itself—a fine atmosphere in which to consider the heritage of this sport.

*Artist: **Neil Cawthorne** AT THE START Courtesy of: **The Artist***

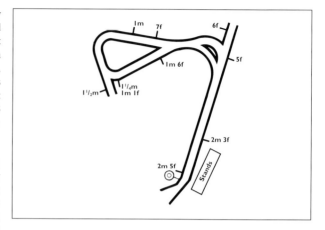

*T*he management team at Goodwood is headed by **Rod Fabricius**, who acts as **Clerk of the Course** and **Managing Director**; **Seamus Buckley** who is **Assistant Clerk of the Course** and **Grounds Manager**; **Sarah Vigneault, Hospitality Sales Manager**; **Frances Barton, Ticket Enquiries**; and **John Thompson** who is Goodwood's **Racecourse Manager**. They can all be contacted at **Goodwood Racecourse, Chichester, West Sussex PO18 0PS, tel: (01243) 755022 fax: (01243) 755025. E-mail:** *racing@goodwood.co.uk* **Website:** *www.goodwood.co.uk*

The racecourse is about 60 miles from London. Chichester, the nearest large town, is five miles away. Chichester railway station is on the Victoria line and there is an efficient bus service from the station to the course on racedays. If you do travel by car from London the journey time is likely to be an hour and a half. The A29 or the A3 doubled up with the A27 should produce a satisfactory result. The A27, which bypasses Chichester, also serves racegoers from the east and west and there are brown tourist signs on it to direct you to the course. Goodwood has ample parking and this is free or at £3 (£6 for the Festival), depending on how far you are prepared to walk. Free owners and trainers valet parking is available from the west entrance. Light aircraft can land at Goodwood Airfield, two miles from the course. Helicopters or taxis can be taken to the course from there.

Major races to note at the Glorious Goodwood meeting are the long distance Goodwood Cup, the Stewards Cup, the Richmond Stakes and the jewel of the year, the outstanding Sussex Stakes.

The annual membership at Goodwood is £275 for new members and £205 for a renewal, admitting the member to the Richmond Enclosure on all Goodwood racedays, reciprocal fixtures on 28 other days and special offers on cricket, show jumping and polo. A Junior Annual Badge is priced at £85 for the under 25s. At the July meeting, daily badges are not on sale to the general public for the Richmond Enclosure but badges for other meetings can be purchased for £21. Entry to the Gordon Enclosure for the Glorious Goodwood meeting costs between £25 and £29, and from £12-£14 for other meetings. Entry to the Public Enclosure costs between £7 and £9 and rises to £11-£14 in July. You can save money on most of these prices if you book for Glorious Goodwood before June 1st. The course also offers a range of

Artist: **Martin Williams GOING DOWN - GOODWOOD** *Courtesy of:* **The Artist**

Artist: **Johnny Jonas POST HASTE** _Courtesy of:_ **The Artist**

ting facilities as well as an expanded parade ring and winner's enclosure that can accommodate 5,000 racegoers.

The third Duke of Richmond organised the first Goodwood race meeting in 1802. It was a friendly competition between himself and other army officers. The event was such a success that in the following year the public was admitted. Glorious Goodwood is now a firm favourite in the sporting calendar and a chance for many to put on their finest summer togs and Panamas and enjoy the garden party atmosphere. Racing is one of the very few sports that encourages its fans to dress up for the occasion and this certainly adds to its appeal, especially to those of the fairer sex. Chester in May, Ascot in June, Goodwood in July, York in August, all provide a wonderful frame for the latest fashion. Dress codes in certain enclosures sometimes come under criticism for being a bit old fashioned and stuffy and we are not quite sure ourselves what the ubiquitous 'smart casual' sometimes refers to. But the fact is that on a wonderful summer day at places like Goodwood the sight of a sea of Panamas and summer dresses provides the visual confirmation that something special is taking place. Long may it last.

group discounts and special deals for students and OAP's. Check with the course for details of which deals apply to various meetings. Goodwood also has its own Racecourse Club for 10-16 year olds, which is something that other courses should seriously consider. It provides some special amusements for the younger set, including a playground and a staffed creche for the little ones.

There are many facilities at Goodwood to suit all tastes and budgets. Enquiries with regard to the catering and restaurant reservations can be made with Payne & Gunter on (01243) 755123. The ever-expanding tented village and the superb racing make for massive crowds at the July fixture, so be warned. Try to arrive at the racecourse in plenty of time, Goodwood always provides a number of worthwhile additional attractions before racing commences.

Goodwood organises various events during the summer meetings which include barbecues, jazz and steel bands, over 65s days and family days—all of which are highly recommended. Other especially laudable points about the course are the lifts and stands for the disabled and numerous bet-

Artist: **Graham Isom ROCK OF GIBRALTAR** _Courtesy of:_ **Rosenstiel's**

Artist: **Peter Smith THREE ABREAST, WARREN HILL** _Courtesy of:_ **Frost & Reed**

There are all manner of good reasons for visiting Goodwood, not least because it is surrounded by some first rate hotels, but make sure you book early as the crowds are enormous. The **Marriott Goodwood Park Hotel** (0870) 400 7225 is a charming hotel with some delightful rooms, a pleasant restaurant and a friendly welcome that makes for a thoroughly worthwhile place to stay. Lovers of golf should make a point of booking here. A visit to nearby Goodwood House should also be fitted in if at all possible. The **Royal Norfolk Hotel** (01243) 826222 in Bognor Regis offers special Goodwood weekly rates. Bognor was incidentally given the addition of Regis after George V recuperated there in 1929. If it was good enough for him, it's good enough for me. The part 16th century **Inglenook Hotel and Restaurant** (01243) 265411 is also a worthy consideration in this tricky field.

Goodwood is situated between Midhurst and Chichester. Both towns have a lot to offer. Near Midhurst the **Spread Eagle** (01730) 816911 is a first class 18th century inn and certainly one of the best of its type. The accommodation is most comfortable and both lunch and dinner in the restaurant are good. There is a number of excellent establishments in and near to Midhurst and the civilized **Angel** (01730) 812421 offers good value bedrooms and an excellent restaurant, the Cowdray Room. Midhurst really is ideal for lovers of the post-race pub crawl. Restaurants are also in abundance. West of Midhurst is Pulborough, home of the **Chequers Hotel** (01798) 872486, an ideal base for some energetic exploration of the countryside, as is the majestic **Amberley Castle** (01798) 831992 which simply oozes history and class. A genuine favourite in any field.

Travelling south on the A286 and entering Chichester, one is confronted with a number of delights including **Comme Ça** (01243) 788724, a confident nap in any field. Meanwhile, lovers of traditional English food should sample **Cassons Restaurant and Bar** (01243) 773294 in Tangmere. The **Ship Hotel** (0870) 330 5193 is a satisfactory place to spend the night. The streets of Chichester are often extremely busy. There are some excellent shops—ideal if you don't wish to attend every day of Glorious Goodwood. At night, the streets have an excellent atmosphere and the cathedral and the **Festival Theatre** (01243) 781312 are worth a visit. **Crouchers Country Hotel** (01243) 784995 is also a thoroughly welcoming selection. Further west one arrives in Bosham, a delightful village which houses the **Millstream Hotel** (01243) 573234, an attractive small hotel which is a convenient place to stay, especially if you like the coast. In Chilgrove, the **White Horse Inn** (01243) 359219 is excellent—a superb pub and also a fine restaurant not to be missed, the wine list here is breathtaking. In case you take the wrong road out of Chichester and find yourself heading east, do not despair, but head instead for Rustington, where the **Kenmore Guest House** (01903) 784634 will ease the most furrowed brow. Finally, in Langrish, near Petersfield, **Langrish House** (01730) 266941 is a little farther afield but is particularly enjoyable.

If, by chance, you anticipate owning or backing a winner, we recommend that you book a table in **Auberge de France** (01428) 651251 in the very pleasant **Lythe Hill Hotel and Spa** in Haslemere, a decent French restaurant and a fine hotel as well. Two pleasant pubs can be located by people trekking northwards. In Lickfold, the **Lickfold Inn** (01798) 861285 is a fine Tudor establishment which offers some excellent

Artist: **Graham Isom** *GOODWOOD* *Courtesy of:* **Rosenstiel's**

Artist: **Jacqueline Stanhope PERSIAN PUNCH** *Courtesy of:* **The Artist**

food and some accommodation. The **Coach and Horses** at Compton (023) 9263 1228 is a friendly local to try as is the **Anglesey Arms** (01243)773474, a particularly convenient local favourite. The **Elsted Inn** (01730) 813662, Elsted Marsh, also offers excellent pub grub and some accomodation—a great choice. For people seeking more liquid refreshment, visit the Chilsdown vineyard. Near Chichester, the Fishbourne Roman Palace is worth a peep while the Weald and Downland Open Air Museum is also something to note. We are grateful to the Goodwood team for suggesting the following places to try: the **Fox Goes Free** (01243) 811461 in Charlton and the **Selsey Arms** (01243) 811465 in West Dean. The **Star and Garter** (01243) 811318 at East Dean is highly regarded. These are recommendations from the horse's mouth so to speak and should definitely be carefully considered when assessing the form. The **Hilton Avisford Park** (01243) 551215, comes with a strong recommendation from the racecourse executive. A great *Travelling the Turf* favourite is **South Lodge Hotel**, Lower Beeding (01403) 891711—a first class hotel and restaurant double and with excellent golf too. There's also a fairly strong local whisper for **Hallidays** (01243) 575331 at Funtington—a fine, characterful restaurant. The **Black Rabbit** (01903) 882828. in Arundel has also been reported to be good.

If you have any energy left and the summer sun still shines, one place you should not miss near Plumpton is **Glyndebourne Opera House** (01273) 812321—the location of the Glyndebourne Festival (May to mid-August). If you can tie in racing with an evening's opera the contrast will be enormous, but the appeal no less great. **Horsted Place**, Uckfield (01825) 750581 provides a luxurious base, depending, of course, on the state of the following day's betting fund! Golfers will find this hotel particularly appealing. The thought of a day or more at Goodwood fills the heart with joy. In contrast try **Severals House** (01730) 812771 two double bedrooms but warmly commended for its quality accommodation and peaceful ambience. Hopefully one of the above will provide good cause for further celebration after a successful day's racing on the South Downs in 2005.

Artist: **Stephen Cook TIGHT FINISH** *Courtesy of:* **The Artist**

*Artist: **Jonathan Trowell** LEADING IN Courtesy of: **The Artist***

*T*he people in charge at Hamilton are **Racing Manager Hazel Peplinski**, **Track Manager George Murdoch** and **Chief Executive Alastair Warwick**, who can be contacted at **Hamilton Park Racecourse, Bothwell Road, Hamilton, Lanarkshire ML3 0DW. Tel (01698) 283806. Fax: (01698) 286621. Website:** *www.hamilton-park.co.uk* **E-mail:** *enquiries@hamilton-park.co.uk*

The course is 10 miles south of Glasgow, in Hamilton, and the track is accessible from Glasgow via the M74, junction 5, or from Edinburgh via the M8, junction 6, and the A723, which runs near the course from east to west. The A776 from East Kilbride may prove an alternative route for eastbound travellers. For punters from the south, the A74 and the M74, junction 5 is an advisable route from Carlisle. Glasgow Central is the city's principal station and trains from London can be caught at Euston. There is a connecting line to Hamilton West which is the course's local station and buses from there pass the course. People with light aircraft and helicopters can't land at the course itself but a shuttle service between Heathrow and Glasgow as well as other major cities, could be of some use. Annually there are 18 days of flat racing at Hamilton Park with plenty of action between May and September, including a Family Night and Ladies Night. Evening meetings are well worth considering here—ideal for unwinding after a hard day's work in Glasgow. The most popular meeting remains the Saints & Sinners Charity Meeting held in June. I imagine a number of both can be found at such events.

The Annual Membership rates are as follows: a single badge is priced at £150 and a double badge is £250 which includes access to the Winning Post Bar and over 20 reciprocal days at other racecourses. A Junior Membership for 17-21 year olds is £100. There is also a corporate rate available at £350 plus VAT with transferable badges. A more fleeting relationship with Hamilton will cost £16 for a Premier Enclosure badge at a standard race meeting and £20 on a feature day or £10 for the Grandstand with a reduced rate if you are a student or a pensioner.

If you are planning a day out for more than 10 people you will receive a discount of 20 per cent and this applies to all enclosures. Full details can be obtained from the racecourse office and there are private boxes of various sizes as well as a sponsors' room. Marquees are also available. There are various restaurants, club dining room, snack bars and a string of drinks bars, but, as one might expect, these are fairly busy areas. In the Premier Enclosure the Duke's Restaurant is quite popular and booking is essential (01698) 283806. In the Grandstand the Panorama Bar has floor to ceiling glass overlooking the course. The Winning Post Bar is an exclusive facility for owners, trainers and Annual Members with a full bar.

Hamilton is always a contender for the best turned out course. The course is compact and the atmosphere is excellent. Those with children under 16 will be pleased to hear about their free admission and the playground. There are various facilities for disabled racegoers including special viewing in all enclosures. There are no banking facilities, although Tote cash and credit facilities are available. So if you intend to make use of the on-course betting shops bring your stake money with you.

Owners and Trainers are well looked after here, with their own room overlooking the parade ring with complimentary tea and coffee served all day. There have been some major developments at Hamilton Park in recent years which include the £2.7 million extension of the Grandstand to accommodate 13 additional boxes and the new Dukes restaurant. Local people should note that the facilities can be used for conferences and receptions throughout the year.

Hamilton Park may not be one of Britain's foremost racecourses but with a situation near to Glasgow, the racecourse is extremely popular; being a part of the throng when your fancy is coming through the field is a happy feeling indeed.

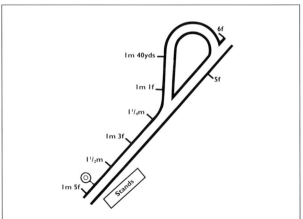

Local favourites

For people wishing to tie a visit in with a trip, try the ever improving **Glasgow Marriott** 0141 226 5577 in Argyle Street which offers pleasant cocktail bars and a wealth of leisure facilities. The **Hilton Glasgow** 0141 204 5555 is another high-rise hotel but is well run and comfortable with a good restaurant, while the **Hilton Glasgow Grosvenor** 0141 339 8811 is a most impressive hotel with a delightful situation opposite the Botanical Gardens. **The Radisson** 0141 204 3333 in Argyle Street offers a contemporary design and is really comfortable. With more contemporary style and ideally placed for the Concert Hall is **Langs** 0141 333 1500 which is also well thought of (great food here as well). Glasgow offers a variety of attractions and an exquisite Victorian hotel in which to stay is **One Devonshire Gardens** 0141 339 2001, home of a renowned restaurant: **Amaryllis** 0141 337 3434 - it's from the mastermind of Gordon Ramsay, and is considered to offer the finest cuisine in the city. Finally, the **Malmasion** 0141 572 1000 is delightfully luxurious and will appeal to those who enjoy contemporary design.

Glasgow has become a veritable Mecca for lovers of fine cuisine with **Rogano** 0141 248 4055 one of its most celebrated restaurants. The **Buttery** 0141 221 8188 in Argyle Street, is convenient for the Holiday Inn and an excellent spot for lunch or dinner. Upstairs is expensive and correspondingly elegant while downstairs has a more relaxed air. **Gamba** 0141 572 0899 in West George Street is a haven for lovers of seafood - it's chic and really good.

A Cantonese restaurant with an extensive menu can be found in Sauchiehall Street—it's called **Loon Fung** 0141 332 1477. **Amber Regent** 0141 331 1655 provides Chinese cuisine of an award-winning standard. Just around the corner, the **Ubiquitous Chip** 0141 334 5007 is fancied and has a great reputation locally. Others to consider include **Rococo** 0141 221 5004 which has a thoroughly relaxing feel whereas **Papingo** 0141 334 2665 is also ideal for a post race celebration.

To the west of Glasgow stands **Gleddoch House** (01475) 540711, a distinguished hotel and restaurant. Built on the banks of the Clyde, this impressive hotel is particularly charming and golfers will be delighted to hear that there is a nearby course. Golf courses, like pubs, are never far away in Glasgow and its surrounds. Those who like pubs and bars should try **Babbity Bowster** 0141 552 5055.

Returning south of the Clyde, in East Kilbride hotels to note are the **Hilton East Kilbride** (01355) 236300 and the **Bruce** (01355) 229771. Both are modern, friendly and relatively convenient for the racecourse. Similarly appealing is the **Crutherland House Hotel** (0870) 381 8710 which boasts first class facilities and a really pleasant situation. Another good restaurant in the area is **Da Luciano** (01698) 852722. Closer to the racecourse, the **Bothwell Bridge Hotel** (01698) 852246 also serves good food, while the **Hilton Strathclyde** (01698) 395500 provides first class accommodation. One final thought from the racecourse team is the nearby Alona Hotel (01698) 333888 it's a chery place to visit by all accounts.

*Artist: **Mao Wen Biao** TURNING FOR HOME Courtesy of: **Osborne Studio Gallery***

*H*aydock Park is the best all-round racecourse in the north of England, just one of the reasons why it has been twice named Travelling the Turf's Racecourse of the Year. **Kirkland Tellweight** acts as **Clerk of the Course** while **Adam Waterworth** is **Managing Director** and **Stephen Mansfield** fills the role of **Operations Manager** with **Dean Martin** as the **Commercial Manager**. They can be contacted at **Haydock Park Racecourse, Newton-le-Willows, Merseyside WA12 0HQ. Tel: (01942) 725963, Fax: (01942) 270879. E-mail:** *haydockpark@rht.net* **Website:** *www.haydock-park.com*

Access to the course is off the A49 close to Ashton. The course is superbly served by motorways and the M6 (Junction 23) and the M62 converge close by. An additional entrance has also been opened to provide easier access to the Owners and Trainers car park from the A580 end of the racecourse. In order to ensure entry through the western gate, M6 traffic from the north can leave at junction 24 and turn left, then right at the lights - the racecourse is a mile further, on the left. To arrive by train, catch the Euston train to Warrington Bank Quay or take the local link to Newton-le-Willows; or catch the 320 bus from Liverpool which will deposit you at the gates. There is also the Haydock Park Xpress, a direct bus from St Helens Central and Newton-le-Willows Merseyrail stations to the course on Saturdays and Sundays. More speedy access can be obtained by using the landing strip or helipad.

Haydock runs year round and has both excellent flat and jump racing. There are several three-day meetings during the summer months, with the Lancashire Oaks and Old Newton Cup held in July, while the Sprint Cup in September is the feature race of the flat season. National Hunt enthusiasts get to see some of the best horses in the jumping game here and a new grade one chase in November promises to become the highlight of the season.

Artist: **Graham Isom ONE MAN** *Courtesy of:* **Rosenstiel's**

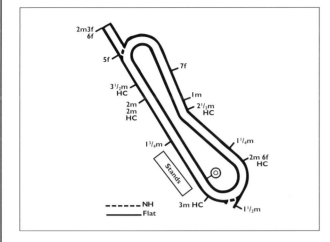

For admission to the Premier Enclosure in 2005 you will pay £32 (£38 at the weekend and £40 on Premium Days) and for the County Enclosure you will pay £19 (£24 on Saturdays and bank holidays and £30 on Premium Days). For Tattersalls the prices will be £12 (£15 and £18) with £6 and £8 for the Newton Enclosure rising to £8 on weekends. Haydock's Harry's Bistro is a panoramic dining facility that will cost you £71.50 pp and a badge must be purchased in advance to confirm your booking. There is a dress code in effect in the Premier Enclosure for which you will be required to wear a jacket and tie (that's the men, of course).

Senior Citizens are admitted to Tattersalls and the Newton Enclosure at half price, while accompanied children under 16 and people confined to wheelchairs are free. To keep the kids busy there is a playground in the Newton Enclosure and other entertainments on summer Saturdays. An Annual Badge for the County Stand offers a definite saving. A single badge for the entire year is priced at £270. This includes a special car pass and 24 reciprocal days racing at different courses. A Junior badge is also on offer at £70. The racecourse also offers discounts in Tattersalls and the Newton Enclosure for parties of 15 or more. Private facilities at Haydock Park are excellent—they include 32 boxes and six function rooms. The boxes are sited on three floors of the Tommy Whittle Stand, and can accommodate up to 20 people. There is also the Premier Suite from whose glass front you can observe the finishing post, opposite. For larger parties the luncheon rooms can be linked together. The Park Suite can seat 450 people but can be sectioned off to accommodate smaller parties. If you wish to use the restaurant, bookings start three months prior to each raceday. A more fun way of catering for a larger party may be to organise a marquee. The Lancaster restaurant in the County Enclosure offers à la carte and tables can be booked in advance by telephoning the sales office. Overlooking the parade ring, the glass encased conservatory holds a seafood and champagne bar and has a fine view of the parade ring.

Whether it's flat or jump racing you never seem to be far away from the action at Haydock. While many improvements have been made to the facilities during the last decade, the course management has wisely managed to retain the ambience of the course's unique park atmosphere. The tree lined parade ring is one of the finest in Britain and the new winner's enclosure now allows many more people to see their heroes when they return.

In Lower Peover, the **Bells of Peover** (01565) 722269 has a delightful setting, and as well as super bar food the restaurant is recommended. North of the Bells, in Plumley, the **Smoker** (01565) 722338 which has an adjoining restaurant as well as serving excellent bar food can be recommended. **Ye Olde Parkgate Inn** (01625) 861455 is also good. In Mobberley, the **Bird In Hand** (01565) 873149 is one of the growing band of good food pubs. Other pubs in the area include the extremely welcoming **Fiddle Inn i'th' Bag** (01925) 225442 at Burtonwood. The **Pickering Arms** (01925) 261001 at Thelwell is an attractive and friendly village local while in Risley, the **Noggin** (01925) 812022 is another popular food pub. However, perhaps the most convenient pub for the racecourse is the **Bay Horse Hotel** 0161 368 2632. An enticing and handy alternative is the **Kirkfield Hotel** (01925) 228196 which is a friendly place and conveniently well placed for the racecourse. Another likely place for the early bird is the **Holiday Inn** at Newton-le-Willows (0870) 4009068 for it stands in parkland fringing the Haydock Park racecourse. For those expectant racegoers travelling from Liverpool on the A580, a **Travelodge** provides a convenient stopover and there are several in the area (08700) 850950. There is also the **Thistle Haydock** (01942) 272000 which lies near to the course. The **Hanover International Hotel and Club** (01925) 730706 at Stretton is one for the notebook . Another first class post race retreat is the **Park Hall** Hotel (01257) 455000, well placed and welcoming.

Manchester has numerous attractions and some excellent hotels and eateries. **Simply Heathcotes** 0161 835 3536 is a good restaurant as is **Brasserie St Pierre** 0161 228 0231 and the **Royal Orchid** 0161 2365183. **The Lowry** 0161 827 4000 is a modern hotel beside the River Irwen. It's sumptuous in every way while its brasserie style restaurant, inspired by Marco Pierre White, produces good cuisine. **The Hotel Rosetti** (0870) 381 9148 is also creating something of a reputation. Another polished hotel is the **Portland Thistle Hotel** 0161 2283400, an elegant establishment which also boasts a good leisure centre. The **Le Meridien Victoria and Albert** (0870) 4008585 in a converted 19th century warehouse is first-class with a television themed interior. **Le Meridien Palace** 0161 288 1111 is also well thought of from the same stable. While another group with a fairly handsome string, offers **The Marriott Worsley Park** 0161 975 2000 - some good golf here as well. **The Copthorne Hotel** 0161 873 7321 and the **Malmaison** 0161 278 1000 are other excellent contenders in this select field. The **Crowne Plaza Midland** 0161 2363333 provides top-class comfort and the French restaurant there is excellent. Manchester boasts an outstanding array of cosmopolitan cooking. **Yang Sing** 0161 2369438 in Princess Street is an excellent Chinese restaurant. **Est Est Est** 0161 8339400 at 5 Ridgefield, is also a welcome Italian addition to the field. **Simply Heathcotes** 0161 835 3536 is also good but for an extraordinary culinary feast head to Altrincham where **Juniper** 0161 929 4008 offers something special for the gastronome to sample. **The Lincoln** 0161 8349000 is an appropriately named restaurant, while near the airport **Moss Nook** 0161 4374778 is one of the most established restaurants in the area. There are some rooms here as well for those wishing to stay. Didsbury Village also offers something a little special in **Didsbury House** (0870) 381 8481 - it's wonderfully designed and has to be one for lovers of contemporary chic and first class accommodation.

At Hereford, **Katie Langdell** is the **General Manager** and she can be contacted at **Hereford Racecourse, Roman Road, Hereford HR4 9QU. Tel: (01432) 273560 Fax: (01432) 352807. E-mail:** _klangdell@hereford-racecourse.co.uk_ **Website:** _www.hereford-racecourse.co.uk_

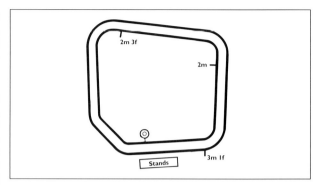

Hereford Racecourse is clearly signposted and there are good roads on the northern outskirts of the city. Indeed, the whole area is bordered by several major roads from the Midlands, South Wales and the south west. From the north, the racecourse can be reached via the A49 from Leominster and the A4110. The main southern approach roads are the A49 and the A495. The A438 through Hereford itself passes close to the racecourse and there's also an approach on the A4103 from Worcester. London is approximately 120 miles away and if you are travelling to Hereford by train then Paddington station is the one from which to make your departure from London. The local station is three miles from the course and a taxi will be required from there. Should you be fairly busy and/or well-off then, subject to prior arrangement, helicopters are welcome. If you decide to take the motor, two large free car parks await you, one of which is a picnic-style park with a complete view of all the racing. Please note however, that the entrance for the Course Enclosure is off the A49, whilst the Grandstand entrance can be found off the A4103. The racecourse holds 16 National Hunt meetings throughout the year and in 2005 five will take place on Sundays. Most of the racing here is bread-and-butter stuff but there are often large fields and racing is competitive. Admission to the Premier Enclosure is £15 and £10 for Grandstand and Paddock. If you want to have a picnic, it will cost you only £5 to get into the picnic parking area. Old

Age Pensioners can claim a 20% discount on all days. Annual Membership here costs £130 and includes all 16 race days, as well as reciprocal fixtures at many other racecourses and reduced green fees at a local golf course. A pretty good deal even if you aren't a golfer! Discounts are available for the Grandstand and Paddock for groups of 15 or more.

Hereford has had something of a facelift in the past few years with brand new entrance facilities and a new pre-parade and parade rings. Boxes are available to hire on a daily basis and differ in size, catering for up to 40 guests. There is a larger room which will take up to 150 guests or marquees can be erected if you wish for an even bigger party. There is also a restaurant in the Premier Enclosure where there is no need to book. Various packages are on offer here from the caterers. The Grandstand bar has been renovated and a brand new Grandstand food court added for those who want a quick snack. If you wish to take your

Artist: **Anne Farrall FOOT PERFECT** _Courtesy of:_ **The Artist**

under 16 children racing they are admitted free. Disabled racegoers will be pleased to note that there is a special viewing area and easy access to the Grandstand. There is a betting shop in the Grandstand as well as an Owners and Trainers bar that serves hot and cold snacks.

Hereford is one of those delightful out-of-the-way county towns where the pace of life is slightly slower than average. The horses may also be of lesser speed than those seen at Ascot or Cheltenham, but racing is still competitive here and should you wish for a peaceful day out, there are few finer courses at which to spend the day.

Local favourites

For those who wish to really soak up the racecourse atmosphere, a five minute walk from the aforementioned track brings one to the doorstep of the **Travel Inn** (0870) 197 7134. Hereford provides a good range of hotels: **Castle House** (01432) 356321, is a tremendous all round stayer and thoroughly recommended. The **Green Dragon** (01432) 272506 and the **Three Counties Hotel** (01432) 299955, dating from 1850, are also safe bets (always a dangerous claim to make). **The Belmont Lodge** (01432) 352666 should appeal to golfers and enjoys some delightful views. **The Pilgrim Hotel** (01981) 540742 at Much Birch is well regarded and also offers a few holes of par three golf to keep you in the swing. Pubs to try amidst the Malvern Hills include the splendid and highly recommended **Bunch of Carrots** (01432) 870237 at Hampton Bishop, a leading riverside pub about three miles from the course. The **Butchers Arms** (01432) 860281 at Woolhope, a

half-timbered building which offers good bar food, a restaurant and some pleasing accommodation. Nearby, in Fownhope, the **Green Man** (01432) 860243 is a popular local fancy with excellent food and good pub accommodation. In Ledbury the timbered **Feathers** (01531) 635266 is appealing. Another Ledbury thought is **The Verzons Country Inn** (01531) 670381 which also has a well thought of restaurant. In the opposite direction - but a journey well worth making just the same - is **The Stagg Inn and Restaurant** (01544) 230221. It's really welcoming and the food is outstanding. Another bustling and rightly popular inn is the **Three Crowns** (01432) 820279 which offers some fine cooking. If you still haven't had your fill you could try the latest hot tips from the racecourse staff: **The Bell** at Tillington (01432) 760395, the perfect place to whet your whistle, or the **Holme Lacy House Hotel** (01432) 870870 for the best in Hereford hospitality.

The county of Herefordshire, characterised by its brown-and-white faced cows, is stunning, particularly as you approach the Welsh border. In this direction, the **Lord Nelson** (01981) 590208 at Bishopstone has a good restaurant and bar food. In Eardisland, the **White Swan** (01544) 388533 is a good stop-off point for people travelling north, while at Whitney-on-Wye, the **Rhydspence Inn** (01497) 831262 offers superb bar meals and some accommodation. Our trip comes full circle at delightful Ross-on-Wye which boasts a clutch of fine hotels. The **Chase** (01989) 763161 is a charmingly personal Victorian hotel and **Best Western Pengethley Manor** (01989) 730211, just outside the village, has a super restaurant. Finally, **Pheasants** (01989) 565751 is a restaurant with rooms to note. It provides another excuse for visiting this gorgeous area.

Artist: **Margaret Barrett OVER THE LAST** Courtesy of: **The Artist**

Clerk of the Course, Secretary and Managing Director at this delightful course are all roles which are admirably carried out by **Charles Enderby**, who can be contacted at: **Hexham Steeplechase Company, The Riding, Hexham, Northumberland. Tel: (01434) 606881, Fax: (01434) 605814. Marketing Manager** is **Dennis Gallagher** who would be delighted to show prospective clients around the course. **Website:** *www.hexham-racecourse.co.uk* **E-mail:** *hexrace@aol.com*

Hexham lies 20 miles and a few furlongs west from Newcastle, about 35 miles from Carlisle and some 300 miles from the bustle of Trafalgar Square. The course itself is a mile south of this delightful market town, sandwiched between the B6305 and the B6306. The road from Newcastle to Carlisle, the A69, is convenient for joining either of these two minor roads. The Newcastle western bypass should speed up your journey considerably if you are using the A1. If you are northbound on the A1 and have a little extra time in which to make your journey, leave the A1 at its junction with the A68 and follow the road through the Durham hills—stunning. The M6 and the A69 are the most direct routes for those travelling from Carlisle and the west of the country, although the A686 through Penrith and Alston provides some excellent scenery. There are bus and train stations in Hexham. Newcastle is on the main King's Cross—Edinburgh route and the journey time is swift. A connecting train can be caught from Newcastle to Hexham. There is a free bus from the train and bus stations to the racecourse on racedays. The majority of racegoers, however, seem to drive to the course where there are acres of free parking. There is also plenty of room to land your noisy helicopter but please notify the course prior to your arrival. To take advantage of the better weather, Hexham now

stages several summer jumping fixtures in June as part of its 16 fixture annual programme. The biggest day of the year is a local derby for point to pointers in the form of the Heart of All England Maiden Hunter Chase in May. In 2005 admission charges will be £12 for Members and £8 for Tattersalls. OAPs are allowed into Tatts for only £6 and children 16 and under are free. If you wish to enrol as an Annual Member in the Hexham Race Club, the price will be £95 for a single and £150 for a double badge, which drops to £75 and £130 respectively for OAPs. This is excellent value as it includes access to your own bar as well as 17 reciprocal meetings, both flat and jumps, and a day out at the nearby Durham County Cricket Club. Anyone introducing three new members can get a full refund of their annual subscription – quite a deal. For those wishing to organise parties, there is a 20 per cent reduction for groups of 20 or more in both enclosures with free badges for the organiser and coach driver.

Although basically a country course set in magnificent scenery, Hexham continually strives to improve its facilities and is now more 'weather proof' than ever. The Ramshaw Stand provides excellent facilities in the ground floor Members' Bar and you can enjoy the carvery and a drink in the Curlew Room on the first floor. A lift accommodates the needs of disabled people. There are also three private boxes on the top floor which can cater for up to 30 sponsor's or private guests. Larger parties can be accommodated by using a large adjoining room, or for parties of up to 180 people, the Henderson Room in the connecting stand may be used. The new stand has extensive Tote facilities and many television monitors. A Tote betting shop with a bar, a 100 seater sponsors' box which can be subdivided, and the Pavilion Restaurant have all been added in recent years. Racegoers may book a table in advance by phoning the course caterers, Ramside Catering 0191 236 4148. A three-course lunch is served for £20.75 per head and the diners may keep their table for the entire meeting. Just above the parade ring is a new Annual Members bar which can be also used by visiting metal badge holders, owners and trainers. The excellent facilities at Hexham are also for hire on non-racedays for weddings, parties, fairs or seminars. Disabled people can enjoy a superb view of racing from their own special car ramp which can be entered next to the owners/trainers gate at the west end of the stands.

This is one of the most scenic of England's National Hunt racecourses and has one of the finest views of any course in Britain. With a watering system to ensure good going supplied by a centre course lake and a fixture list that takes advantage of the summer weather, Hexham is a sure bet for a visit in 2005.

*Artist: **Charles Church POINT-TO-POINT** Courtesy of: **The Artist***

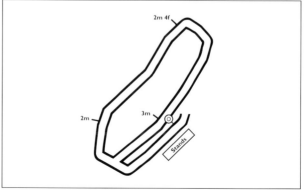

Local favourites

Hexham is a delightful market town and is ideally situated for touring the world heritage site of Hadrian's Wall and the Northumberland National Park with its hundreds of square miles of rugged beauty.

Just to the south of Hexham is the **Lord Crewe Arms** (01434) 675251, hidden deep in the valley of the Derwent River in Blanchland, a delightful place whose setting has gone unchanged for centuries. Just a few miles down the river Tyne lies Corbridge, another picturesque village with some excellent shops. Here the **Dyvels** (01434) 633633 is a popular meeting place and the busy **Corbridge Tandoori** (01434) 633676 is a good bet for an evening meal. Similarly, the **Valley Indian Restaurant** (01434) 633434 is another winner. If you wish to stay in the village, the **Angel Inn** (01434) 632119 has pleasant bedrooms and good food.

Back in Hexham itself, the **Beaumont Hotel** (01434) 602331 overlooks the Abbey grounds and is a convenient place to stay for the racegoer. A pub of note is the **Tap & Spile** (01434) 602039 which has excellent real ales. Almost opposite, on the other side of the road is **Danielle's Bistro** (01434) 601122. A good bet for Italian is **La Famiglia** (01434) 601700 tucked away on St Mary's Chare. For Indian cuisine don't pass by **Diwan-E-Am** (01434) 606575 on Hexham's main street and the bistro at the **Hexham Royal Hotel** (01434) 602270 is a restaurant with real merit and the hotel itself a good value stayer. Just south of the racecourse the **Dipton Mill** pub (01434) 606577 is perfectly placed for a drink and lunch before racing. Excellent home-made food and real ale made in its own brewery. In Wall, a few miles up the North Tyne, the **Hadrian Hotel** (01434) 681232 offers a reasonably priced bed for the night as well as some excellent food. Across the river at Newbrough, **Newbrough Park** (01434) 674545 is a fine country house with rooms, while in the village of Great Whittington the **Queens Head** (01434) 672267 can be highly recommended. Near here and only a twenty minute drive from the course, you'll find a stunning country house hotel - **Matfen Hall** (01661) 886500. It has a good golf course and spa as well and is an ideal spot for the non-racing type. In the opposite direction, **Langley Castle** (01434) 688888 is a splendid building and a good place to consider. A little further down the Tyne, the **General Havelock** (01434) 684376 is well worth a pre race pint or lunch. Also not far away is **The Rat** (01434) 602814 at Anick, where you are sure to receive a warm welcome.

A final thought is **Slaley Hall** (01434) 673350, a five star hotel with excellent leisure facilities and a championship golf course. If you prefer a pleasant pub, the recently refurbished **Travellers Rest** (01434) 673231 on the same road is an ideal place to end your day after a visit to one of Britain's most picturesque racecourses.

Artist: **Margaret Barrett** *COMING INTO LINE* *Courtesy of:* **The Artist**

The **Racecourse Manager Tina Dawson** and the **Clerk of the Course Fiona Needham** can be contacted at the **Huntingdon Racecourse, Brampton, Huntingdon, Cambridgeshire PE28 4NL. Tel: (01480) 453373 Fax: (01480) 455275. E-mail:** *huntingdon@rht.net* **Website:** *www.huntingdon-racecourse.co.uk*

The course lies just outside Brampton, conveniently positioned for travellers from the south (London is 60 miles away) and also from the north, as it is a half mile to the east of the A1 Junction 9, just off the A14, the A1/M11 road link, which takes you right past the course. The nearest railway station is just outside Huntingdon, two miles away. It's on the main 125 line and a very short journey from King's Cross. There is a free bus service from the station to the racecourse that runs two hours before the first race and one hour after the last.

They only race over the sticks at Huntingdon, but a full 18 day fixture list is on offer. The most popular fixtures tend to be Easter Monday and Boxing Day that always guarantee large crowds. Highlights include the Sidney Banks Memorial Hurdle and the Peterborough Chase and often produce excellent fields.

Huntingdon has free parking for cars and coaches, and if a picnic is the order of the day there is no charge for parking adjacent to the rails. The charge for a double annual membership is £245 whereas a single badge costs

£140. You can also get a half-year's membership for only £65. These include 18 days racing and 30 reciprocal days at other course as well as discounts and offers for golf, cricket and greyhound racing. There is a £16 charge for a Daily Member's badge whilst the entrance charge for the Paddock is £12 and the popular Picnic Car Park, £6. Dogs are allowed in the picnic area but must be kept on leads at all times. The latter offers a great view of the action from the rails and is open on weekend, bank holiday and evening meetings. The management offers a 20 per cent discount for parties of 15 or more. Various boxes on the course provide for parties of all sizes. The course has twelve viewing boxes, which can accommodate between 12 and 24 people and have an unrivalled view of the track.

Marquees can also be arranged for larger parties of 50 or more. The course management allows children under 16 to be admitted free of charge and for its bank holiday fixtures provides a variety of children's entertainment on weekends and bank holidays.

In the Members there are a number of bars offering hot dishes and snacks or you may wish to dine in the Peterborough Chase Restaurant that offers a package for a three-course lunch and tea. In Tattersalls you will also find a variety of bars and fast food outlets as well as a champagne and seafood bar. The picnic car park also has its own bar serving drinks and food. There are public telephones on the course but no bank, which makes life frustrating if

Artist: **Philip Toon** DESERT ORCHID *Courtesy of:* **The Artist**

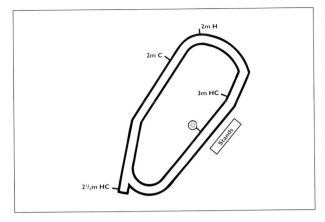

a likely winner and you've blown all your cash! The course's off-track betting shop is, however, a retreat for the hardened punter who wants to keep in touch with racing around the country and escape the outrageous odds that some bookmakers lay when taking money for races elsewhere. This is a friendly, unpretentious racetrack that offers competitive racing and is definitely worth visiting. A new grandstand, planned to open in 2006, should add to its appeal.

Artist: **Jay Kirkman** THE GREY Courtesy of: **The Artist**

Local favourites

The town's foremost hotel is the **Old Bridge** (01480) 424300, where one can enjoy a drink, a quiet lunch, a more comprehensive dinner or a room for the night. Alternatively, the **Huntingdon Marriott** 0870 400 7257 is another popular bar with modern accommodation. The **Stukeleys Country Hotel** (01480) 456927 is five minutes from the course; the bar is always busy and offers, along with the restaurant, a variety of meals. Ideally situated for the racecourse is **The Grange Hotel**, Brampton (01480) 459516 – it's well furnished and the restaurant has a strong local following.

In Fen Drayton, the **Three Tuns** (01954) 230242 is another pleasant drinking establishment—very popular with people in the know. The **Lion Hotel** (01480) 810313 at Buckden, just off the A1 south of Huntingdon, is a 15th Century coaching house offering a friendly, personal wel-

come. The **George Hotel and Brasserie** (01480) 812300 is also well regarded and has recently undergone an excellent refurbishment. In Arrington, the **Hardwicke Arms** (01223) 208802 is a super little pub with some excellent rooms. In St. Ives, another hall which doubles as an hotel has a particularly appropriate name, **Slepe Hall** (01480) 463122. Nearby Needingworth has the **Pike and Eel** (01480) 463336, offering comfortable accommodation and views of the River Ouse, with boats moored in front. The **Old Ferry Boat** at Holywell (01480) 463227 is also good, with fine food and accommodation. A good pub restaurant is sheltered within the **Pheasant** (01832) 710241 at Keyston. For people who are unable to sample these various offerings and need to journey home up the A1, a pint at the **Bell** (01733) 241066 at Stilton may be an idea—a splendid hotel with an excellent restaurant and comfortable bar. Nearby, The **Loch Fyne Oyster Bar** in Elton (01832) 280298 is an informal seafood restaurant to consider. Those going south should try one of three pubs near the A1. Firstly, the **Leeds Arms** (01480) 880283 at Eltisley is a particularly welcoming establishment offering some good food and accommodation. The **Eight Bells** (01767) 677305 in the pleasant village of Abbotsley is also worth a stop and finally, the **White Horse** (01480) 474453 at Eaton Socon is a part 13th Century inn with a pleasant restaurant, good atmosphere and some bedrooms. Two other first class pubs with restaurants to note are the **Three Horseshoes** in Madingley (01954) 210221 and the excellent **Anchor** at Sutton Gault (01353) 778537, the perfect place to celebrate having plundered the bookies. The **Haycock** (01780) 782223 remains a very convenient stop-off point for the A1 and offers a good restaurant, bedrooms and a pleasant bar for barsnacks. Finally a *Travelling the Turf* favourite: **The Falcon** at Fotheringhay (01832) 226254 is a tremendous pub with excellent food.

Artist: **Jay Kirkman** BRIGHT EYED Courtesy of: **The Artist**

*T*his friendly course is exceptionally well run by **Richard Landale** who is the **Managing Director** and **Secretary** and is the person to contact for further information at the following address: **c/o Sale & Partners, 18-20 Glendale Road, Wooler, Northumberland NE71 6DW. Tel: (01668) 280800 Fax: (01668) 281113 E-mail:** *info@kelso-races.co.uk* **Website:** *www.kelso-races.co.uk*

Kelso is easy to find and the course lies to the north of the town itself, off the A6089 and the A699. The journey from London is 320 miles. The A1(M) is the best route to take and the A697 or the A698 both lead to spectacular routes through the Borders and Northumberland. From the west take the M6 to junction 44, from here the A7 and the A698 are the best roads to choose. From Edinburgh the A68 and the A698 is the combination to follow.

There are other options for your journey, but the car has to be the best bet. The nearest railway station is in Berwick, 22 miles away on the King's Cross line, with a limited bus service to the town. Aviators are also diverted to nearby Winfield but helicopters are now welcomed. It seems fairly obvious then, that some form of motor transportation is in order, and there is, after all, the incentive of free parking. Special disabled parking can also be arranged in advance.

Kelso's jump racing fixture list continues to attract some very good horses and it's not unusual to see a horse or two running here that has serious chances in the big Cheltenham and Aintree festivals. The course has one of the longest finishing straights, all uphill, of any course in Britain and close finishes are the order of the day here. Although it's quite far from most of the major cities, Kelso enjoys excellent local support from the Borders' punters and is especially popular on weekends and public holidays. The course has also gained much support from regional businesses and it is rare indeed to see a race at Kelso go unsponsored. With its welcoming atmosphere and unique facilities, Kelso deserves its success.

At Kelso £15 is the midweek price for admission to the Members (£18 on weekends), £10 for the Paddock with discounts for student and OAPs and for those who book a week in advance. Children under 16 are admitted free. Annual Membership, which includes a private bar/viewing room and 92 reciprocal days, costs £200 for a double badge, £100 for a single, £75 for OAPs and £40 for Student Badges.

As far as corporate hospitality is concerned, Kelso offers the Younger Grandstand with five boxes, four to accommodate up to 25 people and one that will hold 45. There is also the Dukes Room (50 people), the Hamilton Room (70 people), the Doody Room (20 people) and three viewing boxes. Please apply to the Secretary. Prices start from £20 a head. Marquees can be erected and will hold up to 850 guests. The catering is provided by two local firms and a very high standard of home cooked delicious food is available at tremendous value—breakfast £3, lunch £10.

Artist: **Klaus Philipp WATER JUMP** *Courtesy of:* **The Artist**

Taking late afternoon tea, or something stronger, in Rosie's Bistro next to the parade ring is a particularly delightful way to pass the last race or two. For a quick snack there is a couple of fast food outlets dotted around the course. Owners are always well treated at Kelso and if you are running your horse you will receive four badges; special arrangements are made for partnerships or syndicates.

The recently built Tweedie Stand in the Paddock enclosure has covered, stepped seating with a new bar and a fast-food outlet. The stand also houses six private boxes on the first floor that can be combined to accommodate larger groups. The facilities for entertaining here are first class and the view of the course excellent. There is a betting shop in the Paddock, together with a Tote building in which to spend your money! There are WCs and viewing ramps for the disabled. One of the more interesting vantage points to watch the racing is from the golf course in the centre of the course, although good viewing is possible from just about anywhere.

Kelso is one of the finest local racecourses in the country and is also one of the best run and many others could learn from the management here. We wish all involved great success in the future.

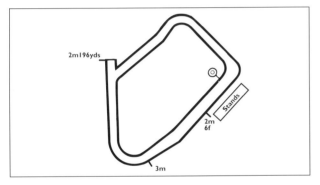

Local favourites

We choose to start our journey at a real favourite, **The Roxburghe Hotel and Golf Course** (01573) 450331—formerly Sunlaws House, a hotel of distinction. You will find this hotel just south of Kelso at Heiton. The hotel is beautifully furnished and the restaurant first rate. The hotel is a great favourite and a trip to Kelso followed by a visit here is about as good as it gets. If you enjoy Golf or Salmon fishing then this is the jewel for you. Further north, in Kelso itself - an extremely pleasant market town - one finds the **Ednam House Hotel** (01573) 224168. The Tweedside setting has obvious appeal for anglers, but the hotel is also convenient for the racecourse. Another place to visit is the **Queens Head Hotel** (01573) 224636—the bar snacks here are good, as indeed they are at the **Cross Keys Hotel** (01573) 223303 in Kelso's town square and an impressive selection of small restaurants. Kelso is a pleasant border town and there are a number of shops, for non racing friends to visit. A little north of Kelso, **Edenwater House (01573) 224070** is a stylish newcomer.

Rain or shine, Melrose is a charming border town and **Burts Hotel** (01896) 822285 is the one to note—good bar meals and more formal meals as well as good accommodation. **Dunfermline House** (01896) 822411 is a splendid guesthouse close to Melrose Abbey. **The Town**

House Hotel (01896) 822645 in Market Square is worth more than a little consideration. A little further south, in St Boswells, two hotels should also be noted. Firstly, the most hospitable **Buccleuch Arms** (01835) 822243 and also the highly recommended **Dryburgh Abbey** (01835) 822261. The **Collingwood Arms** (01890) 882424 in Cornhill and the **Besom Inn** (01890) 882391 at Coldstream (01890) 882391 also come highly recommended by those in the know. A little south of Kelso, Jedburgh offers the Jedforest Hotel (01835) 840222 - a wonderfully well run country hotel which also offers first rate food.

Well warmed up, you may decide to brave the elements and visit Gattonside. Here, the **Hoebridge Inn** (01896) 823082 is appealing. Trekking north towards the uplands, one arrives in Lauder. Here, the **Black Bull** (01578) 712208 is a pleasant, modernised, Georgian coaching inn. Again a fair distance from Kelso, one finds Ettrickbridge. Here, **Ettrickshaws** (01750) 52229 is well worth the journey—good value hospitality and some extremely imaginative set menus. The **Philipburn House Hotel** (01750) 20747 is also a pleasant place in which to stay. The **Wheatsheaf Hotel** (01890) 860257 in Swinton is also a good choice. It's a wonderful restaurant with delightful rooms. Finally, the **Tillmouth Park Hotel** (01890) 885700 boasts nine miles of excellent salmon fishing on the river Tweed and also organises packages for racegoers—a cosy, hospitable, hotel ideal for anyone travelling from far a field.

*Artist: **Charles Church** NOVICE HURDLER Courtesy of: **The Artist***

Kempton Park, the closest racecourse to the centre of London, has enjoyed a long and distinguished history since it opened its doors in 1878 as an up-and-coming rival to nearby Sandown Park. To this day it's little wonder that the majority of its fixtures, whether flat or over the jumps, are well attended affairs.

Julian Thick is the **Managing Director** here, **Beverley Frith** the **Raceday Office Manager** and **Nicky Wiseman** the **Marketing Manager**. They can be contacted at **Kempton Park Racecourse, Staines Road East, Sunbury-on-Thames, Middlesex TW16 5AQ. Tel: (01932) 782292 Fax: (01932) 782044 E-mail:** _kempton@rbt.net_ **Website:** _www.kempton.co.uk._ For **Corporate Hospitality** the contact number is **(01372) 461220**, while those interested in **sponsorship** should get in touch with **Phillipa Haines** on **(01372) 461252**.

The racecourse is situated some 15 miles from central London and is well served by the motorway links. The M25 and the M3 make the trip in from the country especially good. For the popular evening meetings, however, one should consider the rush hour build-up. The A316 and the A308 will take you over the Thames to within a stones throw of the racecourse. The A308 via Hampton Court is the best road from the south. For train travellers, there is an excellent service direct to the course from Waterloo on the Shepperton Line which takes about 35 minutes. For those travelling by bus, there is a bus stop outside the racecourse gates and buses can be taken from Staines and Kingston.

Free parking can be found in the centre of the course, but if you wish to park in the main car park the fee is $5. Those wishing to beat the traffic and arrive by helicopter are requested to land between the dovecote and the lake—but phone in advance and notify the course.

Kempton provides some superb racing throughout the year and the highlight is, without doubt, the Christmas Festival, including the King George VI Steeplechase on Boxing Day. The post-Christmas euphoria always makes for a jovial atmosphere. You can guarantee the King George will provide a memorable spectacle. July features the Gala Evening, an extremely popular night with barbecues, military bands and fireworks to entertain racegoers. These evenings are really popular, the racing is of a very competitive standard.

The rates for Daily admission in the Premier Enclosure range from £17 to £35, depending upon the fixture. It costs between £13 and £25 to enter the Paddock, while the Silver Ring costs between £8 and £11. The latter however is not open on certain days when there is a lack of demand. A special rate of admission is offered to parties of six people or more who receive a 20 per cent discount. The course also offers special package deals for certain meetings and it is worthwhile contacting them about these offers. Accompanied children (16 and under) are admitted free to all enclosures and students can get in for half price if they have the appropriate identification.

Artist: **Philip Toon THE DUKES FLAGSHIP** _Courtesy of:_ **The Artist**

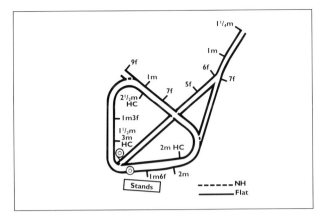

Annual Membership includes both flat and jump meetings and costs £225 and runs from October to the following September. National Hunt membership is £125 and those wishing to purchase a membership for flat racing only can do so for £155. These badges give you free parking in the Members car park, the right to invite guests for half price plus reductions in the Jubilee Panoramic Restaurant and reciprocal meetings at other course. All in all, a great package. Alternatively you can buy a Season's Ticket which provides admission to all summer evening meetings. This costs £65 in the Premier and £50 in the Paddock Enclosure.

The facilities at Kempton are excellent and boxes, suites and conference areas can all be organised. The private boxes are let annually, but they do become available on some quieter days with at least one or two up for grabs for excellent value. They also have balconies overlooking the racecourse and its very attractive grounds. Certainly as far as venues for entertaining go these boxes take some beating.

They can seat twelve people for lunch or about 20 for a less formal buffet. Each box has television monitors, private bar facilities and a number of other perks. The management generally know whether boxes are free two to three weeks in advance.

Meals in the Premier Bistro begin at £8 while the Jubilee Panoramic Restaurant should be booked in advance and will cost you between £50 and £270 per guest. More modest refreshments can be found in numerous snack bars, particularly on the ground floor of the Grandstand. One may also enjoy a picnic in the course enclosure car parks, if you wish to dine al fresco.

Facilities for children include a playground in the centre of the course and a crèche in the Silver Ring (free of charge for children under five years). Good amenities for disabled people including a viewing ramp can also be found. Owners are made particularly welcome with discounts on lunch and a very welcome bottle of bubbly for the successful owners.

Although there was talk a couple of years ago of Kempton abandoning its jumping fixtures, this all seems to have passed – thank goodness. One new development at the course however is its plans for a flood-lit all weather track which have passed the planning permission hurdle. If all goes according to plan, they could be racing on it by early 2006. Given the success of floodlit meetings on Saturday nights at Wolverhampton there is little doubt that such a facility at Kempton would prove equally popular. The improvements to the all weather surface in the past couple of years mean that racing on dirt in Britain no longer needs to be a second class cousin to its turf counterparts. If Kempton's plans work out Londoners will be able to enjoy a great night out in the years to come.

*Artist: **Graham Isom** KEMPTON PARK Courtesy of: **Rosenstiel's***

Racing at either Sandown or Kempton offers a great variety of enticing possibilities for culinary refreshment. Those journeying back to the capital should also find that many of the following suggestions make convenient and relaxing stop-offs.

In Esher, **Good Earth** (01372) 462489 offers a good Chinese menu, while lovers of South East Asian fare will enjoy **La Orient** (01372) 466628. In East Molesey, one finds an extremely popular French restaurant, **Le Chien Qui Fume** (020) 8979 7150, while in Claygate **Petit Pierrot** (01372) 465105 is well worth a visit.

A pub conveniently placed for Sandown is the **Albert Arms** (01372) 465290. Alternatively for Kempton, try the **Kings Head** (01932) 221910 in Shepperton or the **Three Horseshoes Inn** (01932) 225726 in Laleham. If you are staying in the area, then there's a number of possibilities to consider. In Weybridge, the **Oatlands Park Hotel** (01932) 847242 is an ever improving favourite. A well appointed alternative is the **Ship Hotel** (01932) 848364, while **Casa Romana** (01932) 843470 is an exciting Italian affair. Leisure lovers and golfers should note the outstanding country house hotel, **Le Meridien Selsdon Park** (020) 8657 8811 in Sanderstead, a thoroughly delightful venue. **Coulsdon Manor** (020) 8668 0414 is another to consider, more golf, a delightful Victorian Manor House and really impressive food. A smaller but extremely refined establishment is the **Angel Posting House and Livery** (01483) 564555 in Guildford. Excellent cuisine combines well with all the comforts one could wish for—a real find. Restaurants near here include the **Cafe de Paris** (01483) 534896 and the **Gate (01483) 576300**, while at **Shere, Kinghorns** (01483) 202168 is reportedly a very handy and well turned out type.

In Cobham we might consider two options. The **Woodlands Park Hotel** (01372) 843933, at Stoke D'Abernon or if one just wants a post-race pint, the **Cricketers** (01932) 862105. In Ripley, south west of Cobham, another restaurant beckons, **Drakes** (01483) 224777—outstanding French cuisine. Finally, the **Hilton** (01932) 864471 in Cobham is a large, well run concern from the internationally acclaimed stable of the same name.

Turning to London, there is a whole mass of outstanding restaurants, some cheap and cheerful, others cheerful until the bill comes! Outside the capital, however, a number of establishments might be thought of. In Richmond, one finds all manner of good eating places and pubs, and two good hotels as well. There are numerous boozers to sample en route but a little gem with excellent food is the **White Horse** off Sheen Lane in Richmond, ideal for post race fare. The **Petersham** (020) 8940 7471 has a very good restaurant and the **Richmond Gate** (020) 8940 0061, a worthwhile port of call, has been warmly recommended of late. The **Bingham Hotel** (020) 8940 8737 is also well worth considering for both Sandown and Kempton. Richmond itself has good shopping and a range of restaurants and pubs to suit all tastes and budgets. Down by the Thames, **Richmond Pitcher and Piano** (020) 8332 2524 not only offers the 'Old Father' but also provides some good value cooking. In Egham one should note several establishments. The **Olive Grove** (01784) 439494 is a good restaurant to note, while **Great Fosters** (01784) 433822 is an interesting building which houses a good hotel—obviously better value than Central London offerings. The **Runnymede**

(01784) 436171 is more modern and a popular visiting spot for the many who travel this way. In Staines, the **Swan** (01784) 256908 is a fine public house as is the **Harrow** in Compton, south of Guildford—note the racing prints here. Shepperton is also handy for the racecourse where the **Warren Lodge** (01932) 242972 is a good place to stay—its terrace overlooks the Thames. The **Anchor Hotel** (01932) 242748 is another worthy candidate—pleasant bars and bedrooms and not too pricey. One of the largest hotels in the area is the **Shepperton Moat House** (01932) 899988, less intimate than some by virtue of its size, but a worthy recommendation just the same. The **Thames Court** (01932) 221957 in Surbiton is another spot to note. This restaurant offers French cuisine while the bar has a variety of sandwiches and cold meats—excellent. Surbiton also offers the **Warwick Lodge** (020) 8399 5837 for excellent value accommodation. Also note **The French Table** (020) 8399 2365, an enjoyable restaurant in which to dine. Alternatively, **Le Petit Max** (020) 7223 0999 is a good place to visit after an evening at Kempton, or Sandown for that matter. In Hampton Court make a note of the **Carlton Mitre** (020) 8929 9988.

Racegoers who enjoy cricket should seek out the **Swan Inn and Lodge** (01372) 462582 in Claygate in summer as it doubles as the local cricket pavilion—excellent bar food as well.

If you are coming back through London, the following tips should cover most options. The **Kings Arms** (020) 8977 1729, Hampton Court, is a good pub for a pint either before or after racing and we also recommend the **Imperial Arms** (020) 7736 9179 run by racing enthusiasts. It serves first-class food and excellent wine and beer—a real favourite. An outstanding hotel offering style and comfort can be found on Wimbledon Common, **Cannizaro House** (020) 8879 1464. This sumptuous Georgian mansion is an elegant but friendly hotel in which to stay. There is also a variety of pubs and restaurants in Wimbledon, all great fun. If you want to celebrate in style but don't wish to return to the better known West End eating haunts, try the popular **Riva** (020) 8748 0434 in Barnes, the **Blue Elephant** (020) 7385 6595 in Fulham Broadway—excellent Thai food—or the **River Café** (020) 7386 4200, Hammersmith, for unbeatable new-wave Italian cuisine.

Restaurants closer to the racecourse which are well thought of include **Sonny's** (020) 8748 0393 in Barnes, **Crowthers** (020) 8876 372, and **Monsieur Max** (020) 8979 5546. The Glasshouse (020) 8940 6777 is also a great place to go after racing - ideally situated in Kew Village. In Kingston-upon-Thames, **Ayudhya Thai** (020) 8546 5878 is great and **Frere Jacques** (020) 8546 1332 has an idyllic seting and some good French cooking. It's always tricky to keep abreast of these restaurants in London and the home counties, but we hope this is a good selection; if you are a racegoer from this neck of the woods, and have some tips or information on these or other choices, please drop us a line!

Artist: **Anne Farrall** THE WINNER *Courtesy of:* **The Artist**

The **Clerk of the Course** is **Jimmy Stevenson** while **Company Secretary** and **Manager** is **Russell Parrott**. They can be contacted at **The Racecourse, Oadby, Leicester, LE2 4AL. Tel: (0116) 271 6515 Fax: (0116) 271 1746. E-mail:** _info@leicester-racecourse.co.uk_ **Website:** _www.leicester-racecourse.co.uk_

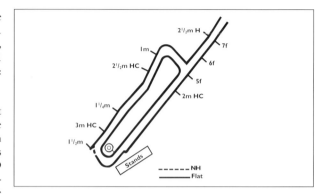

Leicester racecourse is in Oadby, two miles south east of Leicester on the A6 Market Harborough Road. Both the M1, exit junction 21, and the M69 might prove useful in reaching the track. From the west and Birmingham (40 miles away) take the M6 exiting at junction 2 and follow the M69 to the M1. Try to use the B5418 and avoid Leicester's one-way system at all costs. Southbound travellers will find the A46 and the M1 the best routes while the A6 and the M1 are possibilities for the northbound racegoer. People making the journey from Newmarket might wish to use the A47 turn off before Leicester, through Evington. The Southern District Distributor Road links the M1 (junction 21) with the A6 at the entrance to the course. Trains run from St Pancras to Leicester, a journey of about an hour-and-a-half. A bus service runs from the station on racedays and there is a regular service from Leicester City to the track. The ample parking facilities are provided free of charge here and if you have a helicopter, you can land it in the centre of the course by prior appointment by calling the racecourse office.

Leicester enjoys a full year of 32 flat and National Hunt racing fictures. There are no annual memberships available here but daily admission to the Belvoir Stand (formerly the

Club) costs from £15-17, depending on the particular fixture and includes a free race-card. Admission to the Grandstand costs £10-12. Very reasonable for a good day out. Group discounts, available in advance, will reward those fielding parties of 20 or more a £3 discount in both enclosures. Those with a car and four congenial adults can expect to pay between them £25-32 for their combined entry to the Picnic Car Park. Accompanied children under 16 years old are admitted free, while students and OAPs can gain admission for between £7 and £9, depending on the day. Leicester is also part of a scheme called Midlands Racing which offers special deals on admission to various courses. Check with the course for the latest details.

Leicester has more than kept pace with improvements to facilities on British racecourses. The Belvoir Stand has several bars, including Silks Bar where you can enjoy

Artist: **_Johnny Jonas_ RIGHT ON THE MONEY** _Courtesy of:_ **The Artist**

Artist: **Roy Miller LONG SHADOWS** Courtesy of: **The Artist**

tipple with a view over the Weighing Room. The Grandstand restaurant offers lunch and afternoon tea from £23–£29 per person and offers a fine view of the course. In the Grandstand there is the Quorn Room Café which serves a range of snacks and drinks. For corporate entertaining or private groups, the Fernie Room has been refurbished and is available for daily lettings. There are also three double boxes that will take 30 to 40 people quite comfortably. The accommodation is equipped with closed circuit television and private Tote betting facilities. Marquees can be erected in the Paddock area and the centre of the course, if required. On non-racedays, the Nelson Suite provides accommodation for up to 300 people for conferences, seminars, private parties or wedding receptions. Call Maria Szebor at the racecourse office on 0116 271 6515 for box availability and prices.

Children under 16 are admitted free here if accompanied by an adult and there is a special playground area and entertainment on offer during weekend, Bank Holiday and evening meetings. For those with disabilities there are special facilities in the Grandstand and a viewing platform that overlooks the winning post. There are public telephones in all enclosures and a Ladbrokes betting shop in Tattersalls, but there are no banks at the racecourse.

Leicester is a well-situated racecourse and one to bear in mind when scanning the 2005 racing calendar!

Local favourites

If you wish to stay in the city then one suggestion is that you plump for one of the larger hotels in the city centre. The **Holiday Inn Leicester** (0870) 400 9068 is particularly modern but has swimming pools and that sort of thing to

make up for the situation. Less modern, Victorian actually, is the **Ramada** (0116) 255 5599—note here a particularly good coffee shop and some welcoming bars. The **Hilton Leicester** (0116) 263 0066 is another to be considered. The Hilton and the **Belmont House Hotel** (0116) 254 4773 also come highly recommended by Leicester Racecourse themselves. Among the vast number of guesthouses and B&Bs in the area, **Leigh Court** (01886) 832275 and the **Scotia Hotel** (0116) 254 9200 stand out from the crowd. Leisure facilities are reported to be good at the **Corus Time Out Hotel** (0116) 244 4542 - modern, but very appealing. In the restaurant stakes, **Watsons** (0116) 222 7770 also has a good local following. **San Carlo** (0116) 251 9332 is a popular Italian.

In Rothley, the **Rothley Court** (0116) 237 4141 is a manor house with a super setting and restaurant. **The Limes** (0116) 230 2531 also has a good local reputation. In Quorn itself, the **Quorn Country Hotel** (01509) 415050 blends together a combination of traditional hospitality and modern amenities. There are a number of appealing pubs to be found in and around Charnwood and one of them is the **Carrington Arms** (01664) 840228, Ashby Folville—good bar food here. South of the city in Whetstone, the **Old Vicarage** (0116) 278 4247 is a pleasant restaurant close to Leicester. The **Three Swans** (01858) 466644 at Market Harborough is another comfortable and highly recommended establishment. In Old Dalby, the **Crown Inn** (01664) 823134 dates from the 17th century and is a lovely place for a pint and a fireside chat—there's also a fairly handy restaurant. A hotel of note is the **Harboro Hotel** (01664) 560121. The restaurant here is also worth a visit. Alternative accommodation can be found in the **George** (01664) 562112, an extremely comfortable and well looked after inn which is strongly recommended. The **Rose and Crown** (01949) 860424 in Hose is a popular pub with tremendous character and some good food, while on the way to Oakham, the **Noel Arms** (01572) 722931 at Langham is also recommended—a good restaurant here (01572) 722931. A supremely popular pub is the **Bell** at East Langton (01858) 545278, renowned for really first-rate food. Finally, the remotely set **Old Barn** (01858) 545215 offers good food in the evenings and some pleasant accommodation.

'First class' is a description one should also apply to the area's leading hotel, **Hambleton Hall** (01572) 756991. The grounds lead down to Rutland Water and the bedrooms are superb. The highlight of the house is the restaurant—outstanding. Less grand, but no less welcoming accommodation can be found at the **Finch's Arms** (01572) 756575 which serves fine food. In Oakham's market place, the **George** is a good place for a drink. Elsewhere, The **Whipper-In Hotel** (01572) 756971 is a characterful inn to visit and nearby **Barnsdale Lodge** (01572) 724678 and **Barnsdale Hall** (01572) 757901 both enjoy wonderful locations and are both reported to be good, as are the **Neville Arms**, Medbourne (01858) 565288 (some accommodation as well) and the **Marquess Of Exeter Hotel** at Lyddington (01572) 822477. The hotel has a good restaurant and accommodation. **The Lord Nelson (01574) 723199** is also a really good hotel and restaurant double. Continuing the maritime theme, **The Admiral Hornblower Hotel** (01572) 723004 is a good inn to try. A final thought for lovers of over- the-top quality, try **Stapleford Park** (01572) 787522—a really fine choice if you've got a winning jackpot ticket.

The **Clerk of the Course** is **Chris Stickels** who can be contacted at **Lingfield Racecourse, Racecourse Road, Lingfield, Surrey RH7 6PQ. Tel: (01342) 834800, Fax: (01342) 835874.** The **General Manager** here is **Clive Stephens** and the **Sales & Marketing Director** is **Kate Hills. E-mail:** _info@lingfieldpark.co.uk_ **Website:** _www.lingfield-racecourse.co.uk_

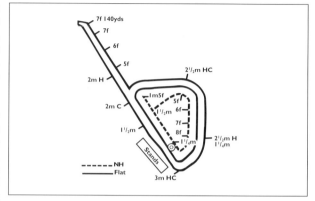

Lingfield is easily accessible from London, which is only 20 miles away. The M25 and the A22 are the best routes to follow from the capital. The racecourse itself is on the B2029. The A22 is the best route for northbound travellers, exiting for the course at Newchapel. Westbound travellers should take the A264 while those heading east should pursue the M25 and the A22, exiting at junction 6. On arrival, there is a choice of car parks with parking for 7,000 cars. The public car park is free while the Members' car park will cost you £5.

If you don't want to take the car then a train from Victoria or London Bridge to Lingfield Station is a convenient option (with combined rail and race tickets available) and a short walk will see you to the racecourse gates. For more local requirements, the 429 bus from East Grinstead to Godstone will take you via the track. If speed is of the essence then helicopters are free to land in the centre of the course provided you make the arrangements in advance on (01342) 831718.

There is no shortage of fixtures at Lingfield as the course holds some 97 race meetings over every month of the year, offering flat racing on the grass course and the all-weather track plus a few national hunt fixtures. From the end of May until August there are quite a number of evening meetings. The most popular event of the year is the excellent Classic Trials meeting in May, featuring the Derby Trial, and the Oaks Trial. The rates for entrance to Lingfield are £16 for the Members and £13 for the Grandstand. The Members rises to £20 on Derby Trial day and the Grandstand to £15. During the winter all weather season from November to March the two enclosures are combined to form one enclosure. Children under 16 who are accompanied by an adult are admitted free. Discounts are available for groups of more than 15 people who receive a £2 discount, but these are only available in advance for meetings between March and November. Annual Membership costs £295 and includes reciprocal race meetings at many racecourses around the country as well as social membership of the Lingfield Park golf club. You can get £25 off this price if you join before December 1st.

Lingfield Park is an excellent place at which to entertain your friends or colleagues as the facilities are good. Boxes for 8 to 400 guests are available and the Members Enclosure Pavilion can handle between 20 and 300 people. The dining facilities here include the Trackside Carvery for which you can book a table on (01342) 834800, the Brasserie in the Members and a Champagne Bar and the Owners and Trainers Bar. In the summer months there is a Seafood Courtyard in operation. You could also try the User Friendly bar in the Grandstand. Both the Members and Grandstand Enclosures have betting shops as well as Tote facilities. There is a play area for children and a crèche, open on specific race days, for 3 to 7 year olds. There are special viewing areas and lavatories for disabled people as well as car parks, and it is good to see the course making an effort here.

Artist: **Susie Whitcombe LINGFIELD PARK** _Courtesy of:_ **The Artist**

Lingfield has improved its facilities year on year and has recently completed a £6 million refurbishment of the grandstand. The quality of racing has improved considerably since the early days of dirt racing as well, with increased prize money on offer and the improvement of the racing surface with the installation of a polytrack which is more user friendly to both horses and jockeys alike. As more all weather tracks come on stream in Britain during the next few years they could do well to emulate Lingfield's success.

Local favourites

Lingfield Park is surrounded by good hostelries. Sampling a different one after each meeting of the year would not be impossible. Some notable examples are the **Hare & Hounds** (01342) 832351 in Lingfield and the **Castle Inn** (01892) 870247 in the delightful village of Chiddingstone. Other suggestions in the locality include the **Crown** (01892) 864742 at Groombridge—a pleasantly situated old inn with some fine ales, a restaurant and some bedrooms if needs be. **The Bottle House** (01892) 870306 and the **Spotted Dog** (01892) 870253 in Penshurst are also firm favourites, as is the **Royal Oak** (01342) 832383 at Dormansland—ideal for a pint or two. In Edenbridge, **Moulin Blanc** (01732) 866757 is a handy place to enjoy good food and wine—be sure to book, and **Haxted Mill** (01732) 862914 is also worth investigating. It has an idyllic situation, great character and first class food. Another good restaurant to consider is the **Old Lodge** at Limpsfield (01883) 714387. This establishment is not cheap but it is extremely well thought of.

If you are keen to stay nearby, then several ideas spring to mind. Firstly, the **Copthorne Effingham Park** (0870) 890 0214 in the village of Copthorne has much appeal, (good restaurant and leisure facilities), while in Tonbridge, the **Rose and Crown** (01732) 357966 in Tonbridge High Street is also a satisfactory port of call. On Mount Ephraim, the **Spa Hotel** (01892) 520331 boasts outstanding facilities and a commendable restaurant, as does the **Royal Wells Inn** (01892) 511188. **Thackeray's** (01892) 511921 is also a chic place for dinner - French cuisine of a high standard is the order of the day here. One should also consider **Hotel du Vin and Bistro** (01892) 526455, which not only boasts an outstanding menu but also has a divine wine list and excellent accommodation. What better place to end up after a successful day's sport? Well, **Gravetye Manor** (01342) 810567, is an outstanding hotel and restaurant double and **Ashdown Park** (01342) 824988 offers relaxation and excellent cuisine. Other less grand, but worthy recommendations in East Grinstead include the **Ramada Gatwick/East Grinstead** (01342) 326992, the **Woodbury House** (01342) 313657, and the **Cranfield Lodge Hotel** (01342) 321251, which are all well worth a visit. In a similar vein, nearby Hartfield offers **Bolebrooks Watermill** (01892) 770425—exceptional value and very charming. Racegoers who thirst after sheer luxury will appreciate **Alexander House** (01342) 714914, located at Turners Hill—not terribly close to the racecourse but well worth a detour. Finally a pub to note: the excellent **George & Dragon** (01892) 863125 at Speldhurst—a fine friendly boozer to count one's ill-gotten gains. If you enjoy historic houses, then Nutfield Priory (01737) 824400 will fit the bill. It's a beautifully restored house that exudes character. Longshott Manor (01293) 786680 is another first class small hotel - ideally situated for the airport (Gatwick) should that be your chosen form of transportation when racing at Lingfield in 2005.

Artist: **Graham Isom LINGFIELD PARK** _Courtesy of:_ **Rosenstiel's**

*T*he **Clerk of the Course** and **Secretary** at Ludlow is **Bob Davies**. He can be contacted at **Ludlow Race Club Ltd, Bromfield, Ludlow, Shropshire SY8 2BT. Tel: (01584) 856221 Fax: (01981) 580181. E-mail:** *mail@ludlow-racecourse.co.uk* **Website:** *www.ludlow-racecourse.co.uk*

The racecourse is situated in beautiful Shropshire countryside yet is easily accessible from major routes, two miles northwest of Ludlow. The favoured routes are the A49 via Shrewsbury from the north or through Hereford from the south. Racegoers from areas west of Ludlow should follow the A4113. Travellers from the east of the country should aim to reach the A44 from Worcester and then make the best use of the A49. Anyone wishing to circumnavigate the town should use the Ludlow bypass. There are both rail and bus stations in Ludlow and the Midland Red runs from Hereford to Shrewsbury on the A49. The railway station is small but the line can be joined from Newport, which in turn is on a direct route from Paddington; or from Euston, via Shrewsbury. There is ample free parking should you decide to drive. Cars can be parked alongside the course in the spring and autumn although this may be restricted during the winter months. Helicopters can also land at Ludlow providing you ask permission first.

The racecourse stages about 16 meetings a year, all National Hunt. Ludlow is one of England's finest market towns, with some excellent local restaurants of the highest standard. This should be reason enough to make a visit and having racing here too is an added bonus for any trip. Most of the fixtures are mid-week and going racing will produce a welcome break from the demands of the ordinary workaday world.

Annual Membership here is priced at £145 and includes 20 reciprocal meetings and two Single day guest vouchers. Daily admission charges are £16 for the Members, £12 for Tattersalls and £6 for the Course. Senior Citizens have the concession of a £2 refreshment voucher for use in Tattersalls and discounts are available for groups of 12 or more in all enclosures if booked in advance (details are available from the website or office). Disabled people in wheelchairs are admitted into the Members at the same price as Tattersalls. There are also disabled toilet facilities in all enclosures and a viewing ramp.

The Members building, the Clive Pavilion, provides bar and restaurant facilities for annual members, owners and trainers. Non-raceday functions for up to 500 people can also be accommodated. The new Jubilee Stand has six private boxes, each with its own balcony, to provide an excellent view of the course and the surrounding scenery. There is also an 80 seat restaurant with its own Tote betting facilities. Bookings can be made through Jenkinson Caterers on (01785) 252247. There are also bars and fast food outlets in Tatts and the Course enclosure.

Children are welcome here and they will be entertained by the free bouncy castle at late spring meetings. For those even younger there is a mother and baby room for Course patrons. Tote credit facilities are available in the Members.

Ludlow is to be applauded for its commitment to provide modern facilities in all areas. It benefits from its splendid scenic location and delights in a peace that is seldom found in Britain.

Artist: **Jay Kirkman JOCKEY IN BLUE** *Courtesy of:* **Rosenstiel's**

Local favourites

A number of fine establishments can be found in Ludlow. **Overton Grange** (01584) 873500 is an Edwardian manor offering really excellent cuisine. The 16th century **Feathers Hotel** (01584) 875261 is extremely popular and offers a good restaurant. More moderately priced accommodation is found at **Cecil** (01584) 872442. A pub to note is the **Church Inn** (01584) 872174, which provides a great

bedrooms here as well) and **Hibiscus** (01584) 872325 (booking is essential here). The modern French cooking at Hibiscus is exceptional - Corve Street is the location for what is surely one of Britain's finest rural collections of exemplary and wonderful cooking.

Just over the border in Wales, the **Radnorshire Arms Hotel** (01544) 267406 at Presteigne is steeped in history—a favourite of Elizabeth I who lived here once. East of Ludlow at Abberley, along the A443, the **Elms Hotel** (01299) 896666 is another hotel with an impressive history and thoughtful service. Just west of Tenbury Wells you find **Cadmore Lodge** (01584) 810044 - an unassuming but nonetheless pleasing hotel. **The Peacock Inn** (01584) 810506 is also well thought of and is good value. In the curiously named Hopton Wafers, the **Crown Inn** (01299) 270372 is a popular pub which provides an excellent bar menu and restaurant. In Clun, the **Sun Inn** (01588) 640559 is a 15th century listed building which also has good value accommodation and bar snacks. Thirteen miles south of Shrewsbury is Church Stretton and in nearby All Stretton you'll find the **Stretton Hall Hotel** (01694) 723224—ideal if you want peace and quiet in a traditional style. **The Studio** (01694) 722672 is also a first class location for good food. Before leaving the area consider The **Roebuck Inn** in Brimfield, whose restaurant (01584) 711230 is first class. In terms of fine dining, Ludlow is to cuisine what Cheltenham is to National Hunt racing. If you enjoy good fare, this pleasant rural trek is an ideal diversion for a few days in 2005.

Artist: **Jay Kirkman JOCKEY IN GOLD** *Courtesy of:* **Rosenstiel's**

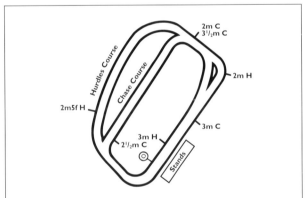

Artist: **Malcolm Coward OVER THE DITCH** *Courtesy of:* **The Artist**

atmosphere for a pre or post-race rendezvous. Another hotel in which to spoil yourself is **Dinham Hall** (01584) 876464 which has a first class restaurant and comfortable rooms. A restaurant for those who delight in excellent food is the **Merchant House** (01584) 875438—but do book. The **Unicorn** (01584) 873555 is a pub worthy of note here, with some accommodation too. Other thoughts for good food are **The Courtyard** (01584) 878080, the really exceptional **Mr Underhills** (01584) 874431 at Dinham Weir (some

Clerk of the Course is **Nick Patton**, while **Pip Adams** is the **Racecourse Manager** and **Amy Fair** is the **Sales/ Executive** at this pleasant Lincolnshire course. All the members of this team can be contacted at: **Market Rasen Racecourse, Legsby Road, Market Rasen, Lincolnshire. LN8 3EA, tel: (01673) 843434, fax: (01673) 844532, E-mail:** *marketrasen@rht.net* **Website:** *www.marketrasen races.co.uk*

The racecourse is some 12 miles north east of the county town of Lincoln, just off the A46, midway between Lincoln and Grimsby. The course is adjacent to the A631 on the eastern edge of the town. The A1 is the closest major road to the course and this, coupled with the A46, is the best route from the south. From the north, use a combination of the M62, M18 and M180 link to the A15, then the A631 at Caenby Corner. Those travelling by train should note that Market Rasen is on the Newark to Cleethorpes line. Change at Newark if you are coming from Kings Cross. The station is about a 10 minute walk from the course. Should you travel by car you will find ample free parking. Helicopters are welcome at Market Rasen but please contact the course for arrangements in advance.

Market Rasen is a popular National Hunt course, hosting meetings throughout the year, including a busy summer jumps season. The big races of the year are the Lincolnshire National held on Boxing Day, and the valuable handicap chase and hurdle races staged at the summer meeting in July. The daily rates for admission are £17, £12 and £7.50 for the Members, Tattersalls and Silver Ring respectively. If you plan to go racing here often, consider joining on an annual basis at £175 single and £265 for a double badge. A

Jubilee Club for pensioners gives reduced admission to Tatts and the Silver Ring as well as to Nottingham Racecourse and costs £5 to join. If you are planning on taking a party of people, special rates are on offer for groups of 15 or more. The course is part of the new Midlands Racing organisation and has special promotional offers that include admission, racecards and betting vouchers. Check with the course for details.

The Club Enclosure's private boxes number an impressive 17, including seven on annual lets and nine corporate rooms let on a daily basis. The County Room can take parties of up to 100 people, or smaller groups if desired, and the Brocklesby Suite can cater for parties of up to 300. You can also book a table here for lunch and afternoon tea. Call the racecourse on (01673) 843434 for reservations. There is an Owners & Trainers private room with food and drink facilities available. Tattersalls and the Silver Ring have a number of bars and catering outlets including the Red Rum Car that offers a hot and cold buffet. Alternatively, you may wish to pack a hamper and use the Picnic Enclosure which charges £6 for your car and £7.50 per adult occupant. It is a good place to watch the action.

If you are disabled there is a special viewing area and two specially adapted lavatories. At the weekend and Bank Holiday meetings a fully supervised crèche is provided on the first floor of the Silver Ring Stand. For older children, there is a playground. All accompanied children under 16 are admitted free of charge. Lincolnshire remains one of England's most unspoiled counties and if you are looking for a new racecourse to visit in 2005, Market Rasen would make a fine choice.

Artist: **Christine M Cancelli LINING UP FOR THE START** *Courtesy of:* **Frost & Reed**

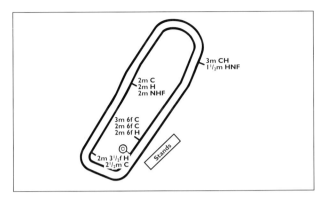

Local favourites

Steeped in history,with narrow cobbled streets, Lincoln is filled with antique and craft shops. Lovers of history should visit the cathedral which holds one of the original copies of the Magna Carta. An appealing place to eat is the **Wig and Mitre** (01522) 535190 on the appropriately named Steep Hill. More convenient and with a city centre setting is **The Castle Hotel**, Lincoln (01522) 538801 which features a very good restaurant. **Lincoln Courtyard** (0870) 400 7213 is also well worth noting. Extremely comfortable but less expensive accommodation can be found in the **Moor Lodge Hotel** (01522) 791366, Branston, a little way outside the city. Lincoln also offers the outstanding, particularly from a price point of view, **D'Isney Place Hotel** (01522) 538881. The **Jews House** (01522) 524851 is an inspired French restaurant. Those wishing to stay close to the racecourse should note the **Limes Hotel** (01673) 842357, Market Rasen, for good accommodation, food and service. **Kenwick Park** (01507) 608806 in Louth is further afield but worth considering. The convenient **Admiral Rodney** (01507) 523131 and the **Petwood Hotel** (01526) 352411 offer special racing packages—check with the hotel for details. The **Washingborough Hall Hotel** (01522) 790340 is also one to note for those who like a little extra luxury. Two hotels to note at Branston are **Moor Lodge** (01522) 791366 and **Branston Hall** (01522) 793305 - two decent staying types.

Those merely looking for a pub for a pre-race pint, or post-race celebration are directed to the **White Swan** (01673) 843356 which is thoroughly recommended, the revamped **Chase** (01673) 842308 or the excellent **Red Lion** (01673) 842424. A more than comfortable bed for the night can be found at Redbourne the **Waveney Guest House** (01673) 843236 and **Beechwood Guest House** (01673) 844043. The **Black Horse** (01507) 343640 at Donnington on Bain is a good all-round performer. Less convenient is Woodhall Spa, but this town should be visited not for racing but for some excellent golf. The **Golf Hotel** (01526) 353535 and the Edwardian **Dower House Hotel** (01526) 52588 are both good. One final thought, consider a trip to Stamford and a night at the **George** (01780) 750750. This really is one of our leading recommendations—a must for all lovers of fine hotels. A fair distance but, if you're planning a weekend to remember after racing at Market Rasen, head north and go to **Winteringham Fields** (01724) 733096. Here the cooking is brilliant and there's some magnificent bedrooms.

Artist: **Brian Stanley JOCKEYS** *Courtesy of:* **The Artist**

Artist: **Katy Sodeau GALLOPS** *Courtesy of:* **The Artist**

The **General Manager** at **Musselburgh** is **Bill Farnsworth** and the **Commercial Manager** is **Claire Sheppard**. They can be reached at **Musselburgh Racecourse, Linkfield Road, Musselburgh, East Lothian, EH21 7RG. Tel: 0131 665 2859 Fax: 0131 653 2083 E-mail:** *musselburghracecourse@eastlothian.gov.uk* **Website:** *www.eastlothian.gov.uk/racecourse*

The racecourse stands proudly around the historic golf course of Musselburgh links overlooking the Firth of Forth and is six miles east of Scotland's capital city of Edinburgh. The major routes to be considered are the M8 and the City bypass from the west and the A1 and A198 from the east. The A7, A68 and A702 should be used by people coming from the south.

Edinburgh's main railway station, Waverley, is on the Intercity 125 line and Kings Cross is little more than three and a half hours away. The nearest station to the course is Wallyford and on racedays a courtesy bus from here will take you to the course. Check with the racecourse to find out which trains it meets. Edinburgh Airport is about 25 minutes drive from the course. If you decide to drive you will be pleased to hear there is an excellent choice of areas in which to park your car and these are all free. Coaches are also welcome. If you are an aviator and happen to be passing in your helicopter, approach the course (by prior arrangement) from the north and land in an area adjacent to the car park.

With a dramatic view overlooking the Firth of Forth, Musselburgh hosts a busy season of both flat and jump racing. The course benefits from its position close to the water by being virtually frost free and can often race in mid winter when other venues are abandoned. Highlights of the year are an Easter Sunday Family Day, a Ladies' Day in September and the Scottish Sprint Cup in May. The course also hosts a very popular Point to Point which attracts some large crowds.

There are two enclosures, the Premier which costs £17 for a day badge (£20 for weekends fixtures) and the Grandstand where a fee of £11 (£13 on weekends) is charged for entry. If you are disabled, a student, OAP or are unemployed—in which case there is a £6 levy (£7 on weekends). Race programmes are provided free of charge to all racegoers – an excellent idea. Accompanied children under 16 years are allowed in free and entertainment is provided for them at some meetings. Group discounts of 20 per cent are available to parties of six or more people. £180 is charged for a single year's membership, £320 double. Membership includes special events and reciprocal meetings at other courses.

Sponsors' rooms are available for hire in the Queen's Stand, where you can entertain in style. Local companies can sponsor fences and hurdles as well as the races themselves. A hospitality complex opened a few years ago comprising 5 private boxes for groups of up to 40, and a large ground floor room for parties of between 60 and 100. The first floor Grandstand has the Members Restaurant overlooking the racecourse. Telephone Sarah O'Sullivan at the racecourse on 0131 665 2859 if you wish to book a table. On the ground floor of the Grandstand, Pinkies Bar serves hot snacks.

As you would expect, there are public telephones, and viewing ramps, loos and some bars for the disabled

Artist: **Katy Sodeau RACING** *Courtesy of:* **The Artist**

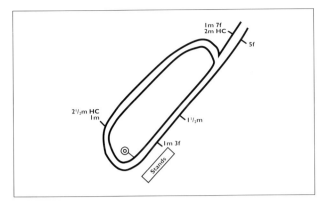

racegoers. 'Cash Back' facilities are available from the racecourse office if you happen to run short of funds. Musselburgh has done a lot to improve its facilities in recent years, including a new parade ring, and deserves a visit.

Local favourites

Outside Edinburgh, one simply outstanding hotel should be visited if at all possible: it has the class of a Derby winner and a history and character as rich as the Grand National—**Greywalls** (01620) 842144. Overlooking Muirfield, this superb hotel and restaurant is thoroughly recommended. Another golfing great is the Links, to be found at North Berwick. Here there is an array of B&B's and guesthouses as well as an imposing hotel, **The Marine** (0870) 400 8129 which offers a range of good facilities. Dirleton offers **The Open Arms** (01620) 850241, a small and good value establishment. South of Gullane in Gifford, the **Tweedale Arms** (01620) 810240 makes a good base—ideal for exploring the East Lothian coast. Remaining outside the city, one finds Howgate and **The Howgate Restaurant** (01968) 670000, a splendid pub for food. Nearby the **Cringletie**

House Hotel (01721) 730233 is an extremely welcoming hotel—comfortable too. The restaurant is also very good. In Haddington the **Waterside Bistro** (01620) 835674 comes highly recommended, and **Maitlandfield House** (01620) 826513 provides a comfortable base.

There is a whole host of restaurants outside Edinburgh. Pride of place goes to the **Champany Inn** (01506) 834532 in Linlithgow where the steaks are said to be among the finest in Britain. You can stay here now and this is a really excellent choice if good food is your passion as well as racing. **Livingston's Restaurant** (01506) 846565 is also said to be excellent. The **Lauriston Farm Restaurant** 0131 312 7071 is another where a slight detour will reap tasty dividends. Another within easy shooting distance is **The Cockatoo** on Old Craighill Road 0131 660 1211. A restaurant within a hotel can be found in Uphall—**Houstoun House** (01506) 853831 is a charming place in which to stay with a delightful restaurant. Finally, mention should be made of the **Cramond Inn** 0131 336 2035 at Cramond, a pleasant place to spend an evening.

In Edinburgh itself the **Caledonian Hotel** 0131 222 8888 is grand—superbly comfortable and the **Pompadour** restaurant is really something to cherish; and the **George Hotel Inter-continental** 0131 225 1251 is first class. The **Balmoral Hotel** 0131 5562414 on Princes Street is a luxurious experience and houses two outstanding restaurants in **Number One** and **Hadrian's**. Less traditional is the **Sheraton Grand Hotel and Spa**, one of the racecourse's major sponsors, 0131 229 9131, which stands opposite the Usher Hall. As you will imagine there is a whole range of hotels in Edinburgh and it is a delightful city to visit. **Channings** 0131 315 2226 is a townhouse hotel and restaurant to savour. **Martin Wishart** 0131 553 3557 in Leith is one of several good restaurants in Leith to consider when visiting Musselburgh in 2005.

Artist: **John Atkins NECK AND NECK** *Courtesy of:* **The Artist**

*I*n 2005 Newbury celebrates its centenary and with the transfer of the King George meeting in July from nearby Ascot, racing promises to be at the highest level. The **Hon Sir David Sieff** is Newbury's **Chairman**. The **Managing Director** at Newbury is **Mark Kershaw** and he can be contacted at: **The Racecourse, Newbury, Berkshire RG14 7NZ. Tel: (01635) 40015 Fax: (01635) 528354, E-mail:** *info@newbury-racecourse.co.uk* **Website:** *www.newbury-racecourse.co.uk*

Travellers from the east and London should use the M4 (junction 12) and complete their journey on the A4. Eastbound racegoers should also use the M4 (junction 13), while those from the south and north converge on the A34. The bypass around Newbury has helped to relieve some of the traffic congestion and there is a new junction open. Signs also direct traffic to the racecourse, which is very handy if you are going there for the first time. There is plenty of excellent parking once you arrive. It's entirely free except for the picnic car park where there is a charge of £5 per car plus £5 per adult.

A good idea for all meetings is to take advantage of the train. Special offers are available with First Great Western trains if you are travelling by rail. If anybody wishes to helicopter or jet in there is a landing strip at the racecourse, situated in the centre of the track. Please contact the secretary for details on (01635) 40015.

With 29 days of racing both on the flat and over the jumps the Newbury racegoer is blessed with some outstanding

fixtures. Races such as the Tote Gold Trophy, the Greenham Stakes, the Lockinge Stakes, the Geoffrey Freer Stakes, the Horris Hill Stakes and November's Hennessy Gold Cup over the sticks make racing at Newbury a delight. As an added attraction, the course hosts an annual Arabian Race Day which, while not part of the Jockey Club calendar, has proved very popular nonetheless. Newbury also has plans to build an all weather course for racing on the dirt and it will be interesting to see how this develops.

Despite the quality of racing, Annual Membership here is priced at a reasonable £230. If you wish to go to flat meetings only the charge drops to £170. Annual jumps membership is a mere £105. Junior Membership is £50 (18-25 year olds). A car park badge is also provided together with 32 reciprocal meetings at some excellent racecourses. Also available is a Grandstand Season Ticket which admits you to all meetings for £120. Daily admission to the Members' Enclosure costs between £17-23, depending on the meeting, rising to £40 on Hennessy Day. The Grandstand is priced at between £11 and £16 (£20 for the Hennessy) and the picnic car park at £5. Parties are encouraged and 20 per cent discounts are offered to groups except in the Members. Credit card bookings are also accepted.

The Newbury racegoer is able to enjoy an excellent view of the racecourse and numerous improvements in recent years such as the refurbishment of the Hampshire Stand and improvements to the Berkshire Stand have added to the racing experience here. The Hennessy Restaurant on

Artist: **Claire Eva Burton HENNESSY GOLD CUP** *Courtesy of:* **Rosenstiel's**

to 1,000) can also be arranged. Corporate entertaining facilities at Newbury are first-class and boxes and function rooms of various sizes can be reserved. There are many other snack bars in all the enclosures and the restaurants and bars are open two hours before the first race.

Children under 18 are admitted free into all enclosures. Younger punters may wish to make use of the Rocking Horse Nursery, which takes up to eight-year-olds. With more and more Sunday meetings in racing, these facilities are now a must for any course. Other important features include lavatories for the disabled and lots of telephones in case your mobile runs down at the wrong time.

Situated near one of the most important training centres at Lambourn, Newbury occupies a strategic place in British racing. In many other countries around the world horses are trained right on the racecourse and move on as meetings go from one track to the other. The racing tradition of Britain is undoubtedly unique in having only three significant training centres in Newmarket, Middleham and Lambourn. With top stables close by, the racing at Newbury attracts some of the best horses you can see, both flat and national hunt. The course has also achieved great success over the past twenty years in attracting the commercial support that finances the prizes in major races. As it approaches its second century we are sure that Newbury will flourish for many years to come.

Artist: **Booth Malone STEEPLECHASE JOCKEY** *Courtesy of:* **Frost & Reed**

Artist: **Katie Sodeau STORM CLOUDS, NEWBURY** *Courtesy of:* **The Artist**

the top floor of the Hampshire Stand has an excellent view of the course. If you wish to book a table you can do so on (01635) 521081. Prices start at £45 per head for an á la carte menu or you can get a package for £85 that includes badges, racecard, champagne, lunch and afternoon tea, but you have to book seven days in advance. Also popular is the Racegoers Restaurant on the top floor of the Grandstand which has panoramic views and offers admission and lunch packages from £38. Call on (01635) 40015 and book a week in advance. Yet another option is available in the Mandarin Restaurant situated next to the pre-parade ring, which offers a lunch and tea package for private tables of ten people. The Champagne Bar and Blewbury Bar are other places to enjoy while the Lambourn and Manton suites provide views of the winning post. Facilities for larger parties (up

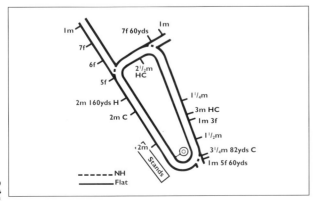

Artist: **Katie O'Sullivan 5 WINNERS** *Courtesy of:* **The Artist**

Newbury racecourse is ideally situated well away from the capital but conveniently placed for folk from Hampshire, Oxfordshire, Berkshire and other ritzy shires of the south. In Newbury itself the **Chequers Hotel** (0870) 609 6141 is most convenient while at Stroud Green the **Plough on the Green** 0870 330 5201 offers a superb garden, covered barbecue area and an excellent bar. Just 500 yards opposite the main car park entrance and five minutes walk across Stroud Green, it is very popular on racedays with those in the know. The **Square Bar & Grill** is also highly thought of locally.

Newbury remains one of the south's growth areas and hotels of excellence include: **The Vineyard** at Stockcross (01635) 528770 (this is a hotel and restaurant double to celebrate a really big win - it's tremendous), the **Newbury Manor Hotel** (01635) 528838 and the **The Hilton Hotel** (01635) 529000 in the town itself, and the recently refurbished **Queens Hotel** (0870) 330 5147 only two minutes from the racecourse. The **Donnington Valley Hotel** (01635) 551199 is one for your shortlist. The **Hilton Newbury North** (01635) 247010 is also worth considering.

Outside the town, but within a decent stone's throw, one finds the **Regency Park Hotel** (01635) 871555, another first class candidate for a visit, as is a hotel that has been warmly recommended by one of our readers—the **Hinds Head Hotel** (0118) 971 2194 in Aldermaston. It sounds tremendous and reminds me to ask readers to let us know of any good information they might have.

Farther afield, a hotel certainly worth an inspection is **Ramada Hotel and Resort** (0870) 850 1768 at Elcot Park - a Georgian mansion set in 16 acres of parkland overlooking the Kennet Valley. The restaurant is good here and some attractive two-day breaks are available.

Slightly farther afield is Hungerford and within its compass are some first class places to visit. The **Bear Ramada Jarvis Hotel** at Hungerford (01488) 682512 is probably the best place to stay. It is a 13th Century inn with an excellent welcome. If you are looking for something to eat then the set lunches are recommended while the evening menu is also good. An alternative eating place to the Bear is an extremely pleasant pub, the **John O'Gaunt** (01488) 683535—a tremendous meeting place before and after racing. There are bedrooms too if you want to stay overnight. **Marshgate Cottage** (01488) 682307 also provides a more than comfortable bed for the night. Hungerford itself is riddled with antique shops and to many it may well be worth a visit on this score alone.

On to Pangbourne, and an old favourite, the **Copper Inn** (0118) 984 2244, which is thoroughly recommended. The **White Hart Inn** at Hampstead Marshall (01488) 658201 has also shown good form—good food and pleasant bedrooms. Another outstanding inn is located in Yattendon: the **Royal Oak** (01635) 201325. Once again, a splendid all-round performer—simple homely bars, a decent fire, cosy bedrooms and a really excellent restaurant. In Goring, the **John Barleycorn Inn** (01491) 872509 and the **Miller of Mansfield** (01491) 872829 are fun pubs, ideal for a post-race celebration. Both offer simple accommodation and good bar food. The **Leatherne Bottel** (01491) 872667 offers a pleasant riverside setting in which to imbibe—a good restaurant as well. Across the Thames and into Streatley more lavish accommodation can be found at the **Swan Diplomat** (01491) 873737. An

outstanding restaurant accompanies the hotel which also boasts fine leisure facilities.

Towards Wallingford, at Moulsford, lies the glorious Thames-side retreat, the **Beetle and Wedge** (01491) 651381. The restaurant here is outstanding. A real must. In Aldworth, the **Bell** (01635) 578272 is a really cosy pub in which to take shelter. Heading towards the rolling Berkshire Downs and the Ilsleys, a number of pubs can be found. In East Ilsley, the **Crown and Horns** (01635) 281545 deserves a particular mention—not least for its excellent collection of sporting prints and racing photographs, with accommodation available too. Racing enthusiasts will also enjoy the **Hare & Hounds** (01488) 71386 at Lambourn—a well-trained landlord there, while in nearby West Ilsley the **Harrow** (01635) 281260 is pleasant and offers good home cooking. The **Sun in the Wood** (01635) 42377 also offers good food. Finally, for the real galloping gourmets, a trip to Great Milton will yield the majestic **Le Manoir aux Quat' Saisons** (01844) 278881. This is a restaurant with rooms of international acclaim. You will need a decent winner to meet the bill here.

A pub with excellent food is the **Dundas Arms Hotel** (01488) 658263 at Kintbury. The restaurant has pride of place here and if you are looking for a place to stay this may be your solution. The bedrooms are located in a converted stable block. Another venue with an extremely popular restaurant and some comfortable bedrooms is the **Five Bells** at Wickham (01488) 657894. The answer has to be to take Friday off—go racing—eat a good lunch and in the evening nestle down in a quiet pub ready for racing on Saturday. If you do, note the **Winterbourne Arms** (01635) 248200—a pub with good food.

Other ideas? Well, in Stanford Dingley the **Old Boot Restaurant** (0118) 974 5213 is worth a visit while the **Bull** (0118) 974 4409 here is a grand pub, a definite if you have won on the last. If you're travelling on the A4, as many people will, one place to pull over at is the **Rising Sun** (0118) 971 2717, Woolhampton—really-first class beer, good bar snacks and, if you are feeling a little more peckish, there is a separate restaurant. In Kingsclere, a particularly strong racing influence exists in the village and a rather good pub as well is the **Crown** (01635) 299558.

If you get round even half of the above for goodness sake don't drive home! To that end, a few more excellent hotels. In Hurstbourne Tarrant, **Esseborne Manor** (01264) 736444 is outstanding—once again a tremendous restaurant, a warmly recommended all-rounder. People heading south might wish to stay at Silchester. The **Romans Hotel** (0118) 970 0421 could be the answer—well priced and very comfortable.

In Pingewood, the **Hanover International** (01189) 500885/ (0845) 744 4123 offers good value. Nearer to Newbury, at Old Burghclere, the **Dew Pond Restaurant** (01635) 278408 is well worth considering. One final thought for those of you who like a good pub: try **The Red House Restaurant** (01635) 582017, a thatched inn at Marsh Benham—an ideal place to lick one's wounds after racing.

We hope you plunder a bounty while racing at Newbury in 2005. Very few racecourses offer as much and these local favourites also make up a select field. Whether you are popping in for a pint or two before or after racing, or organising a weekend away from it all, Berkshire offers no end of distractions.

Artist: **Graham Isom** *DOWN TO THE START* Courtesy of: **Rosenstiel's**

David Williams is **General Manager** at Newcastle Racecourse, with **James Armstrong** as **Clerk of the Course** and **Kay Forster** as **Commercial Manager**. They can be contacted at **Newcastle Racecourse, High Gosforth Park, Newcastle upon Tyne NE3 5HP. Tel: 0191 236 2020 Fax: 0191 236 7761 Website:** _www.newcastle-racecourse.co.uk_ **E-mail:** _info@ newcastle-racecourse.co.uk_

The racecourse is in High Gosforth Park on the northern edge of the city and the course is well posted at the Wideopen junction from the western bypass of the A1 from both north and south. From the east, use the A19 and A1056. The journey to Tyneside from London's Thameside is a good 280 miles and is well served by the main east coast train route. The course is a further four miles or so from Newcastle's Central Station—a fifteen minute taxi journey. The Metro, Newcastle's underground, can be taken to South Gosforth, Regent Centre or Four Lane Ends, and on racedays a free bus service operates between these stations and the course, two hours prior to the first race and for one hour after the last. Quicker transportation can be found by using the nearby airport which is only ten minutes away or, if prior notice is given, you may land a helicopter. There is ample parking for up to 12,000 cars, all free of charge, with areas for Annual Members and disabled guests.

There are now 29 flat and national hunt fixtures throughout the year at Gosforth Park and the highlight of the season is the three-day Northumberland Plate Festival in late June, when the Saturday sees the Northumberland Plate, a handicap over two miles, which always attracts large fields. Highlights of the National Hunt season are the Fighting Fifth Hurdle in November and the Eider Chase, one of the warm-up races for the Grand National.

Premier Enclosure badges cost £16, excluding the Northumberland Plate meeting when they range from £18-

£30. Good value is the Grandstand and Paddock at £11, which rises to £12-£18 for the Plate meeting. There is a concession for advance-booked parties of 14 or more. An Annual Members' Badge is priced at £200. This includes a car park badge and numerous reciprocal meetings across the country.

The Premier Enclosure has the Brandling House, the eighteenth century Grade II listed building at the heart of the racecourse, which contains the Gosforth Park Suite restaurant. Call on 0191 236 2020 to book a table. Please advise your guests that a strict dress code is enforced in this enclosure and they will be turned away if they show up in denim or trainers! The main Colonel Porter Grandstand has private box facilities available for hire, as well as a carvery, and several bars. There is also a separate restaurant for owners and trainers. The Grandstand and Paddock has large grandstands, numerous bars, betting shops, Tote, food take-away counters and access to a Family Foodhall. Numerous snack bars are available for you while you sup the Newky Brown.

Children under 16, with an adult, are admitted free to all enclosures. At weekend and Bank Holiday meetings entertainments are arranged for them—including Punch & Judy shows, funfair rides, face painting and so on.

Since Gosforth Park became part of the Northern Racing group a multi-million pound facelift has taken place. Moving the Winners Enclosure to the front of the stands has been a major benefit for all racegoers. The reinstatement of the first furlong on the picturesque Mile–over which the Blaydon Race is now run–is also a plus for the course. Newcastle is a grade one course and after several years in the doldrums has been restored to its former glory.

Artist: **Graham Isom** NEWCASTLE _Courtesy of:_ **Rosenstiel's**

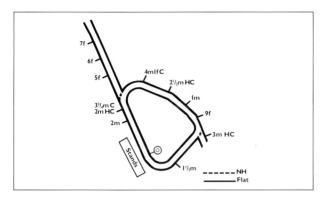

Local favourites

The busy city of Newcastle lies close to the racecourse, but at the same time, Scotland, the Lake District and North Yorkshire are all within striking distance. In the Tyne Valley a Country House to consider is **Newbrough Park** (01434) 674545. A pleasant place to stay in Longhorsley is the **Linden Hall Hotel and Spa** (01670) 500000—it has a delightful setting in 300 acres of parkland, with the added attraction of an 18 hole golf course. The **Granby Inn** (01665) 570228 in Longframlington, further north, is an ideal pub for a visit to the country. **Horton Grange** (01661) 860686 is located five miles from the course, with an excellent restaurant and some fine rooms.

Newcastle Marriott Hotel, Gosforth Park 0191 236 4111 is an excellent and highly convenient hotel where the **Brandling** restaurant offers nouvelle cuisine. There are some fun bars here as well - it's a short walk from the racecourse so is ideally situated. In town, The **Copthorne Newcastle** 0191 222 0333 and the **Vermont** Hotels 0191 233 1010 are excellent, as is **Malmaison** 0191 245 5000 a little further along the Quayside, overlooking the River Tyne. A recent addition to the scene is the excellent Grey Street Hotel 0870 412 5100 from the Niche Hotel group - a really splendid offering. Newcastle is renowned for its nightlife and the Quayside is the place to head for... alternatively, Jesmond offers some good bars and **Osbornes** in the **New Northumbria Hotel** 0191 281 4961 is a good suggestion too.

Newcastle also has a variety of fabulous restaurants. The **Fisherman's Lodge** in Jesmond Dene 0191 281 3281 is a super restaurant while on the Quayside **Uno's** 0191 261 5264 is very popular. Lovers of Chinese food are spoilt for choice on Stowell Street. Sample any of the following; the **Mandarin** 0191 261 7960, the **King Neptune** 0191 261 6657 and the **Palace Garden** 0191 232 3117; and for lovers of Indian cuisine, **Sachins** 0191 261 9035, serves up a tasty treat and **Vujon** 0191 2210601 is a must. Newcastle's finest restaurant is **Café 21** 0191 222 0755 on Princes Wharf virtually beneath the Tyne Bridge. Round the corner, **Treacle Moon** 0191 232 5537 is also very good and **Est Est Est** 0191 260 2291 caters for lovers of Italian cuisine. The **Black Door** 0191 261 6295 is a newcomer but is considered to be excellent.

Some great pubs of note include the **Crown Posada** 0191 232 1269 and the **Shiremoor House Farm** 0191 257 6302 pub and restaurant, which is noted for its beer range. More bar than pub, the **Pitcher and Piano** is worthy of note - it offers a good value menu, a great atmosphere and stunning views over the wonderfully developed Gateshead Quay. A weekend visit in 2005 for lovers of nightlife must include a visit to the quayside as well as the gee-gees and for culture lovers visit the BALTIC... taking in Newcastle's wonderful Millennium Bridge and Sage Music Centre.

*Artist: **Peter Smith** AT THE DISTANCE Courtesy of: **Frost & Reed***

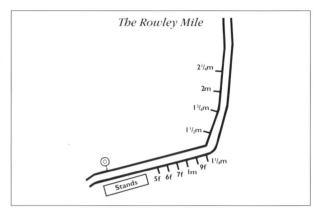

The Rowley Mile

$2^{1}/_{4}$m

2m

$1^{3}/_{4}$m

$1^{1}/_{2}$m

$1^{1}/_{4}$m

9f

5f 6f 7f 1m

Stands

The town of Newmarket seems to breathe racing and is blessed with two of the finest courses in Britain: the Rowley Mile and the July Course. The management team here is headed by **Managing Director**, Lisa Hancock and **Michael Prosser** the **Clerk of the Course**. They are ably assisted by **Damian Thompson** as **Commercial Manager**, **Gaynor Haxby** as **Marketing Manager** and **Christian Mitchell** as **Operations Manager**, who can all be contacted at **Westfield House, The Links, Newmarket, Suffolk CB8 0TG. Tel:(01638) 663482 Fax: (01638) 663044.** If you would like to **order tickets** call on **(01638) 675500. E-mail:** *newmarket@rht.net* **Website:** *www.newmarketracecourses.co.uk*

Crowds flock to Newmarket for their many popular meetings, so an early start is recommended. From London it is a mere 60 mile sprint up the M11—exit junction 9 for the new dual carriageway A11, leaving it at Six Mile Bottom and thence to Newmarket. The A14 links Felixstowe with the M1 and M6, and the A1 will assist both northbound and southbound visitors. Racegoers on busy days should note the back exit via Exning onto the A14, thus avoiding the particularly heavy going. From Norwich and the east, the A11 is the obvious route, while from Bury St Edmunds the A45 can be useful. There are numerous car parks on the Heath for both cars and coaches.

If travelling by train, start at Liverpool Street or King's Cross. Buses meet the trains in Cambridge and ensure prompt delivery to the races. A further innovation is the introduction of a separate free bus service to the course from the station and Newmarket High Street. The CAA have given their permission for use of the July landing strip when there is racing on the July course, although craft must not land or take off over the racecourse buildings. The Rowley Mile strip can also be used. Call ahead on (01638) 675500.

Highlights of the racing calendar include the two three year old Classics, the 1000 and 2000 Guineas. Special entertainment is usually laid on including bands and special children's facilities and an enormous shopping mall—and of course, first class racing. Other highlights include the Cesarewitch, the Cambridgeshire, the Craven Stakes, the Cheveley Park Stakes, the Middle Park, and the Dewhurst.

The ambience of the two Newmarket courses—the Rowley Mile and the July Racecourse—is totally different with the former featuring racing in spring and autumn and the latter creating an excellent atmosphere in beautiful surroundings for the more relaxed summer meetings. Attending one of the popular evening meetings on the July Course is a tremendous

Artist: **Neil Cawthorne** *JOCKEYS GET MOUNTED, NEWMARKET* *Courtesy of:* **The Artist**

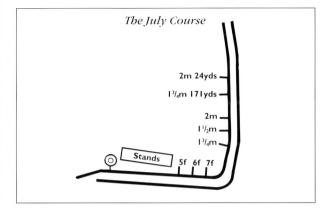

The July Course

2m 24yds
1³/₄m 171yds
2m
1¹/₂m
1³/₄m
Stands
5f 6f 7f

Artist: *Jaqueline Stanhope PRE-PARADE RING, NEWMARKET*
Courtesy of: *The Artist*

way to relax and forget your troubles. Don't plan on leaving early as the entertainment gets going after the racing is over and you could find yourself there the next morning!

Annual Membership rates for all 37 meetings costs £300, with a £50 joining fee and includes free admission and car parking as well as reciprocal days at other courses Day Members' Badges range from £18 to £30, with a £5 charge for preferential parking. Newmarket Nights meetings throughout July and August are a fantastic night out on the July Course with a top band performing after the evening's racing. Tickets for the Grandstand and Paddock enclosure cost between £12 and £20 depending upon the meeting and the Family Enclosure is well priced at between £5 and £8. Early booking and group discounts are available for all but the Family Enclosure and you should check the Newmarket website for cut off dates for special events. Various discounts are also on offer to OAP's, young people and students and vary depending on the meeting. Accompanied children are free and there is a creche available for the tiny ones as well as playgrounds on both courses for those a little bit older.

The Rowley Mile offers fine cuisine in the Champions' Gallery restaurant with unrivalled race viewing from the top floor Millennium Grandstand. There are also some superb private boxes on this level that are available to hire on a daily

basis. Call on 01638 675300 if you wish to book a table or arrange catering. Also in this stand can be found the Birdcage Bar, Millennium Bar and Lounge which serves drinks and light snacks. In the Bistro you can sample some fine wine or champagne and experience a range of dining options. On the July course the marquees add to the summer party atmosphere and many of the bars and other facilities are in the open air. The July Restaurant and the Bistro are also popular venues. The Grandstand and Paddock on both courses also offer a wide range of bars and restaurants.

Artist: *Jaqueline Stanhope MARE AND FOAL* Courtesy of: *The Artist*

Telephones are available as well as extra betting facilities. Disabled people have lavatories, escalators help the elderly and, overall, everyone from junior to senior is well catered for.

Newmarket offers two racecourses that are probably unique in the world. But there is a lot more to Newmarket than that. The flat racing community needs a home base and Newmarket fills the bill admirably. If you go here you should visit some of the off course events and places that really makes it racing's HQ: take a stable tour, go to the Tattersalls sales ring, visit the National Horse Racing Museum and the National Stud, or just take in the gossip of a local pub. There is probably nowhere else in Britain where racing is such an all encompassing experience. You are surrounded by the rich traditions of 350 years of racing history at every turn.

Artist: *Jaqueline Stanhope NATIONAL STUD* Courtesy of: *The Artist*

Artist: **Heather St Clair Davis NEWMARKET MORNING**
Courtesy of: **Frost & Reed**

*I*cannot recommend a visit to Newmarket more highly. If you want to stay in style and don't mind a short drive, **Swynford Paddocks** (01638) 570234 is ideal. This hotel, located in Six Mile Bottom, has elegant bedrooms and an excellent restaurant. Closer to home, the High Street of Newmarket offers a number of places to stay. The **Rutland Arms** (01638) 664251 and the **White Hart** (01638) 663051 opposite the Jockey Club are both comfortable and convenient, while on the Bury Road, the **Bedford Lodge** (01638) 663175 is a popular racing location and offers more stylish accommodation. Bar snacks in all the above hotels are good and dining is also available. Lovers of Chinese food should earmark **The Fountain** (01638) 666255—pricey but good. A less extravagant, although still highly recommended establishment, is **Hill Farmhouse** (01638) 730253 which can be found to the south of the racecourse in Kirtling. A modern, but well located hotel is the **Heath Court** (01638) 667171. The **Bushel** and the **Rookery** are two pubs to note.

There are many outstanding hotels in East Anglia. One thinks of **Maison Talbooth** (01206) 322367 in Dedham near Colchester (note the outstanding Talbooth restaurant—really first class). In Woodbridge, **Seckford Hall** (01394) 385678 is a supremely comfortable country house hotel, while closer to Newmarket in Bury St Edmunds, the **Angel** (01284) 714000 is a fine house with a first class restaurant. Another to note here is the **Priory** (01284) 777181. **Ravenwood Hall Country Hotel and Restaurant** (01359) 270345 at Rougham Green is also well placed for visiting racegoers and a warm welcome is assured. Further south in Broxted, the **Whitehall** (01279) 850603 is another appealing manor with a splendid restaurant. The **Great House** (01787) 247431 at Lavenham should not be forgotten either with delicious French and English cooking. In Mildenhall a couple of suggestions come to mind. **The Riverside** (01638) 717274 is well worth consideration and the **Smoke House** (01638) 713223 is a well regarded alternative. Elsewhere **The Ickworth** (01284) 735350 is a wonderful prospect. Meanwhile at Hintlesham, one finds **Hintlesham Hall** (01473) 652334—a classic stayer with a golf course and some excellent cuisine, a definite *Travelling The Turf* favourite.

Lovers of pub food will also be spoilt. In Dullingham, the **Kings Head** (01634) 507486 is a friendly, extremely busy, racing pub with a restaurant. In nearby Woodditton, another popular pub is the **Three Blackbirds** (01638) 730811, a

mere five minutes drive from the Rowley Mile racecourse. Other excellent establishments include two **Red Lions** - one at Icklingham (01638) 717802 and one at Hinxton (01799) 530601 - good food at both. The **Star** at Lidgate (01638) 500275 is also a good choice and the racing fraternity is particularly keen on the **Old Plough** (01638) 730110 at Ashley. Another real favourite is the excellent **Affleck Arms** at Dalham (01638) 500306—really great atmosphere and good fare. The **Cherry Trees** at Stradishall is also reported to offer good value food.

Artist: **Neil Cawthorne NEWMARKET HEATH** Courtesy of: **The Artist**

Two Cambridge hotels often used for Newmarket meetings are the **University Arms** (01223) 351241 and the **Cambridge Garden House Moat House Hotel** (01223) 259988. The one overlooks Parkers Piece and the other the River Cam—both are excellent. Other thoughts in the University town include **The Hotel Felix** (01223) 277977 - it has a contemporary feel and an excellent restaurant, and the **Cambridge Quay Mill Hotel** (01223) 293383. Cambridge is also the perfect town in which to leave the person who may find a day or a week at the races a trifle tedious. Two excellent restaurants to note in the city are **Midsummer House** (01223) 369299 on Midsummer Common or **Twenty-Two Restaurant** (01223) 351880—ideal for pre-sales, or post-racing discussions.

The **Hole in the Wall** (01223) 812282 in Wilbraham is a fine restaurant, but please remember to book in advance. Also in Bury St Edmunds is the **Butterfly Hotel** (01284) 760884, with a modern, continental feel, and in nearby

Artist: **Graham Isom NEWMARKET** Courtesy of: **Rosenstiel's**

Ixworth **Theobalds Restaurant** (01359) 231707 is there for discovering, open fire and all. North of Newmarket one finds the superb cathedral at Ely. In the same town the **Lamb** (01353) 663574 is comfortable. Restaurants to consider for Bury St Edmonds include **Maison Blene** (01284) 760623 and the **Leaping Hare** in Stanton (01359) 250287.

Artist: **_Jacqueline Stanhope_** _MARE AND FOAL Courtesy of:_ **_The Artist_**

In case you have time between racing and opening time, or whatever you happen to be awaiting in Newmarket, we would strongly recommend you visit the National Horseracing Museum, a well thought-out establishment which owes much to the support of Britain's best known owners. The High Street reveals all manner of interesting shops—saddlers, tailors, bookshops and galleries.

With the fabulous array of weekend meetings as well as midweek occasions we will endeavour to recommend some pleasant inns, or pubs with rooms nearby. In Kennett, north of Newmarket, the **Bell** (01638) 750286 is an idea, while further afield in Lavenham, the **Swan** (01787) 247477 is a delightful 14th century inn which also boasts a first-class restaurant. A free house which is a delight to visit is the **Angel** also at Lavenham (01787) 247388—good food and some accommodation—ideal. While in Long Melford, five establishments are worth considering: firstly, the excellent **Black Lion Hotel and Restaurant** (01787) 312356 is highly recommended and secondly, the **Bull** (01787) 378494. Then the **George and Dragon** (01787) 371285 is a small but pleasant hostelry, while **Chimneys** (01787) 379806 is a restaurant with an excellent reputation and **Scutchers** (01787) 310200 makes up a magnificent five-timer. **Alfonso's** (01787) 280372 in Cavendish is a splendid Italian restaurant opposite the village green. Returning towards Newmarket, the **Bell** (01638) 583511 at Mildenhall is a fine all-rounder and is pretty good value. Also consider the **Green Man** at Six Mile Bottom (01638) 570373, it's a good racing pub and by all accounts an evening here offers that happy combination of quality fare and good company.

One final thought for the racing enthusiast who also enjoys golf and has a taste for style and elegance—**Marriot Hanbury Manor** (0870) 400 7222. It is a fair distance from Newmarket but is outstanding in every way. A place to spoil your non-racing partner! Racing at Newmarket is to be recommended. From the bustling betting shop to the early morning gallops, from a smoke-filled boozer to wide open heath, from the Tattersalls sales to busy restaurants, this is quintessentially a racing town and if you are looking for a day or two away in 2005, Newmarket is a worthy favourite choice.

Artist: **_Klaus Philipp_** **_A CLASSIC VICTORY_** _Courtesy of:_ **_The Artist_**

*T*he course is run by **Manager Patrick Masterson** and the **Estate Manager Jason Loosemore.** They can be contacted at **Newton Abbot Races Ltd, The Racecourse, Newton Road, Newton Abbot, Devon, TQ12 3AF. Tel (01626) 353235 Fax (01626) 336972. E-mail:** *managment@newton abbotracing.com* **Website:** *www.newtonabbotracing.com*

The racecourse is easily accessible via the M5, joined by the M4 and M6. The course is located just off the A380 which joins the M5. If you are journeying from Cornwall then a number of A roads are convenient. The A38 from Plymouth and the A30 via Okehampton are two obvious selections. It is as well to try to time your journey well because the M5 can get ridiculously one-paced on occasions. Despite the rural setting, the public transport services are good. Trains depart from Paddington and a bus can then be taken from the local station to the racecourse. For those feeling a bit fitter, you can easily walk the half mile to the racecourse. Helicopters are welcomed at the course and car parking is free unless you wish to park beside the course rails.

The climax of the season here comes in August with the weekend Summer Festival offering in excess of £180,000 in added prize money. The course has firmly established itself as one of the leading summer jumping courses with a busy season of 19 fixtures throughout the summer.

Newton Abbot has no Members Enclosure and was one of the first courses to simplify its public areas. The two enclosures are the Paddock for which a charge of £14 applies, and £7 for the Course Enclosure. Despite the absence of a Members area, a season ticket can be obtained

for £160 which includes 36 reciprocal meetings. People who are holidaying in groups and local people should note the following discount rates. If you get 5 or more people together you receive a 10 per cent discount; for groups of 12 or more you receive a 20 per cent discount. Both deals have to be booked in advance. The course has a good selection of sponsors and they generally make use of the private function rooms. Eleven private boxes are also available for hire, most by the day, and the Teign Suite, which can accommodate up to 120 people, is ideal for large parties and groups. However, the boxes are very popular and need to be booked in advance.

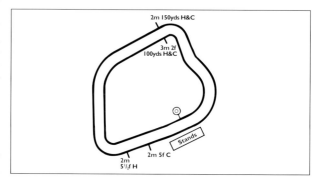

For those wishing to take advantage of some good summer weather, picnics can be enjoyed at the racecourse—a charge of £3 is made for cars parked alongside the rails. If self-catering sounds too much like hard work, then there is the Winning Post Restaurant with fine views across the whole course, serving an à la carte menu. Also the Paddock

Artist: **Graham Isom NEWTON ABBOT** *Courtesy of:* **Rosenstiel's**

Restaurant overlooking the parade ring offers a three course table d' hôte menu. There is a self-service restaurant in the main stand and snacks are served from the newly refurbished Betting Halls. Any prior enquiries with regard to catering should be made to the racecourse. Children are admitted free and there is a crèche in the centre of the course, open throughout the day's racing. There are three public telephones and disabled people have the benefit of a viewing ramp and a lift in the Grandstand and the Teign Suite.

For those looking for a long weekend in the country, this is a fabulous answer. The racecourse is extremely welcoming and the standard of racing is pretty good too. There are also many splendid hostelries nearby in which to spend your ill-gotten gains.

Local favourites

In Newton Abbot the **Passage House Hotel** (01626) 355515—modern but extremely welcoming and the **Queens Hotel** (01626) 363133 welcomes visitors before and after racing as does the excellent **Langstone Cliff Hotel** (01626) 868000. The **Two Mile Oak** (01803) 812411 offers really filling bar snacks. One pub in Kingsteignton to note, is the excellent **Old Rydon Inn** (01626) 54626. Another king this time in Kingskerswell, **Pitt House** (01803) 873374 is a good restaurant in a 15th century thatched dower-house. Another well thought of hotel in close proximity to the racecourse is the **Islington Country House** (01364) 661452–it's a friendly establishment and the food is reported to be good.

Artist: ***David Trundley SLANTING DOWN, NEWTON ABBOT***
Courtesy of: ***Rosenstiel's***

Artist: ***John King THE PADDOCK*** *Courtesy of:* ***The Artist***

If you have the chance, visit Dartmouth, where the **New Angel** (01803) 834842 is a good restaurant to visit. Another excellent port of call in this delightful naval town is the **Royal Castle** (01803) 833033. All along the coast one finds nooks and crannies to explore and eventually one arrives at the larger resorts of Paignton, Torbay and Torquay. In Staverton both **Kingston House** (01803) 762235 and the **Sea Trout Inn** (01803) 762274 are worth visiting–the latter is a particular favourite–ideal for anglers.

There are all manner of activities to be found in Torquay and having played golf, fished or even after a trip to the races, one place to visit is **Ocean Brasserie** (01803) 292359, ideal for dinner. Further round the coast one comes to Teignmouth and the extremely welcoming **Bay Hotel** (01626) 774123. No less excellent is **Thomas Luny House**

(01626) 772976, an award-winning, yet relatively inexpensive guesthouse. For people not wishing to visit the coast there are a number of excellent and secluded places to sample. A quiet country inn in which to spend a night is the **Rock Inn** (01364) 661305 in Haytor Vale. In nearby Haytor, the **Bel Alp House** (01364) 661217 is an extremely welcoming country house hotel to consider, as is the excellent **Leusdon Lodge** (01364) 631304 in Poundsgate. In Ashburton, the **Holne Chase Hotel** (01364) 631471 is a superb place to stay and it also has a fine restaurant. Further afield, but one for pub lovers, is the excellent **Hope and Anchor** (01548) 541294 in Hope Cove which provides a good restaurant and good value accommodation. For a grander offering, **Buckland-Tout-Saints** (01548) 853055 is a class act!

There are seven public houses by the name of **Church House** within a small radius. One you should certainly visit is located in Rattery (01364) 642220—a welcoming place for a drink and substantial bar snacks. Nearer to Newton Abbot is the village of Woodland and the superb **Rising Sun Inn** (01364) 652544. The **Hare and Hounds** (01803) 873119 at Kingskerswell has a good carvery; the **Barn Owl** (0870) 330 5211 is extremely friendly and has bedrooms and the **Chaser's Arms** (01626) 873670 at Stokeinteignhead is also recommended as is **Sampson's Farm** Restaurant on the edge of Newton Abbot (01626) 354913 some accommodation here as well. All in all, a great selection for a really friendly racecourse.

Nottingham is run by **Racecourse Manager, Nina Coverley**, assisted by **Nick Patton, Clerk of the Course, Mark Bemrose** as **Head Groundsman** and **Britt Hauselt** who handles the sales side. The team can be contacted at **Nottingham Racecourse, Colwick Park, Colwick Road, Nottingham NG2 4BE. Tel: (0115) 9580620 Fax: (0115) 9584515, E-mail:** *nottingham@rbt.net* **Website:** *www.nottinghamracecourse.co.uk*

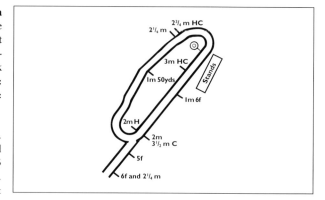

The course lies east of the city off the B686 Colwick road. The M1 offers good going but does suffer from the odd tailback. Southbound travellers should exit at junction 25 and follow the A52 to pick up the A6011 at West Bridgford. From there follow the brown tourist signs and the 'Park & Ride' racecourse signs. The A46 from Leicester is an alternative although renowned for one-paced lorries. From the A46, follow the A606 and the A612. The nearest railway station is in the city, two miles from the course (trains leave London from St Pancras). Bus Number 44 leaves the city centre every 15 minutes. If you do take the wheels, you will be pleased to hear that all parking is free. If you are coming by air, Nottingham East Midlands Airport is quite handy. Helicopters may land in the centre of the course by prior arrangement with the management.

Known locally as Colwick Park, Nottingham often attracts some of the top trainers and jockeys and presents a good standard of flat racing each year with 21 fixtures between April and November.

Daily entrance to the Premier Enclosure is £17 on weekends and evenings and £15 during the week, while the Grandstand costs £12 and £10. There are quite a few special offers available here, including a Jubilee Club for those over 60 who receive entry for £5 on weekdays and £9 on weekends and evenings. Nottingham is part of the Midlands Racing scheme, offering special packages but must be booked in advance. Group discounts are also available to those managing to bring 15 or more people to the racecourse. There is also a Young Racegoer package for those 16-21 that reduces the costs significantly and children under 16 are admitted free if accompanied by an adult. Details of other deals can be found on the course's website. Truly, Nottingham has something for everyone!

The facilities here are also very good with quite a bit of investment on refurbishing the Grandstand in recent years. In the Premier Enclosure you will find the Centenary Bar which also offers sandwiches and other light fare. The Lawn Bar is the perfect place to sample a Pimms and in the Members Rooftop Restaurant you can enjoy a three course carvery lunch or evening meal. Booking tables in advance is strongly advised and you can do so by contacting the caterers at the racecourse number. In the Grandstand, the Champions Bar offers light snacks, while the Bistro and

Artist: **Roy Miller RELUCTANT PARTICIPANTS** *Courtesy of:* **The Artist**

Champagne Bar has seafood and various other offerings. There is a lift to all floors in the Grandstand. The private boxes have capacities of between twelve and eighty people. Prices start at £70 + VAT per person. Packages are available to include badges, bar, Bucks Fizz and a meal—contact the racecourse for further information. There is space for a marquee that will take up to 500 guests. If you are going to Nottingham for the first time, please note that a dress code is in effect in the Premier Enclosure and patrons are requested not to wear denim, T-shirts or shorts

Children have an adventure playground and additional entertainment at weekends. Disabled people have a viewing stand and a lift in the Centenary Stand. Should you wish to book Nottingham's facilities on a non-raceday, the racecourse has developed a Conference Centre providing conference and exhibition facilities. Nottingham is a very progressive racecourse and deserves its success. We recommend it highly to anyone who happens to be passing by.

Local favourites

Nottingham has seen something of a renaissance in the 'where to stay/go' stakes and some hotels to recommend in the city include **Harts** (0115) 988 1900 - a wonderfully elegant Town House Hotel. A similar description and high promise can also go to **Lace Market** (0115) 852 3232 which is an elegant conversion of Georgian buildings - it's a really fine hotel. Ultra modern accommodation can be found at the **Park Plaza** (0115) 947 7200 which is well thought of. There are all manner of Travelodges and Travel Inns in and around the city. The **Holiday Inn Nottingham City** (0870) 400 9061 is a 13-storey hotel which boasts panoramic views of the city. Alternatively, the **Rutland Square** (0115) 941 1114 should not be ignored. The **Nottingham Moat House** (0115) 935 9988 is another up to date hotel. The **Hilton** (0115) 934 9700 offers city centre location (2 miles from the racecourse)

with leisure facilities. Swans Hotel (0115) 981 4042 outside the city is worthy of note. Other restaurants to consider include the excellent **Sonny's** (0115) 947 3041, and **Hotel des Clos** (0115) 986 6566 which also has some pleasant rooms. **Saagar** (0115) 962 2014 is a particularly good Indian restaurant and **Harts Restaurant** (0115) 911 0666 is definitely worth investigation, at the hotel listed previously. Other reccomendations from locals include: **World Service** 0115 847 5587 which offers fine indoor and outdoor eating and **Merchants** 0115 958 9898 in the city centre.

Outside the town, one place definitely to visit is the outstanding public house in Old Dalby, the **Crown** (01664) 823134. If you're a real ale fan then this is the pub for you and the pub food in this gorgeous converted farmhouse is excellent. The **Red House** in Nether Broughton is also well worth a visit. Highly recommended by those at the racecourse is the **Peacock** (01949) 842554 at Redmile Belvoir. The **Martins Arms** (01949) 81361 in Colston Bassett (01949) 81361 also warrants attention—good food and accomodation here the **Red Lion** at Strathern is also a good candidate. There is also a restaurant in which you can dine in the evenings. Although it is a bit of a trek, **Stapleford Park** (01572) 787522 just outside Melton Mowbray is excellent. Although expensive, this 16th century marvel is worth every penny for a luxurious stay and good food. The **Priest House** (01232) 810649 has a delightful setting and is handy for the M1. In Plumtree, **Perkins** (0115) 937 3695 offers a tempting menu off the blackboard and this makes for an ideal post-racing spot. The **Victoria** (0115) 925 4049 at Beeston will appeal to real ale aficionados and **Risley Hall** (0115) 939 9000 is an appealing Victorian hotel. In Castle Donington, the **Cross Keys** (01332) 812214 has good food and a cosy atmosphere and the **Priest House** (01332) 810649 has a delightful river setting. Finally, the **Royal Horseshoes** in Waltham-on-the-Wolds is a pleasant village pub with above average accommodation—ideal for lovers of England's countryside.

*Artist: **John Atkins INTO THE LEAD** Courtesy of: **The Artist***

This friendly course is run by **Sam Morshead** as **General Manager** and **Anthea Morshead** as **Clerk of the Course**. **Morag Reid** is **Secretary** and **Treasurer** and **Julie Manners** is the **Marketing Manager**. They can be found at **Perth Racecourse, Scone Palace Park, Perth PH2 6BB, tel (01738) 551597, fax (01738) 553021 E-mail:** *sam@perth-races.co.uk* **Website:** *www.perth-races.co.uk*

Although Perth is Britain's most northerly racecourse, some 450 miles from London, it is fairly accessible from all quarters of the country. When you reach Perth by car watch out for theTourist Board signs for Scone Palace which will conveniently take you to the racecourse itself. Edinburgh and Glasgow are only an hour's drive away and the M90 can be taken from Edinburgh via the Forth Bridge, making your way through the Ochil Hills and past Loch Leven—a wonderful drive. The A9 struggles through the beautiful Perthshire countryside via Aviemore, Blair Atholl, Pitlochry and Blairgowrie. Even the train picks out numerous beauty spots as it shunts north from Edinburgh and the distant King's Cross in London, and there is a free bus service to the course from Perth town centre. The nearest airports are at Dundee, Edinburgh and Glasgow. Helicopters may be landed by prior arrangement while aircraft should be landed at Scone aerodrome some two miles away. Car parking at the racecourse is plentiful and free.

The wooded parkland of Scone Palace is the setting for this superbly picturesque course. The fixture list is well designed and all the meetings are run over two or three days. The sponsorship at the course is particularly good and this, coupled with the general popularity of the course, ensures some good fields. Meetings take place in late April, mid May and early June, with a new Sunday fixture at the end of June, mid August and September. The main race of the year is the Perth Gold Cup run at the end of June.

The rates for the various enclosures are as follows: Club £15, £10 for the Paddock Enclosure and £5 for the Course Enclosure. The Annual Membership subscription is £115 for a single badge with a £200 charge for a double badge and includes reciprocal meetings at other courses. For the three-day Perth Festival visitors can buy a badge for all days for £40 for the Club Enclosure. There are discounts of £3 per person for clans of 15 strong or more which applies to the Paddock only. All enclosures have excellent views of the course and its sweeping wooded turns. However, if you're one of those people who hate to be parted from your car then centre course parking is an option at a price of £5 a head or £15 per car - fair value for picnic lovers.

The Grandstand is delightfully compact and allows for a superb atmosphere as the well-backed favourite strides by. A new stand is scheduled to open in 2005 and promises to offer even better facilities. Private boxes that can accommodate between 20 and 30 people can be arranged with the General Manager, with full catering facilities to fit the required budget. There is an excellent stand for

*Artist: **Mary Hamilton** UNSADDLING Courtesy of: **The Artist***

corporate hospitality and private parties that can cater for parties from 10 to 60, all with private viewing facilities. The Club Dining Room offers a silver service. To book a table in advance contact the racecourse office on (01738) 551597. For a superb view of the course go to the Champagne and Wine bar upstairs in the Club Stand. The Paddock Enclosure also has comfortable facilities with a wide range of bars and restaurants. Owners and Trainers are well treated here with their own restaurant and bar that overlooks the parade ring and saddling boxes. This is also available for hire on non racedays. There are telephones at the course and viewing ramps for the disabled. Special facilities for children are now provided on major race days and those under sixteen are admitted free on all days.

Perth may be Britain's most northerly track but it is also one of the country's most attractive—it's no small wonder that Perth has been voted the best small course in the North many times in recent years.

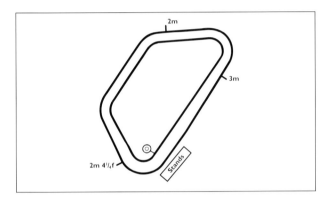

Local favourites

In Perth, the **Hunting Tower** (01738) 583771 is a comfortable place in which to stay. Excellent value accommodation is plentiful in Perth with **Clark Kimberley** (01738) 637406 and the **Clunie Guest House** (01738) 623625 providing comfort and style and the **New County Hotel** (01738) 623355 in Perth is worth a look in. **Let's Eat** (01738) 643377 is an extremely well thought of restaurant featuring the best of local ingredients. Three other restaurants to consider in town are the **Parklands Hotel** (01738) 622451 (good accommodation here as well) - alternatively try **63 Tay Street** (01738) 441451 which is an elegant place to eat. Finally, the **Grouse and Claret** (01577) 864212 is popular local suggestion. **Kinfauns Castle** (01738) 620777, a renowned 17th Century castle, is also first class. An hotel exceptionally close to the racecourse is **Murrayshall Country House** (01738) 551171 in New Scone. The hotel offers a fine restaurant and a championship golf course and comes thoroughly recommended. People making use of the A94 should note Alyth and here the **Lands of Loyal Hotel** (01828) 633151 is a pleasant and reasonably priced country house hotel in which to stay. Eastwards, one finds Blairgowrie, home of a wonderful golf course, Rosemount. Here you will find **Kinloch House Hotel** (01250) 884237, an award-winning Country House Hotel, extremely well run by the Shentall family who are keen racegoers. South of the town in Kinclaven by Stanley, the **Ballathie House** (01250) 883268 has another gorgeous Tayside setting. Another outstanding hotel to consider is **Dalmunzie House** (01250) 885224, family run and welcoming—cottages are

also available in the grounds for those who prefer the more independent life.

Another majestic place is, of course, **Gleneagles Hotel** (01764) 662231. Not only are there superb golf courses but the hotel exudes class—a first rate establishment in every way. More modest, but still friendly accommodation can be found at the **Glenfarg Hotel** (01577) 830241. Other alternatives outside Perth include the **Crieff Hydro** (01764) 655555 which is a very popular destination for those seeking a leisure break. Alternatively **The Royal** at Comrie (01764) 679200 is now a really tremendous place to stay. We should also alert you to two outstanding establishments, one at Dunblane, the other at Dunkeld. **Cromlix House** (01786) 822125 is superb and the restaurant is one of Scotland's finest. **Kinnaird House** (01796) 482440 is another hotel and restaurant that oozes class and is a great place to celebrate if the right horse wins—note the excellent game fishing here. Two miles beyond Perth you find another Scottish classic, on this occasion **Kinfauns Castle** (01738) 620777 - it's beautifully furnished and also offers first class bedrooms and dining. Another hotel to please game fishermen is the **Hilton Dunkeld House Hotel** (01350) 727771 with a delightful riverside setting for this welcoming establishment. Just outside Perth, **Dupplin Castle** (01904) 738859 is family run, extremely welcoming and thoroughly relaxing. Ideal after a tight finish in the last.

Artist: **Charles Church** THE WINNER Courtesy of: **The Artist**

Plumpton is a well run friendly racecourse within easy striking distance of London. **Patrick Davis** is **Chief Executive** of the racecourse, **Clerk of the Course** is **Mark Cornford** and **Moppy Peate** is **Marketing Manager** and **Allison Blake, Hospitality Manager**. They can be contacted at **Plumpton Racecourse, Plumpton, East Sussex, BN7 3AL. Tel: (01273) 890383 Fax: (01273) 891557.** E mail: _racing@plumptonracecourse.co.uk_ Website: _www.plumptonracecourse.co.uk_

Plumpton lies approximately 50 miles from London, midway between Haywards Heath and Lewes. The M23 is the best route south, but after this the motorist is left with various A and B roads. The A23, the A273 and the B2112 seem the best routes to punt on. From Brighton and the south coast, the A27 Lewes road coupled with the A273 should oblige. The course lies in the village of Plumpton Green. The quaint name of this village reflects its unspoilt character but the quiet is occasionally broken by the sound of the trains. This is good news for racegoers though, as the station lies beside the course. The best idea is to catch the Victoria-Hastings train to Plumpton Station. Helicopters are able to land at the racecourse by prior arrangement. For parking there is no charge.

Plumpton racecourse hosts 17 days racing per year from September through May. The New Year's Day, Easter Meetings (Saturday and Monday) and the Sussex National Meeting run in November have proved to be exceptionally popular with families.

The price for entry into Plumpton's Members' Enclosure is £17 per person, Tattersalls is £13 and the Silver Ring £8, except at Easter when it is £10. All prices include a free full-colour racecard – an excellent idea. By booking in advance you can gain entry to the Members at £15, Tattersalls at £11.50 and the Silver Ring for £7. OAP concessions are available on the day and children under 16 are free. Annual membership costs £170 for a single and £320 for a double membership. If you book before December 1st, this drops to £155 and £295. This price includes an Annual Members' car park and racecards. You will also be entitled to many reciprocal days at other sporting events and racecourses around the country.

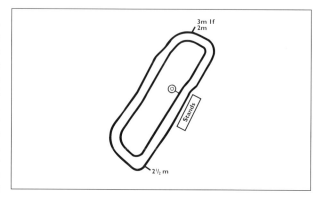

For the best seat in the house, why not take a hospitality box, with a viewing balcony over the racecourse. Hospitality boxes can accommodate from eight up to 80 people. Prices range to about £60 + VAT per person. For larger groups there are other function rooms and marquees. Contact the racecourse for details.

The popular Members Restaurant and Bar overlook the course and tables can be booked in advance with the caterers or by contacting the racecourse office. A three-course silver service lunch costs £27.50. In addition, fast food outlets and bars are available throughout the various enclosures. Many improvements have taken place at the racecourse over the last two years, which have attracted high calibre horses to the track with more prize money on offer.

We would warmly recommend a mid-week winter afternoon visit to Plumpton where exciting racing and a fun atmosphere is assured.

Local favourites

We start at a pinnacle of excellence, some way north of Plumpton—**Gravetye Manor** (01342) 810567 in Gravetye, south of East Grinstead—it's a really outstanding find. Another top hotel can be found at Cuckfield, **Ockendon Manor** (01444) 416111—the building is 16th century and the traditional open fires and panelling add immense charm to the excellent facilities. The restaurant is also particularly well thought of. Ashdown Forest has some delightful scenery and an excellent base from which to explore is the **Chequers Hotel** (01342) 823333 at Forest Row. In Lower Beeding, **South Lodge** (01403) 891711 is an attractive restaurant and boasts some excellent accommodation within. For lovers of luxury, a final recommendation here is for **Horsted Place** (01825) 750581 near Uckfield, where both the rooms and the restaurant are of an excellent standard **Buxted Park** (01825) 750581 in nearby Buxted also offers excellent accommodation and a dining room of merit. Slightly closer to the racecourse–the racegoer can find another English gem–**The Newick Park Hotel** (01825) 723633. It has a majestic parkland setting and offers elegance throughout.

Artist: **Jacqueline Stanhope** AP MCCOY _Courtesy of:_ **The Artist**

Much further south, one arrives in the extremely pleasant Sussex town of Lewes. Here one finds an hotel of excellence - **The Shelleys** (01273) 472361, first class food here as well. There are many of restaurants in Lewes. **Pailin** (01273) 473906 is a fine one where imaginative cooking ensures delightful eating. **Ortry Circa** (01273) 471777–there's some extravagant cooking in this stylsih art deco eaterie. Staying in this part of the world need not cost a fortune and for the avid bargain hunters **Millers** (01273) 475631 should fit the bill. In Ditchling, the **Bull** (01273) 843147 is a pleasant coaching inn.

While restaurants come and go, pubs generally stand their ground. In Fulking, the **Shepherd and Dog** is a pleasant small country pub and the bar snacks here are excellent. Closer to the racecourse at Clayton, the **Jack and Jill** is also a friendly place while the **Rainbow Arms** (01273) 400334 in Cooksbridge is welcoming and provides good bar snacks too. The **Highlands Inn** (01825) 762989 in Uckfield is another establishment popular with those in search of good fare. Not too far away we find Chiddingly's the **Six Bells** (01825) 872227—most appealing with old beams and excellent snacks as well as some good beers. In Horsted Keynes, try the **Green Man** (01825) 790656. Another fairly convenient stop could be made at the **Hare and Hounds** (01825) 890327, a pleasant village pub east of Uckfield. Racegoers who like country pubs with charm, should try **Juggs** (01273) 472523 in Kingston. Rustic to the core, it is a country pub for a country course. Finally, a selection of pubs in Plumpton Green that come recommended by those who run the course - the aptly named **Winning Post** (01273) 890571, **The Fountain** (01273) 890294 and **The Plough** (01273) 890311. In Plumpton itself the **Half Moon** (01273) 890253 also comes highly recommended. Just a few to consider when planning your racing in 2005.

Artist: **Klaus Philipp** *BEFORE RACING Courtesy of:* **The Artist**

A lot of hard work goes into making Pontefract one of the most popular racecourses in the north of England. The man in charge of this most progressive of courses is **Norman Gundill**, who acts as **Clerk, Manager** and **Secretary**. He is assisted by **Richard Hammill** and **Nicola Cawood**. They can be contacted at: **The Racecourse, Pontefract Park, Pontefract, tel: (01977) 702210 (racedays only)**, or at **33 Ropergate, Pontefract WF8 1LE, tel: (01977) 781307, fax: (01977) 781333, E-mail:** *info@pontefract-races.co.uk* Website: *www.pontefract-races.co.uk*

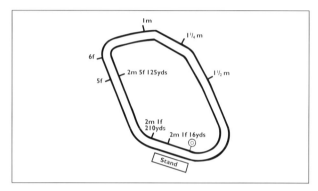

The course is marvellously situated for motorway access, the entrance being only half a mile from junction 32 of the M62, making it an excellent location for racegoers from almost all areas of the country. Leeds lies 20 miles west of Pontefract and the A1 and M1 and M18 are all within 10 miles of the course. Although there are plenty of busy rail stations nearby–Doncaster, York and Leeds–Pontefract is not on a main line station, so this is probably a course where one should take the car. There are vast car parking areas and all parking is free, other than the Special Reserve Park, where a charge of £10 is levied for the season. Buses are an option too, with those from Pontefract and Leeds passing the gates. If you are in a particular hurry, there are ample open playing fields in the park in which to place one's helicopter. You must check with the Secretary first though, just in case some other activity is taking place. The nearest airport, Leeds-Bradford is 27 miles away.

The course has 16 fixtures including three evening meetings in May, June and July, and has three Sunday fixtures (June, July, August) for 2005. Charges for 2004 were £16 for a daily club membership, £11 for entrance to the Paddock, £5 for the Silver Ring and the Third Ring. The best value, however, was the Third Ring car park which costs £8 per car and includes up to four people. Discounts are also available for groups of 10 or more in the Club enclosure. If you wished to become an Annual Member the adult single badge was priced at £145, whilst a husband and wife team could be members for the reasonable sum of £195.

Annual Members are also entitled to 15 reciprocal meetings at Thirsk, Doncaster, Haydock Park, Beverley, Newcastle, Market Rasen, Nottingham and Catterick, to name only a few. The racecourse executive is also to be applauded for reciprocal meetings at a variety of Yorkshire County Cricket Club venues including Headingley and Sheffield. The course also offers special discounts for parties in all racecourse enclosures. Contact the Secretary for further details.

Artist: **Graham Isom NECK & NECK** *Courtesy of:* **Rosenstiel's**

Artist: **Charles Church THREE-YEAR-OLD COLT** *Courtesy of:* **The Artist**

The Park Suite has a superb location with balconies overlooking both the Winning Post and the Parade Ring/ Winners Enclosure. It has closed circuit TV and Private Tote Betting facilities. The Park Suite Restaurant offers a stylish and practical approach to racegoing - once you are shown to your table it is yours for the day. With tables for up to 10 guests, the Park Suite is a particularly good option; however, smaller parties may be required to share a table. Packages of £39.50 (plus vat) a head are available, and include morning coffee, a five-course carvery luncheon and afternoon tea, a complimentary race card and a cash bar and wine list. However, the admission badge is not included.

Other facilities at the course include The Private Room in the Main Stand that looks directly out over the course and larger parties can be accommodated in the Entertainment Suite. The private boxes in the Dalby Stand certainly appear good value. The stand was built on the site of the old Club entrance and Champagne Bar. Each box seats up to 20 and the stand itself faces down the finishing straight, overlooks the horsewalk and has views over the Parade Ring—a superb place at which to make the most of a day's racing. Charges vary so it is best to contact the racecourse for details. Pontefract would certainly be a tremendous place to have a company summer party with a difference. Catering arrangements should be made directly with the racecourse caterers, Craven Gilpin & Sons (0113) 2876387.

Snack bars can be found throughout the course and more substantial food can be had in the Club and Paddock restaurants. Finally, should you wish to have a picnic, the place to go is the Third Ring car park on the stands side. Both the stands serving the Silver Ring and the Third Ring have been refurbished. There is a special playground for the youngsters in the Third Ring and, if under 16, they will be admitted free when accompanied by an adult. A fully supervised crèche operates in the Third Ring at holiday meetings at Easter and August and at evening meetings. Another good reason to go racing at this friendly, well-run racecourse.

Local favourites

Closest, being opposite the racecourse, the **Parkside Hotel** (01977) 709911 provides very handy accomodation, while just a short walk (10 minutes) from the course is **Queens Hotel** (01977) 702228. Pontefract is ideally placed for venturing further north, and one place that should be visited is Ilkley—a little distant but well worth the trek. Here, **Rombalds Hotel and Restaurant** (01943) 603201 is a really excellent place to stay—home comforts and a warm Yorkshire welcome are the order of the day. What's more, if you happen to wake up a little hungry on Saturday morning after an evening at Pontefract, fear not, their Edwardian breakfast is an absolute monster and should keep the largest of wolves from the door. Ilkley is cluttered with some delightful antique shops. The **Box Tree** (01943) 608484 is a celebrated restaurant to note. The **Grove** (01943) 816477 is also well thought of. The **Cow and Calf Hotel** (01943) 607335 is another to consider. Closer to the course again, Leeds has a few good fancies (see Wetherby).

Returning to more local spots, one should consider some places in which to have an ale or two. In Ledsham, the **Chequers** (01977) 683135 is an enormously popular free house, resplendent with oak beams and open fires. In Ledston's Main Street, one finds an equine establishment, the **White Horse** (01977) 553069 and another warm welcome and fire, so I understand. The **Greyhound** (01937) 557202 in Saxton is also a pleasing Yorkshire hostelry. In Wentbridge, the **Wentbridge House Hotel** (01977) 620444 is a glorious, early 18th century hotel, very cosy and well appointed, standing in 15 acres of grounds. The restaurant here is well thought of, a fine place to visit prior to the racecourse and perfect for a post race celebration. Another historic and worthy entry to the Pontefract shortlist is found at Monk Fryston. Here, **Monk Fryston Hall** (01977) 682369 has pleasant interiors and formal gardens as well as a more modern wing. **Rogerthorpe Manor Country House Hotel** in nearby Badsworth (01977) 643839 comes personally recommended by the racecourse management, making it a fine place to stay when visiting Pontefract in 2005.

Artist: **Jaqueline Stanhope FOAL** *Courtesy of:* **The Artist**

*T*he team in charge at Redcar is headed by the **Chairman, Peter Hill-Walker**, ably assisted by **James Sanderson, Clerk of the Course** and **Manager**. They can be contacted at **Redcar Racecourse, Redcar, Cleveland TS10 2BY, tel: (01642) 484068, fax: (01642) 488272, Website:** *www.redcarracing.co.uk*. International Racecourse Management are also part of the impressive executive structure. Together they form as fine a team as you will find in racing and continuing improvements at the racecourse are evidence of this.

Redcar racecourse is located in the south of this coastal town to the north east of the Yorkshire Moors. Redcar is accessible by road from the A19 dual carriageway, which passes within 15 minutes of the racecourse (via the Parkway). The A19 links to the south with the A1 at Dishforth and to the north at Newcastle. Travellers from the east will find the A67 and the A66 routes the most direct into Redcar and the racecourse. The nearest railway station, Redcar Central Station, is in the town itself, a distance of approximately half a mile from the track—a 10 minute walk at the most! A fast train service runs from King's Cross to Darlington where you can catch the local train to Redcar. The bus station is a mere 150 yard hike from the Grandstand—perfect. There are ample free parking facilities with three major areas for cars and coaches. Teesside Airport is the nearest airport, a 30 minute drive from the course and if you wish to land your own plane there is a private air strip at Yearby, a five minute drive away. Contact the racecourse for details. Helicopters should notify the course in advance on (01642) 484068.

Redcar hosts 18 flat fixtures a year from March to October. Two of the feature races are the Totesport Zetland Gold Cup, which is worth some £50,000 in prize money, and also the £150,000 betfair Two Year Old Trophy in October which is the focal point of Redcar's racing calendar.

Annual Membership in 2004 was priced at £110 and £45 for Juniors (under 25). The charge for Joint Membership, was £165. These may rise a bit in 2005. Annual Membership includes a car pass for each meeting plus the use of a private room, bar, catering and Tote kiosk. The use of a private bar is an excellent concept and one that all the racecourses should adopt for their annual patrons. The daily admissions for the Members, Tattersalls and the Course were priced at £15, £10 and £3.50 respectively. OAPs receive discounted admission in Tattersalls of £5 and only £2 for the Course enclosure. The racecourse offers a discount to parties of 12 or more, reducing the daily prices to £11 for the Club, £6 for Tattersalls and £2.50 for the Course and one free ticket is included with pre-booked groups of 20 tickets. The stand facilities are excellent and the colourful flower beds form a cheerful feature—all further indications of the management's eagerness to please.

The course will be happy to provide information with regard to boxes, conference suites and rooms for smaller gatherings. The Paddock Rooms add a new dimension to Redcar's facilities as a fully self-contained entertainment centre with magnificent viewing facilities and suites to cater for between 35 and 140. Much refurbishment has been carried out during the past few years, completely renovating the facilities which include the Crow's Nest dine and view restaurant that combines full table service with a fine view of the racing action, while the Voltigeur restaurant has a carvery. The Classic Suite provides great corporate hospitality and caters for up to 120 guests. The four luxurious executive boxes cater for 8-12 guests (Silver Service) or 15 plus with a Buffet-style menu. In 2004 the Members' Enclosure facilities

Artist: **Peter Smith NOW IS THE TIME** *Courtesy of:* **Frost & Reed**

underwent a renovation as did two of the bars for Owners & Trainers and further modernisation is planned for other areas of this progressive course.

Children are admitted free if under the age of 16 and accompanied (excluding Redcar's Family Funday in August where a minimal charge will be made) and there is a playground provided. Other facilities include a viewing ramp for the disabled opposite the winning post, and lavatories for the disabled in all enclosures. Although there are no special banking facilities, public telephones are available for any necessary credit punts and there is a Tote betting shop and credit shop.

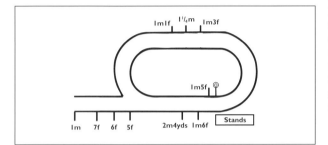

Local favourites

The north east may not enjoy the most illustrious of reputations elsewhere, but in this case ignorance is not bliss. Few who venture this far north are in any hurry to leave. In Crathorne, near Yarm, there is an extremely fine hotel the **Crathorne Hall Hotel** (01642) 700398. It enjoys a splendid setting and is thoroughly welcoming—a good choice. **Judges Hotel** (01642) 789000 at Kirklevington Hall is also extremely

good. In Yarm itself, **Santoro** (01642) 781305 is a good Italian restaurant to note. At Staddle Bridge, **The Tontine** (01609) 882671 is a truly delightful hotel run by the McCoy brothers with a genuine 1930s feel. It is also home to **McCoy's Bistro.** In Stockton-on-Tees, the **Stockton Swallow Hotel** (01642) 679721 boasts extremely comfortable accommodation and is high on the list of visiting business people. In Northallerton, **Solberge Hall** (01609) 779191 is also good.

If the bustle of the city centre hotels is not to your liking then you may care to try the **Grinkle Park Hotel** in Loftus (01287) 640515—the parkland setting of this Victorian hotel is especially attractive. Farther afield in Goathland, the **Mallyan Spout Hotel** (01947) 896486 is recommended. The **Endeavour** in Staithes (01947) 840825 is a really splendid restaurant. **Gisborough Hall Hotel** (01287) 634533 has recently untertaken an £8 million refurbishment and after a quick inspection we can say it is well worth a visit - the food is also excellent. Closer to the racecourse at Saltburn-by-the-Sea, **Rushpool Hall** (01287) 624111 is well regarded. We also hear good things about **Best Western Parkmore** (01642) 786815 at Eaglescliffe - pleasant accommodation and fine food.

There are several pubs to note in the area and one such establishment is the **Ship** at Saltburn-by-the-Sea, splendid seafood, snacks and good views—well worth a trip out. Farther west in Eaglescliffe, the **Blue Bell** (01642) 780358 has good food as well as fine views of the River Tees. The racecourse management also recommend **O'Grady's** (01642) 477624. A little further afield, the **Horseshoe Hotel** at Egton Bridge (01947) 895245 has a lovely setting and good value bedrooms and a similar description can be applied to the **Duke of Wellington Inn** (01287) 660351 in Danby. A peaceful atmosphere in which to peruse your Racing Post and consider the day ahead at Redcar races.

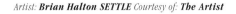

Artist: **Brian Halton SETTLE** _Courtesy of:_ **The Artist**

are given nine days' complimentary Yorkshire cricket, as well as reciprocal meetings at many other northern courses. Membership charge for a double badge is £150, a single £100 and a junior (under 21) is required to pay a £65 subscription. If you are able to justify only the occasional visit to Ripon then daily badges cost £15 in the Club, £10 in Tattersalls, and £3.50 in the Course Enclosure. All are 2004 charges and may rise in 2005. Children under 16 are admitted free as long as they are accompanied by an adult.

Artist: **John Atkins** *MIDDLEHAM LOW MOOR* *Courtesy of:* **The Artist**

The authorities are headed by **Michael Hutchinson** who acts as **Managing Director** and is assisted by **Clerk of the Course, James Hutchinson**. They can be contacted at **77 North Street, Ripon, North Yorkshire HG4 1DS, tel: (01765) 602156 fax: (01765) 690018.**

The most obvious way to get to Ripon is by car for there is no train station at the town itself, and while trains do stop at Harrogate, the nearest major station is at York, some 23 miles away. If you do wish to travel by train then the King's Cross line is the one to board. London itself lies 200 miles away and the best way of reaching the racecourse from the south is to use the A1/A1(M). and turn off at Boroughbridge following the signs for Ripon Cathedral (well worth a visit itself!). The course is two miles east of Ripon, off the B6265, which in turn is just four miles from the A1. The A61 from Leeds and Harrogate is a useful road from the south and this, together with the A19, will assist racegoers from the north east. Similar access is provided by the A61 from Thirsk for those travelling from the east. There are ample parking areas at the racecourse and these are provided free. If people are hurrying to the course then helicopters are a welcome option provided you give prior notice to the racecourse office.

The spring and summer months play host to Ripon's race meetings and August is particularly crowded with excellent fixtures. The William Hill Great St Wilfrid Handicap is the feature race whilst many a good entry is attracted by the Champion Two Year Old Trophy. Lovers of summer sports who enrol as Members of Ripon will also be offered a taste of another splendid summer game—cricket. Annual Members

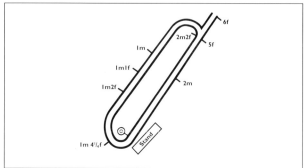

Discounts are available for groups of 20 or more and give £1.50 off the charges for Club and Tatts. If you are looking for an afternoon with slightly more than the average entry badge allows, there are nine boxes available for hire, catering for between 25 and 100 people. If you require precise details, contact the course as they have an excellent printed brochure. These offer good value but don't forget to sort out the catering at the same time. For bigger parties a marquee area is available in the Paddock. Taking a car and four passengers into the course enclosure for £10 offers excellent value.

There are restaurants and snack bars in all enclosures. Parts of the Members and Tattersalls stands have been rebuilt, increasing and improving the facilities available while new railings around the Parade Ring create a smart appearance and give added protection for both horses and people. As an added attraction, music lovers will enjoy a variety of music from Ripon's award-winning re-creation of a Victorian bandstand. Ripon was the first course to have a children's playground and there are now two—one on either side of the course—marvellous. Another first is Ripon's giant screen - the only course in the country to have installed their own permanent screen. This guarantees racegoers a close up view of the racing. Other details to note are

Artist: **John Atkins** *MIDDLEHAM LOW MOOR* *Courtesy of:* **The Artist**

that there are telephones in the Paddock and Course enclosures as well as betting shops. Disabled racegoers are well catered for with reserved car parking and raised platforms for viewing. Those of you who have not visited Ripon should give it a try. It is fondly called the 'Garden Racecourse' and is one of the most pleasing in the country.

Local favourites

Ripon has much to offer the sightseer—notably Fountains Abbey, Ripon Cathedral, Newby Hall and the recently re-opened canal. Ripon's leading hotel the **Ripon Spa** (01765) 602172 is a particularly racing orientated abode, while the **Unicorn** (01765) 602202 is a traditional coaching inn. Less glamorous, but quite agreeable accommodation can also be had at the **Crescent Lodge Guest House** (01765) 609589. One pub within sight of the course **The Blackamoor Inn** comes highly recommended. **The Gallery** at the **Outside Inn** (01765) 602600 is also well worth a visit.

In Markington the **Hob Green Hotel** (01423) 770031 is another extremely restful place to stay with award-winning gardens and excellent food. Great character and some good accommodation can be found in the **Sportsman's Arms** (01423) 711306 in Wath-in-Nidderdale. If you love the country, stay here—it's a charming setting and the food is also first class as is the **Yorke Arms** (01423) 755243 at Ramsgill. Also well thought of is the **Crown Hotel** (01423) 322328 at Boroughbridge. For those of you seeking a really wonderful place to visit, try **Swinton Park**, Masham (01765) 680900 - it's absolutely magnificent.

Harrogate will make a good base while you visit Yorkshire. 'An 18th Century building with an extremely attractive setting' is a fair description of the splendid **Studley Hotel** (01423) 560425 where a good restaurant is complemented by comfortable accommodation. Other small hotels in this celebrated spa town, which boasts a wealth of good shopping, include the **Balmoral Hotel** (01423) 508208 and **Cutlers on the Stray** (01423) 524471 which is also a good 'food and sleep' double. The very civilised **Rudding Park** (01423) 871350 will appeal to golfers as well as racegoers. It's highly luxurious and an ideal post racecourse location. The twin advantages of staying in Harrogate are that firstly one can leave a non-racing partner to browse in this delightful town and secondly, in the evening, one has a number of restaurants to visit. The **Drum and Monkey** (01423) 502650 is good - downstairs, a bustling bar and superb food, upstairs a more formal and extremely popular fish restaurant. **The Courtyard Restaurant** (01423) 530708 is also good.

For people who have to rush home the same day then here are a few options before you set sail. In Staveley, the **Royal Oak** (01423) 340267 is a welcoming country pub with good food while in Roecliffe, the **Crown** (01423) 322578 is another great little pub. Other public houses handy for the A1 include the **Ye Olde Punch Bowl Inn** (01423) 322519 in Marton cum Grafton and the **Ship Inn** at Aldborough—note the Roman connection here. The **Sawley Arms** (01765) 620642 in Sawley is highly recommended for meals. **The Bruce Arms** (01677) 470325 is also a great place for a post race rendezvous. Another real classic place to consider is **The General Tarleton Inn** (01423) 340284 - it's a great place to stay and/or eat. A similar commendation of excellence can be given to the thoroughly charming **York Arms** at Ramsgill (01423) 755243–it's also tremendous. A final tip before we leave this area is the **The Boar's Head** (01423) 771888; this is a charming hotel which exudes character–a real favourite. Racing at Ripon can be competitive and will need a clear head. A trip in 2005 is recommended.

Artist: **Graham Isom** *RIPON RACECOURSE* *Courtesy of:* **Rosenstiel's**

Salisbury is an enchanting racecourse and keen racegoers should definitely make the effort to attend a meeting here in 2005. **Jeremy Martin** runs Salisbury as the **Clerk of the Course**. He can be contacted at **Salisbury Racecourse, Netherhampton, Wiltshire SP2 8PN, tel: (01722) 326461/ 327327, fax: (01722) 412710 E-mail:** *jmartin@salisburyracec ourse.freeserve.co.uk* **Website:** *www.salisburyracecourse.co.uk*

The racecourse is located three-and-a-half miles south west of Salisbury on the A3094. The best plan is to aim for the town and from there you should follow the signs to the racecourse. The A360 is the best route from the north. For people heading from the east or the west of the country the A30 is ideal. Other modes of transport to be considered are the train/bus double. The first leg is the Waterloo-Salisbury line which should be coupled with a courtesy bus from Salisbury station to the racecourse. If you wish to use the helicopter then there is no problem—as long as you telephone the management in advance. There are excellent car parking facilities at the course which are provided free of charge.

The major day's racing here is the Bibury Meeting which takes place in late June. The feature race on the card is the Tote Bibury Cup worth £25,000. Other major races of the season are the Upavon Fillies Stakes (£45,000), the Group 3 Sovereign Stakes in August (£60,000) and the Axminster Carpets Cathedral Stakes (£35,500), Dick Role Stakes and Stonehenge Stakes (£30,000 apiece).

There are three evening meetings and two Sunday meetings when there is entertainment for the children and jazz bands and barbecues add a certain spice to some competitive racing.

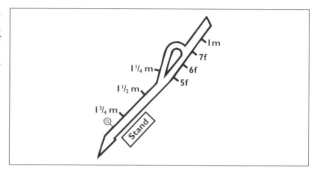

Additionally, the Sunday meeting in May is well worth a visit when plenty of entertainment is laid on for all the family to accompany an excellent programme of racing.

Admission prices will be £16 for the Members, £10 for Tattersalls and £5 for the Course Enclosure. Children are admitted free, if accompanied. If you wish to become an Annual Member the rate is £140. However, in addition you receive a car pass and 20 reciprocal meetings plus, of course, the prestige of belonging to the oldest known racing club still in existence — the Bibury.

If you wish to organise a party at Salisbury, and it's a special place to have one, discounts are available, subject to numbers on advance bookings. Private hospitality boxes located above the Members Bar and the Festival Stand accommodate between 12 and 40 guests. These are available for daily hire from £600 per day or on an annual basis. Daily sublets can be arranged, depending on the day and the

Artist: **Anne Farrall** **DYNAMIC ELEGANCE** *Courtesy of:* **The Artist**

box required. However, it is always worth contacting the racecourse for availability or cancellations. The best idea, however, may be to organise a marquee or chalet located adjacent to the parade ring and the winning post catering for up to 300 guests.

Salisbury runs its own Bibury Club Catering Company and provides an excellent food service to the recently refurbished Members Restaurant where advance booking is essential. There is also a snack bar located in the Bibury Suite if you fancy something less substantial and a seafood bar in the refurbished Paddock Bar. On the drinking front, Members can enjoy the Wessex Bar, while in Tattersalls a temporary Pavilion Bar is erected to cater for the larger crowds in July and August. Disabled people are given the opportunity to enjoy racing by virtue of a raised viewing area—situated in the Members Enclosure. A Tote betting shop is located in Tattersalls and telephones are available. An evening or afternoon at Salisbury is thoroughly recommended.

Local favourites

Hampshire, Dorset and Wiltshire are home to an enticing array of country pubs. Here is a quick listing of some of the various contenders: the **Compasses** (01722) 714318 in Lower Chicksgrove has bar snacks and a traditional atmosphere as well as a separate restaurant and cosy rooms if required. Another pub-restaurant ideal for informal post-race nosh is the **Black Dog** (01722) 716344 in Chilmark. The **Black Horse** (01722) 716251 in Teffont Magna has super food and pleasing accommodation. The same can be said of another critter—the **Fox Inn** (01258) 880328, a lovely village pub. In Broad Chalke, the **Queen's Head** (01722) 780344 is a good stayer and in another gorgeous village, Fonthill Bishop, the **King's Arms** is a picturesque alternative, while the **Victoria and Albert** (01722) 743174 in Netherhampton is very convenient; so too is the **Barford Inn** at Barford St Martin (01722) 742242. The list goes on and on. If you love the country and its traditionally copious cuisine, then this is the area for you. Two local tips worth following are the **Pembroke Arms Hotel** (01722) 743328 at Wilton and **Cricket Field House** (01722) 322595. Both also offer good accommodation. We then come across a couple of tools. Before you take offence, relax—merely a reference to two other excellent pubs in the vicinity, the **Malet Arms** in Newton Toney, and the **Silver Plough** (01722) 712266 in Pitton, a tremendous hostelry with a

*Artist: **Jacqueline Stanhope RICHARD HUGHES** Courtesy of: **The Artist***

restaurant. A good pub to stay in is the **Barford** (01722) 742242—good value and good food.

Then there's Salisbury. A charming city and the county town of Wiltshire. The rivers Avon, Bourne, Wylye and Nadder converge here. Many people visit the area to see the cathedral or shop in the market and the town is a busy and thriving focal point. At Harnham, the **Rose and Crown Hotel** (01722) 339816 has a lovely setting on the banks of the River Avon, overlooking the cathedral. The **White Hart Hotel** (01722) 412761 has great character and is an ideal choice before racing at the Bibury Club. **Milford Hall Hotel** (01722) 417411 is also reported to be of an excellent standard. If you are in search of a pub then the **King's Arms** (01722) 327629 is a sure bet and it offers good value accommodation. **The Red Lion** (01722) 323334 is also a characterful place to meet and stay before racing at Salisbury. Outside the town, a really super pub to note is the **Fox and Goose** (01722) 718437 at Coombe Bissett—well worth a post-race pint. South of the racecourse at East Tytherley is the excellent **Star Inn** (01794) 340225—a few rooms and some excellent fare in a charming old coaching inn.

Some distance from Salisbury, but a definite must if you have time, is the **Sign of the Angel** (01249) 730230 at Lacock—also a possibility for Newbury. Marlborough offers the **Ivy House Hotel** (01672) 515333. Closer to the racecourse, try **Howard's House Hotel** (01722) 716392—a real peach of a place—an ideal port of call for those of you wishing to break the journey before racing at Salisbury. If you can't find inspiration at this absolute gem, we suggest you give the game up!

*Artist: **Graham Isom SALISBURY** Courtesy of: **The Artist***

At Sandown, **David Morris** is the **Managing Director** while **Andrew Cooper** is the **Director of Racing**, tel: **(01372) 461213**. The **Sales Director** is **Ben Gibson (01372) 461208** and the **Head of Marketing** is **Karen Englishby (01372) 461275**. If you wish to contact them, write to: **Sandown Park Racecourse, Esher, Surrey KT10 9AJ**, tel: **(01372) 463072**, fax: **(01372) 465205**, website: *www.sandown.co.uk* There is also a ticket bookings hotline on **(01372) 470047**.

The racecourse is a mere 15 miles from the centre of London in the suburb of Esher. The best route from the capital is to take the A3 out of central London itself. The A308 and the A309 are trunk roads that run nearby, and the racecourse itself lies off the A307, the Portsmouth Road. Racegoers from London are strongly recommended to use the Esher—Waterloo/Clapham Junction line as it passes the course. If you live closer to the course, buses from Kingston, Guildford and Staines all go to Esher and stop in the High Street. Assuming that you are in a car, you will find free parking off the Portsmouth Road. Parking in the Members car park carries a charge of £2. If time is of the essence you can take a helicopter and land on the golf course in the centre of the track—but please check beforehand. Golf is of course suspended on racedays.

Since it opened its doors in 1870, Sandown Park has long been one of the most popular racecourses in Britain. One of its great attributes is the viewing of the course and the fact that everything is close at hand, with just a short hop from the parade ring to the finish line.

Fixtures for 2005 are expected to remain at 26 with meetings both on the flat and over the jumps–with the

famous Gold Cup Meeting, when the combination of the Classic Trial and the Golf Cup itself produces arguably the most exciting day's racing of the year. Both races are sponsored by Betfred. Other highlights at Sandown are the Sunderlands Imperial Cup, the Agfa Diamond Chase and the Coral-Eclipse Stakes on the flat—the first major clash of the generations each summer.

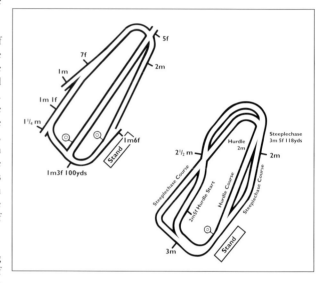

For the two big meetings, the Gold Cup day and Coral Eclipse there is a charge of £35 in the Premier Enclosure and £20 in the Grandstand. For other meetings you will be charged £22 to get into the Premier and £15 for the Grandstand. You could, however, save up to 10 per cent

*Artist: **Graham Isom** SANDOWN PARK Courtesy of: **Rosenstiel's***

on the badges if you booked a week in advance, and 25 per cent on most race days when booking a party of 12 or more. Accompanied children aged 16 or under are admitted free to all enclosures. If you are over 60 you could join the course's Diamond Club which costs a fiver and entitles you to a £5 discount on Grandstand admission for all fixtures bar the big meetings.

Annual Membership in 2005 (for all 26 flat and jump meetings) costs £260. A single membership for the 11 National Hunt meetings is £115, while a similar arrangement for the flat's 15 meetings is £170. Reciprocal arrangements were made for admission by members at Goodwood, Taunton, Lingfield, Newbury, Newton Abbot, Epsom and Sandown.

There are 34 boxes at Sandown Park, and these are let on both an annual or daily basis. They are much in demand and you should book well in advance on (01372) 477747. Numerous private rooms are also available and marquee sites can be organised. If you would like a table for lunch and tea, the Tingle Creek Restaurant can accommodate you and your guests. There are also a large number of snack bars in the Food Court area to suit every budget. Recent additions in the Premier Enclosure include Chaser's Wine Bar and the Wheeler's of St James Champagne and Seafood Bar, which remains open for two hours after racing with live music. If you wish to take your own food and have a picnic you can to so in the car parks. Owners and their connections can enjoy the Winners Enclosure where they can watch a video replay of their race. The Owners and Trainers Club is situated next to the weighing room and includes complimentary refreshments. During the warmer weather there are marquees placed next to the pre-parade rings and winners enclosure that offer some excellent packages for groups of 20 or more.

A Tote betting shop has been installed in both the Premier and Grandstand enclosures. Those with families might wish to use the picnic area in the Course Enclosure. Children are admitted free when accompanied and a creche provides first-class facilities for young children. These are not open at every race meeting so it is best to check the Sandown website for details. Disabled facilities are also excellent here with specially equipped toilets and viewing areas, reserved parking and access ramps to all areas.

Sandown is unique in British racing for hosting a mixed meeting featuring both flat and jumps action on the same day when it hosts the Gold Cup meeting in May. Not only does this bring a dramatic finale to the annual National Hunt season, but there is also the chance to see some top flat horses in action. For fans of Irish racing this is a relatively common occurrence, but unfortunately nowhere else does it happen on this side of the Irish sea. We think these meetings are an excellent way of bringing the 'two solitudes' of flat and jumps enthusiasts together and something that could be extended to other dual purpose courses. In the meantime, go and enjoy Sandown on Gold Cup day and see what we mean.

Artist: **John Atkins** *LEAVING THE PADDOCK, SANDOWN Courtesy of:* **The Artist**

Because of Sandown's proximity to London, many racegoers will inevitably be heading back to the capital after a day at the track so it is difficult to know where to start a selection of hotels and restaurants. For those who want luxury and have the money to spend, **Blakes Hotel** 0207 370 6701 in South Kensington is quite superb as is the renowned **Raffles Browns Hotel** (020) 7493 6020. That bastion of old-fashioned English values, **Claridge's** 0800 7671 7671 on Brook Street needs no introduction–its discreet luxury and elegance are quite unsurpassed. Park Lane delivers a number of excellent hotels. The **Dorchester** 0207 629 8888 is also magnificent and is crying out for a pre-race inspection. The **Grosvenor House** (020) 7499 6363 is another impressive hotel and a star performer. The **Four Seasons Hotel** 0207499 0888 and the **Carlton Tower** (020) 7235 1234 are two other thoroughbreds with outstanding restaurants as well. A great favourite for many years is the **Goring** (020) 7396 9000–it's wonderfully welcoming and the food is spectacular. If the above are slightly out of the range of the impoverished racegoer, then it goes without saying that London provides a veritable multitude of accommodation at vastly varying rates. One highly recommended establishment that combines comfort and value is the **Aston Court Hotel** (020) 7602 9954. Many of the chains are also well represented as you can imagine and here, weekend breaks can be surprisingly good value.

So far, the emphasis has been on central London. A bit farther south on Wimbledon Common, **Cannizaro House** (020) 8879 1464 is a delight, a true country house overlooking the common and superbly appointed throughout. The **Petit Pierrot** (01372) 465105 at Claygate is also well regarded.

Prefer to stay in the Esher area to sample the local delights? Sandown Park has its own on-site hotel (01372) 461201. The **Dining Room** (01932) 231686 at Hersham serves good English food, whilst the **Hilton Hotel,** Cobham (01932) 864471 in nearby Cobham has excellent facilities such as saunas and whirlpool baths. Elsewhere, in Coatham the **Woodlands Park Hotel** (01372) 843933 is an improving type and an excellent choice for visitors to Sandown. Further afield in Weybridge the **Warbeck House Hotel** (01932) 848764 is unpretentious but recommended. The **Oatlands Park Hotel** (01932) 847242 is a strong local fancy and a recent upgrading makes it a handy favourite. **Casa Romana** (01932) 843470 is an excellent Italian to note as is **La Capanna** (01932) 862121 in Cobham. **Good Earth** (01372) 462489 is an extremely handy and first-rate Chinese restaurant. Less convenient, but with outstanding cuisine **Drake's**, Ripley (01483) 224777 is excellent. **Gatton Manor** (01306) 627555 is also a good choice—it's located in Ockley, and the **Cricketers Arms** (01306) 627205 is a good selection.

Artist: **Graham Isom IN THE PADDOCK** *Courtesy of:* **Rosenstiel's**

Artist: **Roy Miller** DANCING BRAVE *Courtesy of:* **The Artist**

Sedgefield

The man in charge here is **General Manager Jim Allen**. He can be contacted at **Sedgefield Racecourse, Sedgefield, Stockton on Tees TS21 2HW, tel (racedays only): (01740) 621925, fax: (01740) 620663. E-mail:** *info@sedgefield-racecourse.co.uk* **Website:** *www.sedgefield-racecourse.co.uk*

The racecourse is approachable from Middlesbrough and the east via the A177 off the A19, while the A1(M) makes the racecourse easily accessible for both northbound and southbound travellers: just follow the brown tourist signs to the course. For racegoers from the larger conurbations to the southwest, the M62 and the A1(M) provide good routes. Major train routes run to the centre of Darlington some 250 miles from London. The closest rail stations are at Stockton-on-Tees (nine miles away), Durham (twelve miles) and Darlington itself. There is ample free parking for a variety of vehicles, although there is a charge of £5 in the Paddock car park. Helicopters are also able to land at Sedgefield, but please call in advance.

Sedgefield is the only course in County Durham and prides itself on being known as 'The Friendly Course'. There were 19 national hunt fixtures on offer in 2004 including a number of summer jumping meetings. The course's major race each year is the Durham National Handicap Steeplechase, a unique long distance event at a unique course. The busiest day of the year is traditionally the Boxing Day Fixture which attracts thousands of local people.

The course has only two enclosures: the Grandstand which is reasonably priced at £12 (OAPs £7) and the Course Enclosure which is equally good value at £6. The course also offers special party rates with a 20 per cent discount for groups of 15. Children under 16 are admitted free in both enclosures. If you wish to take out an Annual Membership the cost is £150. Owners are well looked after here and are entitled to six complimentary badges if they are running their horse. Syndicates are offered eight badges.

During recent years the racecourse management has spent over a million pounds on improvements to the track, stabling

*Artist: **John Atkins SEDGEFIELD, COMING BACK** Courtesy of: **The Artist***

and public amenities. A new weighing room, incorporating two entertainment suites with viewing balconies overlooking the parade ring and winners enclosure have been added, as well as a renovated public bar. There is a new Parade Ring and Winners Enclosure, new offices, toilet block and admission turnstiles. There are now ten private boxes, the six additional ones situated in the new pavilion. All have excellent views of the winning post. Two sponsors suites are available for hire, the first seats up to 100 while the smaller one seats up to 40. The caterers are Ramside Event Catering who can be contacted on 0191 236 4148. Good value lunches are available at Sedgefield in the Pavilion Restaurant which seats 120. There are various snack bars to keep the hunger pangs at bay as well as two restaurants, offering both à la carte and table d'hôte dining.

The disabled racegoer has special ramps provided to ensure a pleasant day. An on-course betting office is in existence as well as telephones, although no banking facilities are available. Sedgefield is well supported by the local community and visitors from further afield are encouraged to visit this unspoilt, well-run racecourse which has been significantly refurbished in recent years. Certainly one to be put in the diary for 2005.

*Artist: **Malcolm Coward MORNING MIST** Courtesy of: **The Artist***

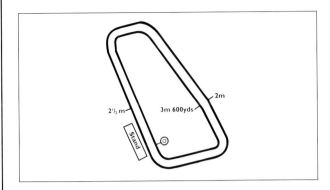

Local favourites

Sedgefield is surrounded by a number of good hotels and a visit in 2003 is well recommended. **Blackwell Grange** (0870) 609 6121 in Darlington is one to note. An excellent Italian restaurant is **Sardis** (01325) 461222—which, given the quality, is well priced. Heading north we find **Headlam Hall** (01325) 730238—a worthy selection—whilst the **Dog Inn** (01325) 312152 is a possibility for a pre-race pint. **Redworth Hall Hotel** (01388) 770600 is a fine hotel—a good restaurant here as well. **Ramside Hall** (0191) 386 5282 outside Durham is also handy. It also offers a good golf course for those who enjoy this sport.

Stapleton offers the **White Horse Hotel** (01325) 382121—not grand but comfortable and convenient. For an excellent post-race nosebag try the **Black Bull Inn** (01325) 377289 in Moulton. It's a mile-and-a-half off the A1 at Scotch Corner and is one of the most celebrated fish restaurants in the area. In Rushyford, three miles from the course, one finds the **Swallow Eden Arms Hotel** (01388) 720541 which receives promising reports from locals in the know. On the doorstep of the racecourse itself, the **Dun Cow Inn and Restaurant**

(01740) 620894 will provide for your every reasonable need! The **Inn on the Green** also in Sedgefield is another popular local favourite. The **George** at Piercebridge (01325) 374576 has a magnificent setting and offers good food and some accommodation. Further afield still, but well worth the trip, is the **Rose and Crown** (01833) 650213 at Romaldskirk - a beautifully set, unpretentious hotel which offers good food and hospitality, ideal for a local post-race evening.

Over in the city of Durham the cathedral is awe-inspiring and the castle is also worth a look. If you are going to stay here, then the better hotels include the stylish **Durham Marriot Royal County** 0870 400 7286 which overlooks the River Wear and the **Three Tuns** 0191 386 4326. If you like a good restaurant try **Bistro 21** in Aykley Heads 0191 384 4354, it's a real gem. If you're looking for a bit of divine inspiration prior to racing, make a visit to Durham Cathedral–it's majestic– good pubs in the nearby locale as well! In Coatham Mundeville –a 15 minute drive from Sedgefield, between Darlington and Newton Aycliffe–one finds a hot favourite–**Hall Garth Golf and Country Club** 0870 609 6131, a well appointed 16th century mansion—thoroughly recommended.

There are two places nearer the course that should also be considered in your each-way plans. Firstly, **Hardwick Hall** (01740) 620253, which lies one mile west of the town making it most convenient for early morning race enthusiasts. Secondly, the **Nags Head** (01740) 620234, an extremely friendly pub which offers good bar snacks as well as having a separate restaurant. In fact it's one of many appealing pubs to be found in the pleasant town of Sedgefield. The aptly named **Ministers** (01740) 622201 is a restaurant to note. If you are the type that enjoys a good pamper as well as the racing, head for **Seaham Hall Hotel and Serenity Spa** 0191 516 1400 - it's a real stunning establishment. A good idea for a pre-race rendezvous when travelling the turf in 2005.

*Artist: **Peter Smith** IN THEIR STRIDE Courtesy of: **Frost & Reed***

The **Clerk of the Course** at Southwell is **Jon Pullin**, **David Roberts** is the **General Manager** and **Adam Grey** the **Marketing Manager**. They can be contacted at **Southwell Racecourse, Rolleston, Newark, Nottinghamshire NG25 OTS, tel: 0870 220 2332, fax: 0870 220 0144, E-mail:** _adam@southwellracecourse.fsnet. co.uk_ **Website:** _www.southwell-racecourse.co.uk_

The racecourse itself has a splendidly scenic setting. A Midlands track, it is situated just outside the Nottinghamshire village of Rolleston some five miles from Newark and within access of various motorway routes. Westminster Abbey is some 138 miles away and the A1 is the most direct route to follow. Northbound travellers should exit for the racecourse on the A6065 and then pursue the A617. The A46, which runs from east to west, serves racegoers from those points of the compass. The A617 should be used by travellers from the north west and is convenient owing largely to its connection with the M1, junction 29. Drivers should also note the new Newark bypass. If you do not wish to travel by car, then the train is a cert. In fact, Rolleston's station is one of the most convenient racecourse stations in the land. Nottingham is on London's St Pancras line and from here one can catch a train to nearby Rolleston. Some of the Mansfield/Newark buses also stop in Rolleston a quarter of a mile from the course. As one would expect with such a rural track, there are plenty of parking areas in the fields around which are free. Helicopters may land in the centre of the course, subject to prior agreement.

With 75 meetings a year, on the all-weather and over the sticks, Southwell is one of the busiest racecourses in the country. Admission to the course is £15 for Daily Members and £8 for Tattersalls. OAP's may get in to Tatts for £6 or the Members' for £13 if they join the Diamond Club for which there is a £2.50 administration charge. The cost of Annual Membership at Southwell is £225 for a single and £350 for a double badge. Membership includes parking, many reciprocal meetings at other courses and the use of the Queen Mother's Restaurant, Paddock viewing balcony and Members Bar and Restaurant. If you live in this part of the country and wish to go racing regularly this is real value. The racecourse offers attractive discounts to Tattersalls according to the size of your party—contact the racecourse management for details. For groups of 15-25 Members badges are £13.50 each, and over 25, £12. For Tatts, badges are £7 for each member of a group of 15-25, and £6 if there are more in the party.

Hospitality boxes at Southwell can accommodate parties from 10 to 50 people. Each will overlook the track and adjoin the Members Suite that can host up to 250 people. Other details to be noted when considering a day's outing at Southwell children under 16 are admitted free if they are accompanied by an adult. If the racing does not grip them then they will be delighted to hear that there is a play area available at no cost. There are two telephones in the Tote hall and one in the Members Bar and Weighing Room. Facilities for the disabled are good. Both floors are purpose built with lavatories, a lift and viewing platform. There is a Tote and Ladbrokes betting shop in the Grandstand too.

Southwell is part of the Arena Leisure group of racecourses and has done much to improve and upgrade its facilities and the course itself over the years. A steady diet of racing on the all weather might not appeal to everyone, but the competition is lively and in the depths of winter can be the only game around.

Artist: **Peter Smith FINAL BEND** _Courtesy of:_ **Frost & Reed**

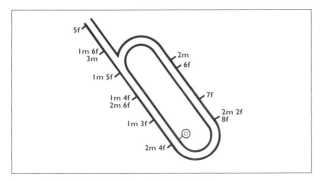

Local favourites

The **Saracen's Head Hotel** (01636) 812701 is the ideal starting point for visitors to Southwell racecourse. The inn dates from the 16th century and its Stuart heritage is displayed in many paintings. Somewhat further afield, **George Hotel of Stamford** (01780) 750750 at Stamford is a magnificent old coaching inn whilst the **Cavendish Hotel** (01246) 582311 occupies a superb setting in the grounds of Chatsworth and has a fine restaurant, with venison a speciality. In Stamford, a super old market town, note the **Lord Burghley** (01780) 763426—a lively pub renowned for its fine ales. Other places to stay include the **Bull and Swan Inn** (01780) 763558 and the **Crown Hotel** (01780) 763136—both are marvellous old inns and make for a pleasant place to stay. For those heading south, the **Ram Jam Inn** (01780) 410776 on the A1 at Stretton is convenient and well recommended as a good stopping place. The **Black Swan** (01636) 626474, is a really good restaurant in Beckingham. The **Square & Compass** in Normanton on Trent is a good pub to remember. Caunton offers the **Caunton Beck** (01636) 636793—good food here.

The **French Horn** (01636) 812394 at Upton, is certainly worth visiting for its good value, quality, pub food and is especially convenient for Rolleston and the racecourse. In Maplebeck, a little further north, the **Beehive Inn** (01636) 636306 is worth a visit despite, or perhaps because, it is a little out of the way in the Nottinghamshire countryside. Travelling in the same direction, the medieval village of Laxton offers the hospitable **Moorgate Farmhouse** (01777) 870274 and the **Dovecote Inn** (01777) 871586 is a friendly place to visit. In Marston, the **Thorold Arms** (01400) 250899, convenient for A1 travellers and for **Marston Hall**, offers a particularly good drop of ale and nice bar meals. In Bottesford, due north of Belvoir Castle, one finds an excellent and intimate restaurant—the **Peacock** at Redmile (01949) 842554. Other than Belvoir Castle itself, Newstead Abbey is a sight worth seeing home of the poet, the sixth Lord Byron, housing numerous personal articles; the gardens too are ideal for a diversion for the less than enthusiastic racing partner. Golfers might care to note the **De Vere Belton Woods** (01476) 593200—a large hotel with good leisure facilities. **Harry's Place** (01476) 561780 at Great Gonerby is top of the handicap in the restaurant stakes—first class. South of Southwell at Lowdham, the **Unicorn** (0115) 966 3612 is a comfortable place in which to stay, as is **Langar Hall** in Langar (01949) 60559, where the dining is really excellent, whilst Southwell's **Racecourse Hotel** (01636) 814481 is excellent value. The **Full Moon Inn** (01636) 830251 just one mile from the racecourse is also a newcomer of note. We also recommend a local favourite; the **Old Forge** at Southwell (01636) 812809. Bed and Breakfast may be had at **Racecourse Farm** (01636) 812176, a five minute walk from the course and finally **Café Bleu** (01636) 610141 in Newark is an excellent eaterie all year round..

*Artist: **Elizabeth Sharp** DIRT TRACK Courtesy of: **The Artist***

Racecourse **Manager** and **Clerk of the Course** at Stratford is **Stephen Lambert**, ably assisted by **Ilona Barnett**. They can be contacted at: **Stratford-on-Avon Racecourse, Luddington Road, Stratford-on-Avon CV37 9SE, tel: (01789) 267949, fax: (01789) 415850, E-mail:** _info@stratfordraceoucrse.net_ **Website:** _www.stratfordrace course.net_

Stratford is fairly easy to reach from all directions and the racecourse lies one mile south west of the town. Access is via the M40 (Warwick turn off) from the north. From other directions, the M5, M42 and M6 are all within a half hour's drive of the course. The new Stratford bypass is handy and there are AA signs to the racecourse to further assist on racedays. If you wish to travel by train from London then you should aim for Stratford-upon-Avon from Euston changing at Coventry, or Paddington changing at Leamington Spa. There is no bus directly from the station to the course but buses from the town heading to Evesham do pass the entrance to Luddington Road. There is ample parking at Stratford with a large free car park. A charge of £2 is made for cars parking in the main car park in the centre of the course from which you can access the new exit route from the racecourse. Members park separately. There are also good facilities for coaches but limited scope for helicopters, so please arrange with the racecourse in advance.

In 2004 there were 15 fixtures, all between March and October, including the popular Monday Irish Day March which precedes the Cheltenham festival, drawing a good crowd; and four Sunday meetings in June and July and a

Countryside Day in October. The major fixture remains the Intrum Justitia meeting in May which features the Horse and Hound Champion Hunter Chase and is now a two day (Friday and Saturday evening) festival. Annual Membership badges cost £125 with an extra £10 required for an annual car park badge. Senior and Junior membership is also available at a reasonable £65. You can save on all annual memberships if they are purchased before March 1st. Daily Membership is now £16. Entrance to Tattersalls is £12, whereas the Course Enclosure costs £6. If you are planning a party, 15 is the minimum required for a 20 per cent reduction. For further details, contact the Manager. Children under 16 are welcomed at no charge. Disabled people are admitted to Tattersalls for £5.

Stratford has plenty of facilities in the way of boxes, conference areas and function rooms. There is an Owners and Trainers viewing gallery right next to the Owners and Trainers room. The Avon Suite is specifically designed for corporate hospitality, catering for up to 90 people. Requests for these facilities should be directed to the racecourse management.

Since it was opened a few years ago, the glass-fronted grandstand provides a fine view of the course and comfortable facilities. Members have a champagne/seafood bar, tea room, Tote and betting shop, while Tatts patrons benefit from a snack bar, Totesport betting shop and bar. Meals before and during racing are available from the Paddock Suite Restaurant in the Club Enclosure and the Winning Post Restaurant in Tattersalls. To reserve a table phone ahead on (01785) 252247 for the Paddock Suite

Artist: **Nikki Moore RACING** Courtesy of: **The Artist**

and (01785) 342234 for the Winning Post. There are some amenities for disabled racegoers for whom a small stand is provided, with excellent viewing. Telephones are located in the Members' Enclosure and Tattersalls but there is no bank at the course so bring plenty of readies with you.

Stratford racecourse is a quite a tight track but attracts some very good national hunt horses. There are all manner of reasons for going racing: a day in the fresh air, a rendezvous with friends, a tilt at the ring or, if you are lucky, to watch your own horse run. Stratford does not profess to being Britain's foremost racecourse but it provides good racing in a convenient location and a visit should be considered in 2005.

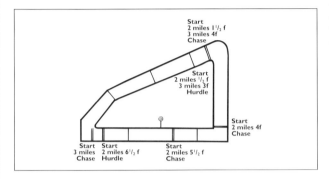

Local favourites

The first production of _A Midsummer Night's Dream_ apparently took place in the grounds of **Alveston Manor** (0870) 400 8181. The house retains much of its Elizabethan charm and is a relaxing place to stay. A Georgian hotel convenient for the theatre is **Caterham House** (01789) 267309, less expensive and with an excellent restaurant. Other hotels to note include **The Stratford Manor** (01789) 731173, **The Stratford Victoria** (01789) 271000 and the **Shakespeare** (0870) 400 8182, which also boasts above average food. A really characterful hotel, if that's your fancy, is the Grade 1 **Salford Hall** (01386) 871300 in Abbots Salford - a really pleasant place to spend a night or two. Back in town the **White Swan** (01789) 297022 and **The Falcon** (01789) 299953 are others for the short list - or perhaps that should be long list. On the Warwick road the **Welcombe Hotel** (01789) 295252 is also well thought of, boasting 18 holes of golf, some delightful rooms and a first class restaurant. Pride of place goes to **Ettington Park** (01789) 450123 in nearby Alderminster. The hotel is magnificent, the bedrooms are charmingly furnished and the bars and library comfortable and relaxing. In Ettington itself, the **Chase Hotel** (01789) 740000 is good value with an excellent restaurant. The racecourse management recommend Ettington Park and The Houndshill (see below). Among the wealth of guesthouses that form an equally important part of Stratford's accommodation industry, **Broad Marston Manor** (01789) 720252 is recommended. Another hotel of acclaim outside Stratford-upon-Avon—the **Billesley Manor** (01789) 279955, is a lovely gabled manor house. Those seeking fine fare might consider **Calland's** (01789) 269304, very good, as is the Indian **Hussains** (01789) 267506.

People who prefer a day out without an overnight stay might wish to sample any one of a number of pubs. In Wellesbourne, the **King's Head Hotel** (01789) 840206 is good for lunch and the National Trust's **Charlecote Park**

(01789) 470277 is a superb Elizabethan mansion which lies close by and can be viewed between April and October. The **Butcher's Arms Restaurant** (01327) 260504 at Priors Hardwick, more of a restaurant than a pub, is handy for the A41 while the A34 reveals the **White Hart** (01789) 450205 at Newbold-on-Stour, an excellent place to have a bar snack. In Oxhill, the **Peacock** (01295) 688060 is an extremely hospitable village pub as is the **Royal Oak** (01295) 680319 in Whatcote. Traditionalists will enjoy the **King's Head** (01789) 488242 at Aston Cantlow, another tremendously atmospheric pub. A strong local rating is given to the Howard Arms, Ilmington (01608) 682226 apparently it's tremendous. If you are keen to enjoy the Cotswolds after the Stratford steeds then a reasonably priced and extremely relaxing hotel to visit is the **Three Ways House** (01386) 438429 at Mickleton—the restaurant is also quietly civilised with a fine wine list. In Chipping Campden, two establishments worthy of note are the **Cotswold House Hotel** (01386) 840330 and its restaurant and the **Noel Arms** (01386) 840317. The **Fox & Goose Inn** (01608) 682293 at Armscote comes hightly recommended with its excellent food, service and dècor. Finally, close by at Charingworth, **Charingworth Manor** (01386) 593555 provides accommodation and service of the highest standard, while the **Houndshill House** (01789) 740267 is a pleasant inn on the A422 and an ideal place to stay. Finally, in Evesham both **Wood Norton Hall** (01388) 425780 and the **Riverside** (01386) 446200 are ideal selections - also handy for racing at Cheltenham.

Artist: **_Charles Church AT THE RACES_** _Courtesy of:_ **_The Artist_**

Managing Director **John Hills** and **Clerk of the Course Michael Trickey** can be contacted via the course at **Orchard Portman, Taunton, Somerset TA3 7BL,** tel: **(01823) 337172,** fax: **(01823) 325881,** website: *www.tauntonracecourse.co.uk.* This is very much a course for the locals, but if you are planning a trip to the southwest this year it is a delightful part of the country and made even better by having a racecourse to visit.

Taunton is 100 minutes from London on a fast train with a direct service from Plymouth and has good connections from the North and Midlands. You can settle most comfortably into a Pullman seat on the train from Paddington. The course is situated close to the M5, 50 minutes south of the M4 intersection, while the A303 is fast achieving near motorway status as a major trunk route giving access from the south coast. Why not travel the day before racing and spend the night in a local hostelry?

All of Taunton's national hunt fixtures are weekday affairs. Buy your day badge and a plentiful supply of Tote vouchers in advance from the racecourse secretary and you won't need to worry about living it up overnight in the Cider County. Admission to the Portman Grandstand will cost you £14, or £10 for Tattersalls. You can save a few pounds if you go with a group, but you must buy the badges in advance. Annual Badges here cost £175 for a double badge and £105 single and include reciprocal days at other racecourses. Cars are free—unless they go onto the centre of the course as the base for a family picnic or portable grandstand, in which case have £3 handy.

Those who know Taunton well are delighted by the new Winners Enclosure which has been returned to the Parade Ring, giving the dedicated punter a much improved view of the horses before and after the race.

When the weather is wet and the wind keen, the Saddle Room on the ground floor of the Paddock Stand is an ideal place to have tea, coffee and a snack while you put your feet up and study the form. Catering is now 'in-house' at Taunton and very popular it is too! You can choose from the 'Racegoers Special' - a two or three-course quick service lunch in the Orchard Restaurant, or you can really indulge yourself and book a table in the restaurant with a birds-eye view of the course. The latter will cost you £36.50 for an all-day table with a three-course lunch, afternoon tea, complimentary racecard and tea and coffee service throughout the day. Admission is also included at a special discounted rate. These tables are popular though, so please book early. There is also a new Paddock Stand that is situated next to the Parade Ring and enjoys a fine view of the course. This houses a first-class Owners & Trainers bar on the ground floor with additional bars and eating areas on the next two floors which are shared with annual Members and their guests.

You may enjoy your day at Taunton so much that you decide to become an Annual Member. They charge £90 for a single membership and £150 double for a Gentleman and Lady. This will give you 13 days racing at Taunton between the end of October and mid April, plus another 14 at other courses around the country including Newbury, Cheltenham, Chepstow and Wincanton.

The course betting shop is run by Peter Jolliffe. This and the Tote betting shops are in Tattersalls, together with two public telephones for credit punters. There is a raised viewing platform for wheelchair users and disabled toilets in the Orchard and Paddock

*Artist: **David Trundley** TAUNTON, EVENING MEETING Courtesy of: **The Artist***

stands as well as in the centre course bar. Managing Director John Hills is a man who clearly loves his racing—if you love yours, take a trip to Taunton and you won't be disappointed.

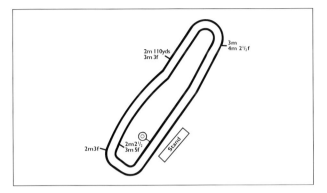

Local favourites

In the town itself, the **Castle Hotel** (01823) 272671 on Castle Green is excellent in every way. **The Corner House** (01823) 284683 is a less expensive, but thoroughly relaxing alternative. One mile outside the town at Bishop's Hull lies the outstanding (and outstandingly reasonable) **Meryan House Hotel** (01823) 337445. Also south of the town is **Rumwell Manor Hotel** (01823) 461902 a quietly elegant hotel set in five acres of parkland. The city centre is changing nearly every day but restaurants are a little thin on the ground although **Brazz** (01823) 252000 is an enjoyable establishment. Some of the many pubs in the area are obviously good places to meet for a post-race beverage. **The Carved Angel Café** (01823) 352033 is another relaxing choice. In Staple Fitzpaine, close to the racecourse, the **Greyhound** (01823) 480227 is a splendid

little pub serving an excellent pint and good bar snacks. It also has an adjoining restaurant, a fine place for post-race dinner. The **Volunteer Inn** (01460) 240126 at Seavington St Michael is a good place both for its cooking and for that extraordinary stuff, Scrumpy. Another good value food pub is the **Square and Compass** (01823) 480467 in Ashill. The **Rose and Crown** (01823) 698235 at East Lyng is also good. Breaking momentarily from the pub scene, it is well worth seeking out **Farthings Country House Hotel** (01823) 480664 at Hatch Beauchamp—an attractive Georgian house convenient for the racecourse. **Nightingales** (01833) 480806 is a well thought of restaurant to consider here. The **Mount Somerset Hotel** (01823) 442500 in Henlade is also well worth a pre race inspection. It's an elegant country house with outstanding cooking - a real gem.

Many people racing at Taunton are locals just out for a quick day's sport. If, however, you have made a bit of an effort to go to Taunton races, then one great place to reward yourself is the excellent **Bindon Country House Hotel** (01823) 400070–it's a delightful establishment full of character and charm. It's also handy for those of you planning to have a horse with the Master of his Craft: Martin Pipe. Towards the delights of the coast, one charming hotel to consider is the **White House Hotel** (01984) 632306 in Williton - great food, great atmosphere. Two splendid pubs are the **Rising Sun Inn** (01823) 432575 in Bagborough, which is especially good for those who enjoy fish, and the **Rose and Crown** (01823) 490296 at Stoke St Gregory, which is an outstanding establishment and very welcoming (some good value rooms here - ask for the cottage rooms). Further north in Nether Stowey lies the **Apple Tree Hotel** (01278) 733238—highly recommended. Take a trip this year to the south west—it's a delightful part of the country. One for the diary in 2005.

Artist: **Graham Isom TAUNTON RACECOURSE** *Courtesy of:* **Rosenstiel's**

Christopher Tetley acts as **Clerk of the Course**, **Manager** and **Secretary**, and **Gaynor Garrity** is **Sponsorship** and **Marketing Manager**. Both can be contacted at **Thirsk Racecourse, Station Road, Thirsk, North Yorkshire YO7 1QL tel: (01845) 522276, fax: (01845) 525353, website:** *www.thirskracecourse.net* **e-mail:** *info@thirskraces.fastnet.co.uk*

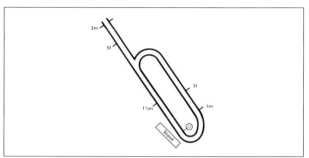

*Artist: **John Atkins RAIN AT MIDDLEHAM** Courtesy of: **The Artist***

The racecourse is situated just off the A61 west of Thirsk. The best route for travellers from the south is to use the A1/A1M northbound and then follow the A61, or the A19 if journeying from York. Southbound drivers should also use the A1, or alternatively the A61 or A19. If travelling from the east, the A170 is convenient whilst eastbound journeyers should take the M62 and the A1 north. There is ample car parking to be found on arriving. If you wish to travel by train, the King's Cross line is pretty swift and Thirsk station is a mere six furlongs away from the course, although you will need to change trains en route. Buses to Thirsk will take you to within a quick canter of the track but there are no special race buses. One other point that should be noted is that there are facilities for helicopters if you're lucky enough to have one but they must be pre-booked with the course.

*Artist: **Martin Williams AT THE START** Courtesy of: **The Artist***

There are 15 days of flat racing at Thirsk and the course enjoys many weekend fixtures. The area around abounds with training facilities and it is no wonder that many races attract large fields. Highlight of the year is the Thirsk Classic Trial, the oldest 1,000 Guineas trial in the country. The course itself is pretty tight and it is not difficult to get close to the action.

There are three enclosures at Thirsk: the Members, Tattersalls and the Family Ring. In 2004, prices were £15, £10 (£5 for OAPs) and £3 (£2 for OAPs). Party bookings are encouraged and must be booked in advance to obtain discounts. This largely depends on your ability to gather 10 or more troops to the fray. Basically, the more the merrier. However, these party terms do not apply to the Members Enclosure. In 2004, annual single Membership cost £120, whilst Associate Membership cost £200—this apparently means a membership plus another member of the family. Annual Members are also entitled to 14 reciprocal days at other northern racecourses and 11 free days at Yorkshire County Cricket Club plus discounts at various hotels and restaurants. Juniors are welcomed and the Annual Membership subscription is good value at £65. On all days cars can be parked beside the course in the Family Ring where you can enjoy a picnic and there is childrens entertainment on Saturdays and during school holidays.

The racecourse rests at the foot of the Hambleton Hills and has an excellent setting, subject naturally to the weather. There are several snack bars around the course and a more substantial restaurant can be found in the Members Stand. The Grimthorpe Hall in Tattersalls combines bars, a tea bar, fast food outlets and Tote facilities. Bookings for lunch should be made through Craven Gilpin & Sons in Leeds (0113) 287 6387.

Thirsk is improving all the time and the latest facility to be upgraded is the building for Owners and Trainers, situated between the pre-parade and main parade ring. The management are rightly proud of it and consider it to be one of the best in the country!

Bars in both the Members and Tattersalls have also been improved and the Manton Suite has hospitality facilities available. Tables for 10 or larger parties can be reserved in advance at an all inclusive price. If you wish to have a picnic then the racecourse welcomes this and if you want to order a viewing box overlooking the winning post, this can also be arranged–there is a choice of five and they can hold from ten to twenty people. Prices range from £250 to £425. Speaking of the winning post, the marquee site overlooking the finish is proving very popular as it's merely a horse's hair from the action. However, sponsors are given first option on the marquee before other parties.

If you do not get in here, don't despair, there are other marquees situated in the garden area around the parade ring. The Manton Suite offers accommodation for parties of 120 at a price tailor-made to suit the individual client or at a fixed price. For larger functions there is an ideal place near the Paddock for a marquee and a function room for Members overlooking the lawns and Parade Ring, catering for parties of 50-100. Individual tables can be reserved for the whole day. Again, arrangements and bookings can be made through the racecourse. This is a friendly racecourse in a beautiful part of England—well worth a visit.

Artist: **Margaret Barrett CLASS AND COURAGE** Courtesy of: **The Artist**

Local favourites

In Thirsk itself, the **Golden Fleece** (01845) 523108 is a convenient place to stay. The hotel is an old coaching inn and it faces onto a cobbled market square. Just outside the town is the small but cosy **Oswalds** (01845) 523655. **The Angel** at Topcliffe (01845) 577237 is another to consider. Climbing into the Hambleton Hills one arrives at Helmsley. Here, there is a number of good hotels, pubs and another scenic market place. This is an ideal base for exploring the nearby Dales and two sights that should definitely be seen are the ruins of Rievaulx and Byland Abbey. The **Black Swan** (0870) 400 8112 is extremely comfortable with a fine restaurant. A similar accolade befits the really excellent **Feversham Arms** (01439) 770766 it has great food, real character and is a real favourite.

Artist: **Karen Davies HANDS AND HEELS** Courtesy of: **The Artist**

Artist: **Harry Matthews HELL FOR LEATHER** Courtesy of: **The Artist**

Another good spot is the **Fauconberg Arms** (01347) 868214 in Coxwold, a first class pub popular locally (always a good sign) with some good bedrooms. In Harome the **Pheasant** (01439) 771241, a pleasant hotel, provides good accommodation in relaxing surroundings and **The Star Inn** (01439) 770397 is also excellent—one of the finest establishments in this book! The cuisine here is legendary. In Kirkbymoorside, the **George & Dragon** (01751) 433334 is excellent for a bar snack and some cosy bedrooms make it an ideal place to stay.

The **Plough Inn** (01751) 4731515 in Fadmoor is first class. Other good restaurants can be found near Northallerton. In nearby Staddlebridge, an outstanding restaurant is **McCoys Bistro** (01609) 882671. An evening here will be one to remember. In Pickhill, the appropriately named **Nags Head Inn** (01845) 567391 is a favourite—good food and some pleasant accommodation. The **Bay Horse Inn** (01845) 577307 in Rainton and the **Fox and Hounds** (01845) 567433 in Carthorpe are also very popular. Another interesting alternative is the excellent **Solberge Hall** (01609) 779191 in Newby Wiske, a really appealing place with delightful views of the moors. A little further afield, but extremely conveniently situated for the A1 is the **Crown Hotel** (01423) 322328 in Boroughbridge. Those who enjoy a really first class inn should sample the delights of the **Worsley Arms Hotel** at Hovingham (01653) 628234–an excellent establishment. Further afield and deep into the heart of Yorkshire racing country we arrive at Malton. Here there are a number of suggestions. **Burythorpe House** (01635) 658200 is a charming hotel with excellent food. The **Green Man** (01635) 600370 and the **Talbot** (01635) 694031 are both long established favourites.

Other selections in this excellent field—all within five miles of the course—include the **Crab and Lobster** (01845) 577286 at Asenby—extremely popular and rightly so—make sure you get there early. Crab Manor, contactable on the same number is a really fun hotel—order a brochure and you will see why! The **Carpenters Arms** (01845) 537369 at Felixkirk and the **Whitestonecliffe Inn** (01845) 597271 in Sutton under Whitestonecliffe are also good. The **Swinton Park Hotel** (01765) 680900 at Masham is well regarded. Slightly further afield, in Kilburn, is the **Forresters Arms** (01347) 868386. Kilburn is the home of the famous 'Mouse Man' furniture maker. Finally, we come to the **George and Dragon**, Melmerby, (01765) 640970. This is a small inn located between Thirsk and Ripon—ideally placed for two of Yorkshire's excellent racetracks.

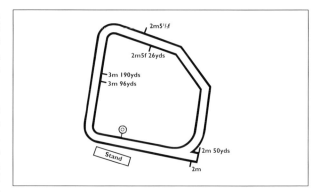

Chris Palmer is the **Chief Executive** at Towcester, while **Kevin Ackerman** is the **General Manager** and **Paul Robinson** the **Operations Manager**. Contact can be made by writing to **Towcester Racecourse, Easton Neston, Towcester, Northants NN12 7HS, tel: (01327) 353414, fax: (01327) 358534, website:** *www.towcester-racecourse.co.uk*

The racecourse itself is situated one mile south east of the town of Towcester which lies at the intersection of the A43 and the A5. Although the course itself has a tranquil setting, the M1 is only a few miles away. People travelling from both the north and south should get on to the M1 and exit at junction 15a. The A43 towards Oxford should be followed for some six miles until the junction with the A5. From the town centre, follow the signs for the racecourse.

The major train routes leave Euston and racegoers are advised to go either to Milton Keynes or Northampton. The former is some eleven miles away and the latter nine. Bus services run from Northampton but only as far as Towcester, half a mile short of the racecourse. A better bet would be to take a helicopter, but make arrangements with the racecourse beforehand by calling Paul Robinson (Mobile: 07801 019157). There is ample free parking space.

During the 2004/5 season there will be a total of 19 fixtures from October to May including three Sunday fixtures. The bank holiday meetings at Easter and in early May are always popular. After the main stand burned down in 2002, Towcester took the brave and unprecedented step of making admission to the course free to all comers. This bold move has paid off handsomely in attendance and the course attracts thousands of punters at each meeting.

Towcester provides lots of entertainment for evening, Easter and bank holiday meetings and this has obviously paid dividends too.

The Grace Stand includes a 150 seater restaurant and six private boxes with lifts to all floors for the disabled. If you prefer more exclusive comfort, there is the Paddock Pavilion, which can cater for groups from 20 to 250. Alternatively you could have a marquee beside the Grace Stand, or hire one of the corporate hospitality boxes. Prices start from £60 per head. The new £5.5 million Grandstand is due to be completed in the spring of 2005 and will round out other course developments that have taken place since the fire destroyed the old stand.

The racecourse has the standard telephone and betting facilities but there are no banking facilities available. Towcester has much to commend it, not least its marvellous setting. It is surely one of the most charming country

Artist: **Margaret Barrett WASHING DOWN** *Courtesy of:* **The Artist**

courses in Britain. It is no surprise that many rate this unassuming course as one of the country's most appealing. A visit for 2005 is an absolute priority.

Local favourites

If you should wish to make a weekend trip to Towcester then the following hotels are to be noted. In Northampton, the **Northampton Moat House** (01604) 739988 is good. Another to remember is the **Northampton Marriott** (0870) 400 7252. The hotel is modern in design but luxurious and the leisure facilities are good. The Racecourse has links with the **Hilton Northampton** (01604) 700666 and the **Saracen's Head** (01327) 350414 in Towcester itself and if you mention you are visiting for the races you can get a special rate. Also, opposite the racecourse is **The Folly** (01327) 350275, which has recently been refurbished and offers quality food. In fact Towcester, a pleasant town, offers a number of good pubs to visit before and after racing. One really convenient port of call for fine fodder is the **Vine House Restaurant** (01327) 811267 - an excellent characterful establishment.

The **Farthingstone Hotel, Golf & Leisure Centre** (01327) 361291 is well placed for the racecourse and is very comfortable. The **Plough** (01327) 350738, on the road out of Towcester, is well worth a post-race quickie and the **Brave Old Oak** (01327) 358255 also merits your attention. In Stoke Bruerne a canal-side stop-off reveals the **Boat Inn** (01604) 862428. The pub itself has a fairly modern interior but the welcome is genuine as is the restaurant—a sound each-way chance. **Bruerne's Lock** (01604) 863654 with its canal-side setting is also reported to be good. One for the lover of motor sports is **Whittlebury Hall** (01327) 857857 in nearby Whittlebury. It's lavishly appointed and has an F1 feel. Another sport can be enjoyed at another hotel handy for Towcester - this time **Hellidon Lakes Hotel and Country Club** (01327) 262550. On this occasion it's golf but it has

many other leisure pursuits as well. Another classic for the notebook is **Fawsley Hall** (01327) 892000–it's a wonderful hotel with exceptional charm–definitely one for that special occasion.

Only six miles from Towcester lies Roade. The aptly named **Roade House Restaurant** (01604) 863372 has a pleasant situation in the village which is only two miles from junction 15 of the motorway. There are rooms here as well. In Horton, **The New French Partridge** (01604) 870033 is an outstanding restaurant. After a cold afternoon's racing, there could be nothing better than sitting down to some quite superb game—a really first class idea. The **Vine House Hotel and Restaurant** (01327) 811267 at Towcester also offers excellent cooking and some pleasing bedrooms, definitely one for the Towcester visitor. **Broomhill Country House Hotel** (01604) 845959 at Spratton also is worthy of inspection. There are several pubs which have appeal: in Akeley, the **Bull and Butcher** (01280) 860257 is friendly and offers superb steaks, in Brackley Hatch, the **Green Man** (01280) 850209 may be inspected. North of Towcester, the **Red Lion** (01604) 770223 at East Haddon offers good bar food, good beer and some pleasant accommodation. In Buckingham, **Villiers** (01280) 822444 is highly regarded for food and accommodation. For those keen on having an outstanding weekend, two somewhat distant thoughts. **Hartwell House** (01296) 747444 is the first—seeing is believing—a classic country house hotel located near Aylesbury. Alternatively, Woburn is a pleasant town where **Woburn Abbey** (01525) 290666 warrants a look, whilst other places to visit include the **The Inn at Woburn** (01525) 290441, an elegant inn and **Paris House** (01525) 290692—a marvellous restaurant with racing connections. Finally, **The Birch** (01525) 290295 is a civilised place to enjoy a pint with bar snack or more formal fare. Finally, a real gem for 2005 is the **Crooked Billet** (01908) 373936–a really great 'gastropub' to spend your ill gotten gains.

*Artist: **Graham Isom** TURNING FOR HOME Courtesy of: **Rosenstiel's***

*Artist: **Graham Isom END OF THE RACE** Courtesy of: **Rosenstiel's***

Uttoxeter has **Julie Harrington** as the **Racecourse Manager** while **Keith Ottesen** is the **Clerk of the Course**. They may be contacted at **Uttoxeter Racecourse, Wood Lane, Uttoxeter, Staffordshire ST14 8BD, tel: (01889) 562561, fax: (01889) 562786, e-mail:** *info@uttoxeter-racecourse.co.uk* **website:** *www.uttoxeter-racecourse.co.uk* Uttoxeter is part of the Northern Racing Group of racecourses, headed up by **Managing Director, Rod Street**.

Uttoxeter is conveniently situated in the heart of the Midlands, equidistant from Stoke-on-Trent and Derby, just off the new A50, which has made the course even more accessible. London is 135 miles away to the south east. The course is a short hop from the town centre, just off the B5017 and is clearly signposted from the A50, A515 and A518. From the north or south of the country, the M6 is the motorway to aim for. Exit at junction 14 and then use the Stafford ring road or take junction 15 and follow the signs for the A50 to Derby. The new M40/M42 link is also a possibility if you do not wish to tackle the M1/M6 combination. All parking at the course is free and there is plenty available.

For those who prefer to travel by train, Uttoxeter Railway Station is right next door—you can walk off the platform straight onto the racecourse. Frequent Intercity services from Birmingham, Glasgow, Liverpool and Manchester run to Derby and Stoke-on-Trent, both of which run regular connecting trains to Uttoxeter. A direct service also operates from Crewe. By air, helicopters may land (by prior arrangement with the management) at the course itself, whilst light aircraft may use Tatenhill Airfield at Needwood, seven miles from the racecourse. Telephone Tatenhill Aviation on (01283) 575283.

Uttoxeter enjoys an attendance of up to 15,000 on busy days and is surely a shining example of what can be achieved in all-round excellence at the races. Uttoxeter has been named "Best Regional Racecourse" for years, as well as the most "Owner Friendly". Prize money each year runs over £1,000,000 and this has played a large part in attracting the best horses for competitive jump racing. The course received our Travelling the Turf Racecourse of the Year Award 2001.

Admission prices at Uttoxeter for 2005 are £18 for the Premier Enclosure, £14 for Grandstand & Paddock and £6 for the Centre course (a great place to picnic or bring your own barbecue). On Midlands Grand National day in March, prices rise to £25, £20 and £10 respectively for this rich marathon event. There are discounts for pensioners and under 16s are admitted free when accompanied by an adult. Annual Membership is excellent value at £195 for a single badge or £285 for a double badge. Juniors pay just £90, while memberships for OAP's are £160 single and £220 double. As well as 21 days at Uttoxeter, membership includes reciprocal fixtures at 28 other courses, free race programmes, entry to the Members car park and complimentary badges for guests at some meetings. Outstanding racing value for the enthusiast. Tickets and annual membership can now be purchased online from Uttoxeter's website.

Uttoxeter is an ideal place for corporate hospitality and the immaculate facilities at the progressive racecourse provide a setting in which companies can entertain in either a formal or informal manner. Sixty-five rooms and boxes are available for parties of between 15 and 1000 guests. There are also five corporate hospitality boxes in chalets overlooking the parade ring and winner's enclosure.

The Members restaurant, the Platinum Suite, has been refurbished to the highest standards and tables may be reserved in advance and retained throughout the meeting. Tables may also be reserved in Hoops Champagne and Seafood bar, adjacent to the Paddock.

At major meetings and on bank holidays, youngsters can enjoy a funfair and playground—an excellent way to distract the kids. There are three public telephone boxes and reserved parking on the rails for disabled racegoers as well as a viewing platform and loos.

*Artist: **Klaus Philipp NECK AND NECK** Courtesy of: **The Artist***

This is a thoroughly well-run and friendly racecourse offering fine facilities—a visit in 2005 should be a high priority.

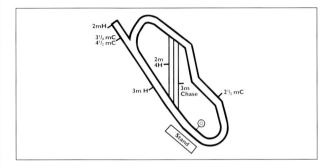

Local Favourites

South of Stoke, in Stone, **Stone House Hotel** (0870) 609 6140 is a former country house and offers some good leisure facilities. **Granvilles** (01785) 816658 is also a wine bar and restaurant to consider. In Ashbourne, note **Callow Hall** (01335) 300900—a tranquil retreat. It enjoys an idyllic setting and its restaurant is also well thought of. Elsewhere the **Hanover International Hotel and Club** (01335) 346666 is a more modern building with some good leisure facilities. In nearby Swinscoe, **The Dog and Partridge** (01335) 343183 is a fun place to visit. Meanwhile, towards Stafford, **The Moat House**, Acton Trossell (01785) 712217 is a really excellent establishment for the Uttoxeter shortlist. A similar comment could be made of the **Boars Head**, Sudbury (01283) 820344. Another really worthwhile hotel to head for, where the food is also good, is the **Izaak Walton Hotel** (01335) 350555. On the subject of restaurants, both **Bramhalls** (01335) 346158 and **The Dining Room** (01335) 300666 are also well regarded. There are many pubs hidden away in these parts and invariably they have superb views.

In Uttoxeter itself, the **White Hart** (01889) 562437 is an historic coaching inn and the bar here makes a good place to meet if you are planning to see friends before the races. Another good inn is the characterful **Ye Olde Dog and Partridge** (01283) 813030 in Tutbury. The building dates from the 15th century and the bars here are typical of this kind of inn, welcoming and refreshing. The **Mill House** (0116) 2536421 is a delightful alternative to consider. Perhaps an even more enchanting place to stay can be found in Rolleston-on-Dove. Here, the **Brookhouse Inn** (01283) 814188 has charming bars, a good restaurant and extremely pleasing bedrooms. Another superb hotel and restaurant double can be found close to here; the **Dovecliff Hall** (01283) 531818 at Stretton. If you are seeking somewhere relatively inexpensive try the **Crown** (01283) 840227 in Abbots Bromley. **The Beeches**, in Doveridge (01889) 590288 is an excellent farmhouse-style establishment offering cosy accommodation and superb meals. Finally, the **Blacksmiths Arms** (01889) 562178 in Marchington offers innovative and realistically priced cuisine in rustic country-pub surroundings and is a favourite with the management of this first rate racecourse.

Artist: **Graham Isom UTTOXETER** *Courtesy of:* **Rosenstiel's**

Nathan Corden is the **Racecourse Manager** here and **Fiona Needham** is the **Clerk of the Course**, while **Kathryn Nield** handles **Sales and Marketing**. They can all be contacted at **Warwick Racecourse, Hampton Street, Warwick CV34 6HN, tel: (01926) 491553, fax: (01926) 403223, E-mail:** _warwick@rht.net_ **Website:** _www.warwick racecourse.co.uk_

Warwick racecourse lies close to junction 15 of the M40, the A46 and the A41 and is convenient for the M1, M5 and M6, a mere eight miles from Stratford (which should be avoided in the summer) and 20 miles from Birmingham—following the M6—M42 (junction 2), thence on the A41. The A46 via Leamington Spa from the north and via Stratford from the south is most convenient. Travellers from the south and west might join the A46 from the A422, (Anne Hathaway's cottage marks the appropriate junction).

The train journey from London has been improved and there is an hourly service direct from London to Warwick and Leamington. The station is a 20 minute walk from the racecourse. There is free parking for 3,000 cars. Coaches are also welcome here. Helicopters may land in the centre of the track at Warwick by arrangement but as for light aircraft, they are somewhat unwelcomingly sent to Coventry.

Racing here includes both flat racing and National Hunt meetings, as well as one mixed fixture in March, one of the few on this side of the Irish Sea. Annual Membership rates for 2004 were £120 for a full badge and £75 for a National Hunt badge. Juniors (16 to 24) are charged £50 but please also note an extra £10 is asked for a car park badge if required. A Half Yearly Membership may be purchased from June 1st at a cost of £60. In addition to racing at Warwick, full Members are entitled to reciprocal arrangements at 10 other courses. Each member is also given two vouchers which admit guests to the Club during the year. The Daily Club badge is £15 on weekends and Bank Holidays but only £11 for weekday meetings. For £6 you can enter the Course Enclosure. Accompanied children under 16 are admitted free. Discounts on a sliding scale are given for parties of 10 or more if booked in advance.

Boxes in the Paddock Suite are available on a daily basis and enjoy spectacular views which are also available from the balcony over the Paddock and racecourse. The elegant Kingmaker Suite accommodates 60 for lunch or dinner and 80 for a buffet meal. The suite may be divided into three rooms if required. The Dukes Room is opposite the winning post, offering entertaining views of the betting ring too. There are snack bars in all enclosures and two restaurants: the Paddock Bar and recently refurbished Members Bar. Booking is advisable on major racedays and can be done by telephoning the course caterers, Amadeus, on 0121 767 2543.

Disabled people are accommodated by means of a raised stand, ramps and lavatories in the Members Enclosure. While it is fair to say that no Midlands course is a major sporting venue, several provide excellent entertainment. Furthermore, Members here can enjoy a variety of racing at under £5 a head and to my mind that represents very good value.

Artist: **Graham Isom WARWICK** _Courtesy of:_ **Rosenstiel's**

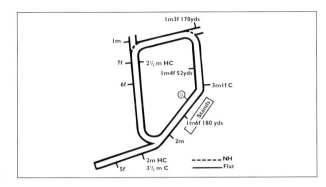

is a better than average location for a post race curry. The **Glebe** (01926) 624218 in Barford has good leisure facilities. **Walton Hall** (01789) 842424 is also a very good hotel with a good restaurant. **Haigs Hotel** (01676) 533004 is a family run hotel situated in Balsall Common. It has very strong claims for great food. The Lord Leycester (01926) 491481, which is handy for the impressive castle, is also good. A really distinguished hotel can also be found at Berkswell's **Nailcote Hall Hotel** (01247) 646 6174 - it's a realy beauty. Another popular local is the **Racehorse Inn** (01604) 631997 in Stratford Road. Kenilworth has two fancied restaurants **Simpsons** (01926) 864567 and the **Bosquet Restaurant** (01926) 852463, while Charlecote offers the **Charlecote Pheasant** 0870 609 6159–a pleasant hotel for a weekend away. The **Case is Altered** (01926) 484206 in Fiveways is delightful (no youngsters though). However, children are welcomed at another fine establishment, the **Bulls Head** at Wootton Wanen.

Further north in Claverdon a friendly place to stay is the **Ardencote Manor House** (01926) 843111, a country house with views over the Warwickshire countryside. In Sutton Coldfield, **Thistle New Hall** 0121 378 2442 offers a stylish haven in the oldest moated manor house in England while **De Vere The Belfry** (01675) 470301 just outside Sutton Coldfield, provides sumptuous comfort and excellent golf. Alternatively try the **Hilton Birmingham Metropole** 0121 780 4242. Elsewhere in Birmingham, **The Hotel du Vin and Bistro** 0121 200 0600 is a sensational townhouse in which to stay and **The Marriot** 0121 452 1144 and **The Malmaison** 0121 246 5000 is another to consider if you're staying in Britain's second city. If you fancy a curry, they're legendary at **Imran's Balti** 0121 449 1370 and **Maharaja** 0121 662 2641, but for opulence **Shimla Pinks** 0121 633 0366 is a classic; for French try **La Toque d'Or** 0121 233 3653–it's first rate. Perhaps the most outstanding place to visit in the area is **Mallory Court** (01926) 330214. Situated in Bishops Tachbrook, south of Leamington Spa, this is a picture of elegance. Bedrooms are sumptuous, while the restaurant provides exquisite French cooking. In the Parade of Leamington Spa itself, one finds a more modest, but no less welcoming hotel: the **Royal Leamington Hotel** (01926) 883777, is also worthy of consideration. **Love's Restaurant** (01926) 315522 is an elegant and accomplished place to eat and **Solo** (01926) 422422 is also extremely popular locally. We trust one of the above appeals whilst visiting Warwick in 2005.

Artist: **Malcolm Coward COMING IN** *Courtesy of:* **The Artist**

Local favourites

If you are staying nearby, a number of hotels stand out. A well thought of hotel is the **Hilton Warwick** (01926) 499555, most convenient for the A46 and the M40. By contrast, the **Old Fourpenny Shop and Hotel** (01926) 491360 is small but appealing. **Saffron** (01926) 402061

Artist: **Katy Sodeau BEND, WARWICK** *Courtesy of:* **The Artist**

Wetherby is an extremely popular racecourse and provides an excellent standard of racing. **Christopher Tetley** is **Clerk of the Course**, **Tim Betteridge** is **Chief Executive** and **Angela Anders** is in charge of **Sales & Marketing**. They can be contacted through **Wetherby Steeplechase Committee Ltd, The Racecourse, York Road, Wetherby, West Yorkshire LS22 5EJ, tel: (01937) 582035, fax: (01937) 588021. E-mail:** *info@wetherbyracing.co.uk* **Website:** *www.wetherbyracing.co.uk*

The course is one of the most accessible in the country, being close to the A1 and thereby providing an excellent route for both north and southbound vehicles. Wetherby is 200 miles from London and close to Leeds, Harrogate and York. York is about 13 miles from the racecourse and buses run there from outside the railway station. The B1224 is the most direct route from York. The M62 runs from the west of the country and it connects with the new A1/M1 link road, which finishes about five miles south of Wetherby. There is a railway station in Harrogate about nine miles away and a bus station in Wetherby which is one and a half miles from the course. The 98/99 buses run from Leeds City Bus Station to Wetherby Bus Station every half hour from Monday to Saturday. Car parking is ample and is provided free of charge.

Eighteen national hunt fixtures are due to be run here in 2005 and it is interesting that the course has plans afoot to build a turf course for flat racing during the summer. Wetherby is such an excellent venue that it deserves to have a summer racing and it is well positioned with the nearby Yorkshire training centres. Not abandoning its jumping roots, it wishes to be primarily known as a jumps course with a bit of flat racing thrown in.

Annual Membership here is good value at £140. Joint Membership for couples is also well priced at £230. There is also a Guest Membership with a transferable badge on offer for £250. The Club 16-25 Membership is only £50. Daily Premier Enclosure rates are £16, the Paddock £10 rising to £20 and £12 respectively on feature days, and the popular Course Enclosure is £4, reduced to £2 for pensioners. Cars are admitted to the centre of the course for £14 (including up to four adults). Children under 16 are admitted free if accompanied by an adult.

The Saddling-up Enclosure, Weighing Room and Administration Complex was built at a cost of £375,000. In addition, the Wetherby Millennium Stand opened in 2000 as its name suggests. Built at a cost of £4.2 million, this development forms the new Members Stand and offers 19 corporate hospitality boxes as well as state-of-the-art facilities and surroundings such as 3 new bars, a restaurant with a Parade Ring view and raised viewing for 500. Other facilities include a children's playground in the Course Enclosure, and viewing facilities close to the winning post for disabled people. There is no racecourse bank but there are public telephones and a betting shop which is located in the Paddock Enclosure.

All in all, Wetherby is a friendly racecourse. It is one of the top jumping tracks in the north and the only one of the nine Yorkshire courses devoted entirely to National Hunt racing. Although this might change with the introduction of summer flat racing, Wetherby hosts so many important jumps races that it will probably always be considered primarily a good home for jumps fans. Whatever the going or weather, we can always recommend a day at Wetherby where racing over the sticks is at its best. Be sure to visit in 2005.

Artist: **Malcolm Coward** *COMING IN Courtesy of:* **The Artist**

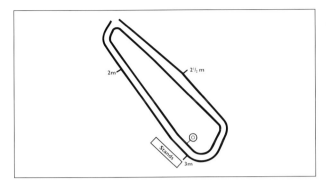

Local favourites

In West Yorkshire, there are relatively few hotels but several pubs. However, the ever more chic Leeds makes up for the lack of hotels elsewhere and a selection includes the **Malmaison** (0113) 398 1000, which is modern and comfortable. A more traditional, 1930s hotel is the **Le Meridien Metropole** (0113) 245 1841 in the city square. There are many good restaurants in Leeds but one with a definite pedigree is **Fourth Floor** (0113) 242 1010; located at Harvey Nicholls it's the ideal port of call for the non-racing type! (but has some pretty hot numbers for racegoers as well). A really well thought of Town House Hotel is **Haley's Hotel and Restaurant** (0113) 278 4446 which is beautifully tasteful and a relaxing place to stay. **Quebecs** (0113) 244 8989 is another nearby stylish establishment in which to stay. The offerings at **Pool Court at 42** (0113) 244 4242, and **Brasserie Forty Four** (0113) 234 3232, make them an excellent places in which to enjoy dinner and **Simply Heathcotes Leeds** (0113) 244 6611, from the highly successful Heathcote stable that should not disappoint, makes this a trio of excellence to challenge any. A winner in the last at nearby Wetherby and dinner in any of these would satisfy the most discerning of punters. An alternative, however, is **De Vere Oulton Hall** (0113) 282 1000, a classy performer with good leisure facilities from the De Vere stable. Other hotels of note in Leeds are the **Leeds Marriott** (0870) 400 7260 and the **Crowne Plaza** (0870) 400 9170, both of which provide top-class accommodation. Another good restaurant is **Leodis** (0113) 242 1010 which offers excellent fare.

If you can escape the city, then run to Harewood where the best known landmark in the village is Harewood House. Open from April to October, the gardens, collections of Chippendale furniture, and superb English works of art are all fascinating. Here the **Harewood Arms** (0113) 288 6566 is ideally placed and reasonable. Good public houses nearby are the **Windmill Inn** (01937) 582209 in Linton and the **White Swan** (01937) 832217 at Wighill, a marvellous country boozer with a fine collection of racing prints—a pleasant restaurant as well. Whilst we are in the vicinity of Linton, **Wood Hall** (01937) 587271 is quite outstanding. This is a converted Georgian manor which has excellent amenities. A good guest house is **Prospect House** (01937) 582428—offering a pleasant welcome to the weary (or exuberant) traveller. **Milford Lodge** (01977) 681800 is a handy prospect–the décor is contemporary in look and the food is well thought of.

There are two hotels convenient for the racecourse, The **Bridge Inn** at Walshford (01937) 580115 and the **Ramada Jarvis** (01937) 583881. A more historic option is the excellent **Hazlewood Castle** (01937) 535353—tremendous!

Much of the countryside in Yorkshire is full of mystery, none more haunting than that surrounding the former home of Emily and Charlotte Bronte. A pub that dates back to well before the birth of the sisters can be found at Bardsey, the **Bingley Arms** (01937) 572462 - a mere four miles from Wetherby - the perfect place to celebrate an historic win at the races.

Artist: **Heather St Clair Davis OUT IN THE COUNTRY** *Courtesy of:* **Frost & Reed**

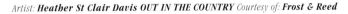

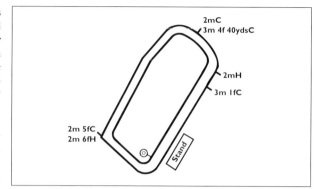

Wincanton hosts some top class National Hunt meetings and if you are going to the southwest you really should make a visit. **Stephen Higgins** is the **Racecourse Manager** here, with **Rebecca Morgan Clerk of the Course** and **Pam Will** the **Commercial Executive**. They can be contacted at **The Racecourse, Wincanton, Somerset BA9 8BJ, tel: (01963) 32344, fax: (01963) 34668.** E-mail: *wincanton@rht.net* Website: *www.wincntonracecourse.co.uk*

The course itself lies just off the A303 bypass, on the B3081 and like many racecourses on racedays is signposted by brown tourist signs as well as the yellow AA ones. If you are travelling from London, some 110 miles away, then the M4 and the M3 both trek in that westward direction. Equally satisfactory is the old A4. Wincanton itself lies on the A303. Travellers north and south should note the A357 and the A37 respectively. A public bus service winds its way to Wincanton, but the nearest railway stations are at Gillingham (six miles from the course) and Templecombe on the Waterloo line four miles away, where a free coach service will meet the London Waterloo train, or at Castle Cary on the Paddington route. There are taxis in good supply at all stations. Large car parks are available and there is no charge for parking. Finally, helicopters may land in the centre of the course by prior arrangement.

On your arrival there will inevitably be some fairly competitive racing. The Boxing Day meeting, including the Mid Season Chase and the Lord Stalbridge Gold Cup, is the most popular. Other leading races include the Jim Ford Challenge Cup and the Axminster 100 Kingwell Hurdle in late February and Elite Hurdle and Badger Chase in November. These races often attract excellent horses and local trainers use them as 'prep' events for more prestigious races later in the year.

In the 2004 season a visit to Wincanton cost £17 for the Premier Enclosure, £15 for the Grandstand and £6 for the Course Enclosure. The price of an Annual Members Badge was £140, Double £270. A car pass was also thrown in which gave you preferential parking plus reciprocal days racing at various tracks around the country including Ascot, Salisbury, Newbury, Taunton, Exeter, Bath, Sandown, Cheltenham, Kempton and Doncaster with a voucher book scheme. For those aged between 17 and 25 Junior Annual Membership was available at £65 and the Junior Club cost £7.50, although this was not available on Boxing Day. If one wished to gather a group of friends together then a 10% discount applied for parties in excess of ten and if you were taking a more substantial number then a 15% discount could be arranged. Bigger parties of 30 to 120 may wish to make use of the private rooms available. Companies or individuals wishing to take advantage of these facilities should contact the racecourse.

You may well be surprised at the excellent value you can receive entertaining at the races. The course has seven boxes which are let either daily or annually. Sited on the top floor they offer splendid views of the course. Another plan for a party at the races is to arrange for your own marquee—an area near the parade ring is ideal. If you like the idea of lunching whilst you fill out your bets, then the Members Restaurant overlooks the Paddock and should serve you well—bookings can be made through the course office. The three course lunch will cost from around £18.50. A new grandstand was completed a couple of years ago in

*Artist: **Peter Curling** TWO MILE CHASERS Courtesy of: **Rosenstiel's***

the Members Enclosure and this houses facilities for the course officials as well as corporate boxes and a restaurant as well as facilities for owners and trainers. Contact the racecourse office for catering information. Alternatively, there are the snack bars and a picnic area in the refurbished Course Enclosure. Car parking on the course costs £5 plus £5 for each occupant. This is a great way to get the best out of racing, particularly for newcomers to the sport.

16s and under are admitted free with children's entertainment and a crèche available at the April and October Sunday meetings. There are plenty of telephones and disabled viewing in the Hatherleigh Stand and Grandstand. Special discounts can be made in advance for disabled people on written application to the course. Wincanton offers exciting and competitive racing with welcoming staff who will ensure you have a happy and—hopefully—successful day at the races.

Local favourites

Wincanton is a first rate jumping track to visit and the following establishments may help stave off a winter chill after a day at the races. An excellent pub to try is the **Unicorn Inn** (01963) 32324 in Bayford, which has a pleasant atmosphere, good bar snacks and a number of bedrooms. In Hindon, one finds the **Lamb at Hindon** (01747) 820573 with some good bar food and comfortable accommodation. **The Angel Inn** (01747) 820696 is another sumptuous place to stay and also find some first class cooking. As the road diverges one has the choice of Warminster or Mere. The town of Mere houses the highly

recommended **Chetcombe House B&B** (01747) 860219 and the **Talbot Hotel** (01747) 860427. In Warminster you have an excellent proposition in the form of **Bishopstrow House** (01985) 212312, an outstanding Georgian mansion. The hotel is a delight and the restaurant is excellent. In Shepton Mallet, **Bowlish House Restaurant and Hotel** (01749) 342022 is much recommended for a pleasant evening after a successful day at Wincanton races. At Evercreech the **Pecking Mill** (01749) 830336 offers good food and some bedrooms. Nearer to Wincanton, several places should be mentioned. Bruton offers **Truffles** (01749) 812255, a restaurant of note. For those of you who enjoy a restaurant with rooms, **The Claire de Lane Restaurant** (01749) 813395 is ideal and very welcoming. The **Bull Inn** (01749) 812200 in Brewham is a hotel with good bar food. And nearby Stourton proves a worthy diversion with a Palladian mansion and superb gardens. The **Spread Eagle** (01747) 840587 is the local to note and it has some accommodation if required. In Bourtons, neighbouring Wincanton, the **Hunters Lodge Inn** (01747) 840439 is popular with racegoers. While in Holbrook, the **Holbrook House** (01963) 824466 is an ideal place to stay. Not quite so convenient, but appealing, is **The George** (01963) 350761; Castle Cary in the marketplace is also good. Nearby, a handy pub for the A30 is the **Queen's Head** (01963) 250314, at Milborne Port, which has excellent value accommodation and some good bar snacks. Our final thought for racegoers considering a visit to Wincanton is the outstanding **Charlton House Hotel and Mulberry Restaurant** (01749) 342008, a superb Georgian house which reveals an outstanding hotel and restaurant double—one to shortlist for 2003.

Artist: **Graham Isom WINCANTON** *Courtesy of:* **Rosenstiel's**

Windsor is a busy racecourse, renowned for its midsummer evening races. The **Clerk of the Course** at Windsor is **David Mackinnon** and he can be reached at the racecourse office, **Royal Windsor Races, The Racecourse, Maidenhead Road, Windsor, Berkshire SL4 5JJ, tel: (01753) 498400, fax: (01753) 830156. E-mail:** *office@windsor-racecourse.co.uk* **Website:** *www.windsor-racecourse.co.uk*

The racecourse is on the A308 between Windsor and Maidenhead. West and eastbound traffic on the M4 should leave the motorway at junction 6. The M3 traffic from the south should leave the motorway at interchange 3 and follow the A332 to Windsor. Travellers from the north and the east will find a combination of the M25, M4 and the A308 the best route. For those who might prefer a slight change from the normal mode of transportation, why not travel by river bus? The summer shuttle boat service operates from Barry Avenue Promenade close to Windsor Bridge in the town centre and takes racegoers to the racecourse jetty, close to the Paddock. The journey takes about ten minutes and there is a bar on board. For further information contact French Brothers (01753) 851900. There are frequent rail services from Waterloo and Paddington to Windsor and Eton (Riverside) and Windsor and Eton (Central) respectively, both two miles away. The Green Line bus terminus is one mile from the course. The main car parking facilities and coach park are free, although the Members car park charges £5. On another plane, helicopter landing facilities are available but permission must be sought in advance.

A few years ago Windsor gave up its jumping fixtures, but with the renovation of nearby Ascot, national hunt racing has returned for the 2004/5 season with several of the Ascot fixtures transferred here. The course hosts 29 meetings a year, including 17 on the flat on Monday evenings. These are very popular affairs with a real atmosphere and many people dash out from London to be there and enjoy the summer evening.

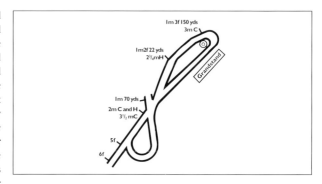

In 2004 Annual Membership Badges for Royal Windsor Race Club were priced at £195 each. This was tremendous value as it included car parking, use of the bar for Owners, Trainers and Annual Members and many reciprocal days at other courses. Daily Members badges were £18 for the Club, £12 for the Grandstand and Paddock Enclosure and £6 for the Silver Ring. The Silver Ring Picnic Area was also priced at £6 a head, plus £6 for the car. The course encourages advance bookings for the Grandstand and Paddock, for

Artist: **Klaus Philipp** *AT FULL STRETCH Courtesy of:* **The Artist**

which discounts are offered for parties and groups over 20. The executive also encourages the reservation of the Churchill Suite and private boxes in the Royal Windsor Grandstand and Paddock Pavilion, overlooking the finishing straight. Lunch and dinner can be reserved by contacting the course caterers, Letherby & Christopher (01753) 832552. The potential for company and business entertainment is particularly interesting when one considers the evening meetings. Corporate hospitality is organised by the racecourse office. It is also worth noting that children under 16 are admitted free and there are public telephones available, but no banks are in attendance as yet although cash facilities are being installed this year. Disabled people are well looked after with a special viewing stand and reserved paddock viewing. Admission for wheelchair users is free of charge, which is excellent.

All in all Windsor has great appeal. The Royal Windsor Stand, housing the Castle Restaurant and viewing boxes, is an excellent addition. We hope the investment is richly rewarded in the years to come.

Local favourites

If you do wish to stay in the immediate area then a hotel that is worthy of recommendation is **Fredrick's** (01628) 581000 on Shoppenhangers Road—the bedrooms are comfortable and the restaurant excellent. The menu changes frequently and one is treated to some splendidly imaginative cooking. A similarly outstanding hotel and restaurant double is to be found along the Windsor road—it is an absolute pearl and its name is **Oakley Court** (01753) 609988. All manner of facilities are complemented by excellent service, gracious surroundings and beautiful grounds. **Sir Christopher Wren's House Hotel** (01753) 861354 is also excellent—the **Strokes Restaurant** has a splendid setting and is definitely one to sample. A further example of good fare and good value service is **Melrose House** (01753) 865328. Two good restaurants to note are **The Bel and Dragon** (01753) 866056 in Thames Street and the excellent Moroccan **Al Fassia** (01753) 855370. **The Royal Adelaide** (01753) 863916 is a highly satisfactory place to stay. **The Monkey Island Hotel** (01628) 623400 is a really characterful establishment with highly regarded food.

In Eton, on the High Street to be precise, the **Christopher Hotel** (01753) 852359 has comfortable bedrooms and a palatable selection of real ales. This is also a good base for exploring the antique shops of Eton if this happens to be to your liking. The **Gilbey's Bar Restaurant** (01753) 854921 is also very good. Returning to Windsor, a number of suggestions arise. There are several excellent establishments that nestle beneath the magnificent castle, the **Castle Hotel** (0870) 400 8300 being a particularly notable example. Another well known landmark in Marlow is the **Compleat Angler** (01628) 484444. Its setting on the Thames is renowned as one of the most superb spots. The **Valaisan** restaurant is also outstanding and visitors can enjoy marvellous views of the river. In Taplow a superb hotel is **Taplow House** (01628) 670056—excellent comfort and once again an elegant formal restaurant—the **Tulip Tree**. Lovers of truly excellent cooking should consider **L'Ortolan** (0118) 988 3783 in Shinfield, it's excellent. Similarly The **Waterside Inn** (01628) 620691 is, on its day, up there with the best - some pleasant rooms here as well. Also consider **Cliveden** (01628) 668561 an incredible hotel with a restaurant, **Waldo's**, for those who came up trumps with a good win. The **French Horn** at Sonning (0118) 969 8727 is an outstanding restaurant and is ideal for a celebration after a big win. The **Marriott Windsor** (0870) 400 7244 is particularly well located for the racecourse.

Also in Bray you find one of the great restaurants The Fat Duck (01628) 580333: it's creative cuisine is almost unsurpassed–if food is your thing and you haven't been, it's a taste sensation. The Riverside Brasserie (01628) 780553 is a less celebrated residence–but excellent just the same. In Cookham Maliks (01628) 520085 is a superb choice for lovers of Indian food, set in an English pub! Also in Cookham, the **Bel and Dragon** (01628) 521263 in the High Street is good—there is a fine restaurant to be found here. **Manzanois** (01628) 525775 is also a fine restaurant to visit. Elsewhere in Cookham, lovers of oriental cuisine should seek out the **Peking Inn** (01628) 520900—where booking is advisable. **The Inn on the Green** (01628) 482638 in Cookham Dean is also to be noted. The **Long Barn** (01753) 521396 in Cippenham, also offers good food and great character. In Dorney, the **Palmer Arms** (01628) 666612 is also excellent, serving really tremendous bar meals. One final thought for those who love great food, golf and a brilliant spa is to sample Stoke Park Club (01753) 717171–it's Group 1 in every way.

Artist: **Philip Toon** *TIME FOR A CHAT Courtesy of:* **The Artist**

Wolverhampton - Dunstall Park

Wolverhampton Racecourse, also known as Dunstall Park, is one of the busiest racecourses in the country and if it's Saturday night you know they will probably be running around here under the lights. **David Roberts** is the **General Manager** and **Claudette Ebanks** the **Business Development Manager**. Enquiries should be made through **Wolverhampton Racecourse, Dunstall Park Centre, Wolverhampton WV6 0PE, tel: (0870) 2202442, fax: (0870) 2200107. E-mail:** *enquiries@dunstallpark .com* **Website:** *www.wolverhampton-racecourse.co.uk* **Restaurant bookings: (0870) 2200140.**

The course lies some 16 miles north west of Birmingham, close to Tettenhall, and the area is well served by motorways. If you are arriving from the north follow the M6 to junction 12 and thereafter the A5 west to the A449 south. Racegoers from the south should exit the M6 at junction 10a and on to the M54 to junction 2 and follow the signs to the course. Welshmen should aim for Wellington and the M54. The course is approximately 130 miles from London. The nearest railway station is in Wolverhampton—take the train from Euston and then grab a taxi for the five minute journey to the course. There is also a bus station in the town centre and buses run to the course. Free parking is provided for cars with 1,500 spaces and plenty of room for coaches. The nearest airport is Birmingham, approximately 25 miles away. Helicopters can land at the course but please contact the estate manager in advance on (07968) 016617.

Racing takes place here almost every week of the year from January to December with a staggering 84 meetings scheduled for 2005. Of course you can only do this on the dirt and a new polytrack surface will be in operation for the first time this year. As the only floodlit racecourse in Great Britain, regular Saturday evening racing makes for a superb night out, and there is a continuing growth of restaurants and style of dining to cater for the course's increasing popularity.

With so many meetings to attend, Annual Membership for the Club Enclosure at £240 is excellent value. A joint membership is £375 and you can save money on both of these if you join before the end of February. Access to the Club Enclosure is for Annual Subscribers, day members, owners, trainers, executive box holders and invited guests.

Admission to the Members on a daily basis is £15, rising to £20 on Boxing Day. Tattersalls costs £10 to get in and £12 on the day after Christmas. You can get 10 per cent off these prices if you book online. Children under 16 are allowed in free of charge. For Saturday evening meetings there is a choice of three restaurants which all offer various deals including your entry, racecard, and dinner. Contact the racecourse for prices and booking. The 400-seater tiered viewing restaurant offers panoramic views of the racetrack for all racegoers with a courier betting service available at each table.

The eight private boxes accommodate parties of 16—64 seated and up to 80 for buffets; they are let on a daily basis. Prices per person range from £52.50 + VAT for a midweek meeting to £65 for Saturdays in December. Larger function suites are also available for corporate and private hire. Packages are tailored to include hire of box, a four course meal, access to the Owners and Members lounge, admission charge and car parking. A courier betting service is also available on request. There are special facilities for disabled people with accessible parking, toilets, lifts, and easy access to ground level bars.

Wolverhampton is unique in Britain and the millions of pounds that have been invested by Arena, the multiple course operator, are beginning to pay dividends. The new polytrack surface, so successful at sister racecourse Lingfield Park, should make racing here even better. No 'kick-back' to worry about if your horse has to come from behind to win!

Artist: **Peter Smith THREE ABREAST** *Courtesy of:* **Rosenstiel's**

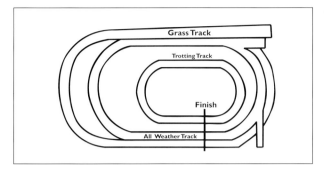

Local favourites

The most obvious recommendation is the **Holiday Inn Garden Court Hotel** at Dunstall Park **(**0870) 400 9068. The 54 rooms are all en suite with TV, telephone, tea and coffee making facilities. Accommodation is specially tailored for the punter, being linked to the main grandstand. The hotel also boasts a relaxing bar and bistro, and disabled facilities—a fitness room is available for use by hotel guests. The **Mount Coutry House Hotel** (01902) 752055 is also well worth a pre or post race inspection. Elsewhere Ely House (01902) 311311 has been well converted and is a friendly place to stay. In Himley. The **Himley Country Hotel** (01902) 896668 is also handy and worthy of consideration.

One of the best known leisure centres in the country is situated at Wishaw: the **Belfry** (01675) 470301—a whole host of pursuits can be enjoyed here aside from golf. Alternatively, you may wish to visit the **Best Western Moor Hall Hotel and Spa**, Sutton Coldfield (0121) 308 3751 which also has strong associations with the nearby golf course and is a most welcoming place to stay. Another Hall also can be found at Sutton Coldfield, **New Hall** (0121) 378 2442. This is an outstanding establishment with an inspiring setting and a fine restaurant—just two good reasons for staying there. If any or all of the above are full then another good place to try is the **Standbridge Hotel** (0121) 354 3007.

In Birmingham, one finds some very large hotels. The **Hyatt Regency** (0121) 643 1234 is extremely good and has a distinguished restaurant—**Number 282.** The same summary could be applied to the **Birmingham Marriott** (0870) 400 7280. Similarly, the **Crown Plaza Birmingham City (**0870) 400 9150 offers excellent leisure facilities. If you get a yen for Chinese food, the **Queens Cantonese** restaurant (01902) 713399 in Queen Street, Wolverhampton comes highly recommended. For a taste of something different the same applies to a local pub with Tex Mex food, the **Bentlands** (01902) 843654 which is in Suckling Green Lane, Codsall, or the **Barley Mow** who specialise in Yorkies. For a taste of Italy, try, **Cataldos** (01902) 428928.

Chaddesley Corbett also offers an establishment of distinction in **Brockencote Hall** (01562) 777876. The house, restaurant and grounds are all worth a pre-race inspection: combined they make up a great favourite. Finally, on the hotel front, another sporting hotel with great appeal is **Patshall Park** (01902) 700100, where the accent is on an excellent golf course. To complete our section on a rather bizarre note, visit the **Crooked House** (01384) 238583 an unusual establishment with good food. One final trip to consider is to Worfield and the **Old Vicarage** (01746) 716497—a delightful setting and good food...it's a cracking place if you're expecting a big win.

Artist: **Rochelle Levy** *STRETCH RUN Courtesy of:* **The Artist**

*T*he people in charge of the course at Worcester are **David Roberts**, **Arena Leisure Regional Manager**, **Fergus Cameron**, the **Clerk of the Course**, **Andrew Bourton**, the **Estate Manager**, **Jenny Cheshire**, the **Corporate Hospitality Manager** and **Katherine Smith-Maxwell**, **Operations Manager**. The course address is: **Grandstand Road, Worcester WR1 3EJ, tel: (0870) 2202772, fax: (0870) 2202882. E-mail:** *worcester-races@btconnect.com* **Website:** *www.worcester-racecourse.co.uk*

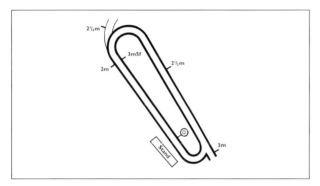

To reach the racecourse, which lies some 120 miles west of London and 20 miles from Birmingham, one might use any one of the following routes. From the west, the M5 (junction 6) and thence the A449 and the A38 provide a winning combination. The course itself rests between Broadheath and Herwick. The A58 from Birmingham provides a smooth route for racegoers from the West Midlands. The M5 (junction 7) is another route which benefits from the A38. From the Cotswolds, the A44 is a pleasant trek—the A443 is a help here. People who consider this to be the age of the train, can use it via the Paddington line. Get off at Worcester Foregate St. If the proverbial flying horse is preferred to the so-called iron horse, then phone the manager in advance who will inform you where to land your chopper. Car parking is free, except for picnic parking where a £5 charge is made.

The 2005 season should enjoy an increased fixture list with 20 meetings, all of which are summer fixtures, with some excellent evening and Wednesday afternoon meetings. A wet and windy Wednesday at Worcester may not immediately appeal but even when the elements prove uncooperative a day out can still be well worthwhile. Annual Membership was priced at £150 in 2004, to include over 70 reciprocal meetings. Members Daily Badges in 2004 were priced at £15, entrance to Tattersalls £10 and the Centre Course £5. OAPs are entitled to tickets at only £2. Something also worth noting is a discount for parties of 10 or more. You get two free tickets if you purchase 10, and four free tickets if you purchase 20. You should book in advance to obtain these prices and you may pay by credit card. Badges can be purchased from the Manager's office but must be paid for at least seven days in advance.

What sounds great fun are the riverboats moored behind the grandstand for parties from 30 to 200. The Worcester management team are clearly refusing to give in to the ravages of the Severn, and are instead harnessing its beauty for their own ends. For landlubbers there are the usual boxes and a new Members' restaurant on the top floor of the grandstand. Punters please note that the Croft Suite also has a restaurant for which reservations can be made through the racecourse office. There are improved club facilities and a corporate lawn area, with additional Tote facilities and catering concessions in the Tattersalls enclosure. Worcester has three private boxes available for hire; prices start at £64 per head plus VAT. It is clear there is plenty of scope for all sorts of additional entertainment and this is reflected in the fact that the racecourse has the support of numerous sponsors.

Other advantages of coming to Worcester are that children are admitted free before their 16th birthday. In addition, there are children's facilities during the summer. Disabled people have special viewing facilities and there is a lift to the Members' restaurant. The course betting shop

Artist: **Susan Crawford** *WE THREE CHAMPIONS Courtesy of:* **Rosenstiel's**

is located close to the grandstand so you won't have to go too far to put on an off course bet. Make no mistake, this is a delightful racetrack—its facilities are good and a day's racing here is to be thoroughly recommended.

Local favourites

The ancient cathedral city of Worcester, which is delightfully peaceful, has some excellent antique shops and a variety of hotels and restaurants, should you be anticipating a large gamble coming off. The **Gifford Hotel** (01905) 726262, overlooking the cathedral's precincts, is modern while **Brown's** (01905) 26263 is a splendidly converted corn mill, ideal for lunch and dinner and situated beside the cricket ground. Returning Cathedral-wards, a thirsty fellow should find the **Farriers Arms** (01905) 27569–a traditional public house, and the **Cardinals Hat** (01905) 22066 on Friar Street for equally good refreshment. The **Bank House** (01886) 833551 is another to note, good leisure facilities here; and also the **Pear Tree Inn** (01905) 756565 — a traditional establishment with modern touches. **The Glass House Restaurant** (01905) 611120 is an alternative restaurant to sample. Still in Worcester, **Worcester White House Hotel** (01905) 24308 is recommended by the racecourse management, as is **Ostlers at Number 1** restaurant (01905) 612300 at **The Moors** in Worcester.

Outside the city itself, amid the fruit trees and the whiff of hops, one finds a feast of delights, starting with the racecourse. In Colwall, the **Colwall Park Hotel** (01684) 540000 stands in front of the old National Hunt course and is a tremendous place to stay. The hotel offers English cooking and the Edwardian dining room is backed up by an extensive bar menu. Some lovely places can be found in and around Great Malvern. In Malvern Wells, the **Croque-en-Bouche** (01684) 565612 is one of the country's finest dining places. Alternatively, visit the **Cottage in the Wood Hotel** (01684) 575859. A really wonderful place to stay, it also has a highly regarded restaurant which is open to non-residents. One commendable hotel in Malvern is the **Foley Arms** (01684) 573397, a charming Georgian edifice in which to slumber. Another great place to stay with a good restaurant is the **Elms Hotel** (01299) 896666 in Abberley. Where next? Try Bromsgrove and **Grafton Manor** (01527) 579007 where tradition and luxury combine to make yours a delightful stay. Whilst in Droitwich Spa, the **Chateau Impney** (01905) 774411 is yet another good idea for those of you seeking refined stabling when visiting these parts.

In Wyre Piddle, the **Anchor Inn** (01386) 552799 is a grand pub cum restaurant. The **Talbot** (01886) 821235 at Knightwick is also a tremendous inn with good value accommodation. Followers of the Archers might care to make a pilgrimage to the **Old Bull** (01386) 792428 Inkberrow whilst those looking for some good pub food should visit the **Bear and Ragged Staff** (01886) 833399 in Bransford or The **Bell** at Pensax (01299) 896677. And don't forget Ombersley, where the **Kings Arms** (01905) 620142 and the **Crown and Sandys Arms** (01905) 620252 provide good food and warm hospitality. A fitting double for visitors to Worcester racecourse.

Artist: **Graham Isom** *WORCESTER RACECOURSE* *Courtesy of:* **Rosenstiel's**

Artist: **Sue Drew PURPLE SILKS** *Courtesy of:* **The Artist**

*T*hose in charge at Yarmouth are **General Manager** and **Clerk of the Course Katherine Self** and **Head Groundsman Guy Woodward**. They can be contacted at **The Racecourse, Jellicoe Road, Great Yarmouth NR30 4AU, tel: (01493) 842527, fax: (01493) 843254. E-mail:** *info@greatyarmouth-racecourse.co.uk* **Website:** *greatyarm outhracecourse.co.uk.*

If you are driving there from the south, Yarmouth is well signposted from the A12. From the west, take the A11 and A 47, or from the northwest the A 149. The course is about 24 miles east of Norwich and lies just to the north of the town centre. Were you to make a seafront promenade the night before, please note that a bus runs regularly from the seafront to the racecourse. Local bus routes run from each of the town's holiday centres. The nearest railway station is in Great Yarmouth itself and is about a mile from the course entrance. London racegoers should use the Liverpool Street line. There is plenty of room for car parking, for which there is a £2 charge. Limited space is reserved for coaches if pre-booked with the course management. Norwich Airport (01603) 411923 is the closest landing strip and if you wish to land your own plane, call (01692) 630886. Helicopters may land at the course by prior arrangement by calling (01493) 842527.

Yarmouth regularly attracts a good crowd of holidaymakers during its summer fixtures. The great Mtoto won his first race here and some superb two year olds make the short trip from Newmarket for their racecourse debut. If you only want a day's racing here a daily ticket to the Premier Enclosure will cost you £16 on most days and £18 on feature racedays. If you wish to be closer to the bookmakers the Grandstand and Paddock will cost £10 and £12. An Annual Membership is also available

for the regular racegoer and costs from £190. Membership includes a car park sticker and reciprocal meetings. Group discounts are also available, and a party of eight or more is admitted at a 20 per cent reduction for each badge if booked in advance. A special three day September Eastern Festival badge is also available at a reduced price if you book ahead: £30 will get you into the Grandstand and Paddock for all three days, while for the Premier Enclosure, £46 is the price.

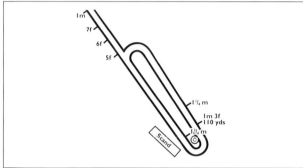

The racecourse is eager to combine business with leisure and there are four hospitality boxes and two large marquees, ideal for corporate entertainment. Hospitality packages can be arranged from £50 + VAT per person. All the boxes are fitted with closed circuit television screens and are located in the centre of the course. The recently completed Lord Nelson Stand is a fine new addition to the course and has numerous bars whose names conjure up stirring reminders of naval history. On the first floor there are eight hospitality boxes and a private function suite.

Artist: **Sue Drew KEIREN FALLON** *Courtesy of:* **The Artist**

For the younger crowd, those under 16 years are admitted free if accompanied by an adult. Indeed, Yarmouth is focusing its attention on families. There are playgrounds, sideshows, a bouncy castle, train rides and extra sideshows arranged for evening and Sunday fixtures. One point you should remember is that there is no bank, so have enough readies to hand. If you wish to bet at the on-course betting shops, you'll find them in the Grandstand and Paddock. There are facilities for disabled people in all enclosures. If the weather holds, British seaside resorts can offer a lot to the holidaymaker during the summer and the chance to go for a day's racing adds to Yarmouth's appeal. Since it was taken over by Northern Racing a few years ago, Yarmouth has gone a long way in improving its facilities and should be congratulated. We wish them a bumper season in 2005.

Local favourites

The **Imperial** (01493) 842000 is a traditional seaside hotel, an ideal meeting place prior to the races. A strong local recommendation comes for the **Furzedown** (01493) 844138—another popular haunt of racegoers. Some local favourites noted by the racecourse management include the **Burlington Palm Court** (01493) 844568, the **Star** (01493) 842294, and **Hotel Elizabeth** (01493) 855551. They are certainly worth a pre-race inspection. Two fine restaurants are **Friends Bistro** (01493) 852538 and **Seafood Restaurant** (01493) 856009 on the North Quay. The latter is fairly pricey but is a great favourite of the Newmarket trainers. In Gorleston-on-Sea the **Pier Hotel** (01493) 662631 has spectacular views along the river, harbour-mouth and across the glorious sandy beach out to sea—ideal when visiting Great Yarmouth. Back in nearby Gorleston-on-Sea The **Cliff Hotel** (01493) 662179 is also a good bet. Ideal for the beach as well.

Norwich itself is a delightful city, over 1000 years old. The better hotels are **Marriot Sprowston Manor Hotel and Country** (0870) 4007229, **De Vere Dunston Hall Hotel and Golf Club** (01508) 470444 (good leisure facilities here) and the **Maids Head Hotel** (0870) 609 6110, a 13th century building ideally situated near the cathedral. Norwich is something of a gastronomer's paradise. Other restaurants for consideration include the best in the field, **Adlards** (01603) 633522 and **By Appointment** (01603) 630730—handy for the impressive cathedral and castle. A final thought goes to the **Wildebeest Arms** (01508) 492497 at Stoke Holy Cross, a good choice when stampeding back from the races! Stayers of merit outside the town include the **Petersfield House** (01692) 630741 at Horning and **Church Farm Hotel and Restaurant** (01493) 780251 at Burgh Castle. If you are wishing to journey further westwards then try the **Park Farm** (01603) 810264 in Hethersett. Good facilities and restaurant make this a most appealing place to stay. A number of good boozers can be found either on the coast or amongst the Norfolk Broads. Lovers of real ale should try the **Fur and Feather** (01603) 720003 at Woodbastwick, it is excellent. In Hickling, the **Pleasure Boat Inn** (01692) 598211 has a charming waterside setting as has the **Eels Foot (01493) 730342** in Ormesby St Michael—both of these serve good food. In appropriately named Horsey, the **Nelson's Head** is a pleasant coastal pub, while at Winterton-on-Sea, the **Fisherman's Return** (01493) 393305 has some comfortable bedrooms and also does good bar food—ideal for escaping the throngs when racing at Yarmouth.

Artist: **Adrian Dent RAMRUMA** *Courtesy of:* **The Artist**

Artist: **Graham Isom YORK** *Courtesy of:* **Rosenstiel's**

York is one of the country's finest racecourses and we are pleased to have chosen it as Travelling the Turf's Flat Racecourse of the last 20 Years. The simple fact is that York has managed to get most everything right over the last two decades about staging some great racing and taking care of its fans. As recognition for its fine facilities and ambience, York has also won the accolade of being chosen in 2005 as the stage for the prestigious Royal Ascot meeting in June.

The successor to one of the best managers in racing in **John Smith**, much of the credit for bringing in Royal Ascot must go to York's current **Clerk of the Course** and **Chief Executive William Derby**, himself a former **Commercial Director** at Ascot Racecourse. He can be contacted at: **The Racecourse, York YO23 1EX, tel: (01904) 620911, fax: (01904) 611071, E-mail:** *enquiries@yorkracecourse.co.uk* **website:** *www.yorkracecourse.co.uk*

The course is located a mile outside the centre of the beautiful cathedral city. York railway station is a mile from the course and is on the Kings Cross line. There are frequent buses to complete the journey to the track, only five minutes ride away. A combination of the A64 and the A1036 is the answer for visitors from south, east and west, or you could try the new M1/A1 link (signed as M1), while from the north, the A19 and York Ring Road help you avoid the busy city centre. York recognises that it has problems with traffic and is working hard with the local authorities to improve access to the course. The best piece of advice is to allow as much time as you can for your journey and arrive at the course as

early as you can. Once you arrive, there are numerous car parks which are well organised and free. One way of avoiding the traffic is to come by helicopter and land at the course but please let the management know beforehand. Landing facilities for light aircraft also exist close to the course, at Rufforth. Full details are available from the racecourse office.

In addition to hosting the Royal Ascot meeting, York's own fine stable of events includes the totesport Dante Stakes, the Tattersalls Musidora Stakes and the Emirates Airline Yorkshire Cup run in May—a platform for racing of the highest calibre including two Classic trials. In August, the Ebor Festival includes some of the most impressive racing of the year with the Aston Upthorpe Yorkshire Oaks and the Group One Juddmonte International Stakes. The overriding popularity and good feeling of the summer meeting is superb but less crowded fixtures can be enjoyed in July, September and October. In all, the course offers a total of 15 days racing with over £3 million in prize money.

Artist: **Margaret Barrett TURNING FOR HOME** *Courtesy of:* **The Artist**

For the 2005 Royal Ascot meeting, York will provide the facilities, but tickets will be issued through the usual channels by the Ascot team. Please see the Ascot course section for details. For all other meetings at York, daily charges for 2005 have yet to be finalised but for the August meeting in 2004 they were £45, £23 and £6 for the County Stand, Grandstand and Paddock, and Course Enclosures, respectively. Other days were charged at £21 and £11 for the top enclosures, but there were small extra charges for the May Meeting and Saturday fixtures where the Course Enclosure was £4. There is a generous saving on three-day badges for the May and August meetings and further details of these are available from the racecourse. Senior citizens are given discounts in the Course enclosure and Grandstand and Paddock—an excellent policy. There is a waiting list for Senior County Stand annual membership, but for those fortunate enough to obtain it, there are reciprocal arrangements included with daily membership at many other courses. Party organisers should also note that the racecourse offers concessions for all meetings except the August Festival but including Saturday fixtures.

York completed a £20 million project to develop the new County Stand and a fine building it has turned out to be. Fortunately though for some of us traditionalists, the old Members stand still sits happily next to it and it remains one of the finest places to watch the racing. The new stand provides

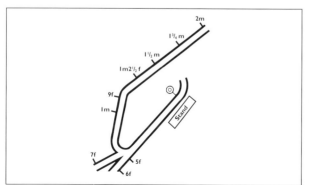

increased viewing and seating as well as more bar and wash-room facilities. With the Knavesmire Stand and the remod-elling of existing facilities, York is almost unrivalled in the choice of quality facilities for private entertaining. Subject to availability, quality 'dining with viewing' suites are available for parties of all sizes. The Dante Suite (200 guests); Knaves-mire Boxes (20, 40 and 50 guests) and Melrose Boxes (16, 30 and 40) are outstanding. A complete gamut of restaurants and bars features the famous Gimcrack Room and the 'dine with view' Ebor and Voltigeur Restaurants (advance booking only) in the new stand where the all-in admission, gourmet luncheon and Grandstand viewing seat package offers real value. Enquiries should be addressed to the hospitality team at the racecourse, (01904) 638971.

The Course Enclosure has numerous places to feed and sup and the latest addition is a new food court. Incidentally, champagne enthusiasts should note that the York racecourse offers a different brand on sale at each meeting at a bargain price on the refurbished Champagne Terrace. Prices start from around £20. Only Ascot sells more champagne than York, but we would bet that York will be the runaway winner in the champagne stakes this year.

York is one of the most successful and best run racecours-es in the country. It is thoughtfully managed and immensely popular. Witness the souvenir shop and disabled facilities. The racecourse has managed to combine the new stands with the more traditional features. By the way, don't forget to visit the York Racing Museum while you are there which gives a fascinating look at bygone days of the turf. The course really tries to take care of the owners and trainers who provide the product too—they now have a club of their own on the first floor of the Melrose Stand and there is a winning connections and sponsors room. Last year saw the addition of an Owners and Trainers terrace serving drinks and sandwiches overlooking the weighing room.

It is just this sort of attention to detail that sets York apart from many other courses. There is no doubt that it has successfully been able to blend the old with the new and extend value for money from the top end to the ground floor. It is no wonder that it is so popular with the racing public in the North. Now of course the racecourse faces a new challenge with so many new visitors to host during the Royal Ascot meeting. We must admit we were a bit con-cerned initially as like many others we have been stuck in traffic trying to get to the course on time for the first race and the swelling tourists from down south will no doubt add to this in June. Still, it's best to judge the course on how well it performs in staging racing and leave the carping about traffic and high hotel prices elsewhere. We are confi-dent that York will provide the best framework possible for a successful Royal Ascot meeting.

Artist: **Graham Isom YORK, PEUGEOT LOWTHER STAKES** *Courtesy of:* **Rosenstiel's**

*I*n 2005 Royal Ascot comes to York - often called the Ascot of the North, York is a truly excellent racetrack. It also lacks the stifling conurbations of Surrey, West London and the M4 corridor. In North Yorkshire you will find a collection of wonderful inns, some great hotels and the traffic until you get to York and hopefully not then will be relatively straightforward. Yes hotels are being snapped up, but in the surrounding Pennines, Moors and further afield into Leeds, Newcastle and other cities, you will find some great accommodation and a really fun time. York City has so much to offer—the racecourse, the castle, the minster and its many quaint streets which now house some super shops. The Shambles is perhaps the best known of these—a delightful warren with tiny lanes running into each other. More recent additions to the city include the Yorkshire Museum, the Jorvik Viking Museum and the National Railway Museum. For racing fanatics looking for a suitable place to 'ditch' loved ones whilst at the course, York is without doubt the most complete choice.

The city's hotels really capture the imagination. However, in order to make the most of the visit, rooms should be booked well in advance. The city's leading establishment is **Middlethorpe Hall** (01904) 641241 which is set in superb grounds and overlooks the racecourse and has an excellent restaurant. Another first class hotel is found within two beautifully kept William IV houses, the **Mount Royale** (01904) 628856. One of the highlights here is the charming dining room which overlooks beautiful gardens. This hotel is a real favourite and is strongly recommended. Another listed building is the excellent **Judges Lodging** (01904) 638733—superbly stylish—and do visit the 18th century wine cellars which now house an exquisite bar. For a prime position opposite the Minster, the **Dean Court Hotel** (01904) 625082 is the one to opt for—very comfortable too. The city straddles the Ouse and a most modern hotel which overlooks the river is the **York Moat House** (01904) 459988. Two further additions to the Yorkshire stable are the extremely convenient **Knavesmire Manor** (01904) 702941—certainly one for the notebook. and the **Grange Hotel** (01904) 644744 in Clifton. The latter boasts an excellent restaurant within its Regency walls. Its newly refurbished seafood restaurant has a racing 'cyclorama' which has to be seen.

A view of the Tote-Ebor start can be gained from the **York Marriot Hotel** (0870) 400 7263. Also in York is the **Le Meridien York** (01904) 653681, a gigantic but elegant edifice right next to the station. Others to make a note of include **The York Pavilion** in Fulford (01904) 622099, **The Clifton Bridge** (01904) 610510–unassuming but well thought of. **The Groves**, Clifton (01904) 559777 and the **Jacobean Lodge** (01904) 762749 and **Heworth Court** (01904) 425156 are others to consider.

York has something to offer every taste and pocket, and those planning a flutter well beyond their means may wish to save a little on their accommodation. If so, they should try the still excellent but relatively modestly priced **Hudsons Hotel** (01904) 62126.

Restaurants in York are not as strong as the hotels but pay special attention to **The Blue Bicycle** (01904) 673990. An excellent venue for a pre-race brunch or post-race tea is the famous **Bettys** in the centre of York—renowned for its truly moreish cream cakes. Another distinguished restaurant is **Melton's** (01904) 634341 which offers outstanding English cooking.

York is unsurprisingly riddled with pubs. The **Black Swan** (01904) 686911 on Peaseholme Green offers a lively atmosphere and some good value bedrooms. For a riverside setting try the **Kings Arms** (01904) 659435. There are numerous pubs beside the Ouse which appeal and for a more central location try the **York Arms** (01904) 624508 in Petergate. Real ale lovers will enjoy the **Tap and Spile** (01904) 656158 in Petersgate, while shoppers can enjoy some refreshment in the **Ye Olde Starre Inne** (01904) 623063 in Stonegate.

Aldwark Manor (01347) 838146 at Alne near Easingwold is well worth considering for those wishing to stay outside York itself. In Escrick **The Parsonage Coutry House** (01904) 728111 is an elegant offering. Another one to pray for a few winners is The **Old Rectory**, Sutton-upon-Derwent (01904) 608548. Further north at Helmsley, the **Feversham Arms** (01439) 770766 offers elegant accommodation and excellent lunches. A trip to Malton can never go amiss, after all this is one of Britain's major racing towns. There are numerous pubs of note here and the **Green Man** (01653) 600370 is a good place to stay. The **Talbot** (01653) 694031 and the **Burythorpe Hotel** (01653) 658200 are also well worth shortlisting. If passing through Hovingham, meanwhile, do not overlook the **Worsley Arms Hotel** (01653) 628234, another great favourite. A pub to note here is the inappropriately named **Gold Cup** (01759) 371354. The **St Vincent Arms** (01904) 608349 in Sutton Upon Derwent is a good boozer and the **Three Hares Country Inn and Restaurant** (01937) 832128 in Bilborough is also one to note—excellent food here—a strong fancy. The **Ship Inn** (01904) 703888 at Acaster Malbis has good food and good value accommodation. Finally, the **Dawnay Arms** (01347) 848345 is a recommended stayer after the last.

The **Crown** (01423) 322328 at Boroughbridge is another racing favourite, and rightly so, drawing racegoers from all the Yorkshire courses. A similar commendation can be made of another excellent **Crown** (01347) 821698 on this occasion at Easingwold–it's a thoroughly welcoming and good value Yorkshire establishment. **Ramada York** (01904) 670222, is also well positioned for the many who choose to visit the Knavesmire. Heading off towards Beverley, an inn of great character is the **Feathers**, Pocklington (01759) 303155–an ideal choice if your trip is on a more restricted budget. The **Londesborough Arms** in Market Weighton (01430) 872214 is another extremely welcoming establishment to add to the shortlist. Another is the **Boars Head** (01423) 771888—a particularly smart establishment. In the picturesque town of Harrogate, the **Majestic Hotel** (01423) 700300 provides a welcome watering hole for racegoers. There are many people who visit York just for the races but it has many other attractions, so do try to book in advance. A combination of racing at York, coupled with a stay in delightful York City itself or the neighbouring countryside is, as ever, warmly recommended.

This luxurious hotel is only 20 minutes from both Leeds and York, within easy reach of all the main motorway networks. Set within 77 acres of delightful parkland and landscaped grounds, the fortified Knights residence offers a distinctly different lifestyle experience in an idyllic rural location.

The Castle, once used by the Carmelite order, has now been elegantly and sensitively restored into a unique 21 bedroom hotel. It boasts two restaurants, superb conference facilites and has been named top wedding venue in Yorkshire.

All bedrooms are beautifully decorated to the highest standards, with great care taken to enhance their natural beauty. Our rooms vary from Suites to Four Poster Rooms; all

are individual and vary in shape and size, designed to provide a relaxing haven full of knickknacks (and little rubber ducks!).

The Restaurant '1086' is a treat not to be missed, overlooking the beautiful grounds of Hazlewood. With two rosette's, the restaurant serves an exquisite à la carte menu using only the finest products and ingredients from around the region.

The Castle has been thoughtfully and tastefully designed, combining the elegance of the Castle with the excellence of the food and service offered to all our guests. Whether visiting Hazlewood for the first time with friends or a a guest at one of our many events, you will always be greeted with a warm welcome.

Hazlewood Castle
Paradise Lane, Hazlewood, Tadcaster
Nr Leeds and York LS24 9NJ
Tel: (01937) 535353 Fax: (01937) 530630
www.hazlewood-castle.co.uk

Travelling the Turf
in Ireland

Artist: **Peter Smith** *GOING FOR HOME* Courtesy of: **Frost & Reed**

Introduction by Alan Lee - UK Times

For me, the journey started in Naas, just before Cheltenham one year. The bug had not taken hold of me then – it was merely a niggle, a sense of curiosity at a different kind of turf life. So, on a track that has more suburbia and less eccentricity to it than most of the breed, I sampled for the first time the characteristics that were to become so familiar. And, once I had been racing in Ireland, I was hooked.

There are certain things about it that are delightfully different from racing in England, or indeed anywhere else in the world. There are the itinerant sellers, for instance - the pen and form men before racing and the women who load old prams with chocolate bars and fruit as the crowds leave. There are the self-service, stand-up eateries that work so slickly I constantly wonder why they have not become a thriving Irish export. There is the Guinness – it really does taste different here. Most of all, there are the smiles. People not only enjoy themselves at Irish racing, they seem genuinely concerned that every visitor should have a ball, too.

And it is not hard. You don't have to drink - I'm told there are people who abstain. You don't even have to bet to appreciate that there is an atmosphere around racing in Ireland that simply does not exist elsewhere. But those who wish to both drink and bet – and there seem to be a few – do so with a genial camaraderie which may even be helped, dare I say, by dealing in those handy euro rather than the quaint old pounds we still persist in using this side of the water.

I never did see a composite figure of how many euro changed hands during the marvellous marathon at Galway in 2002 – I suspect there was not enough room on a newspaper page for all the noughts. But it was one hell of a party, even for those of us who could only sneak in on the Friday evening, when the lifers were already five days into the battle. "It used to take over the city," I was told by the lugubrious manager, John Moloney. "Now it takes over the country." Not bad for a one-liner.

The September shindig in Listowel is just as long but a shade more discreet. The lovely little town embraces the racing but other than on Kerry National day (and why more British trainers do not contest such a giddily valuable race is beyond me) the pace is gentle and the evenings can be spent sampling some of the generous hospitality of this region. Which is another fine reason for getting this bug – in Ireland, you can stay in rural splendour, yet eat modishly and well, near an ever-increasing number of racecourses. It may not be good for the waistline but it does a great deal for the quality of life.

Variety is everything in Ireland. Leopardstown, in January, stages top-notch jump racing with marvellous facilities; Laytown, in September, stages flat racing on a beach, with a couple of tents supplying provisions. You cannot get much more diverse than that. I have seen Killarney in the mists of May, peerless Punchestown in hock-deep mud and steambath sunshine. I even went to Tipperary when the lanes for miles around were adorned with yellow posters joyfully proclaiming: 'Istabraq Returns'. And nobody, native or visitor, had to ask what it meant.

It has become an obsession now, of course. Not only to keep going back to some of the magical perennials but to complete the set. I had never thought of myself as an anorakish collector of racecourses, nor of anything else come to that, but having visited all 59 British courses in a single year – a duty that became an eye-opening odyssey – I have no intention of letting any of the Irish 27 elude me. I am not quite halfway yet, and loving every minute of the trip.

Artist: **Peter Smith** **TURNING FOR HOME** *Courtesy of:* **Frost & Reed**

Artist: **Peter Curling LUSH SUMMER** *Courtesy of:* **Rosenstiel's**

No visit to Ireland would be complete without a trip to the races. The racing experience is a unique one in a country where the horse forms an integral part of the culture and where empathy with the noble creature is unprecedented. The 27 racetracks, which are scattered generously around the country, cater for every need.

All tastes are covered, whether you are looking for the social whirl and cosmopolitan atmosphere of The Curragh (Kildare) or Leopardstown (Dublin) or the more rustic appeal of the midlands venue at Kilbeggan. Whether you want to dress up or dress down there is a racecourse to fulfil your needs.

Travelling the Turf in rural Ireland has been compared to a return to the charm and simplicity of 50's and 60's Britain.

You can sense the affinity with the horse, the intense interest in every aspect of the racing and the inescapable feeling that everyone knows (or pretends to know) everyone else. Racegoers display easy familiarity with visiting Government Ministers (a common sight), rockstars, the Aga Khan, Mick Kinane, Aidan O'Brien and the man on the car park gate.

While the conviviality and enthusiasm recall the best aspects of former days the racecourses themselves have modernised and upgraded significantly in the past decade, so you can reasonably expect a tall skinny latte to be on offer in many places, in addition to rich creamy pints of stout.

For the casual racegoer the goings on of the bookmakers are tremendously interesting and for the regulars they are an integral part of a good day out. Nowhere are the bookmakers busier than at the Galway Festival where huge sums change hands and the betting records tumble regularly. The Tote, which also provides an excellent betting medium with a myriad of wagering options, also sees huge turnover as backers chase the Jackpot on a daily basis.

The Ballybrit track, located on the outskirts of Galway City, is a virtual place of pilgrimage at the end of July when people travel from all over the globe to sample the craic. The words of the song sum it up best:

'There was half a million people there of all denominations The Catholic, the Protestant, the Jew, the Presbyterian Yet there was no animosity no matter what persuasion But failte hospitality inducing fresh acquaintance'

No doubt those fresh acquaintances can be renewed by travelling on to the Tralee Festival in late August. This four day meeting runs in conjunction with the internationally famous Rose of Tralee pageant and the Roses from all over the world will be at Ballybeggan Park rubbing shoulders with the racegoers. Such is the social whirl of 'the Rose' that regular trips to the races during the daylight hours are essential just to keep the system intact.

By the time that Listowel comes around a month later in late September there has been plenty of time to recuperate and just as well because the Harvest Festival in the north-Kerry town is not for the weak-livered. The area is renowned as the source of inspiration for many of the brilliant works of local playwright John B. Keane and for a week at least the outside world also gets an opportunity to draw on that inspiration.

The racecourse, on the island adjacent to the town centre, is within walking distance of all local restaurants and hostelries and by the time you get across the bridge to the track the traditional musicians on the streetside and the kids scurrying for loose change in the waters below, and calling "throw me down something" have already imbued you with the unique atmosphere of the place. Listowel is definitely one of those 'you must do it at least once in a lifetime' experiences.

And so the summer itinerary comes to an end. But before there is time to draw breath the stars of jump racing are limbering up for the winter campaign and festival outings at picturesque Gowran Park, near Kilkenny, and Down Royal afford them ample opportunities to flex their muscles.

Some species may go into hibernation for the winter months but the hardy perennials of the jumping scene only come to life around November or thereabouts. For the following six months they rule the racing world with the unsurpassable thrills and spills of the jumping game.

As the programme gets under way in earnest the star performers are inevitably building towards the four day Christmas festival at Leopardstown and Limerick, where jockeys and horses combine with holly and ivy to provide top class action in a unique festive atmosphere.

No sooner has the festive season passed than the big prizes of the spring are looming large on the horizon. Pre-Cheltenham fever inevitably takes over for a while with big trial meetings at the likes of Punchestown, Naas and Navan. The Co. Meath track presents one of the toughest, and fairest, tests of a jumping horse and anybody taking Cheltenham seriously must closely monitor the Navan results.

Gradually the promised light of spring illuminates and with it comes the Powers Gold Label Irish Grand National meeting at Fairyhouse. One of the traditional highlights on the Irish sporting and social calendar sees the multitudes flock to the course just north of Dublin City.

Finally the dial goes full circle and the highpoint of the season arrives with the Irish National Hunt Festival at Punchestown. Traditional and contemporary styles and values combine almost unnoticed at the Co. Kildare venue which also boasts just about the finest natural racing facility around.

The racing world is almost akin to a well-oiled roundabout, which keeps spinning along. Get on soon – you'll enjoy the ride!!!

Artist: **Peter Curling WINTER RATIONS** *Courtesy of:* **Rosenstiel's**

National Hunt

9 Jan	Leopardstown	Pierse Hurdle Grade A
20 Jan	Gowran Park	Thyestes Handicap Chase Grade B
22 Jan	Naas	Woodlands Park Naas Nov Chase Grade 2
23 Jan	Leopardstown	AIG Champion Hurdle Grade 1
23 Jan	Leopardstown	Arkle Nov Chase Grade 1
27 Jan	Thurles	Kinloch Brae Chase Grade 2
6 Feb	Leopardstown	Hennessy Gold Cup Grade 1
6 Feb	Leopardstown	Dr P J Moriarty Nov Chase Grade 1
6 Feb	Leopardstown	Deloittte Nov Hurdle Grade 1
12 Feb	Gowran Park	Red Mills Chase Grade 3
20 Feb	Naas	Newlands Chase Grade 2
27 Mar	Fairyhouse	Moore Mem Handicap Chase Grade A
28 Mar	Fairyhouse	Irish Grand National (Handicap Chase) Grade A
29 Mar	Fairyhouse	Powers Gold Cup Novice Chase Grade 1
29 Mar	Fairyhouse	Moore Mem Handicap Chase Grade A
26 Apr	Punchestown	Evening Herald Nov Hurdle Grade 1
26 Apr	Punchestown	The Kerrygold Champion Chase Grade 1
27 Apr	Punchestown	Punchestown Guinness Gold Cup Grade 1
27 Apr	Punchestown	Champion Bumper Grade 1
28 Apr	Punchestown	Ballymore Properties Champion Stayers Hurdle Grade 1
28 Apr	Punchestown	Swordlestown Nov Chase Grade 1
28 Apr	Punchestown	Champion 4yo Hurdle Grade 1
29 Apr	Punchestown	Emo Oil Champion Hurdle Grade 1
29 Apr	Punchestown	Tickell Nov Hurdle Grade 1
8 May	Killarney	Murphys Hurdle Grade B
27 Jul	Galway	Galway Plate (Handicap Chase) Grade A
28 Jul	Galway	Galway Hurdle (Handicap) Grade A
25 Aug	Tralee	Denny Handicap Chase Grade C
21 Sep	Listowel	Kerry National (Handicap Chase) Grade A
2 Oct	Tipperary	McManus Hurdle Grade 1
7 Oct	Gowran Park	National Lottery Chase Grade 3
9 Oct	Limerick	Munster National (Handicap Chase) Grade B
30 Oct	Galway	Ballybrit Nov Chase Grade 3
5 Nov	Down Royal	Nicholson Chase Grade 1
6 Nov	Cork	Cork National Grade C
13 Nov	Navan	Fortria Chase Grade 2
17 Nov	Clonmel	Clonmel Oil Chase Grade 2
19 Nov	Punchestown	Morgiana Hurdle Grade 2
19 Nov	Punchestown	Craddockstown Nov Chase Grade 2
27 Nov	Navan	Troytown Handicap Chase Grade A
4 Dec	Fairyhouse	Drinmore Nov Chase Grade 1
4 Dec	Fairyhouse	Royal Bond Nov Hurdle Grade 1
4 Dec	Fairyhouse	Hattons Grace Hurdle Grade 1
11 Dec	Cork	Hilly Way Chase Grade 2
11 Dec	Punchestown	John Durkan Mem Chase Grade 1
26 Dec	Leopardstown	Durkan's New Homes Novice Chase Grade 1
26 Dec	Limerick	Greenmount Park Nov Chase Grade 2
27 Dec	Leopardstown	Future Champion Nov Hurdle Grade 2
27 Dec	Leopardstown	Dial A Bet Chase Grade 2
28 Dec	Leopardstown	Ascon Novice Chase Grade 1
28 Dec	Leopardstown	Lexus Chase Grade 1
29 Dec	Leopardstown	December Hurdle Grade 1

Flat

21 May	Curragh	Boylesports Irish 2000 Guineas Stakes Group 1
22 May	Curragh	Boylesports Irish 1000 Guineas Stakes Group 1
22 May	Curragh	Tattersalls Gold Cup Group 1
25 Jun	Curragh	Pretty Polly Stakes Group 1
26 Jun	Curragh	Irish Derby Group 1
17 Jul	Curragh	Irish Oaks Group 1
7 Aug	Curragh	The Independent Waterford Wedgwood Phoenix Stakes Group 1
4 Sep	Curragh	Moyglare Stud Stakes Group 1
10 Sep	Leopardstown	Baileys Irish Champion Stakes Group 1
10 Sep	Leopardstown	Coolmore Matron Stakes Group 1
17 Sep	Curragh	Irish Field St Leger Stakes Group 1
18 Sep	Curragh	National Stakes Group 1

Festivals

Cork Easter Festival – Sat 26th, Sun 27th & Mon 28th March

Fairyhouse Grand National Festival – Sun 27th, Mon 28th & Tues 29th March

Punchestown NH Festival – Tue 26th - Fri 29th April

Killarney May Festival – Sun 8th, Mon 9th (e) & Tues 10th (e) May

Curragh Guineas Festival – Sat 21st & Sun 22nd May

Tralee June Bank Holiday Festival – Sun 5th, Mon 6th (BH) & Tues 7th June

Curragh Derby Festival – Fri, 24th (e), Sat 25th & Sun 26th June

Bellewstown Summer Festival – Wed 29th (e), Thurs 30th (e) June & Fri 1st (e) July

Killarney July Festival – Mon 11th (e), Tues 12th (e), Wed 13th (e) & Thurs 14th July

Curragh Oaks Festival – Sat 16th & Sun 17th July

Galway Racing Festival – Mon 25th (e), Tues 26th (e), Wed 27th, Thurs 28th, Fri 29th (e), Sat 30th & Sun 31st July

Tramore Summer Festival – Thurs 11th (e), Fri 12th (e), Sat 13th (e) & Sun 14th August

Tralee Rose Festival – Mon 22nd, Tues 23rd, Wed 24th & Thurs 25th August

Galway Autumn Festival – Sun 4th, Mon 5th & Tues 6th September

Listowel Festival – Sun 18th, Mon 19th, Tues 20th, Wed 21st, Thurs 22nd, Fri 23rd & Sat 24th September

Gowran Park 2-day Festival – Fri 7th & Sat 8th October

Down Royal Festival – Fri 4th & Sat 5th November

Fairyhouse November Festival – Sat 3rd & Sun 4th December

Leopardstown Christmas Festival – Mon 26th, Tue 27th, Wed 28th & Thurs 29th December

Limerick Christmas Festival – Mon 26th, Tue 27th, Wed 28th & Thurs 29th December

JANUARY

1	Sat	Fairyhouse
1	Sat	Tramore
2	Sun	Naas
3	Mon	Cork
6	Thu	Thurles
8	Sat	Navan
9	Sun	Leopardstown
13	Thu	Limerick
15	Sat	Punchestown
16	Sun	Cork
16	Sun	Fairyhouse
20	Thu	Gowran Park
22	Sat	Naas
23	Sun	Leopardstown
27	Thu	Thurles
29	Sat	Fairyhouse
30	Sun	Punchestown
30	Sun	Tramore

FEBRUARY

3	Thu	Clonmel
5	Sat	Naas
6	Sun	Leopardstown
9	Wed	Punchestown
10	Thu	Thurles
12	Sat	Gowran Park
13	Sun	Navan
14	Mon	Navan
16	Wed	Down Royal
17	Thu	Clonmel
19	Sat	Fairyhouse
20	Sun	Naas
24	Thu	Thurles
26	Sat	Fairyhouse
27	Sun	Downpatrick
27	Sun	Punchestown

MARCH

3	Thu	Limerick
5	Sat	Navan
6	Sun	Clonmel
6	Sun	Leopardstown
10	Thu	Thurles
12	Sat	Downpatrick
13	Sun	Naas
17	Thu	Down Royal
17	Thu	Wexford
19	Sat	Tramore
20	Sun	Curragh
20	Sun	Limerick
24	Thu	Thurles
26	Sat	Cork
26	Sat	Down Royal
27	Sun	Cork
27	Sun	Fairyhouse
28	Mon	Cork
28	Mon	Fairyhouse
29	Tue	Fairyhouse
31	Thu	Clonmel

APRIL

2	Sat	Navan
3	Sun	Curragh
3	Sun	Tramore
6	Wed	Gowran Park
7	Thu	Tipperary
10	Sun	Leopardstown
10	Sun	Limerick
13	Wed	Fairyhouse
14	Thu	Tipperary
16	Sat	Navan
17	Sun	Curragh
17	Sun	Listowel
20	Wed	Gowran Park
21	Thu	Gowran Park
23	Sat	Naas
24	Sun	Cork
24	Sun	Leopardstown
25	Mon	Sligo (e)
26	Tue	Punchestown
27	Wed	Punchestown
28	Thu	Punchestown
29	Fri	Punchestown
30	Sat	Punchestown

MAY

1	Sun	Gowran Park
1	Sun	Navan
2	Mon	Curragh
2	Mon	Down Royal
2	Mon	Limerick
4	Wed	Ballinrobe (e)
5	Thu	Tipperary (e)
6	Fri	Cork (e)
7	Sat	Kilbeggan (e)
8	Sun	Killarney
8	Sun	Leopardstown
9	Mon	Killarney (e)
10	Tue	Killarney (e)
12	Thu	Clonmel (e)
13	Fri	Downpatrick (e)
13	Fri	Wexford (e)
14	Sat	Naas (e)
15	Sun	Gowran Park
15	Sun	Navan
16	Mon	RoscomMon (e)
18	Wed	Fairyhouse (e)
19	Thu	Tipperary (e)
20	Fri	Cork (e)
20	Fri	Downpatrick (e)
21	Sat	Curragh
22	Sun	Curragh
23	Mon	Kilbeggan (e)
24	Tue	Sligo (e)
25	Wed	Leopardstown (e)
26	Thu	Clonmel (e)
27	Fri	Limerick (e)
27	Fri	Wexford (e)
28	Sat	Punchestown (e)
29	Sun	Gowran Park
29	Sun	Listowel
30	Mon	Ballinrobe (e)
31	Tue	Ballinrobe (e)

JUNE

1	Wed	Leopardstown (e)
3	Fri	Tramore (e)
4	Sat	Kilbeggan (e)
5	Sun	Navan
5	Sun	Tralee
6	Mon	Naas
6	Mon	Tralee
7	Tue	Tralee (e)
8	Wed	Leopardstown (e)
9	Thu	Tipperary (e)
10	Fri	Navan (e)
10	Fri	Wexford (e)
11	Sat	Cork
12	Sun	Cork
12	Sun	Roscommon
13	Mon	Roscommon (e)
15	Wed	Leopardstown (e)
16	Thu	Clonmel (e)
17	Fri	Down Royal (e)
17	Fri	Limerick (e)
18	Sat	Down Royal
19	Sun	Down Royal
19	Sun	Gowran Park
20	Mon	Kilbeggan (e)
21	Tue	Ballinrobe (e)
22	Wed	Naas (e)
23	Thu	Tipperary (e)
24	Fri	Curragh (e)
24	Fri	Limerick (e)
25	Sat	Curragh
26	Sun	Curragh
28	Tue	Sligo (e)
29	Wed	Bellewstown (e)
30	Thu	Bellewstown (e)
30	Thu	Tipperary (e)

JULY

1	Fri	Bellewstown (e)
1	Fri	Limerick (e)
2	Sat	Leopardstown (e)
2	Sat	Limerick (e)
4	Mon	RoscomMon (e)
5	Tue	RoscomMon (e)
6	Wed	Naas (e)
7	Thu	Gowran Park (e)

8	Fri	Cork (e)
8	Fri	Wexford (e)
9	Sat	Fairyhouse (e)
10	Sun	Sligo
10	Sun	Tipperary
11	Mon	Killarney (e)
12	Tue	Killarney (e)
13	Wed	Killarney (e)
13	Wed	Leopardstown (e)
14	Thu	Killarney
15	Fri	Kilbeggan (e)
16	Sat	Curragh
17	Sun	Curragh
18	Mon	Ballinrobe (e)
19	Tue	Ballinrobe (e)
20	Wed	Naas (e)
22	Fri	Fairyhouse (e)
22	Fri	Limerick (e)
23	Sat	Leopardstown (e)
24	Sun	Wexford
25	Mon	Galway (e)
26	Tue	Galway (e)
27	Wed	Galway
28	Thu	Galway
29	Fri	Galway (e)
30	Sat	Galway
31	Sun	Cork
31	Sun	Galway

AUGUST

1	Mon	Cork
1	Mon	Naas
2	Tue	Roscommon (e)
3	Wed	Sligo (e)
4	Thu	Sligo (e)
4	Thu	Tipperary (e)
5	Fri	Wexford (e)
6	Sat	Kilbeggan (e)
7	Sun	Curragh
7	Sun	Downpatrick
8	Mon	Ballinrobe (e)
10	Wed	Gowran Park (e)
11	Thu	Tramore (e)
13	Fri	Tramore (e)
13	Sat	Tramore (e)
14	Sun	Leopardstown
14	Sun	Tramore
15	Mon	Roscommon (e)
17	Wed	Bellewstown (e)
17	Wed	Sligo (e)
18	Thu	Bellewstown (e)
18	Thu	Tipperary (e)
19	Fri	Kilbeggan (e)
20	Sat	Curragh
21	Sun	Cork
21	Sun	Gowran Park
22	Mon	Tralee
23	Tue	Tralee
24	Wed	Tralee
25	Thu	Tralee
27	Sat	Wexford
28	Sun	Ballinrobe
28	Sun	Fairyhouse
29	Mon	Downpatrick
31	Wed	Clonmel

SEPTEMBER

1	Thu	Laytown
2	Fri	Down Royal
3	Sat	Down Royal
4	Sun	Curragh
4	Sun	Galway
5	Mon	Galway
6	Tue	Galway
9	Fri	Kilbeggan
10	Sat	Leopardstown
11	Sun	Killarney
12	Mon	Roscommon
15	Thu	Tipperary
16	Fri	Downpatrick
17	Sat	Curragh
18	Sun	Curragh
18	Sun	Listowel
19	Mon	Listowel
20	Tue	Listowel
21	Wed	Listowel

22	Thu	Listowel
23	Fri	Listowel
24	Sat	Fairyhouse
24	Sat	Listowel
28	Wed	Downpatrick
29	Thu	Thurles

OCTOBER

1	Sat	Curragh
2	Sun	Tipperary
3	Mon	Roscommon
7	Fri	Gowran Park
8	Sat	Gowran Park
9	Sun	Curragh
9	Sun	Limerick
12	Wed	Navan
13	Thu	Tramore
15	Sat	Cork
16	Sun	Cork
16	Sun	Naas
19	Wed	Punchestown
20	Thu	Punchestown
22	Sat	Fairyhouse
23	Sun	Clonmel
23	Sun	Curragh
24	Mon	Curragh
26	Wed	Navan
29	Sat	Naas
29	Sat	Wexford
30	Sun	Galway
30	Sun	Wexford
31	Mon	Galway
31	Mon	Leopardstown

NOVEMBER

2	Wed	Punchestown
3	Thu	Clonmel
4	Fri	Down Royal
5	Sat	Down Royal
6	Sun	Cork
6	Sun	Leopardstown
9	Wed	Fairyhouse
10	Thu	Thurles
12	Sat	Naas
13	Sun	Limerick
13	Sun	Navan
16	Wed	Downpatrick
17	Thu	Clonmel
19	Sat	Punchestown
20	Sun	Cork
20	Sun	Punchestown
24	Thu	Thurles
26	Sat	Gowran Park
27	Sun	Navan

DECEMBER

1	Thu	Thurles
3	Sat	Fairyhouse
4	Sun	Fairyhouse
8	Thu	Clonmel
10	Sat	Navan
11	Sun	Cork
11	Sun	Punchestown
14	Wed	Downpatrick
15	Thu	Gowran Park
17	Sat	Fairyhouse
18	Sun	Navan
18	Sun	Thurles
26	Mon	Down Royal
26	Mon	Leopardstown
26	Mon	Limerick
27	Tue	Leopardstown
27	Tue	Limerick
28	Wed	Leopardstown
28	Wed	Limerick
29	Thu	Leopardstown
29	Thu	Limerick
31	Sat	Punchestown
31	Sat	Tramore

*Status to be confirmed
(e) Donates evening meeting
Dates of fixtures may be subject to alteration.

Sligo

Down Royal

Downpatrick

Dundalk

Ballinrobe

Roscommon

Navan   Laytown

Bellewstown

Galway

Kilbeggan

Fairyhouse

Leopardstown

Curragh

Naas

Punchestown

Limerick   Thurles

Listowel

Tipperary

Gowran Park

Tralee

Clonmel

Tramore   Wexford

Killarney   Cork

Ballinrobe

Contact: Mr John Flannelly, Manager, Ballinrobe Race Committee, Ballinrobe, Co Mayo Tel: 00 353 94 95 41811, 00 353 87 289 5974. Clerk of the Course: PR McGouran, 39 Barton Road, Rathfarnam, Dublin 14 Tel: 00 353 1 4931548 Racedays: Tel: 00 353 94 95 41052, Fax: 00 353 94 95 41406.

Ballinrobe has a very old tradition of racing in various forms with meetings recorded in 1774 and steeplechases included in the 1834 meeting. The present course was purchased in 1921.

Possessing a slightly elevated track, Ballinrobe boasts an exceptional view of the whole course. General facilities updated in 1998.

7 racedates are scheduled for Ballinrobe in 2005 including 4 evening meetings, 1 Saturday and 2 Sunday meetings.

Location
One mile from Ballinrobe Town N84.

Refreshment Facilities
Bars and restaurants

Local Hotels
Ashford Castle, Tel: 00 353 94 95 46003, internationally renowned 5 star Hotel; Ryans Hotel Tel: 00 353 94 95 46243.

Local Restaurants
Flannery's, Ballinrobe, Carney's Ballinrobe, Soprano's Ballinrobe, TE Bhurca, Clonbur.

Places of Interest/Activities
Angling in 60,000 acres of brown trout fishing, golf–18 hole championship course. Also a major area for items of historical and archaeological interest.

Bellewstown

Contact: Mr Kevin Coleman the Secretary/Manager, 9 Palace Street, Drogheda, Co Louth, Tel: 00 353 41 9842111, Fax: 00 353 41 9837566. Racecourse address Bellewstown Racecourse, Bellewstown, Co Meath, Tel: (Racedays only) 00 353 41 9823614 Fax: 00 353 41 9823644.

Bellewstown racecourse, on the Hill of Crockafotha in Co Meath, is beautifully situated in a rural setting with magnificent views of the Mountains of Mourne to the north and the Irish Sea to the east.

Bellewstown is an annual three-day meeting which takes place from Wednesday 29th June – Friday 1st July. The races have always been associated with the smell of freshly mown hay and the taste of strawberries and cream. We do not know exactly when racing started in Bellewstown, but the first record of races appears in the August edition of the Dublin Gazette and the Weekly Courier in 1726.

George Tandy, a former Mayor of Drogheda and brother of the famous Napper Tandy, persuaded King George III to sponsor a race at Bellewstown in 1780. The race was called His Majesty's Plate and was valued at £100.

All the English monarchs continued to sponsor a race at Bellewstown until 1980, when Queen Elizabeth II decided to discontinue the race. However, the Queen continues to sponsor a race at the Curragh called the Royal Whip.

Location
The racecourse is 23 miles north of Dublin, off the main Dublin/ Belfast road and seven miles south of Drogheda.

Public Transport
There is a special bus service from Dublin (Busaras) Tel: Bus Eireann 00 353 1 836 6111 for departure time. Buses also run from Drogheda.

Other Facilities
There is a free area beside the track which includes a carnival for children.

Local Hotels
Neptune Beach Hotel Tel: 00 353 41 982 7107, Bettystown; Old Mill Hotel and Glen Side Hotel, Julianstown; Rosnaree Park Hotel, Westcourt Hotel Tel: 00 353 41 983 0965 and Boyne Valley Hotel Tel: 00 353 41 9837737, Drogheda; Conyngham Arms Hotel Tel: 00 353 41 24155, Slane; Ashbourne House Hotel, Ashbourne, Bracken Court Hotel Tel: 00 353 41 841 3333, Balbriggan. Contact the Irish Tourist Board Tel: 0207 493 3201 for an accommodation list.

Local Restaurants
Bacchus at the Coast Guard, Bettystown; Black Bull Inn, Buttergate and Monasterboice Inn (all Drogheda); Forge, Collon, Co Meath.

Places of Interest/Activities
The racecourse is close to the historic sites of Tara, Slane, Newgrange, Dowth and Knowth and the beautiful Boyne Valley. There are several 18-hole golf courses nearby.

Clonmel

Contact: Mr J L Desmond, Manager, Clonmel Racecourse, Davis Road, Clonmel, Co Tipperary, Tel: 00 353 52 22611/22032 Fax: 00 353 52 26446 Racedays: 00 353 52 21605 Fax: 00 353 52 25719.

Clonmel, an historic town, lies at the foot of the Comeragh Mountains and is situated in the valley of the beautiful River Suir. To the north east lies Slievenamon.

Clonmel racecourse (Powerstown Park) is located in a picturesque setting north of the town. Racing, which had been open and free to spectators for over a hundred years at Clonmel, was enclosed in 1913 by Villiers Morton Jackson and became the commercially run Powerstown Park racecourse.

Morton Jackson also roped in the bookies to a distinct area of the course, banned gaming sideshows, brought in detectives and police to deter pickpockets and provided entry to a roofless grandstand accommodating 1,500 at a charge of two shillings a head!

Since then Clonmel has grown and developed and today it is not uncommon to have in excess of 120 horses running at any one meeting. Extensive refurbishment has been carried out at Clonmel Racecourse during 1998. A new grandstand including a Bar and catering complex has been constructed. Along with a new computerised turnstile entrance, the weighroom/jockeys room has also been extensively upgraded and refurbished.

Location
Clonmel racecourse (Powerstown Park) is situated within two miles of the town centre, off the Waterford-Clonmel road. It is 100 miles from Dublin, 30 miles from Waterford, 24 miles from Tipperary and 12 miles from Cahir.

Refreshment Facilities
Self service restaurant, snack bars and bars.

Local Hotels
Hotel Minella Tel: 00 353 52 22388, Clonmel Arms Hotel Tel: 00 353 52 21233 and Hearns Hotel Tel: 00 353 52 21611.

Local Restaurants
Include La Scala, Emerald Garden (Chinese), Jasmine Court (Chinese), Mulcahys and Sean Tierney's Bar & Restaurant.

Places of Interest/Activities
Clonmel Main Guard, Cahir Castle, Rock of Cashel, Kilkenny Castle and Mitchelstown's Caves, together with scenic drives also golf and pony trekking.

Cork

Contact: Mr Michael Lane, Executive Director/ Secretary, or Michael O'Neill, Commercial Manager, Cork Racecourse (Mallow) Limited Killarney Road, Mallow, Co Cork Tel: 00 353 22 50207 Fax: 00 353 22 50213 Email: *info@corkracecourse.ie* Website: *www.corkracecourse.ie*

There is a long tradition of horse racing in the region. The first ever steeplechase took place in 1752 between the church steeples of Buttervant and Donerail, just a few miles from Mallow. In 1777, six consecutive days of racing were on offer in the Mallow area, "all to be run according to the King's Plate articles".

With the demise of Cork Park in 1917, the need for a new racecourse in Ireland's largest county was apparent. Mallow, formed at the instigation of and under the control of Lieutenant Colonel F F MacCabe, commenced racing in 1924.

The racecourse re-opened at Easter 1997, following a €9 million refurbishment backed by Horse Racing Ireland and local, private and industry sponsorship.

Location
The racecourse is situated one mile from Mallow town on the Mallow-Killarney road (N72). Racegoers coming from Cork and Limerick travelling on the N20 should take the N72 to Killarney at the roundabout in Mallow. Patrons from Dublin and Waterford (N73 & N72) should take the town park bypass to reach the roundabout.

Public Transport
Mallow is well served by bus and rail. Most trains from Dublin (Heuston Station) to Cork stop at Mallow. Tel: Irish Rail (Iarnrod Eireann) 00 353 1 836 6222 for train timetable. Taxi service from Mallow Station to the racecourse.

Refreshment Facilities
Wide range from fast food to self-service; full restaurant and corporate facilities.

Local Hotels
Hiberian Hotel Tel: 00 353 22 21588, Mallow Park Hotel Tel: 00 353 22 21527, Longueville House Tel: 00 353 22 47156 and Springfort Hall Tel: 00 353 22 21278, Mallow; Assolas House Tel: 00 353 29 50015 in Kanturk

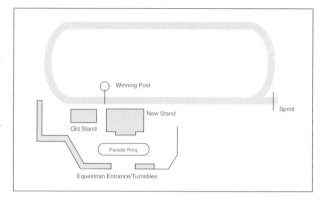

Local Restaurants
The Roundabout Inn & Restaurant and Kepplers in Mallow

Places of Interest/Activities
Mallow Castle and herd of white deer in Mallow; Doneraile Park in Doneraile; Blarney Castle in Blarney; also fishing, golf and pony trekking.

Curragh

Contact: Paul Hensey – General Manager (phensey@currach.ie), Evan Arkwright – Commercial Manager (eark@curragh.ie), Trisha Byrne – Hospitality Manager (sales@curragh.ie) at Curragh Racecourse, The Curragh, Co Kildare Tel: 00 353 45 441205 Fax 00 353 45 441442 E-mail: *info@curragh.ie* Website: *www.curragh.ie*

The Curragh is Ireland's premier international racecourse steeped in history and tradition.

The 17th century saw the Curragh become a sporting resort of the chief governors and administrators of Ireland. Every summer Dublin Castle was almost deserted as the lord lieutenant and his entourage came to Kildare to watch or compete in the racing at the Curragh. The number of King's Plates varied over the two centuries from 1700, but the vast majority of them were contested on the Curragh. Not surprisingly therefore the Curragh became the social centre and administrative headquarters of racing in Ireland over that time.

Artist: **Peter Curling AN IRISH POINT-TO-POINT** *Courtesy of:* **Rosenstiel's**

Artist: **Terence Gilbert CURRAGH** Courtesy of: **The Artist**

At the end of the 18th century, the Curragh had become permanently fringed by the lodges and stables of the most prominent owners, breeders and trainers in the country. These lodges and stables in name and even in fabric have survived in the hands of an equally illustrious racing community today. The first Irish Derby took place at the Curragh in 1866—this famous Classic has a legendary reputation for bringing out the best in horses and riders. It also ranks as Ireland's premier sporting and social event.

Today, as the headquarters of thoroughbred racing in Ireland, the Curragh caters for all five classic races in the country, as well as fifteen other prestigious meetings during the Irish racing calendar.

20 Meetings are scheduled to take place in 2005 from March until October. 42 Stakes races take place at the Curragh including all five Irish Classic races – The Budweiser Irish Derby, Boylesports Irish 1,000 and 2,000 Guineas, The Irish Field St. Leger and the Darley Irish Oaks together with five other Group One contests.

Location
The Curragh racecourse is situated 29 miles south west of Dublin City Centre on the main Dublin-Cork-Limerick road between Newbridge and Kildare town (take exit at junction 10 off M7). It is approximately 50 minutes by car from Dublin airport (take M50 and exit at N7 south) and is easily accessible from all major Ferryports. It is nine miles from Naas and two miles from Newbridge.

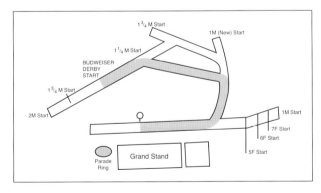

Public Transport
By rail from Dublin (Heuston Station) to the racecourse (approx 500 yards from the entrance). Trains stop at the Curragh on Classic Days and in Kildare town on other days with a free shuttle bus available to transport to and from the racecourse. To check train schedules contact Iarnrod Eireann on 00 353 1 836 6222. A special bus leaves Busaras, Store Street, Dublin 1, for the Curragh on racedays and departs the racecourse after the last race. For further information on departure times contact Bus Eireann 00 353 1 836 6111. Special coaches can be hired for group outings, for further details contact 00 353 45 879007.

Admission Rates
General admission includes access to all facilities excluding the premier level and hospitality suites. Premier Level Access and seats can be purchased on racedays. A reserved enclosure and West End enclosure operate on Budweiser Irish Derby day only. Admission prices can be found by accessing www.curragh.ie or are as follows: regular meetings €15, Group 1 €18, and classic meetings €20. Race tickets for all meetings can also be purchased online at www.curragh.ie Discounts for students and senior citizens are available. Children under 15, accompanied by an adult, gain free admission, except on Irish Derby day. Group discounts for all meetings are available on request.

Owners and Trainers Facilities
Owners and Trainers can utilise a designated section, located beside the main escalator in the centre of the main grandstand, while the owners and trainers bar is located on the Premier Level.

Membership
Membership Club badges are available for purchase. In addition, Membership with Premier Level Access, Member ship with Premier Level Seat and Young Membership (16 to 25 years old) is available. Members can enjoy a variety of exclusive privileges including designated car parking, bar and area on main grandstand. Members can also take advantage of concessions at other racecourses including Newmarket and Doncaster.

Artist: **Peter Curling FROSTY MORNING** Courtesy of: **Rosenstiel's**

Corporate Hospitality
There are a variety of catering options including all-in hospitality packages, etc. Premier Level Suites and Hospitality Rooms are available to cater for 10-160 people. All-in hospitality packages include: Premier Level Access Badge, racecard, reserved seat, pre-lunch reception, four course lunch with wine, complimentary bar, afternoon tea. Contact Trisha Byrne (Hospitality Manager) or Lisa McGoldrick, (Sales and Marketing Executive) at the racecourse on 00 353 45 441205. Suites can be viewed on line at www.curragh.ie.

Sponsorship
There are a variety of race sponsorship and other promotional opportunities at the Curragh including 7 race days with live television coverage by RTE. Race sponsorship packages start from €2,500 and can include a variety of entertainment and hospitality options together with branding, advertising and promotional opportunities. There are also a variety of opportunities for on site sales, merchandise displays, trade stands and on site sampling.

Refreshment Facilities
The Horseshoe Restaurant at the Curragh is open from noon on racedays. To reserve tables for lunch and afternoon tea call 00 353 1 4566046. Within the Tote Hall, located on the ground floor of the main grandstand, there is a self service area with hot meals and snacks served from noon onwards, together with the Weeping Tiger Thai food outlet which also serves delicious coffees and ice creams. There are five bars. The Curragh View Bar and Horseshoe Bar on the first floor have clear views of the course and the finishing post.

The Curragh View Bar also serves hot and cold food from a deli and baguette bar. The Vintage Crop Bar is located under the West Stand next to the bookmakers ring. There is also a bar in the main Tote hall, while the Balcony Bar and Café is located on the Premier Level. There is also the Champagne Bar and Bistro, Horace Pinks Bar with live traditional music and Dan Donnellys Diner.

Other Facilities
A big screen is provided for all fixtures, while a PA system relays full race commentary to all areas of the course. There is a closed circuit TV in all public areas and an on-course betting shop showing British racing via SIS. A Ladbrokes betting shop is located in the main Tote Hall. Plenty of free car parking.

For children a crèche and outdoor playground are provided at the west end of the stand. In both these areas children are supervised by qualified nursing and child care staff. A Gift Shop carrying a range of high quality Curragh merchandise is located in the Tote Hall.

Local Hotels
Keadeen Hotel Tel: 00 353 45 431666 in Newbridge; Stand House Hotel Tel: 00 353 45 436177, Curragh Lodge Hotel Tel: 00 353 45 522144, Kildare; Kilkea Castle Tel: 00 353 45 503 45156, Castledermot; Ardenode Hotel Tel: 00 353 45 864198, Ballymore Eustace; Tulfarris House Tel: 00 353 45 867555, Blessington; Barberstown Castle Tel: 00 353 1 628 8157, Kildare Hotel and Country Club Tel: 00 353 1 601 7200, Straffan; Kilashee House Hotel Tel: 00353 45 879277, Naas; City West Hotel, Golf, Conference and Leisure Resort Tel: 00353 1 4588566, The Osprey Hotel, Naas, Tel: 045 881111

Local Restaurants
Red House Inn, all in Newbridge; Silken Thomas and Kristianas in Kildare; Hangmans Arch, Milltown Berney's, Kilcullen and Poulaphouca House close to Ballymore Eustace, Ballymore Inn, Lemongrass, Naas and Citywest, and Weeping Thaiger . Contact the Irish Tourist Board Tel: 0207 493 3201 for a full accommodation list.

Places of Interest/Activities
Irish National Stud; Japanese Gardens in Kildare; Castletown House in Celbridge; Lakeside Leisure Centre in Blessington; also golf, fishing, hunting, horse riding.

Down Royal

Contact: Mr Michael Todd, at Down Royal Racecourse, Maze, Lisburn, Co Down BT27 5BW Tel: 02892 621256 Fax: 02892 621433.

Home of the Northern Ireland Festival of Racing held in November each year, Down Royal attracts the cream of the National Hunt world.

Florida Pearl, Looks Like Trouble, See More Business and Moscow Flyer, a three times winner at the Festival, top the list of leading horses that have competed at Northern Ireland's top race meeting.

The history of Down Royal goes back over 300 years to the reign of James II. Created by Royal Charter in 1685, The Down Royal Corporation of Horse Breeders was tasked with "Encouraging the Breed in the County of Down". Undoubtedly the most famous horse to race at Down Royal was the "Byerly Turk" one of the three foundation stallions of the Stud Book. Down Royal Racecourse is the home of the Northern Ireland Festival of Racing.

Location
Down Royal Racecourse is situated 2½ miles from Lisburn and 10 miles south of Belfast. It is adjacent to the A1 which is the main Belfast/Dublin route. The Racecourse is twenty minutes from Belfast International Airport and thirty minutes from Belfast City Airport.

Corporate Hospitality
Corporate hospitality packages are available for all race meetings.

Refreshment Facilities
The Racecourse has a modern Grandstand with a capacity for 2,500 people and incorporates the following public amenities: Large Island Bar, Fast Food Counters, Carvery Counter, Tote Hall, Seating and Tables, Toilets, Close Circuit T.V., Viewing Windows overlooking Parade Ring

Local Hotels
Beechlawn Hotel Tel: (02890) 612974, Dunmurry; White Gables Hotel, Hillsborough; Ballymac Hotel Tel: (02892) 684313, Stoneyford, Lisburn

Artist: **John King AT STUD** *Courtesy of:* **The Artist**

Local Restaurants

The Racecourse Inn, Maze, Lisburn; The Hillside Restaurant, Hillsborough (Egon Ronay Recommended); The Plough, Hillsborough (Egon Ronay Recommended); The Tidi Doffer, Ravernet, Lisburn (Winner of the British Airways Award for best hostelry).

Places of Interest/Activities

Irish Linen Centre/Lisburn Museum, Lisburn (award-winning attraction). Tourist Information available - (02892) 660038. Hillsborough - a beautiful Georgian village with many speciality shops, pubs and restaurants.

Downpatrick

Contact: Mr Iain Duff, Doonhamer, 71 Lismore Road, Downpatrick, Co Down Tel: 02844 841125 Fax: 02844 842227. c/o Ballydugan Road, Downpatrick, Co Down, Racedays: 02844 612054 Fax: 02844 615923.

The first race meeting to be held at Downpatrick was over 300 years ago–1685. Racing has continued to take place with few breaks since, and on the present course for the last 200 years which is situated one mile away from the centre of this historic town.

A tight, undulating track of 1¼ miles; many top National Hunt horses have started their careers at Downpatrick including the dual National winner Rhyme n' Reason and Cheltenham winners Rathgorman, Tourist Attraction and Sparky Gayle.

Downpatrick is possibly the friendliest course in Ireland with a strong local following. It has a supporters club which was formed in the early '70s and has raised substantial sums since its inception. Notably, Downpatrick is one of the few racecourses where all races are sponsored.

A new grandstand completed in 2000 holds over 2500 racegoers. Facilities include: Fast food restaurant, Tote, on-course betting shop, bar. Corporate facilities are available. For further details contact the racecourse.

Local Hotels

Burrendale Hotel and Country Club, Newcastle Tel: (02844) 722599

Dundalk

Contact: Margaret Bothwell, Manager, at Millgrove, Ballymascanlon, Dundalk, Co. Louth, Tel: 00 353 42 9371271.

Closed for major refurbishment until 2004.

Fairyhouse

Contact: Dick Sheil, Manager at Fairyhouse Racecourse, Ratoath, Co. Meath, Tel: 00 353 1 8256167 Fax: 00 353 1 8256051. E-mail: *info@fairyhouseracecourse.ie* Website: *www.fairyhouseracecourse.ie*

Fairyhouse is the home of Ireland's premier National Hunt race, the Powers Gold Label Irish Grand National, which is run every year on Easter Monday. In 2005 it will be on the second day of our popular Easter Festival which will run from Sunday 27th to Tuesday 29th March.

The first meeting held in Fairyhouse was in 1848 when the Ward Union Hunt held their point-to-point at this venue. From these small beginnings Fairyhouse quickly established itself as one of Ireland's premier racecourses. In 1870 the Irish Grand National was run and the winner was 'Sir Robert Peel'. The Grand National quickly became Ireland's most valuable and prestigious steeplechase and each success has its own rich tale, none more amazing than the win in 1929 of a six year old mare 'Alike', owned and ridden by 5'4" Frank Wise who was missing three fingers and who rode with a wooden leg.

Fairyhouse has always been one of the finest and fairest racecourses and continues to attract the leading horses both on the flat and over jumps. Arkle, Desert Orchid, Flying Bolt, Captain Christy, Prince Regent, Persian War, L'Escargot, and more recently Istabraq, See More Business and Bobbyjo are just some of the legendary greats that have graced the almost 2 mile circuit.

The racecourse is located 12 miles north west of Dublin, just off the N2 or the N3. The racecourse is within half an hour's drive

*Artist: **Booth Malone** FIRST LOT Courtesy of: **Frost & Reed***

from Dublin Airport and City Centre, and is easily accessible via the Westlink motorway and Blanchardstown bypass. Bus Eireann provides a special bus service from Busaras for race meetings. Tel: 00 353 1 8366111.

In 2005 Fairyhouse will host 19 days racing with the feature being the three day Easter Festival featuring the Powers Gold Label Irish Grand National, the Menolly Homes Handicap Hurdle and the Powers Gold Cup. The Winter festival (Dec 3rd – 4th) features three Grade 1 races and is now firmly established as Ireland's first major National Hunt fixture each new season. Fairyhouse also races on New Year's Day (Jan 1st).

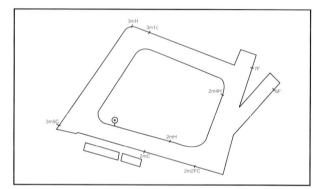

Fairyhouse has an annual membership package, which includes admission to all race meetings in 2005, access to the Members car park, admission to the Members Room in the Jameson Stand, with a Members only area in the grandstand. Fairyhouse has a long established reciprocal arrangement with other Irish and UK racecourses. Fairyhouse Members are entitled to all members facilities on specified dates each year at Navan, Punchestown, the Curragh, Newcastle and Uttoxeter. Annual Membership for 2005 is €175.

Fairyhouse has a fully supervised and equipped crèche for children aged up to 9 years of age, with both indoor and outdoor play areas.

The racecourse opened The Powers Gold Label stand and the refurbished Jameson Stand in November 1999. Fairyhouse is now firmly established as one of the most modern facilities in the country, providing an outstanding level of comfort and service.

Throughout the year, Corporate Facilities, including private suites and corporate function rooms, are available for numbers from 10 to 1,000. All function rooms have Tote, CCTV and either silver service or buffet style dining.

Artist: **Heather St Clair Davis HARD HELD**
Courtesy of: **Frost & Reed**

Artist: **Heather St Clair Davis OUT IN THE COUNTRY**
Courtesy of: **Frost & Reed**

Local Hotels
Ashbourne Court Hotel, Ashbourne Tel: 000 353 1 8359300; Ashbourne House Hotel, Ashbourne Tel: 00353 1 8350167; The Ardboyne Hotel, Navan Tel: 00353 46 23119; The Newgrange Hotel, Navan Tel: 00 353 46 74100; The Glenroyal Hotel, Maynooth Tel: 00353 1 6290909; The Straffan Lodge Hotel, Maynooth Tel: 00353 1 6285002; Barberstown Castle Hotel, Straffan Tel: 00353 1 6288157.

Refreshment Facilities
The Panoramic Restaurant in the Powers Gold Label Stand with views of the racetrack and parade ring/winners enclosure offers four course silver served lunch for €38 per person. For festival prices please contact the racecourse. Other catering facilities include a Self-Service Restaurant and fast food outlets and a choice of six bars.

Local Restaurants
Big Cicero's in Ashbourne, Grandstand Restaurant, Ryan's Steak House and Mulan Chinese in Ratoath; The Mill House in Clonee; The County Club in Dunshaughlin; Chez Francis, Kilbride; Caffreys, Batterstown.

Places of Interest/Activities
The racecourse is close to the historic sites of Tara, Slane and Newgrange as well as the beautiful Boyne Valley. Fishing and golf are available nearby.

Galway

Contact: **Mr John Moloney, Manager at Galway Racecourse, Ballybrit, Co Galway Tel: 00 353 91 753 870 Fax: 00 353 91 752 592, Web site: www.galwayraces.com. E-mail: information@galwayraces.com**

Records of organised race meetings in Co Galway go back to the middle of the 18th century and, according to local tradition, steeplechase races were run annually at Kiltulla, east of Ballybrit, for many years prior to 1868. In 1868, due to flooding of the course, they were transferred to Bushfield, beyond Oranmore. These, we are told, were the forerunners of the Galway races.

Sources record that there was an attendance of around 40,000 on the opening day at Ballybrit on Tuesday, 17th August 1869, and that 35,000 people turned up on the second day of the meeting. It is reported that the park in Eyre Square was used as a camping site to accommodate the huge crowds that arrived for the occasion. The first meeting was an overwhelming success and the Galway Races have gone from strength to strength ever since. The Galway Plate is one of the most important steeplechases in Ireland.

The new Millennium Stand with its viewing terrace for 8,000 people and a second floor seating balcony for 2,000 people also features a wide range of amenities. The 1999 summer festival meeting became the first festival in Ireland to run for a full week–where new records for both attendances and betting were set.

Artist: **Peter Smith FLOOD-TIDE** *Courtesy of:* **Frost & Reed**

Location
Galway is 136 miles from Dublin. The racecourse is situated three miles outside the city centre off the Galway-Tuam road. Directions to the course from the city are clearly marked with AA signs.

Public Transport
Regular train service to Galway from Dublin (Heuston Station). Tel: Irish Rail (Iarnrod Eireann) 00 353 1 836 6222 for train timetables. Special continuous bus service from Galway city centre during racing.

Admission Rates
Admission for the festival in July will be €15 - €25, September Festival €10 - €15, and the October festival €15. For further information contact Galway Racecourse Tel: 00 353 91 753870.

Corporate Hospitality
Throughout the festival week the programme of National Hunt and flat racing including the famous Galway Hurdle and Galway Plate guarantees exciting racing for seven days. The Galway races 'Hospitality Village' offers a choice of packages in the Blazers Pavilion (ideal for groups of 10 or more) or Blazers Private Suite (for groups of 50 or more). Marquees are erected for the Summer/ Autumn Festival, providing hospitality suites for all entertaining guests. There is also a new panoramic restaurant on the top level of the new Millennium Stand which caters for 200 people.

Refreshment Facilities
Self service carvery restaurant, seafood wine bar, snack bars and bars within the Millennium Stand.

Local Hotels
Ardilaun House Hotel Tel: 00 353 91 521433, Corrib Great Southern Hotel Tel: 00 353 91 755281; Galway Ryan Hotel Tel: 00 353 91 753181, Oranmore Lodge Tel: 00 353 91 794400; Victoria Hotel Tel: 00 353 91 564924; Great Southern Hotel Tel: 00 353 91 564041; Park House Hotel Tel: 00 353 91 564926; Radisson SAS Hotel Tel: 00 353 91 539300; Quality Inn Tel: 00 353 91 792244; Oyster Manor Hotel Tel: 00 353 91 796777 and Connemara Coast Hotel Tel: 00 353 91 592108, Galway; and Ashford Castle Tel: 00 353 92 46003, Cong, Station House Hotel Tel: 00 353 95 21699, Clifden. Renvyle House Hotel 095- 43511.

Local Restaurants
Park House, Eyre House, Malte House and Archway Restaurants in Galway; Twelve Pins, Donnelly's and Ty ar Mor in Barna; Drimcong House in Moycullen

Places of Interest/Activities
Walking tours of Galway, Connemara, Burren, Co Clare, Coole Park, Gort and the Aran Islands; also golf, fishing and pony trekking

Artist: **Peter Smith FINAL WORK** *Courtesy of:* **Frost & Reed**

Gowran Park

Contact: Ms Jane Williams, General Manager at Gowran Park Race Company Limited Gowran, Co. Kilkenny Tel: 00 353 56 7726225 Fax: 00 353 56 7726173. E-mail: *gowranpk@eircom.net* Website: *www.gowranpark.ie*

Since the first race meeting was held in June 1914, the course has become recognised as one of the best trial courses for both steeplechasing and flat racing in the islands. Levmoss, who pulled off the unique double of the Ascot Gold Cup and the Prix de L'Arc de Triomphe, first won on the flat at Gowran. Arkle, Nicholas Silver and Foinavon all ran at Gowran before going on to greater success overseas. Recently, Danoli and Doran's Pride have raced against each other at the brand new October Kilkenny Racing Festival.

The Thyestes Chase (January) is the big event of the calendar, the first major steeplechase in the year. The Red Mills trial Hurdle (February) has become one of the classic Cheltenham Trials, and if Cheltenham week has not satisfied your taste for racing, the Tetratema Cup, which has been run since 1918, takes place in April.

In May the flat racing kicks off with The Glanbia Classic trial over the bank holiday weekend, and in June the Victor McCalmont Memorial Stakes and the McEnery Cup are run. The ever popular mid-June Jack Duggan Handicap Hurdle keeps the national hunt fans happy. Mid-October is the Kilkenny Racing Festival, a 2-day event which draws big crowds, The Langton House Handicap Hurdle and the National Lottery Agents Champion Stakes.

Location
The racecourse is approximately ¼ of a mile outside Gowran village on the Dublin-Waterford road. Gowran is 8 miles from Kilkenny, 80 miles from Dublin, 15 miles from Carlow and 5 miles from Thomastown. In addition to its racecourse, Gowran Park, with its scenic setting and natural features, have now opened an 18-hole championship golf course. Five holes are located within the racetrack itself and feature two lakes, and the remaining holes are set among the magnificent nature and extensive woodlands for which Gowran Park Track has long been renowned. Membership is currently available, please contact the golf administration office Tel: 00 353 56 77 26699 for further details.

Public Transport
Bus Eireann provides a special bus service from Dublin (Busaras) for most race meetings. Tel: 00 353 1 836 6111 to check times of departure. Also Rapid Express Tel. 00 353 51 872 149 and Tom Duffy (special raceday coaches from Dublin) Tel. 00 353 1 832 8169

Corporate Hospitality
The racecourse has recently opened its superb new Grandstand and refurbished Private Members Club Room. These new facilities overlooking the racecourse include silver service restaurants, self service restaurants, Tote hall, snack bars and bars. In addition we have the Helen Sheane Suite, which caters for 30-100 people.

Refreshment Facilities
Self service restaurant, snack bar and bars

Local Hotels
Ormonde Hotel Tel: 00 353 56 77 23900 Kilkenny; Langton House Hotel Tel: 00 353 56 77 65133, Kilkenny; Kilkenny River Court Hotel Tel: 00 353 56 7723388, Kilkenny; Mount Juliet Hotel Tel: 00 353 56 7773000, Thomastown; Kilkea Castle Tel: 00 353 503 7745156, Castledermot.

Local Restaurants
Langton House and Kyteler's Inn in Kilkenny; Lord Bagenal in Leighlinbridge; The Long Man of Kilfane in Kilfane

Places of Interest/Activities
Kilkenny Castle, St Canice's Cathedral, Rothe House, Castle Yard, all in Kilkenny; also fishing, horse riding and golf, shopping and plenty of festivals.

Kilbeggan

Contact: Mr Patrick J Dunican, Manager at Kilbeggan Racecourse, Kilbeggan, Co Westmeath Tel: 00 353 506 32176 Fax: 00 353 506 32125 E-mail: *info@kilbegganraces.com* Website: *www.kilbegganraces.com*

Ireland's only all-National Hunt Racecourse – the only racecourse in Ireland where races are over jumps under national hunt rules – the type of racing the Irish love best. That makes for an entertaining and heart-stopping spectacle and you are close enough to see the skill, excellence and bravery of man and animal.

Kilbeggan Races is a truly Irish occasion. The quiet midlands town is transformed on race evenings into a festival of social and sporting pleasure, drawing admirers from every corner of Ireland. You can meet friends, circulate freely; you can eat drink or cheer without restriction, you can bring the family or whoever; where for your few pounds the odds are much better than a lottery ticket, and where you can boast afterwards it was sheer skill that made you pick the winner.

If you are bright, witty and rich you will enjoy Kilbeggan Races and if you are not, you will enjoy them just the same. Westmeath County Council sponsor a feature hurdle race in May. The Midlands National is a July highlight and Bank of Ireland sponsor a major hurdle race, Thornton recycling sponsor a feature chase in May also Max Premium Dog Food sponsor a Handicap Steeplechase during the season, attracting hundreds to the racing the Irish love best, National Hunt. The only racecourse in Ireland where all races are over jumps under National Hunt Rules, the friendship and atmosphere give Kilbeggan the edge over other events. The neighbourly attitude makes it even easier for visitors to join in and savour the excitement of real racing enjoyment.

In the heart of Ireland this is a unique course with a natural setting, both easy on the eye and ideal for viewing. The development of Kilbeggan Racecourse is a great credit to the local community which is reflected in the increasing numbers of visitors who attend - it really is worth a visit.

Location
By road: Kilbeggan is situated on the crossroads of Ireland, easily accessible from all directions. The racecourse is approximately one mile from the town centre, on the north side. It is 13 miles from Mullingar, 20 miles from Athlone, 8 miles from Tullamore, 57 miles from Dublin, 313 miles from Cork and 198 miles from Belfast. By rail: Tullamore station.

Public Transport
Bus service from Dublin (Busaras) Tel 00 353 1 8366111 for time of departure. Taxis from town centre to racecourse.

Corporate Hospitality
Hospitality in the Balcony Suite – the glass fronted Balcony Suite on the first floor of the new Pavilion has first class hospitality facilities to accommodate up to 200 guests, it can also be subdivided or let in tables for 10. The Balcony Suite is superbly located opposite the winning post, adjacent to the Bookmakers Ring and also has its own private balcony with a Panoramic View overlooking the entire racetrack.

Hospitality in the Tented Village – the Tented Village at Kilbeggan is regarded as the jewel in the crown of Irish corporate hospitality facilities, superbly located on the hill with a panoramic view overlooking the entire racecourse and also adjacent to the parade ring, main tote and bookmakers. It has facilities to cater for groups from 100 people to 2000 people.

Refreshment Facilities
The facilities at Kilbeggan are now on a par with the best available in Ireland and include the new Pavilion bar overlooking the winning post, self-service restaurant, snack bar and, of course, the tented bar with live music on the hill overlooking the entire racecourse. The bars are a popular meeting place with visitors and locals alike, and make the ideal place for post race analysis as well as a nice relaxing pint.

Local Hotels/Restaurants

Bridge House Hotel Tel: 00 353 506 22000, Tullamore. Bloomfield House Hotel Tel: 00 353 44 40894, and the Greville Arms Hotel Tel: 00 353 44 48563, Mullingar.

Places of Interest/Activities

Locke's Distillery, Museum, Belvedere House and Gardens, Mullingar (Genesis) Tullynally Castle, Birr Castle and gardens, also numerous golf courses and lakes for both coarse and fly fishing.

Other Facilities

So much more than a racecourse – Kilbeggan racecourse is the perfect venue for any event; the magnificent new Pavilion forms the centrepiece of the Events and Leisure facilities. There are facilities to accommodate conferences, party nights, exhibitions, seminars and product launches. In addition, acres of hard standing and grassed areas are available for open-air exhibitions, team building events and corporate fun days.

Killarney

Contact: Mr John Looney, General Manager, Killarney Race Co. Ltd., Killarney, Co Kerry Tel: 00 353 64 31125 Fax: 00 353 64 31860.

The ideal opportunity to get away from it all, Go racing in Killarney you will keep coming back.

Renowned in verse, song, literature and paintings - the lakes and mountains of Killarney surround the Killarney race track, making it the most spectacular setting of any racecourse in the world.

The tradition of Killarney Races goes back over 150 years with racing at the current location since 1936. Throughout the years a host of international celebrities and thousands of locals alike are drawn to the May and July Festivals to witness an exciting mix of flat, hurdle and national hunt racing. The warmth of welcome as well as the quality of entertainment ensures crowds return year after year. Killarney has two of Ireland's fastest growing festival meetings which just get bigger and better each year.

Location

The racecourse is less than ½ a mile from Killarney Town Centre. There are literally hundreds of Hotels or Bed & Breakfasts within walking distance and with major road access, regular train service and a local airport, Killarney is the ideal destination for that getaway trip to the races.

Public Transport

Regular train service from Dublin (Heuston Station). Tel: Irish Rail (Iarnrod Eireann) 00 353 1 836 6222 for train timetables. For Bus services call Bus Eireann at – 00 353 1 836 6111.

Corporate Hospitality

Given Killarney's spectacular setting and facilities it is the perfect location to impress clients, reward staff or just to have a great, unique company day out. Please contact John Looney at 00 353 64 31125 for details.

Refreshment Facilities

A variety of bars and snacks kiosks spread throughout the facility as well as hot lunches served in the main bar area mean all tastes are catered for.

Local Hotels/Restaurants

Killarney is the tourist capital of Ireland and is awash with quality hotels and restaurants. Lakeside five-star hotels, B & B's and self catering units are all available – for more information contact The Killarney Tourist Office at 00 353 64 31633. Killarney also boasts some of the finest restaurants to cater for the most discerning of culinary palates.

Places of Interest/Activities

When you are not at the races you are spoilt for choice as to how to fill your time in Killarney. Kerry is a golfer's paradise – possibly the golf capital of Europe with 99 championship holes of golf within a 9 mile radius. The Race Course is home to Ireland's premier 9-hole course which is open up to raceday and reopens immediately after racing. Outside that you can choose from boat trips, hill walking, pony trekking, fishing, mountaineering, jaunting car rides, as well as the Ring of Kerry and old world architecture.

We will be delighted to see you.

*Artist: **Booth Malone** IN THE PADDOCK Courtesy of: **Frost & Reed***

Laytown

Contact: Mr Kevin Coleman, the Secretary/Manager, at 9 Palace Street, Drogheda, Co Louth, Tel: 00 353 41 984 2111, Fax: 00 353 41 983 7566.

Local folklore has it that it was the parish priest who, in 1876, organised the first race meeting on Laytown's three miles of golden strand. Held intermittently since then, it was not until 1901 that local landowner, Paddy Delaney, established the meeting as we know it today.

Laytown races have not changed very much through the years, but they are unique because they are the only grandstand races held in Europe which have the approval of the governing bodies. The enclosure consists of a three acre field, elevated above the beach. Steps have been built up into the face of the sand dunes and these form the Grandstand. Marquees are erected on the day before the races and these are used to provide a weigh room, bars and snack bars.

On Race Day, the strand is closed from early morning and work on the course then commences. By the time the first race is ready to start the tide has gone out, and racing can begin.

Location
Laytown is a small seaside resort on the east coast of Ireland, 29 miles north of Dublin. To reach the course, turn off the N1 Dublin-Belfast road at Julianstown.

Public Transport
Regular train services from Drogheda and Dublin (Connolly Station). Special bus service from Drogheda. Tel: 00 353 1 836 6111 Irish Rail (Iarnrod Eireann) for train timetable.

Refreshment Facilities
Snack bars and bars provided in the marquees.

Local Hotels
Neptune Beach Hotel Tel: 00 353 41 9827107, Bettystown; Old Mill Hotel, Julianstown; Rosnaree Park Hotel, West Court Hotel Tel: 00 353 41 983 0965 and Boyne Valley Hotel Tel: 00 353 41 9837737, Drogheda; Conyngham Arms Hotel Tel: 00 353 41 9884444, Slane; Ashbourne House Hotel, Ashbourne.

Local Restaurants
Bacchus at the Coast Guard, Bettystown; Monasterboice Inn, Drogheda; Forge, Collon; Bay Leaf, Laytown.

Leopardstown

Contact: Matt O'Dwyer, General Manager, Tom Burke, Racing Manager, Leopardstown Racecourse, Foxrock, Dublin 18. Tel: 00 353 1 289 0500 Mobile: 087 234 7183 Fax: 00 353 1 289 2634. E-mail: *info@leopardstown.com* Website: *www.leopardstown.com* Aertel Teletext Page 277. Office hours are 9.30am – 5.30pm Monday to Friday and from 8.00am on racedays.

Leopardstown Racecourse hosts 22 race meetings throughout the year, providing a mixture of National hunt and flat fixtures. The four-day Christmas Festival at the end of December and the Hennessy Cognac Gold Cup in February are the highlights of the National Hunt season.

The most prestigious flat races are The Derrinstown Stud Derby Trial and The Baileys Irish Champion Stakes – part of the World Series Racing Championship, which is run in September each year.

Racing at Leopardstown is a popular and effective vehicle for corporate sponsors. All of the major National Hunt and Flat races are sponsored – The Pierse Hurdle, The AIG Europe Champion Hurdle, The Hennessy Cognac Gold Cup, The Derrinstown Stud Derby

Artist: **Terence Gilbert FLORIDA PEARL** *Courtesy of:* **The Artist**

Trial and The Derrinstown Stud 1000 Guineas Trial. In December, The Lexus Chase, The Paddy Power Chase and The Bewleys Hotel December Festival Hurdle are an integral part of the four-day Christmas Festival.

Location
Leopardstown Racecourse is the only remaining racecourse in the greater Dublin area and is located just six miles due south of Dublin city centre. It is set in superb surroundings, nestled in the foothills of the Dublin mountains overlooking Dublin Bay.

Access to the racecourse is via the M50 – coming from the north, west and south-west of Dublin; via the N11 – travelling southbound from Dublin city centre or northbound from Co. Wicklow. The web site gives detailed directions to the track, including an interactive map. We advise those planning to visit the racecourse to leave ample time for the journey, as traffic can be congested approaching the track. Car parking is free and there is a designated area for coach parking.

Public Transport
A racing bus operates from Busaras, Store Street, Dublin 1 on race days. The bus departs one hour before the first race and returns to Busaras 15 minutes after the last race. Contact Dublin Bus – Tel: 00 353 1 703 4420 to confirm time of departure. The Luas light rail is also in operation to Sandyford Terminal which is just 15 minutes walk from the racecourse.

Admission Tickets
Grandstand Admission includes access to the Parade Ring, the Bookmakers' Ring, Tote facilities, the Paddy Power SP Betting Shop, Grandstand seating and viewing areas, Club 92, Madigans Bar and Mc Guirks Golf Shop.

In addition to the Grandstand facilities above, the Reserved Enclosure comprises the Paddock Food Hall, Tote Hall, Tetrarch Bar, Jodami's Bar, Silken Glider Restaurant, Fillies Café Bar, Members Bar, the Reserved Stand viewing area and numerous snack bars and fast food outlets.

A Top Level Seat offers a superb view overlooking the finishing straight and includes access to the Champions Bar and the Larkspur Bar, located on the Top Level of the Reserved Stand.

Details regarding admission prices, race times, Tote Jackpot Guarantee/Rollover and racecard competitions can be found in the News & Events Section on the Home Page at www.leopardstown.com prior to each race meeting.

Membership

There are two Annual Membership options at Leopardstown. Annual Seat Holder membership incorporates a personalised viewing seat overlooking the finishing straight and includes access to the Champions Bar and the Larkspur Bar, both of which are situated on the Top Level of the Reserved Stand.

The Annual Members Badge includes entry to all fixtures, as well as access to the private Members Bar located within the Reserved Stand.

Corporate Hospitality

Leopardstown Racecourse is a thriving entertainment venue offering a choice of superb facilities. In conjunction with our caterers, your event will be skilfully organised and managed. There are many different hospitality options available catering for small parties, or large groups up to 1,000 people both on racedays and throughout the year.

Racedays: A Single Private Suite accommodates 12 for a silver service meal and 24 for buffet style dining. A Double Private Suite accommodates 24 for a seated silver service meal and 40 for a buffet. These suites are located on the Top Level of the Reserved Stand and each suite has its own bar counter, private balcony overlooking the finishing straight, CCTV service and Tote facilities nearby.

The Levmoss Room and the Centenary Room can cater for 120 and 90 people respectively and, combined, up to 220 people. These hospitality rooms are located on the Top Level of the Reserved Stand and have their own private bar, CCTV service and nearby Tote facilities.

The Leopardstown Pavilion caters for groups ranging from 200+ to 1,000, and is unrivalled in the greater Dublin area in terms of facilities and sophistication. Strategically located overlooking the finishing straight, this superb glass fronted building has its own balcony area and provides excellent viewing on racedays. Tables can be reserved in the Silken Glider Restaurant on racedays, which will be available to you and your guests for the whole day. The restaurant, part of which overlooks the Parade Ring, accommodates up to 400 people and is located on the second floor of the Reserved Stand

Raceday bookings for Private Suites, Hospitality Rooms and the Leopardstown Pavilion are taken by Leopardstown Racecourse - Tel: 00 353 1 289 0500 Fax: 00 353 1 289 2634 E-mail: info@leopardstown.com.

Non-racedays: Many of the outstanding facilities at Leopardstown are utilised throughout the year. The purpose-built Leopardstown Pavilion allows for a myriad of uses making it the perfect venue for conferences and seminars, product launches and presentations, as well as receptions and gala evenings.

Anniversaries, 21st birthdays and office parties are celebrated in style in the Levmoss and Centenary Rooms, the Silken Glider Restaurant, the Champions' Bar and Jodami's, while the Private Suites provide a tranquil setting for confidential meetings and seminars. For details on non-raceday events please contact Bravo on Tel: 00 353 1 6745930.

Refreshment Facilities

Leopardstown offers an extensive range of bars and restaurants including Fillies Café Bar, which operates pub hours throughout the year – and on racedays, the Silken Glider Restaurant, Paddock Food Hall, Jodami's, Club 92, Tetrarch Bar and Madigans, as well as private bars for our Leopardstown Seat Holders and Annual Members.

Other Facilities

There is a free crèche facility which is operated on racedays. Located in close proximity to the main entrance building, it caters for children between two and ten, and opens an hour before the first race and closes before the last race.

A permanent AIB ATM Banklink facility is situated between the main entrance building and the crèche.

For those golf enthusiasts, there is a McGuirks Golf Shop which supplies a wide range of golf equipment and accessories.

For the more active, there is the West Wood Health and Fitness Centre, which also provides a special children's centre – Fit Zone. Tel: 00 353 1 289 3208

Leopardstown also boasts its own Golf Centre, an 18 hole, 'pay as you play' golf course situated within the in-field of the track, incorporating a 48 bay floodlit driving range. Tel: 00 353 1 289 5341

Within the Leopardstown complex is Club 92, a very popular Dublin night club, which operates four nights a week (Thursday to Sunday).

As you can see from the above, Leopardstown Racecourse is a thriving entertainment and leisure complex in its own right, with an estimated one million people utilising the facilities throughout the year.

Local Hotels

Bewleys Hotel, Leopardstown – Tel: 00 353 1 2935000, Fitzpatrick Castle Hotel, Killiney – Tel: 00 353 1 284 0700, Stillorgan Park Hotel, Stillorgan – Tel: 00 353 1 288 1621, Radisson SAS St Helen's Hotel, Blackrock – Tel: 00 353 1 218 6000, The Merrion Hotel – Tel: 00 353 1 6030600, Jurys Doyle Hotel Group (a chain of hotels in Dublin, many of them within easy reach of the racecourse) – Tel: 00 353 1 607 0000.

Local Restaurants

Leopardstown Inn in Leopardstown, Beaufield Mews in Stillorgan, The Goat Grill in Goatstown, La Casa in Stepaside and Coopers in Kilternan.

Places of Interest

Leopardstown Racecourse is just six miles from Dublin city centre which provides a wide range of attractions for visitors – galleries, museums, theatres, cinemas, cathedrals and shops, as well as Dublin Zoo in Phoenix Park, the largest enclosed public park in Europe.

Limerick

Contact: Mr Angus Houston, General Manager at Limerick Racecourse, Greenmount Park, Patrickswell, Limerick Tel: 00 353 61 320000 Fax: 00 353 61 355766. Website: *www.limerick-racecourse.com* E-mail: *info@limerick-racecourse.com*

Ireland's first new Racecourse for over fifty years, Greenmount Park opened its doors in October 2001 to over 18,000 on its inaugural raceday. The seventh location for Limerick races since 1790, following Bruff, Rathkeale, Newcastle, Lemonfield, Ballinacurra and Green Park, the track is built on a 400-acre site of an old stud farm on the outskirts of Limerick City, and is home to Grade 1 National Hunt and Flat racing all year round.

The Oval Track is right handed, 1 mile and 3 furlongs long on the outside and at 70 metres across at its widest point, it can provide fresh ground for most meetings. With 17 days programmed for 2005 including the 4 day Guinness Christmas Festival, Limerick continues to build its race programme in profile and prize money.

Schooling
All round schooling facilities include a 1-mile oval Euro track all weather gallop running on the inside track, schooling paddocks with fences and starting stalls complement to the racing activities.

The Hugh McMahon Stand
The magnificent new stand, on four levels can accommodate up to 6,000 people. It includes excellent Tote facilities and an S.P. shop on the ground floor and a state of the art Panoramic Restaurant with a capacity for 400 guests located on the third floor. There are 3 bars, fast food outlets and self-service restaurants within the complex. On the fourth floor there are thirteen hospitality boxes which may be rented on an annual or daily basis and accommodate up to 30 in each.

Non-Racedays
The development of the non racing business has seen Greenmount Park quickly become one of the premier leisure venues in South-West Ireland, hosting numerous conferences, exhibitions, public events and concerts. The stand is designed for multi-purpose use matching any top hotel facility. Packages can be tailored to suit any event from product launches and seminars to boardroom meetings. The natural beauty of the location, together with its ease of access and car parking add up to make this the ideal choice.

Local Hotels
The Radisson SAS – Ennis Road Limerick 061- 326666
The Woodlands House Hotel – Adare 061- 605100
The Dunraven Arms Hotel – Adare 061- 396633
The Adare Manor – Adare 061 396566
The South Court Hotel – 061 487487

Local Restaurants
The Locke Bar & Restaurant – Charlotte Quay Limerick 061- 413733
Tao Tao Chinese Restaurant – Patrickswell 061 – 355999
The Blue Door – Adare 061 – 396481
The Wild Geese – Adare 061 – 396451

Places of interest / Activities
King John's Castle in Limerick, Bunratty Folk Park, The Burren, The Cliffs of Moher, Clonshire Equestrian and Polo Centre, Golfing and Fishing.

Listowel

Contact: Mr Brendan Daly is the Secretary, c/o William Street, Listowel, Co Kerry, Tel/Fax: 00 353 68 21144.

Racing commenced at Listowel in 1858. The races were held previously at Ballyeagh, near Ballybunion, but due to faction fighting they had to be moved and Listowel was chosen as the new venue. Due to the popularity of races, known originally as the North Kerry Hunt Steeplechase, the meeting was extended from the original one-day event until it became a six-day fixture in 1992.

Listowel Races is one of Ireland's oldest and most successful racing festivals and is held in the last week of September. In addition there is a 2-day weekend race meeting in April.

Location
Listowel is 16 miles from Tralee and 50 miles from Limerick. The course is situated five minutes from the town centre.

Public Transport
Regular train services from Dublin (Heuston Station) to Tralee and Limerick. Tel: 00 353 1 836 6222 Irish Rail (Iarnrod Eireann) for train timetables. Special bus services are provided daily from Tralee and Limerick railway stations to Listowel during the festival meeting.

Corporate Hospitality Rooms
Hospitality room available to cater for 40-100 people. The new grandstand complex offers great facilities for all racegoers.

Refreshment Facilities
Dining room, self-service restaurant, snack bars, fast food outlets and bars.

Local Hotels
Listowel Arms Hotel Tel: 00 353 68 21500, Listowel; Cliff House Hotel Tel: 00 353 68 27777, Golf Hotel and The Marine Links Hotel Tel: 00 353 68 27139, Ballybunion. Contact the Irish Tourist Board Tel: 0207 493 3201 for a full accommodation list.

Artist: **Graham Isom ISTABRAQ** *Courtesy of:* **Rosenstiel's**

Local Restaurants
Three Mermaids, Horseshoe Bar, Elite Grill Room, Quirkes and Mamma Mia - all in Listowel.

Places of Interest/Activities
Town Park and Listowel Castle in Listowel. A local festival is held to coincide with the races providing nightly entertainment in the town; also golf and fishing.

Naas

Contact: Mrs Margaret McGuinness, Racecourse Manager or Sinead Cassidy, Marketing & PR Executive, Naas Race Company Plc, Tipper Road, Naas, Co Kildare, Tel: 00 353 45 897391 Fax: 00 353 45 879486. Website: *www.naasracecourse.com* Email: *goracing@naasracecourse.com*

Naas racecourse, located in the heart of Thoroughbred County of Kildare and just a walk from Naas town, is situated on the main dual carriageway on route N7 southbound. Dublin City is within an easy 20 miles reach from Naas Racecourse, just 35 miles drive from the Airport and within an hours drive from the Ferryports.

Naas boasts a Grade 1 National Hunt Track together with a Grade II Flat Track, with the stiff uphill finish making a true test for Cheltenham bound contenders. There are 15 exciting race meetings planned for 2005, with the famous 'Cheltenham Trial Day' occurring in February, the Swordlestown Stud Sprint Stakes in June and the top class 'Birdcatcher Day' taking place in October.

Facilities
Since 1998 Naas Racecourses has invested over €5 million in new facilities that have transformed the racecourse into a comfortable "people friendly" track. The new facilities have added a new dimension to a popular racecourse.

Facilities now on offer include a superb new Grandstand that features an indoor Tote betting hall, public bars, a Panoramic Restaurant and Corporate Suites. A self-service restaurant, public bars, a parade ring snack bar area, the themed Summer BBQs, a

*Artist: **Philip Toon** MORNIING RIDE Courtesy of: **The Artist***

members/owners and trainers bar, plus live bands at most meetings makes Naas the "place to race" if near by.

The facilities at Naas are also available for functions on non race days, i.e. functions, product launches, seminars, wedding receptions and exhibitions.

Admission
Sundays & Bank Holidays – Adults €15 / Students & OAPS €9/ Children Under 14 yrs FREE. All other days – Adults €12 / Students & OAPS €7 / Children Under 14 yrs FREE

Public Transport
Naas Racecourse is located just off the N7 en route into Naas town, just twenty five minutes drive from Dublin city. From Dublin Airport (M50, N7) 25 miles. From Dublin City (N7) 18 miles. Take the N7 (Naas Road) to Naas, racecourse gates are on you left as you enter the town.

Bus
A special return Bus Eireann service is available for racegoers, departing from Busaras in Dublin, straight to the track.
For more information, telephone (00 353) 01-8366111.

Train
A train service is available from Heuston Station in Dublin to Sallins located just minutes from Naas. A feeder bus system is available from Sallins to Naas. Taxi service is also in operation.
For more information, telephone (00 353) 01-8366222

Local Hotels
The Osprey Hotel Tel: 00 353 45 881111, The Ambassador Hotel Tel: 00 353 45 877064, Kill, Naas. Court Hotel, Naas. Town House Hotel, Naas. Harbour View Hotel, Naas. Hotel Keadeen Tel: 00 353 45 431666, Newbridge. Kildare Hotel and Country Club Tel: 00 353 1 601 7200, Straffan and Setanta House Hotel, Celbridge. Killashee House Tel: 00 353 45 879277 and The Stand House Hotel, Tel: 00 353 45 436177.

Local Restaurants
The Storehouse 00 353 45 889333, Butt Mullins 00 353 45 874252, Johnstown Inn 00 353 45 897547, Lemongrass 00 353 45 871544, The Red House 00 353 45 431516 and La Primavera 00 353 45 897926, Maloti Indian Restaurant 00 353 45 883660

Places of Interest
Irish National Stud. Japanese Gardens in Kildare. Fishing, golf, hunting and pony trekking.

Navan

Contact: Richard Lyttle Racing Manager c/o, Navan Racecourse, Proudstown, Navan, Co. Meath. Tel: 00 353 46 9021350, Fax: 00 353 46 9027964. E-mail: *info@navanracecourse.ie* Website: *www.navanracecourse.ie*

Navan Racecourse is 181 acres set in the heart of Co. Meath. From humble beginnings in 1920 Navan Racecourse has become a very special track in the minds of owners, trainers, jockeys and punters alike. Well established as an excellent pre-Cheltenham track, many of our greatest National Hunt horses have raced and won at Navan. Navan is recognised as one of Ireland's fastest growing tracks. It is a left handed one mile four furlongs long with a stiff uphill finish. There is also a straight six furlong track. Very often horses that win at Navan go on to perform very well in major races; examples include Limestone Lad, Like a Butterfly, Davids Lad, Solerina, Balapour, Kenilworth, Dutsdale Dancer and Emotional Moment.

The last few years have seen many changes at Navan Racecourse as it completed the first phase of its development plan in 1999, providing top class suites and restaurants. The racecourse is situated 2 miles from Navan town, 30 miles due north of Dublin City on the N3 and within easy reach of Drogheda, Dundalk, Newry, the Midlands and the N4 Dublin-Galway Road. Continuing its success over the past

Artist: **Heather St Clair Davis SCHOOLING CHASERS** *Courtesy of:* **Frost & Reed**

couple of years, Navan has established itself as a racecourse with great racing, great hospitality and great fun. Corporate racedays at Navan are tailored to individual company needs and are guaranteed to provide great racing, superb hospitality and excellent live entertainment after racing, it's the ideal opportunity for entertaining clients or employees.

Navan racecourse is primarily a National Hunt track and will host 16 meetings in 2005, it's main days are "The McCabe Builders Ltd Boyne Hurdle", Fortria Day and Navan's flagship meeting is the "Stanleybet Troytown Chase" in November, named after the famous Aintree Grand National Winner Troytown who was bred close by.

Navan's recent development has provided new bars, a large self-service restaurant and new corporate facilities overlooking the racetrack. These new facilities have been welcomed by Navan's loyal patrons who come again and again to this friendly welcoming track. Admission to the racecourse varies between €11 and €15. Day membership is also available. There is on course catering ranging from snack bars to full dining facilities. Corporate tables and private function rooms can be booked by arrangement. Restaurant and bar facilities are open seven days a week.

In addition to its racecourse, Navan has a fantastic 18 hole Golf Course with 9 holes lying alongside the track and the newer 9 being within the track itself. The thriving Golf Course brings new people to the racetrack throughout the year and membership is currently available– please contact the Administration Office at 00 353 46 90 72888 for more details. A 12 bay Golf Driving Range is also in operation.

Public Transport
Buses from Dublin depart from Busaras from 7.30am (9.00am on Sundays) and leave at approximately 1 hour intervals, arriving at the Mercy Convent in Navan approximately 1.5 miles from the racecourse. Bus Eireann also provide a service directly to the racecourse. Full details from Bus Eireann at 00 353 1 8366111 Web site - www.buseireann.ie

Local Hotels
Navan now has a number of excellent hotels, namely the Newgrange Hotel Tel: 00 353 46 90 23119, and the Ardboyne Hotel Tel: 00 353 46 90 73732 within the town offering excellent accommodation opportunities. Navan Tourist Information Office is located in the town centre Freephone 050300781, or by e-mail at info@meathtourism.ie; they will be very happy to provide advice on accommodation, bookings and attractions in the Meath district.

Local Restaurants
Being located close to Dublin, Navan has benefited from some exciting developments in the town. There are many excellent pubs and restaurants. The popular restaurants include Hudson's Bistro

Tel: 00 353 46 90 29231, the Loft Tel: 00 353 46 90 71755; China Garden Tel: 00 353 46 90 23938; Scanlon's of Kilberry Tel: 00 353 46 90 28330 and, of course, Navan Racecourse's own Bective Restaurant with catering by O'Brien Lynch Catering available for all types of functions.

Places of Interest
Other local attractions include the Passage Tomb of Newgrange (only 10 miles from the racecourse). Older than the Pyramids of Egypt, the tomb is over 5,000 years old and is one of the most famous megalithic monuments in Western Europe. Visit the recently renovated Trim Castle, parts which have been restored to its original state, and also the Kells Heritage Centre which will host the famous 'Book of Kells' at certain times of the year. Nestled in the Meath Valley is of course the River Boyne, which lends itself to many scenic walks and fishing opportunities. The famous Battle of the Boyne took place in 1690, and its site is now a popular tourist attraction.

Artist: **Peter Smith MORNING BANTER** *Courtesy of:* **Frost & Reed**

Punchestown

The management at Punchestown is headed by Manager Dick O'Sullivan who together with his capable team is contactable at the racecourse office. Tel: 00 353 45 897704 Fax: 00 353 45 897319. The address is Punchestown Racecourse, Naas, Co Kildare. E-mail: *racing@punchestown.com* **Website:** *www.punchestown.com*

As everyone already knows, Ireland is renowned for its unique and friendly atmosphere. No place is this seen to better effect than at Punchestown where even banks and schools are closed without question or complaint to enable everyone to participate in the festivities that take place each year! Peerless Punchestown, as it is often referred to, conjures up something special in the minds of all who have been fortunate enough to attend and sample the unique atmosphere that has made it famous. It has been a huge success story with growth beyond the stone walls and big banks which were used at the first meeting held in 1854 over two days, to what is today one of the premier National Hunt venues in Europe. Fences and hurdles were first introduced in the early 1950s but over 50 years on, Punchestown still maintains its famous bank course which is seen at its best in late April when it is raced over three times in four days. These races are truly unique to Punchestown and provide a great challenge for horse and rider as well as a wonderful spectacle for all National Hunt enthusiasts.

The racecourse has recently undergone a £20m redevelopment, which has seen it transformed into a state of the art complex, capable of catering for the huge crowds which are now attracted each year. It boasts top class restaurant facilities in the panoramic, glass-fronted restaurant overlooking the racecourse, the de Robeck restaurant, together with a self-service restaurant, seafood bar, and champagne bar as well as numerous snack food outlets throughout the grandstand. These are supported by the various hospitality marquees which are always packed to capacity and have a special atmosphere all of their own.

In the recent past, a concerted effort has been made to increase the number of both overseas horses and racegoers coming to the Irish National Hunt Festival Meeting, which takes place in late April each year. Situated close to airport and ferry terminals, it is no wonder that Punchestown attracted almost 6,000 overseas visitors in 2004 and with nearly €2m in prizemoney on offer and substantial travel incentives for overseas runners, the quality of the Festival's premier races has been the highlight of recent years. Stars such as Moscow Flyer, Hardy Eustace, Lord Sam, Rhinestone Cowboy, Iris Gift, Beef Or Salmon, Brave Inca and First Gold have ensured that the Irish National Hunt Festival provides a fitting end to the season and allows National Hunt fans everywhere a chance to witness a Cheltenham rematch on Irish soil!

The racecourse is easily accessible and is only 30 minutes from Dublin City centre travelling via the N7 to Naas which is only 3 miles from Punchestown. During the four day National Hunt Festival a special bus service is available from the Central Bus Station (Busaras), Store Street, Dublin 1 Tel: 000 353 1-836 6111. Punchestown is well signposted with well laid-out car parking facilities to ensure the ever increasing attendances are continually satisfied and sufficiently well catered for. The racecourse has a landing facility suitable for helicopters; however, the office must be notified prior to your intended arrival.

Racegoers will be able to enjoy 17 racedays in 2005, including the four-day National Hunt Festival (26th April – 29th April). Rates of admission vary throughout the year starting from €12 to €25 for entry to the Grandstand Enclosure. Prices are naturally at the higher end of the scale for the National Hunt Festival but discounts are available for advance and group bookings by contacting the ticket office at the racecourse. Senior citizens and children are also allowed entry at reduced admission rates on the day. Car parking is free, however to avoid any possible delays it is advised to arrive early. Annual membership is €190, which provides access to the members car park and Reserved Enclosure for all racedays, representing great value for the regular racegoer. Disabled racegoers are well catered for with a reserved car park close to the entrance. The racecourse is completely wheelchair friendly with reserved areas overlooking the parade ring and racecourse, and lifts provide access to all levels of the grandstand.

Location
Punchestown racecourse is approximately three miles from Naas on the Naas-Ballymore Eustace Road. It is just 45 minutes (23 miles) from Dublin (Route N7), just over an hour's drive from Dublin Airport and Dun Laoghaire, and two hours from Rosslare.

Corporate Hospitality
Corporate hospitality packages are available in the Festival village at the Spring National Hunt Festival. For further information contact Punchestown Racecourse 00 353 45 897704.

Artist: **David Dent STONE WALL AT PUNCHESTOWN** _Courtesy of:_ **The Artist**

Refreshment Facilities
Panoramic restaurant dining room/self service restaurant, snack bars, bars, and a reserved dining room facility available at the Spring Festival.

Local Hotels
Killashee House Tel: 00 353 45 879277, Osprey Hotel Tel: 00 353 45 881111, Hotel Keadeen Tel: 00 353 45 431666, Newbridge; Moyglare Manor in Maynooth; Rathsallagh House Tel: 00 353 45 403112, Dunlavin; Ambassador Hotel Tel: 00 353 45 877064, Kill; Naas Court Hotel, Harbour View Hotel and Gregory Hotel, all in Naas; Kildare Hotel and Country Club Tel: 00 353 1 601 7200 in Straffan; Curryhills House and Country Club in Prosperous. Visit www.punchestown.com for a comprehensive list of Guest Houses and Hotels.

Local Restaurants
Lawlors and Butt Mullins, Naas; Silken Thomas, Kildare; Johnstown Inn, Johnstown; Ballymore Inn and The Thatch, Ballymore Eustace.

Places of Interest/Activities
Irish National Stud; Japanese Gardens in Kildare; Castletown House in Celbridge; Russborough House, Lakeside Leisure Centre in Blessington; also fishing, pony trekking and golf.

Roscommon

Contact: The Manager at Roscommon Racecourse, Racecourse Road, Roscommon Tel: 00 353 90 66 26231 (Racedays) Fax: 00 353 90 66 30462.

Roscommon racecourse is steeped in National Hunt tradition. The first ever recorded race meeting took place in 1837 and was organised by the British military which then had a base in the town. Racing proper began in 1885 and has continued ever since, with the exception of a 12 year period from 1936 to 1948. Roscommon racecourse is now recognised as a true test of a horse's ability with Cheltenham Gold Cup winner, Imperial Call, and Ascot Gold Cup winner, Enzeli, both having run at Roscommon in the last few years. The atmosphere at Roscommon races and indeed in Roscommon town after races makes it a very special occasion.

Location
The racecourse is situated one mile from Roscommon on the Castlebar Road. Roscommon is 90 miles from Dublin, 47 miles from Galway, 20 miles from Athlone and 50 miles from Sligo.

Public Transport
Regular train services from Dublin (Heuston Station) to Roscommon. Tel: Irish Rail (Iarnrod Eireann) 00 353 1 836 6222 for train timetable. Taxi service from Roscommon Station to the racecourse.

Corporate Hospitality
Hospitality rooms available to cater for 20-60 people. Area now available for "Tented Village".

Refreshment Facilities
Dining room, self service restaurant, snack bar, tea room, bars.

Local Hotels, Restaurants and Bed & Breakfast
Abbey Hotel Tel: 00 353 90 66 26240, Royal Hotel Tel: 00 353 90 66 62016, Gleeson's Tel: 00353 90 66 26954 and Coachmans Inn Tel: 00353 90 66 26459.

Local Restaurants
Gleeson's and Westdeli in Roscommon.

Places of Interest/Activities
Lough Key Forest Park in Lough Key; County Heritage and Genealogical Centre in Strokestown; burial place of the kings of Ireland and Connacht in Rathcroghan; Arigna scenic drive; also boating, fishing, wind-surfing in Hudson Bay; Munsboro Equestrian Centre; River Shannon Cruises.

Artist: **Philip Toon WELCOME GALLOP** *Courtesy of:* **The Artist**

Sligo

Contact: Mr Brian Kennedy, Manager at Ballymote, Co Sligo, Tel: 00 353 71 91 83342 Fax: 00 353 71 91 83342 Racedays Tel: 00 353 71 91 62484.

Sligo town, in the heart of Yeats country, boasts one of the most scenic racecourses in the country. William Butler Yeats regarded Sligo as the Land of Heart's Desire. On either side of Sligo town stand the giant sentinels—Benbulben and Knocknarea. Round about are all the other places immortalised in Yeats' poetry—Hazelwood, Innisfree, Lissadell, Slish Wood, Dooney, Drumcliffe, etc.

Racing at Sligo has been taking place for over 180 years, being founded at the time when racing enjoyed great prosperity in the country. Indeed so great was the proliferation of race meetings over the period 1805 to 1815 that the organising committee of the Sligo Races decided that its 1814 meeting "will commence in August so as to give the racehorses time to travel to Bellewstown, Maze, Derry and Monaghan, and to come to Sligo".

The programme at all meetings is comprised of both National Hunt and flat races.

Corporate Hospitality
The Cleveragh Room is available to cater for 60 to 100 people.

Location
The racecourse is situated at Cleveragh, half a mile from the town centre, just off the Dublin-Sligo Road. Strandhill Airport is six miles away and Knock Airport is 35 miles.

Public Transport
Regular train service to Sligo from Dublin (Connolly Station).Tel: Irish Rail (Iarnrod Eireann) 00 353 1 836 6222 for train timetable. Taxi service from train station to the racecourse. Also served by Bus Eireann from Dublin (Busaras) Tel: 00 353 1 836 6111 for departure times.

Refreshment Facilities
Bar, restaurant, snack bar.

Local Hotels
Sligo Park Hotel Tel: 00 353 71 91 60291, Southern Hotel Tel: 00 353 71 91 62101 in Sligo; and Yeats Country Hotel Tel: 00 353 71 91 77211 in Rosses Point.

Places of Interest/Activities
Within a five mile radius of Sligo town are the contrasting beaches of Rosses Point and Strandhill; also golf at Strandhill, Tubbercurry and Ballymote Golf Clubs, surfing, angling and horse riding also at Strandhill.

Thurles

Contact: Mr Pierce Moloney at the Racecourse, Thurles, Co Tipperary Tel: 00 353 504 22253 Fax: 00 353 504 24565 Racedays Tel: 00 353 504 23272 Fax: 00 353 504 23245 or mobile 00 353 86 2515882. E-mail: thurles@iol.ie

Thurles, situated in the sporting county of Tipperary, is celebrated as the centre of the Gaelic Athletic Association. It is also the heart of the famous Scarteen hunting county. Earliest records show a three day meeting in June 1732. In October 1760, there was a six day meeting .

The end of January meeting is renowned as a major trial for the forthcoming National Hunt Festival meetings at Cheltenham, Fairyhouse and Punchestown.

Location
The racecourse is situated one mile west of Thurles town, five miles west of the main Cork-Dublin Road. Thurles is 10 miles north of Cashel, 30 miles west of Kilkenny, 40 miles east of Limerick, 60 miles north of Cork and 60 miles south of Athlone.

Public Transport
Regular train service from Dublin (Heuston Station) and Cork. Tel: Irish Rail (Iarnrod Eireann) 00 353 1 836 6222 for train timetables. Free minibus service to racecourse.

Corporate Hospitality
Hospitality room available to cater for 50-100 people.

Refreshment Facilities
Self service restaurant, bars, tea room.

Local Hotels
Horse & Jockey Tel: 00 353 504 44192 Thurles; Anner Hotel Tel: 00 353 504 21799, Thurles; Cashel Palace Hotel Tel: 00 353 62 62707, Cashel; Dundrum House Hotel Tel: 00 353 62 71116, Dundrum.

Local Restaurants
Jumbo Chinese Tel: 00 353 504 22873 Thurles; Inch House Tel: 00 353 504 51348 Thurles; Bella Notte Tel: 00 353 504 22070 Thurles; Thurles; Horse & Jockey Inn, Tel: 00 353 504 44192, Thurles, Chez Hans Tel: 00 353 62 61177 Cashel.

Places of Interest/Activities
Rock of Cashel; Holycross Abbey; Devil's Bit Mountain; also hunting, local equestrian centres and an excellent 18-hole golf course in Thurles.

Tipperary

Contact: Peter Roe at Tipperary Racecourse Limerick Junction, Co Tipperary, Tel: 00 353 62 51357 Mobile: 086 820 8870 Fax: 00 353 62 51303, Website: *www.tipperaryraces.ie* E-mail: *info@tipperaryraces.ie*

The first recorded meeting of Tipperary Races at Barronstown Course was Monday, 27 March 1848. In 1871/72, the races were abandoned due to smallpox, but were revived in 1881. In the early days of Barronstown (the predecessor to Limerick Junction racecourse) there was only one bookmaker, who also had a roulette table.

The first races at Limerick Junction took place in September 1916 promoted by Mr T Gardiner Wallis, the celebrated racing personality, and his trainer Senator J J Parkinson and colleagues Stephen Grehan and Charles Moore.

A major incentive to the commencement of Limerick Junction was the promise of a special railway siding from the Great Southern and Western Railway Company.

The name was changed from Limerick Junction to Tipperary Racecourse for a meeting on 8 May 1986. In December 1999

Tipperary Supporter's Club, in conjunction with local businessmen, took a short-term lease on the racecourse from the Irish Horseracing Authority. The aim of the newly formed company is to re-establish Tipperary as a leading provincial racecourse. The facilities underwent a major refurbishment in the spring of 2000.

Tipperary stages Super Sunday which is the best mixed card in Ireland and the features are The John James McManus Memorial Hurdle (Grade 1) and the Coolmore Concorde Stakes (Group 3). This meeting has 5 pattern races and is run on the first Sunday of October each year. Throughout the history of Tipperary many of the champions of the turf run at Tipperary and in 2001 the 2002 Derby first and second High Chaparral and Hawk Wing both won their maidens at the Junction.

Location
Situated off the main Tipperary-Limerick road, the racecourse is two miles from Tipperary, 24 miles from Limerick, 40 miles from Shannon Airport, 64 miles from Cork and 1½ miles from Dublin.

Public Transport
Regular train services from Dublin (Heuston Station) and Cork to Limerick Junction Station, which is within easy walking distance of the track. Tel: Irish Rail (Iarnrod Eireann) 00 353 1 836 6222 for train timetables.

Corporate Hospitality
Corporate hospitality is available for groups from 10-150. The newly refurbished hospitality area has Tote facilities; CCTV and either silver service or buffet style dining. The room overlooks the parade ring and racetrack.

Refreshment Facilities
The Winning Post Bar has full drink selections while the Istabraq Bar and Members Bar have full snack facilities as well as usual drinks. There is also a self service restaurant.

Local Hotels
Aherlow House Hotel Tel: 00 353 52 56153, Glen of Aherlow; Dundrum House Hotel, Dundrum; Cashel Palace Hotel Tel: 00 353 62 62707, Cashel; There's also the Royal Hotel Tel: 00 353 62 33244, Tipperary.

Local Restaurants
The Ballykisteen Golf and Country Club opposite the racecourse has restaurant and bar facilities.

The Bit & Bridle opposite the racecourse is a popular venue for a bit to eat before or after racing. Kiely's, Main Street, Tipperary Town or The Stables Restaurant, Main Street, Tipperary – (062) 82080 are also popular venues to eat at before or after a race meeting. Tipperary Town also has a diversity of other restaurants ranging from traditional to Chinese. Donovans (O'Brien Street) is excellent for lunch and hosts Irish music. Others include the Brown Trout (Bridge Street), and Chez Hans (Cashel).

Places of Interest/Activities
Rock of Cashel; Cahir Castle; Mitchelstown Caves; scenic Glen of Aherlow; also golf, fishing, hunting and shooting

Tralee

Contact: Mr Timothy P Griffin, General Manager at Tralee Racecourse, Ballybeggan Park, Tralee, Co Kerry, Tel: 00 353 66 712 6490 Fax: 00 353 66 712 6090 Mobile: 087 929 2736. Website: *traleehorseracing.com* **E-mail:** *traleeraces@hotmail.com*

Racing is recorded in Tralee as far back as 1767, when a week-long meeting was held, the results of which are recorded in the Turf Club.

Great pride was taken in these meetings as is indicated by the organisers of the August 1805 meeting when they observed "The thanks of the meeting was unanimously given to the Steward for his uniform politeness and attention and his daily punctuality in paying the plates." Various venues in the locality were used until the present site, in Ballybeggan Park, was first opened to racing in 1889.

The park was formerly a deer park, and the stone for the surrounding limestone wall was quarried out of the land in the infield area of the course. The estate was formerly the property of Daniel O'Connell, The Liberator, in whose honour the Liberator Handicap is run annually.

The Tralee August meeting is the centrepiece of the International Rose of Tralee Festival. The festival sparkle spreads to the course for four days of great racing—this is a unique experience and is not to be missed. The three day June bank holiday meeting is an ideal way to get into the summer with traditional Kerry hospitality and scenery.

Location
Tralee racecourse is one and a half miles from the town centre, off the Tralee-Killarney road.

Public Transport
Regular train service from Dublin (Heuston Station). Tel Irish Rail (Iarnrod Eireann) 00 353 1 836 6222 for train timetable. Tralee railway station is approximately 1 mile from the racecourse.

Corporate Hospitality
Hospitality suite available to cater for 60-120 people

Refreshment Facilities
Dining room, snack bars and a fast food outlet

Local Hotels
Abbey Gate Hotel Tel: 00 353 66 7129888, Brandon Hotel, Tel: 00 353 66 7123333 the Earl of Desmond, the Grand Hotel Tel: 00 353 66 7121499, Imperial Hotel, Ballygarry House Hotel, Meadowlands Hotel, and Quality Hotel Tel: 00 353 66 7121877—all in Tralee. Contact the Irish Tourist Board Tel: 0207 493 3201 for a full accommodation list.

Local Restaurants
Aisling Geal, Numero Uno and the Oyster Tavern in Tralee, Kirbys Brogue Inn; The Tankard in Fenit; Nick's in Killorglin.

Places of Interest/Activities
The town also boasts the highly acclaimed high-tech county museum, a refurbished working windmill, an aquadome, the Geraldine Experience, Tralee Steam Railway, Siamsa Tire, and the National Folk Theatre.

Tralee is the gateway to the Dingle Peninsula and the starting point for the Ring of Kerry. There are also magnificent beaches nearby at Banna and Inch; an 18 hole golf course designed by Arnold Palmer at Barrow; and sea angling at Fenit.

Artist: **Peter Smith OUT OF THE SHADOWS** *Courtesy of:* **Frost & Reed**

Tramore

Contact: Sue Phelan, Manager, Waterford & Tramore Racecourse, Tramore, Co Waterford, Tel: 00 353 51 391425 Fax: 00 353 51 390928. E-mail: *racing@tramore.ie* **Website:** *www.tramore-racecourse.com*

Tramore Racecourse, located at the picturesque seaside town, outside Waterford, has gone from strength to strength since new owners took over in 1997 after housing developments threatened the closure of the track. At that stage an ambitious development plan was undertaken to modernise all the facilities for all sectors of the racing industry, with the result that over €5 million has been spent to date on the track and enclosures.

In 2000 Tramore Racecourse led racing into the 21st Century when it became the first racecourse to host a race meeting in the western world and history was made again in 2001 when Tramore was the first European racecourse to introduce the euro currency to race goers.

We look forward to welcoming you to Tramore where the number of race fixtures has increased to eleven and the racecourse has now firmly become established as a leading multi-purpose venue in the South East. Enjoy the best of National Hunt and Flat racing where the Turf meets the Surf.

Location
The racecourse is situated 8 miles from Waterford City on the main Tramore road and one mile outside Tramore town.

Public Transport
The racecourse is located eight miles from Waterford Airport with daily flights to London Luton Airport. Regular daily train services from Dublin (Heuston Station), Tel; Irish Rail 00 353 1 836 6222 for timetables. Local bus service to the racecourse from Waterford City. Contact Bus Eireann 00 353 51 879000.

Corporate Hospitality
The Front Room is available to hire to private groups of up to 150 people. The Deise bar is available for smaller groups.

Refreshment Facilities
Three Bars, One self-service restaurant and one take-away restaurant.

Local Hotels
Local Tramore hotels include O'Sheas Hotel, The Grand Hotel, and the Majestic Hotel. Waterford Hotels include The Tower Hotel, The Granville Hotel.

Local Restaurants
In Tramore; Coast Restaurant, 051 393646, The Esquire, 051 386237

Places of Interest
Waterford Crystal Factory, Funfair and amusements in Tramore, Dunmore East Fishing Village, 16 Golf courses within 40 miles, incl. Tramore, Waterford Castle, Faithlegge.

Wexford

Contact: Michael Murphy, Racecourse Manager Roseville, New Ross, Co. Wexford, Tel: 00 353 51 421681 Fax: 00 353 51 421830 Racedays Tel: 00 353 53 42307 Fax: 00 353 53 43702. Administrative Secretary, Mary Ballantyne, Tel: 00 353 53 43412, Fax: 053 43853 or Mobile: 087 3828099 Website: *www.wexfordraces.ie* **E-mail:** *info@wexfordraces.ie*

Steeped in tradition and deriving its name from its Viking heritage, Wexford has always been foremost in the breeding of horses in Ireland. Jumping is particularly associated with Wexford and many of Wexford's native sons as well as her horses have achieved outstanding National Hunt success. The earliest records of racing here took place on reclaimed boglands in the 1870s. By 1902, however, this had ceased and racing commenced again on the present course in 1951.

The course is only 15 miles from the major sea port of Rosslare.

Location
Wexford racecourse is situated just outside the town off the Dublin-Rosslare bypass.

Public Transport
Regular Dublin-Rosslare train service. Tel Irish Rail (Iarnrod Eireann) 00 353 1 836 6222 for train timetables. Good taxi service from Wexford train station to the racecourse.

Corporate Hospitality
The Carriglawn room is available to hire for private groups of up to 80 persons. An area is also available for marquees for corporate entertainment.

Refreshment Facilities
Self service restaurant, snack bar and bars

Local Hotels
Whitford House Hotel, Talbot Hotel, Quality Hotel, Ferrycarrig Hotel, Stanville Lodge in Wexford, Riverside Park Hotel in Enniscorthy.

Local Restaurants
Heavens Above, Mange 2, Vine Thai restaurant, Steps in Whitford House Hotel, Dragon Hein Chinese Restaurant.

Places of Interest/Activities
Wexford Wildlife Reserve in Wexford; Irish National Heritage Park in Ferrycarrig; Johnstown Castle Park in Johnstown; John F Kennedy Arboretum in New Ross; Dunbrody Famine Ship, New Ross; also golf and fishing.

To find out more about horse racing in Ireland contact:
The Marketing Team,
Horse Racing Ireland,
Thoroughbred County House, Kill, Co. Kildare
Tel: 00 353 45 842800
Fax: 00 353 45 842881
Website: www.hri.ie
E-mail: info@hri.ie

For a full list of accommodation contact:
Tourism Ireland,
150 New Bond Street, London, W1Y 0AQ, UK.
Tel: (0044) 0207 518 0800
Fax: (0044) 0207 493 9065
Accommodation/brochure line (free phone):
(0044) 0800 0397000
Website: www.tourismireland.com
E-mail: info.gb@tourismireland.com

Useful Websites:
www.itm.ie
(Irish Thoroughbred Marketing) 045 443060
www.tote.ie
(Irish Tote Betting) 045 842800/ 1850 238669
www.buseireann.ie
(Bus timetables and routes) 01 8366111
www.irishrail.ie
(Train timetables and routes) 01 8366222
www.meteireann.ie
(Weather forecasts) 01 8064200
www.aerrianta.com
(airport information) 01 814 1111
www.irishferries.ie (Sea) 01 6610511
www.stenaline.ie (Sea) 01 204 7777
www.tourismireland.com
(UK based) 00 44 207 5180800
www.ireland.travel.ie
(Bord Failte) 01 6024000
www.goffs.ie (Sales Company) 045 886600
www.tattersalls.ie
(Sales Company) 01 8864300

(International dialling code for Ireland –
00 353, e.g. 00 353 45 842800)

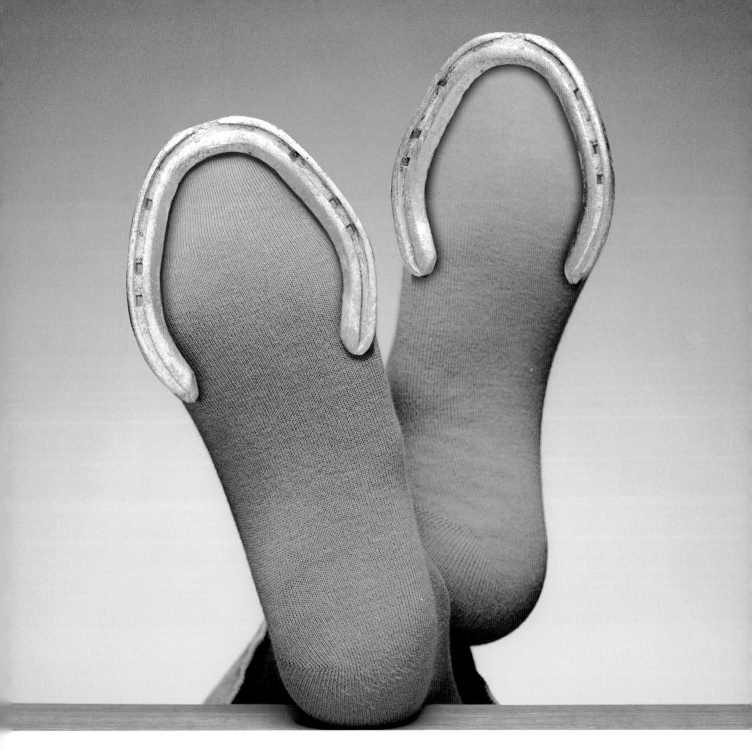

Get your shoes on - you're going racing.

Wherever you are in Ireland you're never far from a race meeting. And if you want to understand one of the country's great passions and meet the Irish at play, get yourself to one of 300 race days at one of 27 racecourses around the country - you'll soon be punting and partying with the best of them!

You haven't really discovered Ireland until you've been racing. So go on - check it out for yourself and kick back for a great day out.

There are countless racing gems throughout the year. For full information on all Irish racecourses and complete fixture details log on to: **www.hri.ie** or phone 00 353 45 842 800.

It shows when you've been racing

HORSE RACING IRELAND

Travelling the Turf Around the World

Artist: **Peter Smith** *CONTINUING THE CONVERSATION* Courtesy of: **Frost & Reed**

Twenty years ago it was a relatively rare occurrence for a British trained horse to venture overseas to contest a major race. For only the very best it would most likely have been for the Arc weekend at Longchamp in Paris; only the very brave, or foolhardy, ever ventured farther. Now top racing at the international level takes place on a year-round basis, with trainers thinking little of shipping their horses to the farthest corners of the racing world to capture the huge prizes on offer.

So today we are not really shocked to see a South African horse running in Hong Kong, a Japanese champion shipped over to contest a major European pattern race, or a dream that began in an Irish field become reality in the crazy carnival that is the Melbourne Cup.

After now twenty years, the brave experiment that was the first Breeders Cup has matured into a world championship event of the highest quality. Similarly on the other side of the world, in fewer years, the Dubai World Cup meeting provides a middle east counterpoint of excellence earlier in the year as much as the December meeting in Hong Kong does at the end of it.

Though far less heralded, jump racing too has followed suit, with events as diverse as the Pardubice in the Czech Republic and the Grand Nakayama Jump in Tokyo attracting British and Irish horses, while the top French trained hurdlers and chasers regularly make forays to Kempton and Cheltenham.

With more televised international racing than ever before and the tumbling cost of travel reducing the barriers to actually being there, the punter can see and enjoy the exciting action of the world's best horses competing against each other. No one this side of the pond had heard of Lone Star Park in Texas until last October when it produced one of the best Breeders Cup meetings in years. Unfortunately there were probably fewer foreign visitors in attendance than ever, but we are sure that those that made the journey to see victories by two British trained raiders will never forget it.

Artist: **Hubert De Watrigant LE ROND DE PRESENTATION** *Courtesy of:* **Osborne Studio Gallery**

Dubai World Cup	March	**Nad Al Sheba, Dubai**
Australian Derby	April	**Randwick, Australia**
Derby Italiano	May	**Rome, Italy**
Poule D'Essai des Poulains	May	**Longchamp, France**
Poule D'Essai des Pouliches	May	**Longchamp, France**
Kentucky Derby	May	**Churchill Downs, USA**
Preakness Stakes	May	**Pimlico, USA**
Belmont Stakes	June	**Belmont Park, USA**
Prix du Jockey Club	June	**Chantilly, France**
Prix de Diane	June	**Chantilly, France**
Japanese Derby	June	**Tokyo, Japan**
Deutsches Derby	July	**Hamburg, Germany**
Durban July Handicap	July	**Durban, South Africa**
Prix du Jacques Le Marois	August	**Deauville, France**
Prix Morny	August	**Deauville, France**
Travers Stakes	August	**Saratoga, USA**
Prix du Moulin	September	**Longchamp, Paris**
Prix de La Salamandre	September	**Longchamp, Paris**
Prix Vermaille	September	**Longchamp, Paris**
Grosser Preis Von Baden	September	**Baden-Baden, Germany**
Prix du Cadran	October	**Longchamp, Paris**
Prix de L'Arc de Triomphe	October	**Longchamp, Paris**
Velka Pardubicka	October	**Pardubice, Czech Republic**
Canadian International	October	**Woodbine, Toronto**
Cox Plate	October	**Flemington, Melbourne**
Breeders' Cup	October	**Belmont Park, USA**
Melbourne Cup	November	**Flemington, Melbourne**
Japan Cup	November	**Tokyo Racecourse**
Hong Kong International Races	December	**Sha Tin, Hong Kong**
New Zealand Derby	December	**Ellerslie, New Zealand**

Artist: **Harry Matthews OUT OF THE STALLS** *Courtesy of:* **The Artist**

While most of our Racing Around the World concerns seeing the great events in the international racing calendar, there are other times and places during the year when you might want to get away for a quick sporting fix in a somewhat unusual locale. No one would pretend that places such as Barbados, the Czech Republic or Switzerland are worth visiting solely for the quality of horses, jockeys or trainers, but, as racing occasions, they are all first class places to visit at the right time of the year. True racing people have taken them to their heartS and celebrate them in style.

Barbados Gold Cup

While steeplechase fans will be in their element come January, many of the flat world's leading owners and trainers look to sunnier climes for a bit of rest and relaxation. Nowhere has been more popular with the sun worshippers than Barbados in recent years because that warm Barbadian welcome mixed with a few rum punches is the perfect antidote to the winter blues. The sun, sea and sand might be perfect, but the icing on this cake comes with a bit of racing thrown in as well. Given that the timing is right, you might even be able to take in a cricket Test Match.

Barbados is the place where Sir Michael Stoute got his start in the training business and the local racetrack has a familiar ring about it too–Garrison Savannah–the same name of the horse that won the Cheltenham Gold Cup for Jenny Pitman in 1991! You'll find the course just a couple of miles outside the capital of Bridgetown and it has been the home of horse racing here since 1845 when British officers raced their horses on what was then the parade ground. Things are a bit more organised now with three racing seasons a year, from January to March, May to August, and October to December, organised by the Barbados Turf Club, St Michael, Barbados, West Indies. Tel: (246) 426 3980, Fax: (246) 429 3591, e-mail: barturf@sunbeach.net website: www.barbadosturfclub.com.

The track is a three-quarter mile oval grass strip, with races from five to 11 furlongs. The most important races in the calendar are the '5000', run in February, the Sandy Lane Gold Cup and the Banks Guineas in March, the United Barbados Derby in August and the Heineken Stakes on Boxing Day. The emphasis at all meetings is on family entertainment and you can enjoy a picnic under the shade of the tall trees ringing the course and sample some Barbadian cuisine in the form of pudding and souse, rice and stew or fried fish and fish cakes. All of this can be washed down with a Planter's Punch, the main ingredient of which is the local rum, which is excellent.

The more serious punter can enjoy the view of racing from either the Grand Stand, Field Stand, Sir John Chandler Stand, or if you can wangle an invitation, one of the corporate boxes overlooking the paddock bend. Admission to the Grand Stand will set you back $10 BDS or about $5 US on normal race days, which rises to $20 BDS on Gold Cup day. The Club House charge is $25 BDS and $50 on Cup day.

Artist: **D M Dent MAIS, MAINTENANT, MONTJEU! THE ARC** *Courtesy of:* **Frost & Reed**

Barbados' economy depends more on importing tourists than exporting sugar and rum these days, so as you would imagine there is a wide range of places to hitch your hammock on this tropical isle. Many are on the south and west coast, the 'Caribbean' side of the island where the white sand gives way to calm blue waters. Here you will find the Almond Beach Club & Spa at Vauxhall, St James (246 432 7840), a low-key group of pastel buildings set amidst palms right on the beach. It has all the facilities and three pools, but families with children under 16 will have to look elsewhere. Any age, however, will be welcomed at its sister hotel, the Almond Beach Village near Speightstown, St Peter (246 422 4900), which has equally fine accommodation. Club Rockley at Worthing (246 435 7880) is set in 70 acres of tropical gardens, has seven swimming pools and a nine hole golf course; a free shuttle bus will take you to the hotel's beachside bar and restaurant. If you don't mind a bit of self catering, you could try the Rainbow Reef at St Lawrence Gap (246 428 5110). Its apartments are right on the beach and there's also a pool and nine hole golf course. One of Barbados' landmark hotels is the famous Sam Lord's Castle (246 423 7350) at St Philip on the south-east coast which has a large complex of rooms, pools and tennis courts around the castle. A few other choices which are definitely in the luxury category, are that watering hole of the rich and famous, the Sandy Lane Hotel, as well as the Colony Club, Royal Pavilion and Treasure Beach, all of which are in St James on Barbados' 'platinum' east coast.

Velka Pardubicka (Czech Republic)

It's known as the "European Grand National", and the sight of a large field of jumpers negotiating the 31 obstacles–which include stone walls, banks, hedges and a monster known as the Taxis fence–that are strung out along the twists and turns of this four and a quarter mile race is a truly thrilling experience. Thanks to international television coverage, inexpensive flights and the sporting participation of a regular flow of horses, trainers and jockeys from Britain, Ireland and sometimes France, the event has grown in stature to a 'must do' for the ardent jump racing enthusiast. Some of the local stars go on to return the favour by tackling the banks course at Cheltenham and have achieved considerable success. We won't however, dwell on the brave mare whose jockey took the wrong course three fences from home when in a commanding lead! She was twice a winner of the Pardubice and will probably add another to her list of victories this year.

You can swill as much of the local Pilsner brew as you wish in the pleasant confines of the quaint old town of Pardubice itself before taking in the Czech St Leger on the Saturday and if your stamina matches that of the horses, return the next day for the Velka Pardubicka itself. The best connections to get there are probably through the delightful city of Prague, just an hour to the west.

Held each October, 2004 marked the 130th running of the Velka Pardubicka and interestingly it was a British

Artist: **Rochelle Levy GOING FOR THE TURN, FAIRHILL** *Courtesy of:* **Frost & Reed**

professional jockey, L Sayers, who won the very first race in 1874 on Fantome. Another well-known rider in his day who rode in the Velka was Count Karel Kinsky; he is the only Czech to have also won the Grand National at Aintree in 1883. That should be good enough to win any pub quiz!

The capital of the Czech Republic, Prague, is a lively city to visit and one that has become increasingly popular with visitors from western Europe since many airlines began introducing cheap flights. Last year the Czech Republic officially became part of the European Community along with many other former eastern bloc countries, making travel to it even easier. Here you will find a wide range of hotels and restaurants from which to choose, as well as many pubs and bars where you can sample the famous Pils. Prices for hotels aren't cheap but the cost of eating and drinking evens things out a bit.

Closer to the racecourse itself, take a few hours and visit Pardubice Castle, a Renaissance castle and Museum near the old Pernstyn square in the old part of Pardubice. Just a few miles outside the town is the Kuneticka Hora, a Gothic castle from the 15th century. A bit further away, about 12 miles west of Pardubice, real horse people will find Kladruby nad Labem - the original six hundred year old stables established in 1579 for breeding the famous Kladrubian white horses; another must see is Slatinany Castle with its Museum of the Horse. It's located in a large old park with walks through the forest about 10 miles south from Pardubice

Some of the hotels recommended by locals in Pardubice include: the 160 room Hotel Labe, which has its own large restaurant and casino; the smaller Clubhotel Harmony, Belehradska, 00420- 40- 6435020; the Hotel Zlata Tika on Trossova, 00420-40-6613478; the 17 room S.M.G. Sporthotel, Sukovo 00420-40-512082 which has a sauna and spa facilities; Hotel u Andela Zamecka 00420-40-514028; the 50 room Hotel Bohemia Masarykovo in Chrudim 00420-455- 620351; or the larger 200-room Hotel Cernigov Riegrovo, 00420-49-5814111, e-mail: cernigov@hk.anet.cz, http://www.cernigov.cz, which has its own night club, restaurant and casino right on the premises. If you are getting a bit hungry after the races try U Nouzu, Hradite na Pmsku 22, a restaurant, with its terrace and wine cellar, about 3 miles north of Pardubice towards Kuneticka Hora, 040 45005; or right in the old part of Pardubice near the castle on Zamecka 24 is Na Kovarne with its restaurant, pub and terrace, 040 514028.

If you want someone else to do the work for you, tour firms such as Horse Racing Abroad offer package deals that include air connections, hotels, admission to the course and local transportation. Czech out the latest details on their website: www.horseracingabroad.com.

St Moritz (Switzerland)

Swiss racing might sound like a contradiction in a land better known for skiing and fondue, but each year mother nature completely freezes over the lake at St Moritz and the good burghers of the town stage a racing spectacular on ice! The sight of horses and jockeys flying across the white packed snow against an Alpine backdrop is truly a unique experience, and the hospitality adds a new dimension to aprés racing.

Artist: **Sir Alfred Munnings AT THE RACES** *Courtesy of:* **Rosenstiel's**

Of course you'll have to be here in January and February to take in the action and hope that a sudden thaw doesn't halt the proceedings! This is one of the few places in the world where you can go skiing in the morning and racing in the afternoon. Surprisingly, the quality of the racing is probably a far cry better than that on show at many of our all-weather meetings at the same time of the year, and the horses adapt remarkably well to the conditions underfoot. Several top jockeys from other countries are also usually on hand and the meetings have a winter carnival air about them. Some jump races over hurdles are also usually put on to keep fans of racing over the sticks happy.

The Swiss practically invented good hotel keeping so you won't be pressed to find some excellent accommodation. It's best to book early though, as St Moritz is a traditional watering hole for the rich and famous at this time of the year, and of course skiing is the name of the true winter game. Although it's usually not cheap, and nothing is in Switzerland, there is a good choice of hotels, apartments and guest houses in St Moritz itself. Some favourites include: Badrutts Palace Hotel, a luxurious resort with old world hospitality overlooking the lake, (41 81837 1000); also overlooking the lake and mountains is the Carlton Hotel (41 81832 1141); the excellent Kulm Hotel (41 81832 1151) on Via Veglia which has welcomed guests since 1856 and also has a fine view of the lake; or the elegant five star Park Hotels Waldhaus (41 81928 4848) which features art nouveau fireplaces and is set in its own 60 acre private park.

If accommodation is booked up here, you could also try another ski resort, Davos, which is not too far away, or the very smart Klosters, another haunt of the rich and famous. The nearest big city and major international airport is to be found in Zurich, which also offers a wide choice of accommodation and is quite interesting in its own right. Here the family-run Baur au Lac Hotel (220 5020) on Talstrasse combines luxury with old-world elegance, while just outside the city the Dolder Grand Hotel (251 6321) on Kurhausstrasse is a fairy-tale castle set in the woods with pretty views over the Zurichsee. Right in the centre of the city you could also try the Savoy Baur En Ville (215 2525) on Am Paradeplatz, Zurich's oldest hotel, or the cosy elegance of the Widder (224 2526), a converted row of townhouses on Rennweg. Another option is the friendly family run Hotel Seidenhof (211 6544) on Sihlstrasse which is close to many of the smart Zurich shops.

Carolina & Colonial Cup
(South Carolina, USA)

When 50,000 jump racing fans assemble each spring at Springdale Race Course near Camden, South Carolina for the Carolina Cup, it's probably the world's biggest point to point. Timber fences, some five feet high, are the name of the game and it has become such an event that people come from hundreds, if not thousands, of miles away to enjoy a massive tail-gate party while they witness the thrills and spills of some of the best steeplechasers in North America. Grab your picnic hamper, pack the beer in ice and you can be a good ol' boy or gal for the day.

You'll probably fly in to the South Carolina state capital of Columbia, which is just a half hour's drive from Camden on Interstate Highway 20, or you could take the more leisurely and historic US Route 1.

Springdale Race Course is part of a 600-acre training facility that was given by Marion duPont Scott to the State of South Carolina. The Carolina Cup is part of a six-race card and dates back to 1930; this is steeplechasing over a long galloping course with stiff timber fences and quite a bit different than what is found in Britain and Ireland, some of the fences on the banks courses excepted.

The Carolina Cup is held at the end of March, while in the autumn at the end of November, the Colonial Cup is also held on the same course. A $100,000 steeplechase, it has produced some good winners such as Lonesome Glory who went on to win at Cheltenham, and usually attracts some good horses from the UK. The whole day has a fairground atmosphere with terrier trials, a market, classic cars, rides and special exhibitions. To find out more, contact their web site at www.carolina-cup.org. General admission for the Colonial Cup is about $10-15, with general parking at $5 or $50 for preferred parking which includes two tickets. Reserved parking in the infield is $75, which also includes two tickets, or $125 for Front Row Paddock Side. $300 will get you a six-seater box in the Grandstand and covers all admission and parking, while $400 will get you the same deal with lunch included. While you're in the area you should also pay a visit to the Carolina Cup Racing Museum, which has interactive exhibits and memorabilia relating to the history of steeplechasing in North America.

Part of the Confederate old south, South Carolina has a lot going for it to entertain and amuse the visitor. If you want more information on where to see or what to do from your armchair, just log on to the excellent website at www.travelsc.com. Camden itself is in the state's 'Olde English District', which perhaps not surprisingly has counties such as Lancaster and York! Here you can find a room for the night at the Colony Inn on US 1 (803 432 5508), the Knights Inn on DeKalb St and US 1 (803 432 2453) or the Plantation Motel on Jefferson Davis Highway (803 432 2300). There are lots of other smaller guesthouses and B&Bs to choose from. Columbia is the nearest main city and also has lots of hotels and restaurants. South Carolina's coast is not to be missed and we strongly suggest a visit to historic Charleston which dates back to 1670 and has lots of Civil War connections, as well as Georgetown, and the seaside beach resorts of Myrtle Beach and Hilton Head Island.

Artist: **Roy Miller THE ARC** *Courtesy of:* **The Artist**

Racing in *France*

Thousands of British racing fans come to Longchamp in Paris each year for the Arc weekend in early October. Perhaps fewer go to Deauville in the summer for some sea air with their sport, Chantilly for the French Derby, Auteuil for some great jumping action or some of the many other provincial courses dotted around the country. No matter which course or event you attend, racing in France has its own joie de vivre and should not be missed.

French racing has taken some positive steps in the last few years to improve the appeal of the sport, and has never been keener to welcome the visiting racegoer from abroad. Taking into account the very high class racing on offer and the first class facilities for the visitor, racing in France is good value. Admission prices to courses are incredibly cheap by British standards and it will set you back only about £7 to attend some of the top events such as the Arc itself. After a few winners, you can load up your car with some firstclass Bordeaux and Brie for the trip home. What are you waiting for?

The organising body for much of thoroughbred racing is France-Galop and they can provide details on the courses and fixtures. Drop them a line at France-Galop, 46 place Abel Gance, 92655 Boulogne, France. Tel: 1 49 10 2030. Fax: 1 47 61 9332. They also have a website at www.france-galop.com

There are several British companies which run regular trips to French racecourses such as Longchamp, Chantilly and Deauville. They enjoy the benefit of being able to block book whole sections of the course for their clients to enjoy private facilities at big events such as the Arc weekend. In October literally thousands take up the offer and the British presence can often dominate proceedings at Longchamp. If you wish to let someone else make all the arrangements you could contact Horse Racing Abroad, 24 Sussex Road, Haywards Heath, West Sussex RH16 4EA. Tel: (01444) 441661. Fax: (01444) 416 169 web site: www.horseracingabroad. The company are experts in arranging racing trips around the globe and Paris is their most popular venue.

Longchamp

The surrounding Bois de Boulogne gives Longchamp a country feel and it is sometimes hard to remember that you are close to the centre of Paris. Reflecting its pre-eminence as the course of France's capital city, Longchamp is the course for many of the most important races in the country's racing calendar. From the French Guineas for colts and fillies in the spring, to the end of season European championship that is the Prix de L'Arc de Triomphe, Longchamp is the home of French racing at its best.

The Clerk of the Course at Longchamp can be contacted at Hippodrome de Longchamp, Route des Tribunes, Bois de Boulogne, 75116 Paris. Tel: 0821 213 213. Fax: 1 44 30 7599.

To get to the course, you can either take the number 244N Bus (Porte Maillot) or hop on the free shuttle bus provided by the racecourse from the Porte d'Auteuil. If the Metro is your choice, take the direction Porte d'Auteuil-Longchamp. Once you have reached the racecourse, compared with

*Artist: **Rochelle Levy** CHANTILLY SPRING AT THE GALLOPS Courtesy of: **Frost & Reed***

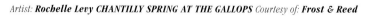

most major British courses it is relatively inexpensive to get in. There is one large public enclosure which covers the entire course and it costs only a few Euros to attend for a mid-week meeting and perhaps another Euro or two for weekend fixtures or bank holidays. Even some of the biggest fixtures of the year such as the Arc de Triomphe cost about 10 Euros. Even better still, those 18 years old or younger get in for nothing, while if you are 18-25 years old or over 60 years young, the price of admission is reduced by half. There is also a large public enclosure in the centre of the course, which is free to everyone!

There will be additional costs if you wish to reserve a seat in one of the restaurants, which you can do by telephoning ahead on 1 44 30 7590. For those who enjoy the luxury of a private box, you can arrange one by contacting 1 49 10 2287.

Each year Longchamp hosts over 30 racing fixtures. Prime amongst these will be Arc day itself on the first Sunday in October, with a fine supporting card that also includes the Abbaye sprint over five furlongs, a race that often goes to an English invader. Get there a day earlier and you can watch one of the best stayers' races of the year, the Prix du Cadran which often attracts some of Britain's best long distance specialists. Leading up to the Arc, in early September there are several Arc trials that try to establish some form for the big race itself. They are fascinating contests in themselves and well worth going to see live. If you do go on the first Sunday in September, you will be able to watch the Prix du Moulin de Longchamp, the race named after the windmill that provides a unique land mark at the far bend. Come to Longchamp in the spring and you will be able to take in the first of the French classics for colts in the form of the Dubai

Poules d'Essai des Poulains and its counterpart for fillies, the Essai des Pouliches. A couple of weeks earlier, and one of the first Group races in the calendar awaits you in the form of the Prix Ganay.

Longchamp is a right handed track of 2,400 metres (about a mile and a half) whose principal characteristic is the sweeping bend before the finishing straight. So there is in effect, a turn for home into a 'false straight', and then another turn for home in the run to the finish line itself. Just to add some interest there are actually two finishing lines, so don't tear up your betting ticket until the race is well and truly over! The outside course is bisected by a straight course upon which the famous Prix de l'Abbaye sprint is held over five furlongs.

Paris Local Favourites

No doubt if you are a racing fan, you will be coming either in the Spring or the Autumn when the major races at Longchamp take place, and it is also a time when this vibrant city is at its finest. The Arc de Triomphe, Champs Elysees and Eiffel Tower are Paris' most famous landmarks but the way to really feel Paris is to walk amongst some of the smaller streets in either Montmartre, Le Marais or the Quartier Latin, the famous left bank on the other side of the Isle de Notre Dame. For anyone surfacing from the Metro for a very first view of Paris, it should be taken at night from the Trocadero overlooking the Seine and la Tour Eiffel. Hopefully the fountains will be playing under coloured floodlights to ensure a magical moment that any visitor to this city of lovers will never forget.

Artist: **Rochelle Levy CHANTILLY, GOING BACK TO THE YARD** *Courtesy of:* **Frost & Reed**

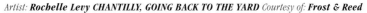

There is an incredible number of excellent restaurants in Paris, and hotels by the bucketful, so recommending just a few is tricky. Naturally, a lot depends on your budget. If time is tight and money no object then try The Crillon (1 44 711500), The Bristol (1 53 43 4300) or the Hotel Vernet (1 44 31 9800), all outstanding hotels with restaurants of superb quality. The Parc (1 44 05 6666) is also excellent and conveniently situated, as is the St-James Paris (1 44 05 8181). Finally, if you are into art nouveau try Alain Ducasse (1 47 27 1227) - a real jewel!

Chantilly

With its connections to French royalty going back centuries, Chantilly is perhaps the most elegant of French racecourses and home to some of the country's, and Europe's, leading Group races for three-year-olds such as the United Arab Emirates Prix du Jockey Club (French Derby) for colts, and the Prix de Diane Hermes (French Oaks) for fillies. A dramatic backdrop is provided by the magnificent 18th century chateau and the Grandes Ecuries, the stables which housed the steeds of nobility in days gone by.

Chantilly also has added interest as the locale is one of the top training centres in France, and home to the operations of such notables as Andre Fabre, Criquette Head-Maarek or Ellie Lellouche - the French Newmarket, one could say, but vive la difference!

If you wish to get in touch with the course write to 16, avenue de Générale Leclerc, BP209, 60631 Chantilly. Tel: 0821 213 213.

Chantilly is situated about 30 miles north of Paris and is easily accessible from the capital. It also handy for Charles de Gaulle airport if you are flying in directly. If you are driving from the direction of Paris, take the A1 autoroute and exit at Survilliers. Alternatively, you could take the trains which run directly to Chantilly from Paris' Gare du Nord station. There are also trains which make other stops along the way and it might be best to check before you set off with the SNCF, Tel: 3 42 80 0303.

Despite the architectural opulence of the surroundings at Chantilly, like most French racecourses it is quite cheap to get into. The public enclosure in the centre of the course is absolutely free, while general admission to the remainder of the course and grandstand area costs a few Euros during the week, or a bit more on Sundays and bank holidays. To see the French Oaks will cost you about 10 Euros–a great bargain. Children and teenagers under 18 are free and those 18-25 years old and over 60s enjoy a fifty per cent reduction on the normal price. If you wish to book a seat or table in the restaurant, call ahead on Tel. 3 44 58 9001.

Chantilly holds about 20 days of racing spread from the end of April until the third week of September. You could get off to an early start with a visit on a Sunday in May to see the running of the Prix Hocquart. The main action of the year of course takes place in June with the running of the French Derby and Oaks on consecutive Sundays. Other fixtures are scattered throughout May, June, July and September, but most often on weekdays.

Chantilly is a sweeping, right handed course of 2,000 metres (about a mile and a quarter) and provides a true test of ability.

Chantilly Local Favourites

As an overall place to pay a visit in the area just outside Paris, Chantilly ranks right up at the top along with such other marvellous venues as Fontainbleau or Versailles. It is connections with the horse though, that make it a must for those with an interest in racing and you should really make a point of visiting the highly-regarded Musee Vivant du Cheval (the Museum of the Living Horse). Other notable places to visit nearby include the Abbaye de Chaalis at Hermenonville, the town of Senlis, and of course the Musee Condee and the park and Chateau de Chantille itself.

If you wish to find a bed for the night in a place that maintains the aristocratic theme of Chantilly, try the Chateau Mont Royal (Tel: 3 44 54 5050) a charming chateau hotel that was built at the turn of the century as a hunting lodge and sits in its own forest about six miles outside Chantilly. It has an excellent restaurant and the hotel will very kindly arrange golf, riding or fishing for you nearby. Another highly rated hostelry is the Golf Hotel Blue Green de Chantilly (3 44 58 4777) a good place for an extended stay if you like to try a round on the fairways. Although perhaps not quite as luxurious as these choices, either of the Hotel du Parc (3 44 58 2000), close to the centre of the town, or the baronial Chateau de Montvillargenne Hotel situated in the midst of a pretty forest, will not see you stuck for a bed for a night. For fine dining, one restaurant to put into the notebook is the Chateau de la Tour (3 44 62 3838). Other first class restaurants include the Tour d'Apremont (3 44 25 6111) and Verbois (3 44 24 0622) on the route de Creil.

If you wish to get more information on what to do while you are in the Chantilly area, contact the local tourist office on, Tel: 3 44 57 08 58.

Deauville

Everyone loves to go to the seaside for the summer, and with Deauville you can paddle your feet in the sea in the morning, gorge yourself on fine cuisine and wines at lunch, play the ponies in the afternoon and then try to double your winnings at the casino all night. Though not as ancient as say Chantilly, Deauville is not without its connections to royalty as racing was first started here in 1864 by the Duc de Morny, the Emperor's younger brother and after whom one of the major races of the year, the Prix Morny, is named.

The Clerk of the Course at Deauville may be contacted at Hippodrome de Deauville-La Touques, 45 avenue Hocquart de Turtot, 14800 Deauville, France. Tel: 2 31 14 2000. Fax: 2 31 14 2007.

To get to Deauville from Paris where you might begin your journey when in France, you could drive there taking the A 13 Autoroute that goes from Paris to Caen. By train, you would start your journey at the Gare St Lazare, getting off at Deauville Station. Of course you could also fly there directly if you had your own plane and then you would head for the airport at St Gatien. For landing information, Tel: 2 31 65 1717. Alternatively, mariners may enjoy a trip on the ferry which docks at Le Havre, fairly close to your destination.

The surroundings and hotels in Deauville might be on the luxurious side, but like most French courses, it won't cost you very much to get into the course, just a few

Euros. Those under 18 and over 60 are free, while the 18-25 year-olds get in for half price. Of course a private box would be more and if you would like to arrange one, call ahead on Tel: 1 49 10 2287. Deauville has three fine restaurants, La Toque, Les Jardins du Paddock and Les Haras, and if you would like to book a table call Tel: 2 31 14 3114.

Racing at Deauville takes place from the middle of July to the end of August, and again for an all too brief couple of days in October. The main action takes place though in August when all of Paris has deserted its streets to find a place for the annual vacation. Racing is put on just about every Saturday and Sunday during the month and the big day is the Sunday when the Group 1 Prix Morny is staged, one of the top races for two year olds in France. In the past this race has been won by such stars as Machiavellian, Arazi and Hector Protector and almost always throws down vital clues to the future classics.

Another top class race is the Prix Jacques le Marois for older horses. Perhaps you too could find a future star here if you go to the Agence Francaise Yearling Sales which are held each August in Deauville. If all this doesn't satisfy your appetite for looking at horses, you could always take in a polo match!

Each year, this right-handed course of about 2,000 metres (a mile and a quarter) hosts about 20 fixtures, the bulk of which are in August, the month when many take place on both Saturdays or Sundays of 'le weekend'.

Deauville Local Favourites

Being an elegant seaside resort that has always attracted the well-heeled Parisian, it is not surprising that Deauville boasts a good complement of excellent hotels. After you've spent some time on the beach, perhaps bought a yacht at the sales, done some shopping at designer boutiques and gambled the day and night away at the course and casino, you might consider bedding down at any one of the following recommended hostelries: the Hotel du Golf (Tel: 2 31 14 2400) is a rambling Tudor chateau that has been recently renovated and enjoys splendid views of the River Seine as it meets the sea. True to its name, you can also get in a round of golf on the hotel's own course; the Golf's sister hotel, the Royal (2 31 98 66 22) is also run by the Lucien Barriere group, enjoys sea views and is handy for the centre of town and the casino; others you could try are the Mercure (2 31 98 6633), the L'Amiraute (2 31 88 6262) and the Hotel Yacht Club (2 31 87 3000) overlooking the quayside near the town centre, or L'Augeval (2 31 81 1318). You don't have to be Greek to stay at the Helios Hotel (2 31 14 4646), but you might take home your winnings to the Hotel Le Trophee (2 31 88 4586). Deauville accommodation tends to get fully booked up when the racing is on during the summer, so it's best to reserve ahead if you can.

There is a delightful atmosphere in Deauville and there are numerous restaurants - many are very relaxed and dinner just seems to go on and on. Try Le Garage (2 31 87 2525) or the appropriately named Yearling (2 31 88 3337) which is well regarded. At nearby Touques the Village (2 31 88 0177) is good, as is Aux Landiers (2 31 88 0039)–a real gem in which to plan your winning bets in real peace.

If the pace is a bit hectic in Deauville, you might take a break and do a bit of a tour to nearby Trouville, the delightful Honfleur, with yet even more outstanding restaurants, or Caen–both of which offer some interesting sight-seeing and some museums worth a visit. If your horse has won or money is no object come what may, try the Ferme St-Simeon (2 31 89 2361), a spectacular restaurant. If you can't get enough of the equine action in Deauville, you might pay a visit to the nearby course at Clairefontaine which usually offers a mixed card of both flat and jump racing.

Artist: **D M Dent IN FULL FLIGHT** *Courtesy of:* **The Artist**

If you need any advice on some of the many attractions that Deauville has to offer, contact the Office du Tourisme on Tel: 2 43 42 6926 or visit their web site at www.deauville.org

Racing in *Germany*

After some years in the doldrums, racing in Germany made a real come-from-behind finish a few years ago and now is one of the top places in Europe to go for some quality racing. In addition to Berlin's historic Hoppegarten the illustrious fold of German racecourses includes: Hamburg, the home of the German Derby held each year on the first Sunday of July; Cologne, where the German 2,000 Guineas is staged and one of the country's leading training centres; as well as other major tracks at Munich, Hannover, Bremen, Dortmund, Dusseldorf and Frankfurt, which provide a variety of top notch flat and jump racing. In high summer the action moves to Baden-Baden where the proceedings are conducted with a distinctly relaxed holiday atmosphere.

With their high prize money, German Pattern races have become major targets for top European owners and trainers since they were opened up to foreign competition and there are few Group races which will not see a runner from the top British or French stables. Germany has long had some top trainers of its own and with the right breeding stock they are now going overseas to take on the world at meetings such as the Breeders Cup. German bloodstock continues to improve and many of the horses are now sought after for export to Britain for both flat and jump racing. By most yardsticks, top amongst German racecourses for racing, hospitality, scenery and a generally great time comes Baden-Baden, a real gem of a place on the edge of the Black Forest.

Baden-Baden

Baden-Baden is one of Germany's most popular and prettiest of courses, with a long history of racing going back to 1858. Back in Victorian times it was visited by those who came originally to take the waters at the town's spa, but is now really a year-round resort. Nestled between the Black Forest and the Rhine, it's a delightful place to escape to no matter what the time of year, but for the racing fan, it is the spring and late summer/autumn when Baden-Baden's two main racing festivals take place that make a visit to the town particularly appealing. The racecourse is considered by many to be the country's number one course: Germany's answer to Ascot, in a beautiful parkland setting.

The course is run by the private Internationaler Club, which has about 130 members, and can be contacted at Internationaler Club e.V., Lichtentaler Allee 8, 76530 Baden-Baden, Germany. Tel: 07221 21120. Fax: 07221 211222. On racedays you can reach the course on Tel: 07221 211216. Web site: www.baden-galopp.de

If you are driving there, the quickest way is to take the A5 Autobahn which links Basel in Switzerland with Karlsruhe and take the exit signed Baden-Baden – Iffezheim and you will find the course about 8 miles north west of the town, next to the village of Iffezheim. If you are travelling by train, head for the Baden-Baden – Oos station and board the special buses laid on for racedays which will take you the last five miles to the course. Otherwise, a taxi will cost you only about ten or so

Euros. If you are lucky enough to come by private aeroplane, you should land at the new airport at Solingen which is only about 20 minutes away. For those taking commercial flights, Strasbourg is the nearest airport with regularly scheduled flights and it is about a half hour's drive away. Foreign owners and trainers are treated particularly well here and if you let the officials know in advance, they'll line you up with a badge and even make arrangements to collect you from the airport or railway station.

Less elevated visitors though won't find the tariff too high to spend a day at the races, with general admission only 5 Euros. If you want a reserved seat it will cost you more depending upon where you sit. There are six days of racing during each of the two annual meetings and you can buy badges which cover the entire meeting. Children will find various things to entertain them during their visit here, including a children's playground. There is also a baby care room which is free.

Although the whole course and setting really is first class, Baden-Baden lets you enjoy your racing any way you like it, from the casual pleasure of a beer and bratwurst on a park bench next to the track, to a fine meal in the more formal surroundings of a private box. You could start the day with an early morning breakfast on the Clubhouse Terrace and watch the horses work out on the course and come back later for a big lunch in the Black Forest Terrace with a view of the real racing action in the afternoon.

Although Baden-Baden is probably best known for its flat racing, the course also holds jump racing over hurdles and fences. In fact, there are no fewer than five different courses here, including the Old Course, New Course and Straight Course, which have a total of two miles of excellent turf racecourse between them, with a two furlong final straight. The Steeplechase Course is two miles and three furlongs around, with sixteen fences with a short, steep hill known as the Kapellenberg, while the Hurdles Course is a tighter one with a quarter mile circumference and completely flat.

There are usually nine races a day on each of the twelve days of racing held at Baden-Baden of different classes and distances. Included in these are no fewer than ten European pattern Group races, so the standard of racing is really quite high. Highlight of the spring meeting is the Group 2 Baden Airpark-Grosser Preis der Wirtschaft. In late summer and early Autumn, the Mercedes-Benz Grosser Preis von Baden is a Group 1 contest that has been won by some outstanding horses.

Putting a bet on your selection on the Tote here will be familiar to most punters, with win, place, Forecast and Tricast wagering. If your German is good enough, the racing paper "Sport-Welt" will help you with your selection. For those used to racing in Britain, Ireland or Australia, there are also on-course bookmakers who will take your bet. If you aren't in the stands when the stalls fly open, there are over 100 TV monitors to help you follow the race. Don't worry if you get to the course without having changed your pounds into euros as there is a foreign exchange and cheque cashing service at the on-course Deutsche Bank branch.

With some of the finest racing in Europe at the highest level, a visit to Baden-Baden is a must for every racing enthusiast. Like the spa town, the racecourse prides itself on looking after its guests!

Baden-Baden Local Favourites

If you are visiting Baden-Baden for the races, you will be fortunate to be staying in a place that has some of the finest hotels and service in the world, with over a century of catering for just about anyone's personal whim. Spa towns tend to pamper their guests and this is one of the ultimate places to be pampered. You could take the waters before or after racing, play a round of golf at one of the resort's many courses or, if you are on a roll with a few winners, try your luck at the world famous casino in the Kurhaus. For updated information visit www.baden-baden.de before you go.

The Caracalla-Therme and the Friedrichsbad are the two best known bathing spots where a garden of earthly delights awaits those wishing to take the cure before taking in a more cultural experience at the theatre or concert hall. Right in Baden-Baden, the Lichtentaler Allee and historic old town is filled with elegant boutiques and shops just waiting to relieve you of your winnings from the course or casino.

Baden-Baden is right on the doorstep of the region's wine growing district, the Rebland, which has some of the finest wines in Germany as well as some extremely good eating places in addition to some glorious scenery. A day touring around here, or a short hop over the Rhine to neighbouring Alsace would be sure to prompt a trip to the gym when you return home.

In the very top rank of hotels here, there is the famous Brenner's Park Hotel (07221 9000) which is firmly in the luxury category and is an excellent nearby hotel on the outskirts of Baden-Baden. Also top class is Monch's Posthotel (07083 7440) in nearby Bad Herrenalb. First-class accommodation can be found in either the Europaischer Hof Hotel (07221 23561) or the Badischer Hof hotels, both run by the quality Steigenberger hotel chain which also provides on-course catering services at Baden-Baden.

If you fancy a stay in the heart of the Black Forest, try the Hotel Bareiss (07442 470) near Baiersbronn-Mitteltal - it's a complete resort with all kinds of sports facilities. Here you won't be too far away from the fabulous Restaurant Schwarzwaldstube (07442 4920) with its classic fine French cuisine.

One thing you should really do before leaving home though is to book ahead, as racing at Baden-Baden has had a resurgence in popularity in recent years and you might be disappointed if you don't have a reservation at the hotel of your choice.

Artist: **Klaus Philip THE PARADE** *Courtesy of:* **The Artist**

Racing in *Canada*

Woodbine

As one of the handful of courses that have hosted the Breeders' Cup, Woodbine has staked its place in international racing and is Canada's leading thoroughbred track. Built on peaceful farmland north west of Toronto in the 1950s, it is now almost engulfed by this fast growing city and as you sit in the grandstand the roar of jet engines signals the approach of yet another flight bringing visitors to the busy international airport nearby.

Woodbine is a first rate facility that has transformed itself recently into an 'entertainment complex', combining flat and harness racing, operating both day and night, with simulcast inter-track betting on other courses. It has also added a huge casino that has 1,700 slot machines on the main floor of the grandstand that is open 365 days a year from 11:00 am until 3:00 am. This may not be everyone's cup of tea, but it does provide the funds for increased prize money on the track and subsidises the free admission to the course.

The course is run by the Woodbine Entertainment Group and they can be contacted at 555 Rexdale Boulevard, Rexdale, Ontario, Canada M9W 5L2. Tel: (888) 675 6110. Fax: (888) 213 2126. Web site: www.ojc.com.

The course is very easy to drive to by car. Just a few minutes from Toronto International Airport, follow Highway 409 to Highway 427 and the main entrance. Allow about an hour to cover the 15 miles from downtown Toronto, taking the Queen Elizabeth Way west to Highway 427 right to the track. Alternatively you could take Toronto's efficient subway system and hop in a taxi or connect with the free Racetrack buses which leave from Kipling Station just under an hour before the first race to the main entrance and returning after the last race. Seating is on a first-come, first served basis. If you need any assistance with directions, give the course a ring on (888) 675-RACE.

Thoroughbred racing takes place at Woodbine from the end of March through to the first week in December, although there is Harness Racing here seven months of the year. There are usually ten races a day of varying calibre and distances, mostly on the dirt track but some held on the turf course. There are big stakes races held on Saturdays, Sundays and holidays throughout the year, with the Queen's Plate for Canadian bred three year olds, the first leg of the Canadian Triple Crown in late June providing the highlight of the summer season and the EP Taylor Stakes and Canadian International with a guaranteed purse of Can $1.5 million in mid October.

Admission to the large Grandstand and course itself is free, but there are admission charges to access various restaurants and other facilities. There are also thousands of free seats in the Grandstand on several levels offering excellent viewing of all parts of the track. Some sections have reserved seating which has a small charge on the big race days. A race programme costs Can $2.50 and contains past performances plus a brief form guide; for the purist handicapper, a copy of the Daily Racing Form is also a must for racegoers. The minimum bet on the pari-mutuel is $2 Canadian (about $1.50 US), so you don't have to bring loads of cash to enjoy yourself.

At the top end of the scale is the Woodbine Club, an exclusive member-only private club whose panelled lounges and bars offer luxurious accommodation. If you are just visiting Toronto for a few days it might be worth your while to find a member who can take you as a guest. If you get lucky and cash in a big daily double, you might want to stump up the $1,000 for your own membership!

Woodbine has a number of restaurants and bars to choose from but reservations are advised for busy weekends and holiday meetings, Tel 888-675 7223. Favourite on the second floor is a restaurant with panoramic views that overlooks the finish line. Each table has its own TV monitor showing track odds and racing. On the third floor Clubhouse level is Champions, a bar and delicatessen counter serving soup and sandwiches, which has an outdoor patio and casual dining. No reservations required here but there is a $5 admission surcharge. On the first floor, the Finish Line bar also offers light snacks. The Grandstand complex also contains a food court with a wide choice of snack and fast food outlets, the hot roast beef sandwiches at the carvery are a safe bet.

Having fully satisfied your appetite, why not spend a while visiting the Canadian Horse Racing Hall of Fame. In addition to celebrating such equine heroes as Northern Dancer and the great 'Big Red' Secretariat, who had his last race at Woodbine, you can explore the rich history of the turf in Canada.

Toronto Local Favourites

Toronto is well worth a visit in itself, with a multitude of first-class hotels and a fabulous range of restaurants that reflect the city's multi-ethnic population. In fact, there are more restaurants per capita in Toronto than any other city in the world! You might never leave the airport strip of hotels and eateries, but you would be missing much if you did not try and stay downtown. It's a clean, safe walking city with lots of shopping, sites and nightlife, so why not enjoy it to the maximum? The Yorkville area in mid-town Toronto is an excellent bet with hotels such as the classic Park Hyatt (416 925 1234) on Avenue Road with its fifties roof garden bar. The Four Seasons Hotel (416 964 0411) opposite offers all the luxury that chain usually provides. Not far away on Cumberland is the classy Sassafraz restaurant, bistro and bar (416 964 2222) on Cumberland Street where visiting film stars hang out. For a fun night out and a lot of local colour try the Brunswick Tavern on Bloor Street West, a favourite watering hole. Dip south on Spadina Avenue between College Street and Queen and you are in Chinatown, one of the largest in North America and packed with many excellent restaurants. The area has many other good nightspots including Grossman's Tavern on Spadina which features an array of talented jazz and blues artists.

There are many hotels right downtown and a safe bet is the Fairmont Royal York Hotel (416 368 2511) opposite Union Station or for a bit of turn-of-the-century elegance try the Royal Meridien King Edward Hotel (416 863 3131) on King Street, handy for shopping in the vast Eaton Centre or exploring the nightlife. Toronto is right on Lake Ontario and the Harbourfront area hops night and day. Stay at the Radisson Hotel (416 203 3333) right on the water and take a ferry to the Toronto Islands for a bit of green quiet and the best view of the city skyline. See the sights from the top of the CN Tower or take in a baseball game in the covered Sky Dome at its foot. Toronto and Woodbine are a winning daily double.

US Racetracks at a Glance

Arizona
Turf Paradise 1501 W. Bell Road
Phoenix, Arizona 85023 (602) 942-1101
www.turfparadise.com
September to May

Arkansas
Oaklawn Park 2705 Central Avenue
Hot Springs, Arkansas 71902 1-800-
OAKLAWN *www.oaklawnpark.com*
January to April

California
Bay Meadows 2600 South Delaware
Street San Mateo, California 94402 (650)
574-RACE *www.baymeadows.com*
April to June, September to November

Del Mar Via De La Valle & Jimmy
Durante Blvd. Del Mar, California 92014
(858) 755-1141 *www.dmtc.com*
July to September

Golden Gate Fields 1100 Eastshore
Hwy Berkeley, California 94710 (510)
559-7300 *www.goldengatefields.com*
November to March

Hollywood Park 1050 South
Prairie Avenue Inglewood,
California 90301 (310) 419-1500
www.hollywoodpark.com
April 23 to July, November/December 21

Santa Anita 285 W. Huntington Drive
Arcadia, California 91066 (626) 574-
7223 *www.santaanita.com*
December to April

Delaware
Delaware Park 777 Delaware Park
Blvd Wilmington Wilmington,
Delaware 19804 (302) 994-2521
www.delpark.com
April to November

Florida
Calder Race Course 21001 NW 27th
Avenue Miami, Florida 33056 (305) 625-
1311 *www.calderracecourse.com*
April to January

Gulfstream Park 901 South
Federal Highway Hallandale,
Florida 33009 (800) 771-TURF
www.gulfstreampark.com
January to April

Tampa Bay Downs P.O. BOX 2007
Oldsmar, Florida 34677 1-800-200-4434
www.tampabaydowns.com
December to May

Illinois
Arlington Park Euclid Avenue &
Wilke Road Arlington Heights,
Illinois 60006 (847) 255-4300
www.arlingtonpark.com
May to September

Hawthorne Race Course 3501 S. Laramie
Cicero, Illinois 60804 (708) 780-3700
www.hawthorneracecourse.com
March onwards

Kentucky
Churchill Downs 700 Central Avenue
Louisville, Kentucky 40208 (502) 636-
4400 *www.churchilldowns.com*
April to July, October/November

Keeneland 4201 Versailles Road
Lexington, Kentucky 40510 (800) 456-
3412 *www.keeneland.com*
April, October

Turfway Park 7500 Turfway Road
Florence, Kentucky 41022 (800) 733-
0200 *www.turfway.com*
January to March

Louisiana
Fair Grounds 1751 Gentilly Blvd. New
Orleans, Louisiana 70119 (504) 944-
5515 *www.fgno.com*

Maryland
Laurel Park Racetrack Road & Route 198
Laurel, Maryland 20725 (301) 725-0400
www.laurelpark.com
October to December

Pimlico Hayward and Winner Avenues
Baltimore, Maryland 21215 (410) 542-
9400 *www.pimlico.com*

Massachusetts
Suffolk Downs 111 Waldemar Avenue
East Boston, Massachusetts 02128 (617)
567-7511 *www.suffolkdowns.com*
January to June

Minnesota
Canterbury Park 1100 Canterbury Road
Shakopee, Minnesota 55379 (612) 445-
7223 *www.canterburypark.com*
May to September

Nebraska
Horsemen's Park 6303 "Q" Street
Omaha, Nebraska 68117 (402) 731-5122

New Jersey
Meadowlands 50 Route 20 East
Rutherford, New Jersey 07073 (201)
935-8500 *www.thebigm.com*
January to August, November/December

Monmouth Park 175 Oceanport Avenue
Oceanport, New Jersey 07757 (732)
222-5100 *www.monmouthpark.com*
May to September

New York
Aqueduct 110th Street & Rockaway Blvd
Ozone Park, New York 11417 (718) 641-
4700 *www.nyra.com/aqueduct*
January to March, October to December

Belmont Park 2150 Hempstead
Turnpike Elmont, New York 11003 (718)
641-4700 *www.nyra.com/belmont*
April to July, September/October

Saratoga Union Avenue Saratoga
Springs, New York 12866 (718) 641-
4700 *www.nyra.com/saratoga*
July to September

Ohio
River Downs 6301 Kellogg Avenue
Cincinnati, Ohio 45230 (513) 232-8000
www.riverdowns.com
April to September

Thistledown 21501 Emery Road North
Randall, Ohio 44128 (800) 289-9956
www.thistledown.com
April to December

Oklahoma
Fair Meadows PO Box 4735 Tulsa,
Oklahoma 74159 (918)743-7223
www.fairmeadows.com
April to June

Remington Park One Remington Place
Oklahoma City, Oklahoma 73111 (405)
424-1000 *www.remingtonpark.com*

Oregon
Portland Meadows 1001 North
Scheemer Rd. Portland,
Oregon 97217 583-285-9144
www.portlandmeadows.com

Texas
Lone Star Park 1000 Lone Star Parkway
Grand Prairie, Texas 75050 (972) 263-
RACE *www.lonestarpark.com*
April to July, October/November

Virginia
Colonial Downs 10515 Colonial Downs
Parkway New Kent, Virginia 23124 (804)
966-RACE *www.colonialdowns.com*
June/July

Washington
Emerald Downs PO Box 617 Auburn,
Washington 98071 (253) 288-7000
www.emeralddowns.com
April to September

West Virginia
Mountaineer Park PO Box 358 Chester,
West Virginia 26034 1-800-804-0468
www.mtrgaming.com
April to November

Racing in **New York**

The three principal thoroughbred racetracks of Belmont and Aqueduct near New York City and Saratoga in upstate New York are run by the New York Racing Association Inc., PO Box 90, Jamaica, New York, 11417. Tel: (718) 641 4700. E Mail: nyra@nyra.com. They also have an excellent web site giving details of all three tracks, updates on big race entries and general news; well worth a visit at www.nyracing.com

Belmont Park

Home to the 2005 Breeders Cup, Belmont Park has been the scene of some memorable moments in turf history. No one will forget the immortal Secretariat powering home by a record margin to win the Belmont Stakes, or Lester Piggott urging Royal Academy to get up by a nose in the Breeders Cup mile.

Any way you look at it, Belmont, like New York City itself, is a big place. The main grandstand which was built as part of a major refit in the late 1960s is awesomely large and stretches most of the finishing straight. On big race days such as the Belmont Stakes they can fit in upwards of 90,000 people and at least 33,000 of those will not have any trouble getting a seat. By North American standards the course itself is also pretty impressive with a mile and a half dirt track, while the Widener turf course is just over a mile and a quarter. Of all racetracks in America Belmont is probably the one best suited to the running style of British and European horses, so

visitors from across the Atlantic might have an even chance of making a few bob if they spot any imported runners here.

Belmont is on Long Island and to get there from Manhattan take the Queens Midtown Tunnel to the Long Island Expressway, east to Cross Island Parkway and south to Exit 26-D. From Connecticut take any route to the Throgs Neck Bridge to the Cross Island Parkway, or from New Jersey you can use the George Washington Bridge from the north or from the south the Interstate bridge to the Staten Island Expressway and the Verazzano Bridge. From Manhattan you could also take the 8th Avenue subway to connecting buses at 169th or 179th streets, or by rail via the Long Island Railroad from Penn Station to make connections at Jamaica.

Once you've reached the track it will cost a mere $2 to park the car, or an additional $2 for preferred parking closer to the entrance. A courtesy shuttle bus will take you to the admission entrance. If you're feeling really quite lazy it's worth paying an extra $4 for valet parking. There is special parking available for both the grandstand and clubhouse. Admission to the Grandstand is only $2, but it's probably worth spending another $2 to get into the Clubhouse, then you can go anywhere you like. Children under 12 are free. Prices for the Breeders Cup meeting can be found on their website: www.breederscup.com.

Racing is held at Belmont over long stretches in the spring and summer and again in the autumn and, apart from the month of August when everyone moves to Saratoga,

*Artist: **Rochelle Levy** SARATOGA, AFTER MORNING WORK Courtesy of: **Frost & Reed***

alternates with Aqueduct. So if you're visiting New York City at any time other than August, you can get some local action. No racing is usually held on Mondays (except bank holidays) and Tuesdays, as well as the occasional Wednesday on a bank holiday week. Watch out for Palm Sunday and Easter Sunday though, as they are both 'dark', as is Yom Kippur.

There are big races just about every weekend, but one to catch in April would be the Wood Memorial, a Kentucky Derby trial for three year-olds, followed by the highlight of the season, the Belmont Stakes in June, which forms the third leg of the American triple crown. It's by far the biggest day of the year with a supporting card of excellent Group 1,2 and 3 races. The crowds pack in and the course looks at its glorious best. In addition to the Breeders Cup, the regular autumn programme has its own rewards with the Man O'War and the Woodward weight-for-age stakes providing excellent quality racing in September followed by the Jockey Club Gold Cup in October and its fine supporting card of Group races.

Belmont is big, but even on the biggest races days there seem to be acres of space in the cavernous Grandstand and getting something to eat or drink is little problem. The Clubhouse has several restaurants, including the glass-enclosed Garden Terrace Dining Room on the fourth floor with its great view of the track. There is a $2 seating charge, a $10 minimum order and you are required to wear a sports jacket or suit. The Paddock Dining Room on the second floor overlooks the paddock (naturally!), while the Belmont

Cafe on the first floor offers lighter fare and also breakfast for those who like to get up early and watch the horses go through their morning paces. On weekends its best to reserve, so call ahead on (516) 488 1740. There's also a food court with a choice of fast food snacks and the backyard picnic area for you to bring your own picnic. There are bars throughout the complex on all levels, some as long as your mother- in- law's last visit!

If you happen to be in New York City during the winter, from December to early March, and are desperate for some action, you could spend an afternoon at Aqueduct. which is not that far from Manhattan in Jamaica (Long Island that is!). It's probably easiest to go by subway - take the 'A' train to the Old Aqueduct station and pick up a free bus to the track. The big "A" will always be a favourite with some Noo Yawkers, but it's really a bit like the all-weather at Lingfield on a cold, wet January day. Come to think of it, you should be where anyone else with a bit sense in the Big Apple has already gone - to Florida!

New York City Local Favourites

For New York City, you've really got to be in the heart of the action, and that means mid-town Manhattan. Shopping at Saks, Bergdorff-Goodman or Brooks Brothers on Fifth Avenue, taking in a concert at Carnegie Hall or seeing a show at Radio City Music Hall, it's all right here. Put a bit of breathing space between you and the skyscrapers by taking a stroll through Central Park (by day, please!) and drop down

Artist: **Booth Malone SARATOGA, REVEILLE** *Courtesy of:* **Frost & Reed**

to Greenwich Village or SoHo at night for some great dining, drinking and music. The flagship of Manhattan hotels is of course the Plaza Hotel (212 546 5493) at Central Park South and Fifth Avenue, made famous by scores of movies –remember Lisa Minelli and Dudley Moore in "Arthur"? If you find the tariff for the night a bit steep, try lunch in the Palm Court instead or sample a few oysters Rockefeller in the Oyster Bar downstairs.

Sunday lunch could take you to the Tavern on the Green in Central Park; it's a rambling, way-over-the-top sort of place but lots of fun. A visit to Rockefeller Plaza is a must and the café overlooking the skating rink in the late autumn and winter is a great place to people watch over lunch. In the evening dine and dance in art deco style in the magnificent Rainbow Room–a great way to blow your winnings. Late night hunger pangs can be satisfied at one of the many delis around town; try Wolfs Famous Delicatessen on Sixth Avenue where the wafer-thin roast beef is piled high on rye. Wherever you stay in New York, go out in the morning to one of the many local diners for breakfast where a couple of dollars will get you eggs sunny side up or easy over with your bottomless cup of coffee. New York offers an incredible choice when it comes to hotels of every size and description. Wouldn't it be better to stay in a place that offers some character with a convenient location? For some Edwardian elegance and connections to the New York literati try the Algonquin (212 840 6800) on West 44th street. The Carlisle (212 744 1600) on Madison Avenue is a real gem and only one block from Central Park. Although it has a mere 60 rooms The Lowell (212 838 1400) on East 63rd Street has working fireplaces to enjoy in its bedrooms and art deco elegance. For a great afternoon tea and fine views over Central Park go to The Pierre (212 838 8000) on famous Fifth Avenue.

Saratoga

The song might say "I like New York in June", but you will love Saratoga in August. That's the month that this sleepy Victorian spa town in upstate New York is transformed into the racing centre of North America. Virtually the whole of the Big Apple is transported three hundred miles north to escape the swelter of the city in summer, joined by many racing professionals and enthusiasts from around the world attracted by the quality of racing, sporting art exhibitions and summer yearling sales. There has been racing at Saratoga since 1863 and the racetrack just like the town itself oozes Victorian charm.

Saratoga is just under an hour's drive north of Albany in upper New York state and is easily reached from New York City or western New York using the New York Thruway to Exit 24 at Albany, then the Northway (87) to Exit 14 and Route 9P to just outside the track entrance. From Vermont or New Hampshire take Route 40 to Schuyerville and Route 29 to Saratoga. When you arrive, $5 will get you trackside parking but it's only $2 in the main parking areas where many pack a picnic and barbecue and have a tailgate party.

A great way to start the day is to have breakfast on the Clubhouse porch and watch the early morning workouts. Admission is free and breakfast is served between 7:00 and 9:30 am every racing day. Expert commentators describe the training sessions; afterwards you can hop on a tram for a free tour of the barn area or catch the Paddock show and starting gate demonstration.

A holiday atmosphere pervades Saratoga, with lots of people bringing their fold-up chairs and coolers into the track to sit among the tall pine trees, listening to the strains of a Dixieland band while watching the betting shows and races on TV monitors slung from the trees. It costs only $2 to get into the track, or $4 for the Clubhouse with children under 12 admitted free. To be sure of a seat overlooking the course it's best to reserve one well in advance–$6 in the Clubhouse and $4 for the Grandstand. Write before April 1st (January 1st for the Clubhouse seat lottery) to Saratoga Reserved Seats, PO Box 030257, Elmont, NY USA 11003 Tel: (718) 641 4700. A few Grandstand seats do go on sale each morning at the track entrance from 8:00 am.

Any day at Saratoga is a great day, even though it's just as hard as any other place to pick a winner. Racing starts at the end of July and runs through to the Labour Day bank holiday which is the first Monday in September–six days a week (Tuesday's are 'dark' days). The quality of the racing is excellent with a top handicap or group race almost every day. Highlights of the meeting include the Group 1 Whitney Handicap and Sword Dancer Invitation Handicap and the Travers Stakes for three year olds over a mile and a quarter run towards the end of August. Thrown in here and there are also some steeplechases, just to make things even more interesting if you're a jumping fan at heart! If you have an hour or so to spare before racing, a visit to the racing museum across the street from the main entrance is also a good bet. For $10 you can take a tour each morning that includes the Oklahoma training track.

Saratoga offers a wide choice of fast food outlets and you can get just about anything you want from steaks to grits and ice cream. There are also several restaurants and bars from which to choose including the Turf Terrace, Club Terrace, Carousel Restaurant and Lounge, Paddock Tent and At The Rail Pavilion most of which should be reserved in advance and carry seating charges. Call Service America (718) 529 8700 before July 20 or (518) 587 5070 during the race meeting.

Saratoga may be very laid back, but America does insist on a little formality with its racing and gentlemen are expected to wear suits or sports jackets in certain areas such as Box Seats, the Turf Terrace and the At The Rail Pavilion. Show up here in shorts or jeans (even designer labels) and you will be turned away! The rest of the course is a lot more relaxed, but you're supposed to keep on your shoes and shirts at all times–that goes for the ladies too!

Saratoga Local Favourites

Saratoga Springs is extremely busy during the entire month of August when the racing community descends en masse, many people staying in the same place every year. If you want to stay right in town then it is advisable to book as early as possible–up to a year before you visit! One top-notch hostelry right in Saratoga is the Ramada Renaissance (518 584 4000). One of the few surviving grand hotels of the spa's glory days is the Adelphi (518 587 4688) which has a lot more charm and has been refurbished in late 19th century style. Another option for a bed for the night is scenic Lake George, just about an hour's drive north. Here you will find the delightfully pricey Sagamore (518 644 9400) which offers a full range of sports; there are also lots of other small motels and B&B's from which to explore the lake by paddlewheel steamer. You could also escape to the cool mountains of neighbouring Vermont where you will find many good inns around Woodstock. There are also many hotels in New York's state capital of Albany if you have trouble staying in Saratoga itself.

There is a wide range of dining and drinking right in Saratoga. A best bet is Siro's restaurant on Lincoln Avenue near the track where you can have breakfast (another one!) on the patio and listen to a panel of handicap experts take you through the coming day's racing. Siro's is only open the six weeks of racing, but it really packs in the punters who wish to spend their winnings on good food each evening. Other places recommended include the Wishing Well in nearby Wilton; Hatties on Philadelphia Street; Bruno's for pizza and the Mexican Connection on Nelson Avenue. Many racing people head for Sperry's on Caroline Street.

Saratoga has lots of other delights, beside the racing, and those who are more culturally minded might take in a performance at the Performing Arts Festival, or visit historic battlefields from the Revolutionary War or President Ulysses S Grant's summer house. One thing's for sure, you won't be short of things for amusement!

Racing in **Florida**

When the temperature dips in eastern North America late in the autumn, sensible racing folk pack their binoculars and form books and head for the sunshine state of Florida. Decades before Godolphin began using the warm climate of Dubai as a winter headquarters, some of the most famous thoroughbreds in North American racing history were trained under Florida palms to go on to glory in the US triple crown.

Thoroughbred racing centres around Miami, where the main winter meeting now takes place at Gulfstream Park. If you do end up in Miami at other times of the year, you could also catch some thoroughbred action at Calder, just south west of the city, where racing is held from the end of April to November.

Gulfstream Park

There is some seriously good racing at Gulfstream and it holds the prime time of Florida racing when the weather is at its worst in the rest of North America. Its lush, tropical setting also makes Gulfstream one of the world's most beautiful courses and it offers a variety of entertainments and a great day out in the sunshine for the serious or casual racegoer. Gulfstream has hosted the Breeders Cup meeting but with its hot, steamy climate we are afraid our European horses don't seem to relish it after the end of a long season.

Gulfstream is located in Hallandale, between Fort Lauderdale and Miami, and it's very handy for both places using the I-95, US 1 and Hallandale Beach Boulevard. You could use either Miami International or Ft Lauderdale/Hollywood International airports to reach your destination.

Artist: **Rochelle Levy SARATOGA** Courtesy of: **Frost & Reed**

For information write to Gulfstream Park, 901 South Federal Highway, Hallandale, Florida, USA 33009. Tel: (954) 454 7000. Fax: (954) 454 7827 www.gulfstreampark.com.

Gulfstream holds its major meeting of the year from early January to the middle of April. There is racing every day except Tuesdays and post time is 1:00 p.m. Admission to the Grandstand is $3 or $5 for the Clubhouse. Both include a free programme and parking. As many trainers use the Florida racing season as a prep for the US Triple Crown for three year olds, the highlight of the season at Gulfstream is the Grade 1 Florida Derby held in the middle of March. It carries a purse in excess of $1 million and usually attracts some top members of the classic generation. There are three gourmet dining rooms to satisfy your hunger, two in the Clubhouse and one in the Turf Club, all with terraced seating for a view of the track. There is also a large, air-conditioned (of course!) cafeteria in the Grandstand as well as no fewer than 21 other restaurants and snack bars and also 14 bars.

Florida Favourites

There's no shortage of places to stay, eat or drink in South Florida, after all it has been the favourite sun destination for North Americans for almost a century now. First time visitors might be surprised at the amount of Spanish that is spoken everywhere, but it gives Miami its unique flavour as the major gateway to Central and South America and provides the Latino punch in the pina colada. Two great centres of interest are the Art Deco revival area of Miami Beach and the laid-back delights of Key West, a hundred and odd miles to the south. Both are sure bets for accommodation, food, drink and fun people-watching.

Handy for Gulfstream are several top notch hostelries including the Turnberry Isle Resort (305) 932 6200 on West Country Club Drive and just 10 minutes from the track, the Sheraton Bal Harbour (305) 865 7511 on Collins Avenue about 20 minutes away in Bal Harbor, and the Marriott Harbor Beach (954) 525 4000 and Pier 66 Hyatt Regency (954) 525 6666 both in Fort Lauderdale, a half hour away. Closer to the track, in fact only five minutes away and a bit less expensive, is the Hollywood Beach Clarion Hotel (954) 459 1900 on South Ocean Drive. The nice people there also give discounts to people connected with racing. There are many top notch restaurants in the Miami area and just a few that come highly recommended are: Manero's on East Hallandale Beach Boulevard (954) 456 1000; Chef Allen's (305) 935 2900 on NE 29th Avenue in North Miami Beach, Las Brisas (954) 923 1500 on Surf Road in Hollywood or Joe's Stone Crabs (305) 673 0365 in Miami Beach. If you need any advice on where to stay or what to do close to the racing action you could contact either the Greater Miami Convention & Visitors Bureau Tel: (305) 539 3000 or that of Fort Lauderdale (954) 765 4466.

Florida really does have everything for the visitor - sun, sand and lots to see. If you have time to spare, take the Tagmeme Trail through the Everglades to the west coast and collect some sea shells on Signable Island. Of course if the kids are along on the trip you won't be able to leave the sunshine state without a stop off at Disney World in Orlando. Actually, big kids seem to like it too!

Racing in **Kentucky**

Kentucky is the spiritual home of racing in America. This is Bluegrass Country and perhaps the most important breeding place for top notch thoroughbreds on the continent. The annual Keeneland Sales attract horse people with fat wallets from all over the world and yearlings sold here go on to fame and glory in most parts of the globe. Of course the racing is top notch here, but just to tour around the countryside following mile after mile of white fencing around the stud farms is the experience of a lifetime for those who love horses and racing, a feeling similar to that found around Newmarket or in much of Ireland.

Churchill Downs

There are five racetracks in Kentucky but the daddy of them all is Churchill Downs, home of the Kentucky Derby, held on the first Saturday in May and the first leg of the US triple crown for three year-olds. Around one hundred and forty thousand people pack the Downs on Derby Day and as the first strains of My Old Kentucky Home waft over the crowd as the horses come out to parade for the big race, spirits and emotions run high. This is mint julep time, when everyone can be a Kentucky Colonel for the day.

Louisville lies on the banks of the Ohio River and is about an hour's flying time from Chicago, just under two hours from New York and about four from Los Angeles and is served by many different airlines so there isn't much problem getting there.

The world famous twin spires of Churchill Downs can be found at 700 Central Avenue, Louisville, Kentucky, USA 40208. Tel: (502) 636 4400. Fax: (502) 636 4430. Website: kentuckyderby.com. The track first opened in 1875 and has one of the longest and most illustrious histories in the annals of the American turf and the Derby has been held here every year since.

The Kentucky Derby is actually a week-long affair, with many other activities going on. For early risers there's 'Dawn at the Downs' where you can breakfast track-side each day and watch the contenders and other horses go through their morning workouts. There are special jockeys autograph sessions, the 'Festival in the Field' concerts with rock bands, handicapping contests and seminars and backstretch tours, just to mention a few. Away from the track, all of Louisville gets into the swing with hot air balloon races, one of the largest firework displays on the continent and a steamboat race down the Ohio River–all part of the Kentucky Derby Festival.

Like most tracks in North America, admission to Churchill Downs on racing days won't break the bank, but on Derby and Oaks days general admission rises to about $40 and $25 respectively. If you wish to sit down anywhere it's best to reserve a seat ahead of time–contact the course for details. A great tradition of the Oaks and Derby days is the tailgate party which sees 80,000 people enjoying their barbecues and beer in the forty acres of the infield. The main grandstand area has many bars and restaurants for those non-tailgaters and a mint julep on Derby day will cost you about $5, but that's not bad because you get to keep the souvenir glass!

Of course the Kentucky Derby week is the highlight of the year at Churchill Downs, but the track stages many more days racing in both the Spring and the Autumn. The Spring meeting covers abut 48 days racing, from the end of April until the end of June. Race days are normally Wednesday through Sunday, all week during Derby Week, and with a few Mondays and Tuesdays thrown in. The Autumn meeting has 24 days racing held daily except Mondays and runs for the month of November. Post time is normally 3:00 pm on weekdays in the Spring and 1:00 on weekends and holidays but on Kentucky Derby and Oaks days the first race is moved up to 11:30 am. The Autumn meeting has a daily 1: 00 pm start, except on Thanksgiving (the third Thursday in November) and closing weekend when it is brought forward to 11:30 am. No excuses now to miss the daily double! In 2006, Churchill Downs will also be hosting the Breeders' Cup, another great excuse to come to this lovely part of the world.

In the Spring, the annual 'Run for the Roses' is just the icing on the cake of a whole week of great racing here which kicks off the Saturday of the week before with the Derby Trial stakes, the last prep race for the big event itself and runs through the Kentucky Oaks for three year old fillies on Derby eve Friday. Each of these and other graded races are championships in their own right. If all of this flat racing is a bit much for those who prefer the jumps, take heart and stick around for Churchill Downs' annual Steeplechase Racing day on Sunday at the end of June. Three jump races are part of a ten race card including the $100,000 Grade 1 Hard Scuffle Steeplechase.

Kentucky has several other racetracks which host racing at other times of the year. Keeneland at Lexington of course also holds the annual summer yearling sales in July and is the centre for breeding; you could spend days or weeks visiting famous stud farms such as Gainesway, Shadwell Stud, Darby Dan Farm, Calumet Farm, the Kentucky Horse Center or Spendthrift Farm. Tours can often be arranged if you enquire ahead of time.

Kentucky Local Favourites

Getting around Louisville can be an experience in itself. For something different, why not hop on a horsedrawn carriage for a tour by Kentucky Carriage (802) 944 6065 or by horsedrawn trams by Louisville Horse Trams (502) 581 0100. There are lots of choices of places to stay in Louisville. The Aleksander House B&B on First Street (502) 637 4985 might be the cosy spot for the November racing at Churchill Downs as it features open fireplaces, gourmet breakfasts and four-poster beds in an old Victorian house. The Camberley Brown Hotel on West Broadway (502) 583 1234 is much larger with 300 four-star rooms. Another Victorian house hotel is the Columbine Inn (502) 635 5000 on South Third Street, where you can sit on the porch overlooking the gardens. The Inn at The Park on South Fourth Street (502) 637 6930 also offers Victorian elegance with your B&B.

Within walking distance right downtown is a host of eateries. You could go for a pizza and beer with some live entertainment at Bearno's by the Bridge on West Main Street (502) 584 7437 or if seafood is your choice try Joe's Crab

Artist: **Booth Malone** SCHOOLING *Courtesy of:* **Frost & Reed**

Shack on River Road (502) 568 1171 which is loud, lively and a lot of fun. A bit more up-market is the Bristol Bar & Grille at Riverfront Plaza (502) 562 0158 serving American and international cuisine; slightly more relaxed and reasonable is Deke's Marketplace Grill on West Market Street (502) 584 8337. Right on the river you can dine aboard the Star of Louisville at West River Road (502) 581 7827 or on the decks of Towboat Annies River Café (502) 589 2010 with its great view of the Ohio River.

If you'd like to take home a souvenir of your visit to Kentucky, why not stop off at The Festival Gallery on Fourth Avenue in Louisville (502) 581 1986 which stocks a wide range of racing art on the Derby and its heroes. Another place to relive some memories and pick up some memorabilia is the Kentucky Derby Museum (502) 637 1111 which has three floors of exhibits on thoroughbred racing and the Derby itself, as well as a gift shop.

If you need any information on where to stay or what to do, contact the Louisville Convention & Visitors Bureau, 400 South First Street, Louisville, Kentucky, USA 40202. Tel:(502) 584 2121 or visit their web site at www.louisville-visitors.com.

Racing in _California_

Southern California's normally benign climate makes racing a year round pleasure. Don't worry about earthquakes or the El Nino effect, here in lotus land some of North America's top trainers such as D Wayne Lukas ply their trade, sometimes venturing farther afield to pluck top prize money. Actually it's surprising that they actually leave at all, given the level of racing right at home. This is a spot to go racing under the palms in first-class comfort before you head off to Malibu for some surfing, tour the big movie company's lots, see the original Disneyworld, shop on Rodeo Drive or cruise down Sunset Strip. California's got it all, and more! This State actually has nine racecourses and if you were visiting San Francisco for example it would be a shame not to put on a few exactors at Golden Gate Fields, or do the daily double at Del Mar in San Diego. The two top bets though are Hollywood Park and Santa Anita in the Los Angeles area.

Santa Anita

Racing at Santa Anita goes back to 1907 but it was in 1933 that the present course was built and, while many changes have been made over the years, it still maintains its classic Art Deco design and park-like setting.

Santa Anita Park covers 320 acres and is situated in the suburb of Arcadia, about 14 miles north east of downtown Los Angeles and 30 miles from LA International Airport. Any one of a number of freeways will connect to the Interstate 210 Freeway to take you there by car; exit at Baldwin and turn right. When you arrive there is a choice of three parking areas: General Parking is $3, Preferred (a bit closer to the track) is $5, or you can have someone else park your car for $8 for Valet Parking.

You can contact the track at Los Angeles Turf Club, PO Box 808, Arcadia, California, USA 91066-0808. Tel: (626) 7223. Fax: (626) 574 9860 Website: santaanita.com

Two race meetings are held here each year. The Oak Tree meeting runs for six to seven weeks in October and November, with about 32 days of racing. The longer winter/spring meeting traditionally opens just after Christmas and runs through mid-April. The Grade 1 Santa Anita Derby is California's 'Spring Classic' for three year-olds and is a major stepping stone to the Kentucky Derby. It is held on the first Saturday in April, exactly a month before the Derby, and many winners such as Triple Crown hero Affirmed have gone on to win the Run for the Roses after success in California. Other top races are the Santa Monica Handicap for older fillies and mares, also a Grade 1 race run at the end of January, the half million dollar Strub Stakes in early February, the San Luis Obispo Handicap over a mile and a half on the turf for four year olds and up in mid February and the $1 million Santa Anita Handicap over a mile and a quarter in early March. Santa Anita hosted the Breeders' Cup in 1984 and 1993 and will probably do so again, a testimonial to this excellent venue.

There are three levels, and prices, of admission to Santa Anita. A $5 General Admission allows you to wander around the Grandstand with its excellent views of the track and finishing line, the Infield, with its picnic grounds and playground for the kids, the Paddock Room which is the ground floor of the Grandstand with lots of betting, food and beverage facilities as well as the Paddock Gardens around the parade ring. The Club House will set you back $8.50 and also has excellent facilities including dining tables overlooking the first turn on the track after the finish line. At the upper end of the scale at $10 on weekdays and $15 on weekends and holidays, the Turf Club is quite luxurious if a bit more formal, with reserved seats at the finish line and fine dining while you put on your bets. Reserved Club House and Grandstand seats are available only at busy weekends and holidays. If you go into the Grandstand and wish to upgrade to other areas you can do so by going to the Reserved Ticket Booth and Terrace Gate for the Club House or the Turf Club. Children under 17 are allowed in free if accompanied by an adult, as are those over 65 on certain special days. Box seats holding four to six people are also available for hire and most include a private television set. If you would like to reserve one, call (626) 574 6400.

There are numerous dining rooms and terraces, snack stands and bars located throughout the park. Dining facilities with full-service menus are located in the Club House and Turf Club. The Terrace Food Court, near the main Grandstand entrance, feature a variety of self-service food. In the infield at the centre of the track, the Wine Shed offers deli-style food, beer and wines.

Santa Anita runs a number of programmes for people who like racing, including a 'Clocker's Corner' where you can watch the early morning workouts and have a bit of breakfast as well as handicapping classes with experts who will share their wisdom in picking winners. They are all free of charge. In fact if you need any information about anything at the track, check with the Patron Service Desks that are located throughout the Grandstand.

Hollywood Park

You certainly don't have to be a movie star to visit Hollywood Park, but you might just bump into a few while you are there. The course has been nicknamed "The track of Lakes and Flowers" and you will see why when you step inside. It has a beautifully picturesque setting and a spectacular view of the hills surrounding Hollywood. The movie star connection is in fact a very real one as the Hollywood Turf Club was founded by Jack L Warner of Warner Brothers films in 1938 and its original shareholders included Walt Disney, Bing Crosby and Sam Goldwyn. Always one step ahead of the pack, Hollywood boasts a number of 'firsts' including the introduction of the film patrol camera for use by the stewards in 1941, the first Sunday racing in 1973 and now the first racetrack to have its own casino.

Hollywood Park is to be found just three miles east of Los Angeles International Airport at the intersection of Century Boulevard and Prairie Avenue. Take the 105 or 405 Freeways to get there. If you need to contact the course, write to PO Box 369, Inglewood, California, USA 90306-0369, otherwise the street address is 1050 South Prairie Avenue, Inglewood, California USA 90301-4197. Tel: (310) 419 1500. Fax: (310) 419 8022. A virtual visit to their website can be arranged at www.hollywoodpark.com.

Hollywood gives you a choice of three different places to watch the racing, dine or have a drink. General admission to the Grandstand and parade ring is only $6, while you could pay $9.50 to step up into the Clubhouse. For those wishing a little bit more luxury, try the Turf Club which carries a $25 admission charge. Parking is all free no matter where you go and you get a free programme on entry. If you arrive by foot or bus, they knock $1.50 off these prices. Anyone under 30 years old gets in on Friday nights for only $1 and if you're over 62 you can attend on Wednesdays and Thursdays for a $3 discount. If you bring the kids, they are free of charge under 17 years and there is lots to keep them occupied with a playground and carousel at the North Park. Once you're inside, Hollywood offers a choice of over 30,000 seats in the grandstand and clubhouse, with another 3,000 in the Turf Club. There is also a wide variety of places to eat and drink, from a hot dog and beer to a four course meal in the Winners Circle dining room in the Clubhouse.

Hollywood has seen some notable stars of the equine variety over the years including the great Citation, the perennially tough John Henry and champion Affirmed who became racing's first $2 million winner in 1979 with a victory in the Hollywood Gold Cup. This was also the course that hosted the very first Breeders' Cup meeting in 1984, the first of three held here, when 65,000 people jammed the place and bet almost $12 million! Hollywood completed a $100 million expansion in the 1990s which included a golf and sports centre and the Hollywood Casino where you can play poker, blackjack or bingo as well as bet on the simulcast races from as far away as Hong Kong–24 hours a day of gambling pleasure.

There are two seasons of racing at Hollywood Park, from the end of April to July and November through December. Daily post times are 1:00 pm except Friday when racing moves to the evening with the first race at 7:00 pm. The big race of the spring and summer meeting is the $1 million Hollywood Gold Cup staged at the end of June with a fine supporting card. Some legendary horses have won the Gold Cup over the years, including the great Cigar, Round Table, Swaps, Citation and Sea Biscuit. In the Autumn there

is a three day Turf Festival held over the Thanksgiving Weekend that features six group races on the grass and attracts turf stars from across North America and Europe–a sure winner. There are lots of stars in Hollywood, but Hollywood Park has to be one of the biggest and brightest!

Southern California Local Favourites

There are so many things to see and do in southern California, you could spend a lifetime here–small wonder so many people move here for the good life. Hollywood Park is only ten minutes from the beach and 20 minutes from Beverly Hills and there are thousands of hotel rooms close at hand. Despite the traffic jams on the freeways, you really do need a car here to get around. Handy for either racetrack, the Beverly Wilshire Hotel (310) 275 5200 on Wilshire Boulevard in Beverly Hills offers the ultimate in luxury and star spotting possibilities. Also firmly in the top bracket are the Beverly Hills Hotel (310) 276 2251 also on Wilshire and the Radisson Plaza (310) 546 7511 in Manhattan Beach. A bit further away from Los Angeles, you could try the Ritz-Carlton (310) 823 1700 on Admiralty Way in Marina Del Ray. If you wanted to save a bit of money to play the ponies, try the budget priced Embassy Suites Hotel (310) 215 1000 on Airport Boulevard in LA or Motel 6 (310) 419 1234 on West Century. If you need any assistance with local information or hotels, there is a tourist information bureau in Los Angeles Airport

There is a wide choice of hotels that are all handy for a trip to Santa Anita, including the Doubletree Hotel (626) 792 2727, Ritz-Carlton Huntingdon Hotel(626) 568 3900 or Hilton Hotel (626) 577 1000, which are all in Pasadena. In Arcadia where the track is located you could stay at the Embassy Suites (626) 445 8525, the Hampton Inn (626) 574 5600 or the Santa Anita Inn (626) 446 5211. Arcadia also has a good choice of restaurants. You could try Anthony's for Italian food (626) 446 3171, go to Peppers (626) 446 5529 or the Arroyo (626) 821 2021 for Mexican specialties. If you like steak and seafood (known here as 'Surf and Turf') drop in to The Derby (626) 447 2430. A taste of the orient can be found at Tokyo Wako for Japanese (626) 351 8963 or the Panda Inn for Chinese in Pasadena (626) 793 7300. For more information about the Santa Anita area, call the Pasadena Convention and Visitors Bureau on (626) 795 9311.

If shopping is your game, you can do it 'til you drop and rub shoulders with the movie stars on Rodeo Drive in Beverly Hills. The Farmer's Market on West 3rd Street in Hollywood is also lots of fun and probably a lot less expensive, as is the Olivera Street area downtown with its Mexican-style marketplace with lots of shops, artisans and restaurants. Little Tokyo, the largest Japanese area in the USA, is not far away, on First and San Pedro Streets, as is Chinatown, north of Sunset Boulevard between Almeda and Hill streets. While you're here you should make a pilgrimage and wish upon a star at Disneyland (714) 999 4565, stroll along the Hollywood Walk of Fame on Hollywood Boulevard and Vine Streets or take the tour at Universal Studios (818) 622 3801. If you've got time, hop on down to San Diego and play a few horses at Del Mar or cross the desert to Las Vegas for unlimited action, day and night.

Artist: **Harry Matthews RED HOT** *Courtesy of:* **The Artist**

Racing in *Australia*

The Australian horse race that everyone in the world seems to know best is the Melbourne Cup. Held at the beginning of November at Flemington Racecourse in the city that gives its name to the prize, the Cup is the event that caps a month-long series of races and brings the entire country to a halt for the day. In antipodean terms it's Royal Ascot, The Derby and Kentucky's Run for the Roses all rolled into one big blast of fun.

From an international perspective, it is also a race that more and more trainers and horses are taking a tilt at from far afield. At face value, the conditions for foreign contenders are horrendous - a long and tiring trip probably halfway around the world to a different hemisphere, and then you face a two mile handicap probably carrying near top weight against a field of twenty or so top locals who have been primed to their best condition for weeks. But an Irish horse lifted the prize a few years ago and the names of Vintage Crop and Dermot Weld will forever be etched in Australian racing history. He's tried to win it again since and came close last year when Media Puzzle managed second place.

For the foreign visitor the equine action leading to the Cup begins a month earlier at Caulfield with the 1,000 Guineas and Caulfield Cup, moves to Moonee Valley for the WS Cox Plate and continues at Flemington for the Victoria Derby. All of these races are major local events that bring out the Aussie punters in droves and provide a holiday atmosphere to some pretty top-notch racing action.

There are about twenty major racecourses in this sports loving nation and they are spread from Tasmania to the Northern Territory and across to Western Australia. The foreign punter, though, can find many a day's pleasure in those located in and around Sydney and in Melbourne, which has four courses including Flemington, Caulfield, Sandown and Moonee Valley, where they hold night racing under the lights.

The thoroughbred racing season stretches year round in Australia, with action both over the sticks and on the flat. The major flat races that will catch the visitor's eye, though, take place between the middle of August and the end of May, which is summer 'Down Under'. As the breeding season flip-flops with the Northern Hemisphere there is also a growing business in shipping stallions from Europe and North America to the land of Oz to do double hemisphere duty. There are many stud farms around the major Australian racing and training centres and they are well worth a day out in themselves. If you want more information on the breeding side or stud farms, contact Thoroughbred Breeders Australia, 571 Queensberry Street, North Melbourne, 3051, Victoria Tel (+613) 9326 3966 Fax (+613) 9326 3866

To get into the mood before you go racing in Australia, try to dig out the video of the film that was made about the Aussie wonder horse, Phar Lap. He won just about everything worth winning in Australia, including the Melbourne Cup in 1930 under record top weight, before being shipped to the USA where his career ended somewhat tragically.

Flemington Racecourse

Flemington is situated about four miles west of the state of Victoria's capital city, Melbourne, next to the Maribyrnong River. It is easily accessible from the city by car or tram and on race days by special trains or by boat along the river. The train arrives upsides the back of the main stands; if you're driving use Entrance A on the opposite side at the junction of the Smithfield and Ballarat roads to enter the large free parking area in the centre of the course; trainers and their horseboxes, and the disabled can use Entrance B, which takes them right next to the stand to the "Birdcage". This is the stabling area where horses are installed before racing and it got its name because it's here that Gentlemen racegoers used to show off their 'birds' or lady friends. You don't have to take your bird these days and it is open to the public.

The track is run by the Victoria Racing Club and can be reached at 400 Epsom Road, Flemington, Australia, 3031. Tel: (03) 9258 4666. Fax: (03) 9258 4605. If you need to get in touch with the track itself call (03) 9371 7171. They also have a helpful website at www.vrc.net. au

Flemington has been the home of the Melbourne Cup since it was first run in 1861 and the race has been run each year here since on the first Tuesday in November. The main course itself is a wide, sweeping ellipse of about a mile and a half in circumference and is used for both flat and hurdle races. There is also a steeplechase course, with all brush fences, used for jump racing. Although it can hold up to 100,000 people (and does on Cup day!) it's a pretty course with a country feel to it. The best viewing of the course is from the Hill Stand opposite the winning post, which has four levels and has full facilities for betting both with the bookmakers and the Tote, as well as restaurants, bars and snack bars. The newer Prince of Wales Stand next to it was opened by Prince Charles in 1985. There are also on-course shops selling souvenirs, clothes, books and videos, so you have no excuses not to bring something back for a friend.

Australia is one of the few places in the world outside Britain and Ireland that has private bookmakers on course and you can either bet with them or the Tote. The bookies here have already entered the computer age though, using electronic boards to record the bets. They also take bets by phone from off-course punters.

Although getting into the course on regular race days only costs a few dollars, understandably admission prices do go up a bit when it comes to the big days of racing at Flemington for the four day Melbourne Cup Carnival which features the Cup itself, the Derby and the Oaks. Admission on Cup day with a reserved seat in the Lawn Stand will set you back A$100, while admission alone is about A$30. The course offers various package deals which include reserved seats on each of the big race days, and a two day package of admission and a reserved seat in the covered Hill Stand for the Derby Cup will cost you A$200 for example. The Hill Stand also has two top notch restaurants, The Panorama and The Skyline, but you will have to fork out about A$1,200 for a Panorama/Skyline 4-day package (Single days N/A).

Melbourne Cup day brings out all kinds of people to the racetrack and offers lots of fun and entertainment, a lot like Australia and its people themselves. It's both the formal recognition of a champion in the making and a great excuse to squeeze a few tinnies, put a shrimp on the barby and let your hair down, so no matter how conservatively or crazily you dress to go there, you will be sure to have a good time. Just be sure to say G'day to your neighbour!

Melbourne Favourites

Despite the high rise buildings which first catch the eye, Melbourne still retains much of its Victorian architecture and this gives the city a pleasant, old-fashioned feel at street level. You can 'go walkabout' here as there are lots of pedestrian malls with interesting shopping and a wide variety of restaurants and bars. The Sovereign Hill area of the city is a place where you can go to relive the city's gold rush days. If you are a real sports fan, be sure to visit the Melbourne Cricket Ground, which is Australia's biggest sports stadium and can hold 100,000 spectators. It was built for the 1956 Olympics which were held here and also contains a fascinating Cricket Museum. Not far away from Melbourne is the Yarra Valley which is famous the world over for its vineyards and wineries, some of which you can visit to sample the tipple before it's exported. For those who'd like to see the local wildlife a bit closer, take a trip to Philip Island where you can cuddle a Koala, try to catch a Kangaroo or just watch the seals or penguins at play.

To find a bed for the night in Melbourne, you could try either the Grand Southern Cross Hotel (03 9653 0221) or The Sofitel Melbourne (03 9653 0000). Accommodation is also available at the popular Crown Towers Hotel (+613) 9292 8888 which is part of the Casino. Other possibilities are The Windsor (03 9653 0653) or the Hotel Como (03 9824 0400) in South Yarra. If you want to step out of an evening and sample some local brew, try the Victoria Hotel in Albert Park, the Palace Hotel, a favourite local hang-out, or the Fawkner Club which has an open-air courtyard. Restaurants abound in this city, with a wide choice of different types of cuisine. The Melbourne Oyster Bar (03 6702745) on King Street will do for seafood lovers, or they could try The Last Aussie Fishcaf (03 6991942) on Park Street in South Melbourne. For a taste of the orient try the Bamboo House (03 6621565) or the Flower Drum (03 66325313) which are both on Little Bourke Street.

Racing in Japan

If racing in Hong Kong seems all about large amounts of money changing hands, in Japan its more yen than most people can count. Huge crowds generate equally huge betting turnover and that in turn makes for exceptional prize money. The average prize money on offer for each race at top courses like Tokyo rings up well in excess of £100,000. If you were a foreign owner this might seem like the veritable pot of gold, but racing in Japan has long been closed to foreign horses except for a few Group races such as

*Artist: **Harry Matthews** HEAD STRONG Courtesy of: **The Artist***

the Japan Cup and the big jumps race of the year the Grand Nakayama. Japanese breeders have spent the rich pickings at the courses buying some expensive horseflesh for many years and you can go and visit studs such as Shadai Farm. Their breeding efforts have paid off and Japanese bred horses by top stallions such as Sunday Silence are now finding success on their world travels in Europe and elsewhere.

Japan has ten racecourses run by the Japan Racing Association spread around the country, including two, Tokyo Racecourse and Nakayama, which are near the capital. Racing takes place largely around the weekends from mid-March to mid-June and again from October to the end of the year when the international flavour is added in the form of the Japan Cup. There are also another thirty or so racecourses that are run by local authorities which offer various levels of thoroughbred racing in settings that range from large urban centres to small country courses.

Tokyo Racecourse

Tokyo Racecourse, or Fuchu as it's known to local punters, is the Newmarket of Japanese racing. Originally built in 1933, it has been updated and expanded ever since, most recently in 1993, to a commodious complex that attracts equally huge crowds of people when racing is held on Saturdays and Sundays during the season. The course actually lies in the Forest of Fuchu from which it derives its local name and from the stands you get a superb view of the famous Mount Fuji and you will be able to enjoy the racing in complete comfort either live or captured on huge television screens around the park. It's here that they hold the Japanese Derby for local three year-olds in the spring and cap it all off in the autumn with the International Japan Cup which sees horses from all over the world going for glory under their equally famous jockeys.

The General Manager of Tokyo Racecourse can be contacted on Tel: 423 63 3141, Fax: 423 40 7070. You can visit the Japan Racing Association website, which has information on all the courses they run on www.jait.jrao.ne.jp which will give you the English language version.

To get to the racecourse it's probably best to take the metro underground train. Fuchu-keibaseimonmae Station on the Keio Line which departs from Shinjuku Station has a concourse that directly connects with the racecourse. It takes about thirty minutes to get there from Shinjuku. Alternatively, Fuchi-Honmachi Station also has a direct overhead passageway leading into the track's West Gate.

Basic admission to the course is only Y200 (about £1) which gives you access to all areas of the course except the reserved enclosure. Y500 (£2.50) gives you a reserved seat in the E area, while prices from Y1,500 (£7.50) (C area) to Y3,500 (£17) (S area) will provide you with admission and a reserved seat in various areas of the reserved enclosure. Some of the S reserved seats on the fifth and six floors are in pairs for couples (sounds cosy) and have a built-in TV monitor. The Grandstand can hold a staggering 200,000 people, just to put some scale on things and what's really amazing is that they actually have room to move around, see the horses and place their bets. It's called Memorial 60 as it was completed to commemorate the 60th anniversary of Tokyo Racecourse in 1993, and extended to stretch 460 metres or well over two furlongs - practically the entire

length of the home stretch. Small wonder that this is the largest grandstand in the world! The course itself has four tracks. The turf track is the biggest at about a mile and a half around and inside are a dirt track, a steeplechase course (jump fans take note) and a training track. State-of-the-art might be an over-used expression these days but the facilities for fans here really qualify. Two giant Turf Vision screens give you an excellent view of the action down the backstretch and the run to the finish line from any part of the grandstand. There is a large amphitheatre around the paddock so you can check on the condition of the horses before the race. Some of them wear some pretty strange looking headgear, but don't be put off! The winner's circle is a large area directly in front of the grandstand.

There are no fewer than 1,100 closed circuit TV monitors scattered throughout the racecourse and these provide information on the horse's weight (not a bad idea), pari-mutuel odds and dividends, as well as paddock views of the horses and the racing itself. In the first floor of the basement is a Video Hall with a giant screen. The course has its own video and book store called the PR Corner as well as an FM radio station just for racegoers on track. Try a bit of sushi in the Fast Food Plaza downstairs in the basement, or for something a bit more formal there is the Restaurant New Tokyo on the third floor or the Restaurant Hotel Okura on the sixth floor.

No doubt you might come to Fuchu for the Japan Cup in November as it usually attracts a top-notch field of international stars with their owners, trainers and jockeys. Under the guidance of Sir Michael Stoute in 1997 Pilsudski capped an incredible season by doing the Breeders' Cup - Japan Cup double, a truly remarkable achievement for a British horse. The top races of the spring season are the Yushun Himba (Japanese Oaks) for home bred three year old fillies, the Tokyo Yushun (Japanese Derby) for local colts and the NHK Mile Cup which is also open to foreign bred horses. Other Grade 1 races which also attract invited international horses are the Yasuda Kinen over a mile for older horses and the Emperor's Cup for three year olds and up. For National Hunt fans, there is at least one jump race included in the programmes for both spring and autumn, but you'd have to go to Nakayama to see the Japanese version of the Grand National!

While you're here be sure to visit the JRA Racing Museum at the racecourse. It has some incredible hands-on displays where you can experience what it's like to be a jockey riding in a race and shows depicting the world's great races. Go into the Epsom Promenade where they have a 1/50 scale walk-through of Epsom Racecourse, Tokyo's sister course, where British punters can check out a bit of old Blighty. There's lots of things for children of all ages to do here as well, with pony and carriage rides in the infield as well as a miniature railway to take you around. If all this becomes a bit much and you need a bit of peace and quiet to study the form or contemplate zen and the art of motorcycle maintenance, sneak away to the Japanese Garden in the woods behind the paddock.

Tokyo Favourites

There's no shortage of things to see and do in sprawling Tokyo. The Ginza is this city's famous shopping area and most famous landmark for visitors and it's busy both day and night. You might want to leave your chequebook or credit card at home though, as many of the imported goods are more expensive here than at home. No wonder Japanese tourists do some hard shopping when they are out of the country on holiday. Still you could just go into some of the big Japanese department stores and enjoy being greeted by the staff with a bow when you enter or take the elevator - that doesn't happen in too many places anywhere else, but it certainly does in Japan! No trip to Japan would be complete without sampling some of the local fare and there are sushi bars dotted around everywhere. If you are daring try a bit of the Fugu. It's a puffer fish and if the chef has left in just a bit of the liver, you won't see the next sunrise! Perhaps a safer bet and often more palatable to western tastes is tepanyaki cooking where your party sits around a horse-shoe table sipping sake while the chef grills prawns or Kobe beef in front of you. Too much sake and the karaoke will no doubt beckon!

Not too far away from the racecourse, there is a number of superior hotels in Shinjuku, all catering to western tastes, including the Hotel Century Hyatt Tokyo (3 3349 0111), the Hotel Park Hyatt Tokyo (3 5322 1234), the Tokyo Hilton (3 3344 5111) and the Keio Plaza InterContinental Tokyo (3 3344 0111). Of course these are just a few of the many possible places to stay and if you wanted something a little bit closer to the Tea House of the August Moon, take a trip outside Tokyo to the countryside and you will have little problem finding a place to leave your shoes at the door. While eminently worthwhile, visiting Japan is certainly not cheap and let's hope you have a few winners at the races to help replenish your wallet!

Racing in **Hong Kong**

Perhaps it is the counterfoil to their otherwise industrious and conservative natures, but the people of Hong Kong love a punt on the horses and this makes racing, and betting, a big business in this former British colony. Of course it was the Brits who exported their rules and regulations for the Sport of Kings back in the early nineteenth century and thoroughbred racing is organised here by the Hong Kong Jockey Club. You can contact them at 1 Sports Road, Happy Valley, Hong Kong. Tel: (852) 2966 8111. Fax: (852) 2577 9036. E mail: jcinfo@hkjc.org.hk. web site: www.hongkong jockeyclub.com

Some might say sadly not 'Royal' any more, but even though the Union Flag was lowered a few years ago, it's business as usual under the new regime and it will probably see thoroughbred racing spread rapidly throughout China during the coming years. Racing means money, money, money and here the profits from racing not only generate a thriving sport, but are used to support social services and run good causes which directly benefit the local population, including hospitals, clinics, schools, parks and swimming pools. The Jockey Club operates the Tote as well as the local lottery and generates a surplus after taxation of about HK$2 billion per season. Racing here, though, is also a lot of fun and the quality of racing is excellent, with many trainers, horses and jockeys coming from around the world to capture some big prize money.

Hong Kong has two racecourses in Sha Tin and Happy Valley and between them 78 race meetings will be held between early September and late June. Meetings are held most Saturdays and Wednesdays and some Sundays, each attracting an average crowd of 38,500 racegoers on-course

who stake several million betting tickets a race meeting. Betting turnover here is the highest in the world per person. The highlights of the year and probably of most interest to visitors are the Hong Kong International Races which attract leading horses, trainers and jockeys from all over the world.

Sha Tin Racecourse

Sha Tin is the modern showpiece of Hong Kong racing, having been built on reclaimed land and opened in 1978. It's here during the first half of December that the big races are held around the course's large sweeping oval. The big date of the year here is the Hong Kong International Races which include the Hong Kong Cup (G1), Hong Kong Mile (G2), Hong Kong Vase (G2) and Hong Kong Sprint (L). Horses competing in these races come from Australia, Europe, New Zealand, Malaysia & Singapore as well as North America, Japan and the United Arab Emirates, so you might be excused if you don't get the form right at first try. Accompanying the race meeting is also a top international sale of thoroughbreds which attracts buyers from almost as far afield. Other highlights of the year include the Hong Kong Derby run in March, the Hong Kong Gold Cup in March, and the Queen Elizabeth II Cup held in the middle of May.

Hong Kong prize money is well endowed by the high tote turnover and some of the world's top jockeys are invited to come here to compete for a season or two on a regular basis, while others fly in for the big races.

Located in Hong Kong's New Territories, you can get to Sha Tin from the centre of town very easily by bus, train or taxi. Once there it will cost you HK$10 (about £1 or US$1.60) to get into the course or HK$50 (£5) to get into the Members' Enclosure. If you are a visitor to Hong Kong, take your passport with you if you wish to buy admission to the Members at the main gate.

Sha Tin hosts a total of about 45 race meetings throughout the season, split between day and night racing. Most are run over the main turf course, but others take place on the all-weather track and a few are mixed all-weather and turf. A nine-race card in the afternoon starts at 1:30 pm, while for a ten-race fixture the first race is moved back to 1:00 pm. Night meetings begin at 6:30 pm and take place on Saturday or Sunday.

Inside the course, which can hold up to 85,000 people, there are lots of restaurants and fast-food stalls to choose from. There are two huge grandstands where you won't have any problem finding a seat, as well as the Club Building overlooking the winning line with a view straight down the finishing straight. A huge colour TV screen also helps the view from ground level. Grandstand 2 connects directly with the railway station, while Grandstand 1 has the parade ring to its rear. There is also a special visitors box for tourists to use, as well as a number of private boxes.

Happy Valley

Despite its verdant, almost pastoral, name, Happy Valley's situation makes Longchamp or Belmont Park seem way out in the middle of the country. The course is right in the centre of the city, surrounded by tall buildings and making it an absolutely unique urban amphitheatre of equine action. Some have claimed the land on which Happy Valley is situated is the world's most expensive piece of real estate and it would be hard to disagree, judging by the buildings which frame it.

Happy Valley is so close to the centre of Hong Kong that you could just as easily walk there as take a bus, subway train or taxi. Admission follows the same pattern here as Sha Tin at HK$10 (about £1 or US$1.60) to get into the course or HK$50 to get into the Members Enclosure. Don't forget to take your passport with you to buy admission to the Members at the main gate. The course also has the usual array of wining and dining possibilities in restaurants and fast food stalls, as well as a visitors box for tourists. There is a high-rise complex of stands overlooking the straight and the finish line and with a large colour TV screen in the middle of the infield, you won't miss a thing at this relatively tight track. Make sure you back a jockey who knows his way around!

Happy Valley holds about 30 meetings a year, also split between day and night racing and all on the turf. A nine-race card in the afternoon commences at 1:30 pm, while for a ten-race fixture the first race is moved back to 1:00 pm. Night meetings begin at 6:30 pm on Wednesdays and sometimes the odd Tuesday, and an hour later if held on a Saturday.

The course also contains the fascinating Hong Kong Racing Museum, situated next to the Happy Valley stand, which is well worth a visit if you can spare the time. For those more interested in flexing their credit cards than racing, the Causeway Bay shopping and entertainment complex is just a five minute walk from the course.

Hong Kong Favourites

There is so much choice in Hong Kong, you could easily spend weeks here and still not find your shopping list exhausted. Anything made to measure, from shirts to suits, is an absolute bargain compared with prices anywhere else and once they've got your measurements you can re-order from anywhere in the world (provided your shape stays the same!). If you want a suit try William Cheng (2739 7888)– outstanding value and they can make them in three days! There are hundreds of restaurants to choose from and a lot of the better ones are housed in the plethora of first class hotels that can be found in Hong Kong.

The Excelsior (2837 6840) situated in the harbourfront in Causeway Bay is an excellent choice with numerous restaurants. Have a drink in Tutts on the 34th floor for a view that will take your breath away. Another choice is the Mandarin Oriental (2522 0111) for more fine dining, breathtaking views and true elegance. You could also try the Hong Kong Renaissance (2375 1133) or the Hotel Nikko (2739 1111). Closer to Sha Tin, the Regal Riverside Hotel and the Royal Park Hotel also come highly recommended. There is also a large shopping mall in Sha Tin, about a five minute ride from the racecourse.

The pace of Hong Kong is extremely frenetic. Visit the Banking Centre and, if you can, go up the Peak in a tram –there's a fantastic harbour-view and find the little bar and restaurant which nestles here - it's an absolute beauty. When arranging a visit to Hong Kong , talk to the major airlines –they offer some tremendous fly and stay deals at some really first class hotels. The flag may have changed in Hong Kong but so much still remains the same - it is a city that is thoroughly recommended.

Racing in *Singapore*

Racing has been taking place in Singapore since the very first meeting contested a prize of $150 in 1842. The purse was a King's ransom in those days, and little has changed in what is today one of the most modern centres of commerce in the Far East. Prize money is still high in Singapore, a fact which has helped racing attract some of the best flat horses in this part of the world as well as a few globe-trotting European and American thoroughbreds for the year's big races. Racing is organised by the Singapore Turf Club and it's an interesting testimonial to the colonial past that members of the public were only allowed to attend their meetings in 1960. Before then the only people allowed in were members and owners. We can only presume that jockeys and trainers were also in attendance!

Things have come a long way since then in Singapore and female jockeys were given their licenses in 1981, the same year a new grandstand was built to provide facilities for up to 50,000 people at the Bukit Timah racecourse. The first million dollar (that's Australian dollars) race was held in 1993 and an entirely new $40 million racecourse and training complex was planned, built and opened in 1999 at Kranji, Tel: (65) 879 1000 Fax: (65) 879 1010, in the northern part of Singapore. State of the art technology enables the Singapore punter to get his bet on in what must be one of the most up to date horse racing emporia in the world. Visit the Singapore Turf Club website at www.turfclub.com.sg if you'd like a tour.

Kranji Racecourse

Kranji Racecourse is a massive new complex about a dozen or so miles from the centre of the city. Those who planned it borrowed the best features from the leading racecourses around the world. The four storey grandstand can hold 30,000 racegoers in comfort, with a fine view of the mile and a quarter, left-handed oval track. The slight incline to the finish line produces some exciting racing. Kranji also has three training tracks providing both turf and fibresand surfaces, as well as modern stables for 1,000 horses. Visiting trainers should take note that their horses are treated like kings here, with their own air-conditioned facilities and stabling that is guarded twenty four hours a day!

Kranji's about 30 minutes from the centre of Singapore and getting there is no problem. The easiest way is probably to take the MRT, the rapid transit system that takes you right to the course and provides links the rest of Singapore. Taxis, a private coach service and public buses also go to the track on race days. If you have a car, there's a multi-storey car park that will take over 2,000 cars and costs S$5.

Racing at Kranji is held at night under the floodlights when it's a bit cooler for punters and horses alike with meetings held on Wednesdays, Saturdays and the occasional Sunday throughout the year. Post time is 7:00 pm for the first race, except on Sundays when it's moved up to 5:30 pm. About 25,000 usually show up to take in the local action as well as live telecasts of racing from across the straights in Malaysia and Perth in Australia. Racing from other venues starts a bit earlier in the afternoon and it's best to check the local papers for exact times. There's a giant outdoor video screen, as well as monitors dotted throughout the grandstand. Admission to the lower grandstand will set you back a mere five Singapore dollars, while ten will buy you air-conditioned comfort upstairs. If you are just visiting Singapore, you can buy admission to the exclusive Hibiscus Room on the third level for 20 Singapore dollars, but you'll need your passport handy when buying the ticket. You won't have any problem getting a bet on the tote as there are over 400 windows, as well as electronic ACCESS terminal points. Electronic dividend boards constantly update the latest odds. Four food courts are located in the grandstand for snacks and drinks and if you want to dine a bit more elegantly try the restaurants in the Club level.

As you will find out, Singapore has a bit of an authoritarian streak in its culture. It wasn't that long ago that the government banned chewing gum and going racing is no exception. At Kranji there are dress codes that should be followed: no shorts, singlets (funny Australian sleeveless shirts) or slippers in the lower and upper grandstands; those attending in the Gold Card members, Hibiscus Room and Owners are not allowed to wear shorts, collarless t-shirts, slippers (best left with the dog at home anyway) sandals or jeans. Don't plan on bringing the kids either as you have to be 18 years old to get in to attend racing in Singapore.

Despite a bit of Ascot-like fussiness about dress, it's well worth leaving your slippers at home to go racing. The standard of horses competing here is getting better all the time. Other highlights of the racing calendar include the Queen Elizabeth II Cup which is held on the annual Ladies Day in August. The very first running was won by Lester Piggott on Jumbo Jet back in 1972. The Singapore Derby in May is open to international entries as are the Singapore Cup in September, Raffles Cup in October and the Singapore Gold Cup, held later that month and worth over S$1 million.

Singapore Favourites

A visit to Singapore evokes the romance of its founder Raffles (337 1886), the intrepid British colonial officer who first developed this part of the Malay peninsula as a centre for trade. Raffles the man has been immortalised by the hotel of the same name, although today you may have to look a little harder to find that famous verandah on which to sip your pink gin as the property is now overshadowed by the looming skyscrapers that offer testimonial to Singapore's booming economy. Singapore is jammed with excellent restaurants, serving a unique blend of local and other oriental cuisine and it's probably worth going there just to eat!

Of course, if you really want to step out in style and back in history, you can still stay at the Raffles Hotel and rub shoulders with the ghosts of Noel Coward, Joseph Conrad and the other illustrious guests of days gone by. You may need a few winners at Kranji to foot the bill though as room rates start at $650 and go up to S$850 per night. It's bang in the centre of the city and has been recently renovated to restore its former glory. Not too far away is the much more reasonable option in the Peninsular Excelsior Hotel (337 2200), and what it might lack in character is more than made up for by convenience and facilities. A bed for the night here is in the S$150 range. Also centrally located and of a superior quality is the The Mandarin Singapore (737 4411) on Orchard Road as well as the Four Seasons Singapore (734 1110) which is close to the main shopping area on Orchard Boulevard. A few more to consider are the 600 room Imperial Hotel which is perched on a hilltop surrounded by greenery and offers a panoramic view of Singapore; the Marina Mandarin (338 3388) on Raffles Boulevard which offers fine facilities or the Metropole Hotel (336 3611) on Seah Street—not far from the Raffles Hotel, but considerably less costly.

Artist: **Rochelle Levy SINGAPORE, THE BUKIT TURF COURSE** *Courtesy of:* **Frost & Reed**

Imagine a green oasis in the middle of the desert; imagine also the finest selection of the world's thoroughbreds; imagine also a watering hole of genuine excellence–well this is racing in Dubai. The richest race in the world, the Dubai World Cup, may attract your immediate attention, but in racing terms it is just a single barrel from the well in this land of oil, sheikhs and stallions. Although everything in Dubai might look shiny, new and modern on the surface, it really just masks the long history of racing in this part of the world. It is, after all, where the modern day thoroughbred originated and where the power behind one of the most successful thoroughbred operations in the world lies today in the form of the rulers of Dubai, the Maktoum family, led by its head Sheikh Mohammed.

It may be rather ironic that when British aristocracy went shopping for horses to be bred for racing in the eighteenth century they ended up in this part of the world and the sires they brought home formed the original stock from which all thoroughbreds racing today are descended. Now, fuelled by the wealth of black gold, Arab sheikhs and princes comb the world for the best horses money can buy and bring some of them home to breed and race.

During the past decade, Dubai has sprung up almost magically to be one of the top tourist destinations in the world, and now it's also a place where the visitor can enjoy some excellent racing during the winter months. The most important factors contributing to this have been the formation of the Godolphin Stable by Sheikh Mohammed which now sees some of the world's best horses returning here for a bit of rest and recreation each winter, the building of Nad al Sheba as the country's showpiece track, and the institution of the world's richest race, the Dubai World Cup to tempt foreign owners and trainers to bring their champions here to win the big prize

Racing in the United Arab Emirates is run by the Emirates Racing Association and you can contact them at Suite 203, City Tower 1, PO Box 1178, Dubai. Tel: (9714) 313311. Fax: (9714) 313322. Perhaps reflecting their keen interests in horses and racing the UAE actually has five racecourses, Nad al Sheba, Jebel Ali, Abu Dhabi, Sharjah, and the Ghantoot Racing and Polo Club and they all have fixtures on various days of the week during the winter season, run under the auspices of the Emirates Racing Association. If the action at these five doesn't quite satisfy your appetite, you could always take in a bit of camel racing which is held a stone's throw from Nad al Sheba at the Dubai Camel Racetrack - it's an amazing sport!

Nad al Sheba

A patch of scrubby desert on the edge of the town of Zabeel just a decade ago, Nad al Sheba now glistens in the sun as a green jewel for equestrian sport. Of course it has taken enormous amounts of money to build this fine complex, but it is now reaping dividends as a new centre of world class racing and, lured as ever by rich prize money, owners and trainers from around the world now bring their best stock to race each March, joined by some of the best international jockeys. Where the best go, the rest usually follow and Dubai is now firmly on the map as a place where the lover of horse racing is pencilling in his next trip.

Although he might be one of the richest men in the world, Sheikh Mohammed is very much a hands-on horseman and

he has applied the same approach to building and running Nad al Sheba. Since the first race was run here in 1992, there have been many improvements and additions that make the expression 'state of the art' an understatement.

Nad al Sheba is run by the Dubai Racing Club and you can contact them at Suite 203, City Tower 1, Sheikh Zayed Road, PO Box 1178, Dubai, United Arab Emirates. Tel: (9714) 329888. Fax: (9714) 329777.

You could probably spot this oasis from a satellite orbiting the earth, but to be a little more precise the racecourse is located about three miles south east of the city of Dubai and if you are driving there it is signposted on the Dubai to Abu Dhabi Road at the Metropolitan Hotel junction or from the roundabout close to the Dubai Polo Club and Country Club. When you get there you can park your car for nothing in the general area; if you already have a badge there is a special area reserved for you at the rear of the grandstand.

General admission to the course is free and this allows you to go just about anywhere. You also get a complimentary programme and form guide! However you will probably wish to go into the Club House area as well and you can buy a day badge at the entrance to it for the price of entrance to most British course grandstands. Club House admission also gives you access to the Dubai Golf and Racing Club's members box on the second floor of the grandstand with its great view of the course. There is a total of 4,000 seats for spectators in the grandstand and they cost Dhs 350 for World Cup Day. There is a wide variety of food and drinks in the Club House, as well as the Spike Bar and Links Steakhouse restaurant where you can dine surrounded by cowboy memorabilia. There are also some 14 private boxes for hire; the availability of these might be somewhat limited as they are sold primarily to the corporate market, but it might be worth enquiring with the course if you wish to entertain a group of people.

In the public enclosure you can dress casually, but those in the Club House or private boxes are encouraged to don 'smart casual' attire. Of course, Dubai being an Arab country, women are expected to dress 'modestly', which means the extremities should be appropriately covered. The course has a Ladies Day during the racing season and it's an event when the smartest clothing is pulled out of the wardrobe.

The high rolling punter will have a bit of difficulty getting a bet on here as gambling per se is not allowed under Islamic law. However, to give everyone a sporting chance at winning something, there is a free 'competition' to win big cash prizes. A Pick 6 (selected winners of all six races) competition is held every race meeting and carries a prize fund of DHs 40,000 (£7,000 or $11,000). There are also other prizes for picking the forecast in the Fifth race, as well as a Big 5 Jackpot where you have to name the first five horses home in correct finishing order. In the third and fourth races there is a Daily Double, although here you are invited to select the first three finishers in correct order to claim the loot. You may not be able to battle with the bookies or tap into the tote in Dubai, but you might just come away with some extra cash and one thing's for sure, as it's free to enter you won't lose your shirt!

There are usually six or seven races per fixture and as it would be unwise for man or beast to exert themselves in the heat of the desert sun, racing is held at night under the lights when things cool down a bit. Post time for the first race is at 7:00 pm, except during Ramadan in January when it moves to 9:00 pm. Four of Dubai's trainers use Nad al Sheba as their training base and they usually work out the horses between 6:00-9:00 am each morning. You can have breakfast at the track in the morning and watch them go through their paces.

Racing at Nad al Sheba is staged from the beginning of November until the third week in April on Sundays and Thursdays. The only exception to the usual fixture arrangements is the Dubai World Cup meeting itself which is held on a Saturday at the end of March. The World Cup has established itself as a major Group 1 fixture in the international racing calendar. In addition to the 30,000 spectators on-course, it is beamed to millions around the world who watch eagerly on television. Tense anticipation and exciting finishes have been the order of the day so far.

The World Cup is supported on the same card by the mile and a quarter Dubai Duty Free, which, although it serves as a consolation race for horses not qualified for the World Cup itself, would be the feature race on any other card with US$ 2 million in prize money to be won. Horses from Britain and Europe may always be at a bit of a disadvantage when running on dirt, but the way some of them have adapted gives hope for the future. If you want to see how the Sheikh Mohammed Godolphin blue silks fare over the winter season this is the place to go. The added attraction of a host of world class jockeys in action is another great bonus.

For more information on the Dubai World Cup, write to Suite 213, City Tower 1, PO Box 1178, Dubai, United Arab Emirates. Tel: (9714) 322277. Fax: (9714) 322288. E-mail: dubaiwcp@emirates.net.ae. Website: www.dubai worldcup.com.

Dubai Favourites

Although the racing might be the sport that lures you to this part of the world, as many thousands of people have already found out, it is now one of the top destinations in the world for an allround winter holiday with some almost-guaranteed great weather. The second running of the Dubai World Cup may have been a washout but it only serves to prove the general rule that in Dubai the sun always shines. This means that you can partake of any other sport at your leisure including sailing or windsurfing, golf on several different courses, polo, or treks into the desert on all-terrain vehicles or by camel! With many people coming here to work from all over the world, Dubai has quite a cosmopolitan flavour and the choice of restaurants, from Mexican or Lebanese to Indian and Italian, as well as bars and nightlife is also pretty impressive.

If you have taken the children with you, or feel a bit young at heart yourself, you could visit the new Wonderland theme park on the edge of Dubai Creek. Not too far away, but worth a visit, is Sharjah with its Arabic souk or marketplace where you can shop for antiques, jewellery or oriental rugs.

There should be little problem finding accommodation here as there is a wide range of choice and location, almost all of it to high international-class standards. Some to note in the luxury category would be the Hatta Fort Hotel ((085 23211), the Hilton Beach Club (9714 445333) or the Metropolitan Hotel (9714 440000) which is closest to the racecourse itself. The Jumeriah Beach (9714 480000) as its name suggests is close to the seaside. A little less luxurious perhaps and at a lower tariff, you could try the Imperial Suites Hotel (9714 515100), Astoria Hotel (9714 534300) or the Palm Beach Hotel (9714 525550). Anywhere you choose, you are likely to come to the conclusion that Dubai is a future winner for a holiday.

*Artist: **P J Bailey SEA & SAND** Courtesy of: **The Artist***

ROBERT AINSWORTH

Robert Ainsworth was interested in art and drawing from an early age, in fact he first exhibited his work at the age of 12.

He now concentrates his artistic skills on painting equestrian, sporting and wildlife scenes. He exhibits in London and at regional game fairs and shows, painting in watercolour, acrylic and pastels.

ANTHONY ALONSO

One of America's foremost racing artists for over twenty-five years, Anthony is well known for his meticulous commissioned portraits of thoroughbreds and racing personalities. His most inspired and original paintings are his backstretch and paddock scenes, which he observes around America's racetracks. His work features in many private collections internationally and is on view in the public collections of many North American racing organisations. Commissions and prints available from the artist.

JOHN ATKINS

John Atkins lives and works in Middleham, where several hundred racehorses are a constant source of inspirtion in this ancient centre of training in North Yorkshire.

John is a painter and sculptor of animals and sporting studies but the horse is his favourite subject, either in paint or in bronze.

Atkin's work is in many private collections in the UK and abroad and commissions for paintings and sculptures are undertaken. The intention of the artist is to achieve a sense of movement without sacrificing the anatomical integrity of the subject.

MARGARET BARRETT

Born in a house overlooking the Derby course at Epsom, Margaret Barrett cannot remember a time when she did not draw and paint horses. She holds a degree in Fine Art and her paintings have since been exhibited in London, Tokyo and New York. She won the Society of Equestrian Artists prize for best Oil Painting in an exhibition held at Christies. Her work is published as limited edition prints and also appears as book illustrations.

Her work shows a lifetime's love of horses and the countryside, but her speciality is in racing scenes. She responds to the power and grace of these magnificent animals by capturing a sense of movement that can almost be heard as well as seen!

Margaret accepts commissions for people, horses and racing scenes. Prices on application.

KATERINA BARTOVA

Katerina Bartova studied at two Prague Artistic Collages (Artistic Collage of Restauration, Collage of Sacral Art), she works as an artist in pastels, acrylics and oils, She specialises in portraits of stallions, racing and hunting scenes.

Her interest in horses dates from an early age, when she was riding in the Czech Pony Club, which developed an interest in breeding, raising and training her own horses.

Katerina now lives in Ireland. She has ridden out for the racehorse trainer Paddy Mullins for over a year and then she worked for dressage trainer Gisela Holstein as a student.

Katerina is now a full time artist and she exhibits her work in the Redmond Fine Art Gallery.

BEACONSFIELD GALLERY

Beaconsfield Gallery is an artist-run gallery situated in West Yorkshire. The gallery features a large selection of Brian Halton originals, prints and greeting cards. Brian taught art and sculpture up to A level standard until recently but now concentrates solely on his painting.

He spends much of his time working on commissions of all sporting themes

Artist: **Heather St Clair Davis COMING OFF THE HEATH** Courtesy of: **Frost & Reed**

Artist: **Graham Isom** THE MINSTREL _Courtesy of:_ **Rosenstiel's**

including greyhound racing, football, boxing and cricket as well as all aspects of racing. Further examples of his work can be found at _www.beaconsfieldgallery.co.uk_

CAROLINE BROMLEY GARDNER

Caroline studied at Bath Art School, Corsham Court, for one year's Pre-Diploma, followed by three years in Italy under Nerina Simi, receiving a scholarship grant from Delta Metal for the last year.

She has been working on equestrian portraiture and related subjects, exhibiting at both the Tyron Gallery in London and Frost and Reid in Bristol, and the Society of Equestrian Art at the Mall Galleries in London. She has also been working on landscape and conversation pieces, and has had work accepted at the Royal Institute of Oil Painters, also at the Mall Galleries, and has shown work in various mixed exhibitions both locally and in the Costswolds and in Yorkshire.

CLAIRE EVA BURTON

Claire Eva Burton has always been interested in horses and racing. She began by sketching horses at local point-to-points and this led to full-time study at Medway College of Art. On leaving college, Claire worked for trainers Mick Haines and Tommy Gosling at Epsom but after a nasty fall she decided to study horses from the ground. She attends many race meetings where she sketches scenes and later completes the paintings in her studio.

Claire has held many exhibitions in London and is kept busy with commissions, including one for 12 pictures to decorate the Queen Mother's Box at Cheltenham. Claire's work is extremely popular and many limited editions of her work have been published. Please see our print section for further details. Commission prices on application.

CHARLES CHURCH

Charles Church is one the leading equestrian Artists in the UK, his work is hanging in numerous private and public collections around the world.

Born in 1970, Charles studied Classical Realism and Portraiture at the renowned Charles Cecil Studio in Florence. With a comprehensive training in the techniques of the old masters, Charles returned to Englnd in 1994, since when he has had a ceaseless stream of commissions.

Charles has since settled in Dorset and now divides his time equally between commissions and exhibition work. He paints mainly from life, which he finds essential for obtaining a true understanding of the colour and tone, as well as the character of his subject. He has exhibited widely in the USA, UK and Ireland. _www.charleschurch.net_

ALEXANDRA CHURCHILL GALLERY

Alexandra Churchill is an international artist whose works are in collections all around the world. She works from her own studio/gallery in Gloucestershire's Chipping Campden, exclusively in oil, often to a large scale.

Her work is strong, immediate, and beautifully portrayed. Racing is of particular interest but her paintings of riding, polo and hunting scenes are eagerly sought after.

Alexandra puts an almost human look into her smaller animals, her foxes, hares and hounds have quite unique expressions. _www.alexandrachurchillgallery.com_

ANGELA CONNER

Angela Conner spent her childhood travelling. She sold her first sculpture at the age of eight. She worked as an illustrator and journalist in New York and then spent nine months as a paid apprentice to Dame Barbara Hepworth after winning a scholarship to Rhodes.

Her first one man show was held in Bond Street, London when she was only twenty. It was followed by a one man show at the Lincoln Centre, New York; the first of many.

Though Angela Conner's work is often mobile and abstract on a large scale, she's made the biggest mobile in the world -- her lifelong passion for horses has resulted in her producing many equine sculptures and paintings.

Her works are on both sides of the Atlantic and have been included in many serious collections, for instance: she has sculpted and painted winners for the Duke of Devonshire and she is in the collection of Anne, Duchess of Westminster. Angela has done 21 bronze sculptures for John Gaines, Gainesway Farm, Kentucky; three day Eventors for leading riders; and also horse sculptures with an unusual use of water, which is her speciality.

Angela Conner has been awarded the Best Sculptor of the Year Award by The Royal Society of Equestrian Artists and is a Fellow of the Royal Society of British Sculptors.

ROSEMARY COATES

Rosemary studied at the Ruskin School of Fine Art and Drawing in Oxford, having been brought up in the heart of Berkshire where she spent her time with horses. Rosemary has worked on commissions for over ten years and specialises in equestrian field sports.

Her pictures sell in the USA and through sporting shops and the racecourses as well as through the National Horse Racing Museum in Newmarket. Commission prices on application.

PETER CURLING

Peter Curling was born in Waterford in Ireland in 1955; he was educated in England and Florence and now lives permanently in Ireland.

He has been fascinated by horses since his earliest childhood and began to sketch

Artist: **Peter Curling RACING IN IRELAND** Courtesy of: **Rosenstiel's**

and paint at his local stables whilst he was still at school. He later lived for a time in Newmarket, riding out with the eminent trainer Michael Stoute. Peter Curling rode his own horse, Caddy, to Victory at Limerick Junction in 1985. His originals are now exhibited all over the world.

SUE DREW

Sue is a London born Fashion Design graduate who studied at the Somerset and Gloucestershire Colleges of Art. She worked as a designer in London but, growing tired of the rat-race, eventually moved back to Somerset, bought the first of her two horses and taught herself to paint.

She now specialises in painting racehorses, as portraits or in action. She has been pleased to donate other work in support of Charity Racedays at Newbury and Wincanton and for Lambourn Open Day. Her paintings are hung permanently at West Country racecourses. Sue belongs to Taunton Art Group and the Society of Equestrian Artists. Commission prices on application.

ROBIN FURNESS

Robin Furness farms in North Yorkshire with his son Michael, and has painted all his life. He specialises in racing and hunting commissions, working in both oils and gouache media. He married into a Devon racing family and is steward at Sedgefield N.H. racecourse. He learnt painting under Ian Fleming-Williams at Charterhouse, where he was a contemporary of Peter Walwyn.

TERENCE GILBERT

Born in London he began his artistic training at Camberwell Art School and studied the Old Masters at the National Gallery.

He started working in various advertising studios until 1965 and for the next ten years become a freelance illustrator working in Europe and the USA. After a successful exhibition in America in 1975 he decided to paint purely for galleries.

Besides his much loved London cityscapes, Terence is a very talented portrait painter. Numerous commissions include a portrait of HM The Queen and President Reagan on horseback at Windsor which was presented to the late President at the White House.

He is also an equine painter of note, among commissions were Nashwan, Generous, Istabraq, Florida Pearl and Rooster Booster.

PETER GOODHALL

An acclaimed professional equestrian and wildlife artist working in oils in a traditional style, tending towards achieving an almost photographic likeness. Using a technique combining a strong sense of draughtsmanship with a subtle use of colour, his work is to be found in collections worldwide. Much of his work is commissioned and varies from the heavy, working horse to the thoroughbred. A variety of his paintings has been published as limited edition prints.

Peter's website is to be found at _www.watchhousestudios.co.uk_

JANICE GORDON

Janice Gordon is a professional artist specialising in equestrian paintings. Working mainly in oil and pastel, she is known for capturing the character and personality of her subjects using a realistic but not photographic approach. She also paints dogs, farm animals and conversation pieces, one of which was a finalist in the NOT the Turner Prize competition.

REFNA HAMEY

Refna is no stranger to horses. A keen observer of all equine sports and a natural draughtswoman, her paintings show innate compositional skills, firmness of touch and vitality of colour. She is immensely capable of showing the moods and movements of her subjects and they are depicted from a great variety of angles.

Refna studied at Cambridge and Kingston Schools of Art. She trotted off to Newmarket regularly to paint from life. It was the painting of Mill Reef, which started the success story. This led to more commissions: Observe, Celtic Shot, Saxon Farm and Kibah Tictoc, to name a few.

Refna has had work accepted by the Royal Academy. Her most recent exhibition was at the Tryon and Swann Gallery.

PAUL HART

Paul Hart studied illustration at Medway College of Art and Design, learning mainly figure work in a variety of mediums. After leaving college he worked as a freelance illustrator carrying out commissions for companies such as IPC magazines, Longmans Educational Books and Readers Digest.

His first equestrian paintings were of shire horses at ploughing matches and he has had some of them reproduced as greeting cards by Medici and Gordon Fraser. Since then he has concentrated mainly on horse racing subjects, starting with a commission of Desert Orchid and more recently a commission for Sir Mark Prescott. Some examples of his work have been reproduced as limited edition prints.

MICHAEL HESLOP

Michael Heslop is one of the foremost sports artists in the world, having studied at Somerset College of Art and Design for four years, followed by a final year at Brighton College of Art and Design. He has exhibited and won awards in England, America, Spain, Sweden, Switzerland and Australia, and is collected by many of the world's leading professional sportsmen and women. His career spans a period of some twenty-five years.

His commitment and intense love of the subject stems from his active participation in many sports, both as a competitor and a coach. His work is meticulously researched and composed and is based on a sound technique and an interest in detail and atmosphere.

He now lives and works from Topsham, a picturesque village in Devon, having returned from a successful eighteen months as resident artist in Sweden. Michael now concentrates on sporting subject commissions and limited edition prints.

JACQUIE JONES

Jacquie Jones' responsive and enlightened style is a result of the incredible passion and confidence with which she paints, employing unnerving strokes of colour and joy in a variety of mediums. Her works range from the serene and tranquil, as seen in 'Salukis and Hawks', to the raw, energetic power of 'Racing Vigour'.

Jacquie's work is very much influenced by all cultures associated with the horse, especially that of the Arab world. The freedom that the horse enables man to enjoy is the primary focus of Jacquie's style and it is this freedom that she paints.

Alongside her special interest in racing and the racehorse, Jacquie portrays every aspect of the equine world, through equestrian sports into Arabian images, horse portraiture, hunting, eventing and dressage scenes. In addition Jacquie paints other countryside pursuits and is much influenced by her love of working dogs. This variety of subjects keeps her energy and artistic diversity at the highest possible level.

Jacquie is a Friend of the Equestrian Artists Society of England. She has illustrated three books, Racing Dreams, Ponies and Dreams and Badger Creek. Jacquie has previously exhibited in Newmarket and the United Arab Emirates. In 1997, Jacquie was appointed the first ever artist in residence to the National Horseracing Museum in Newmarket and had her first London solo exhibition in 1998 at The Park Gallery. Her latest exhibition, 'Racing Silk', held in June 2002 at the FarmiloFiumano 21st Century Art Gallery was a huge success. Her work is collected by racing aficionados and art lovers alike. *www.farmilofiumano.com*

JOHN KING

Born at West Tytherley near Salisbury, where he still lives. Due to the influence of Lionel Edwards, a close neighbour and family friend, he became a full-time artist. Having always hunted and point-to-pointed, he specialises in all equestrian and field sports, portraits, family groups, military and ceremonial, and recently a lot more bronzes. Hunting and commissions take him all over the UK, Ireland, Europe, South Africa, the USA and, more recently, the Middle East. Also painting landscape and architecture in France, Spain and Italy etc. Many hunting works and others have been reproduced as limited edition prints. He has done illustrations for the Illustrated London News, Horse & Hound and has also illustrated books by Michael Clayton, Jim Meads, Robin Page and others. He has had 10 one-man exhibitions and many shared in London since 1966. He has exhibited with the R.I., The Society of Wild Life Artists and is a founder member of The Society of Equestrian Artists.

War artist in Aden in 1965 for the Illustrated London News. Also regimental pictures in Germany and Cyprus and also for the Royal Tournament.

In 2000 he was commissioned by Sheikh Mohammed Al Maktoum to paint a picture of his famous racehorse, Dubai Millennium. This picture, now hanging in Dubai, measures 16ft x 8ft and is believed to be the largest equestrian picture painted in the UK in the last two hundred years.

Patrons include The Duke of Beaufront, The late Duke of Northumberland, The Royal Bodyguard, Household Cavalry, The Palace of Westminster, Livery Companies and Tattersalls etc.

Artist: **John King** THE RACE THAT NEVER WAS *Courtesy of:* **Rosenstiel's**

DENNIS KIRTLEY

Dennis Kirtley, born in Sunderland, is entirely self-taught. Throughout his life he has nursed a passion for horses, in particular the English thoroughbred, and his drawings and paintings of the noble animal are scattered worldwide. His patrons from the racing world are numerous and include the late Prince Aly Khan and the late Sir Victor Sassoon.

His subjects range from Derby winners Crepello and St Paddy in the fifties and sixties to champions Known Fact, Be my Guest and the brilliant Golden Fleece in more recent times. Dennis has exhibited at numerous galleries and in 1977 published a limited edition print entitled Lester showing the champion jockey surrounded by many of his greatest winners. Prices on application, web site: _www.denniskirtley.co.uk_

ELIZABETH KITSON

Elizabeth Kitson rode and taught riding from an early age, horses being a major part of her life. Later she started painting seriously, starting with military actions, then specialising in portraits of people and animals, particularly horses and dogs, in oils and pastels–always getting a good likeness–action, movement and light being her special interest. She works mainly for commission.

She has exhibited in London and the provinces. Commissions have included the 'Battle of Waterloo' which is now a limited edition print. Her pictures have sold in many different countries. She is a member of the Society of Equestrian Artists and runs their Devon Art Workshop. She is also a member of the Society of the Armed Forces Art Society and the Army Art Society.

SUSAN LEYLAND

Susan Leyland is an accomplished British-born sculptor and artist. She lives in Italy, where her sculpture has successfully sold for many years. Working in Tuscany, in close proximity to the great classical sculpture she so loves, is the unifying fulfilment of her two lifelong passions: horses and art. As inspirational ideas, her drawings form an integral part of her sculpture, yet with great ease they stand as complete works of art in their own right. Her drawings have already found a keen audience in Italy and in the UK and her work has sold through Frost & Reed's Saratoga Springs Exhibition and in their London Gallery.

ROCHELLE LEVY

Rochelle Levy is one of Philadelphia's most respected and versatile artists. She has shown her work in a number of solo and group exhibitions in the USA over the years and is included in leading private collections, not just among horsemen but across a wide spectrum of life. She is well known for lively beach scenes, but the emphasis of her work is on horses and riders–exercising and at the track. Horse-related art was Levy's first calling, and her own familiarity with the world of racing has endowed her treatment of the genre with a particular authenticity. She is a modern painter with a keen sense of form, light and colour, who brilliantly captures the magic of her subject.

Artist: **Roy Miller SHERGAR, W SWINBURN** _Courtesy of:_ **The Artist**

ASAD KURI MONTANA

Asad's interest in horses began at an early age when drawing cowboys and Indians. Since studying fine art in London, he has exhibited at the RHH summer exhibitions, and other galleries in Dubai and Canada, and he now teaches equestrian art in Salisbury.

His view is that painting horses is easy but capturing the movement and characteristics of each individual horse is the key point in equestrian art.

He attends some of the major horse shows and trials, but his main passion in life is British racing with all its beauty, colour, fullness and ups and downs. Over the years he has painted for many breeders, owners and trainers in the UK, Dubai and Canada. Commission prices and other details are available on application.

JANE LAZENBY

Jane was born in Barnsley in 1969, and grew up horse mad, getting her first pony on her 13th birthday. She still competes in a variety of disciplines on her homebred mare.

She studied fine art at Newcastle, graduating in 1992, and was one of nine UK finalists to have their work chosen for exhibition in New York.

Jane spends the majority of her time working on commissions, specialising in equestrian portraits and scenes. She has exhibited in London with the Society of Equestrian Artists, and throughout Yorkshire.

She has work in private collections in New Zealand, Australia, the USA and across the UK. Commission prices on application.

BARRIE LINKLATER

Barrie Linklater specialises in human and equine portraiture and covers a broad range of equestrian and portrait subjects. He particularly likes racing scenes and free action studies of horses and riders in oils and watercolour.

His main commissions have come from Her Majesty The Queen, HRH Duke of Edinburgh, The Committee of York Racecourse, Sir Michael Oswald, Sheik Ahmed-al-Maktoum, Queen's Tennis Club and the City of London. Ascot Authority commissioned him to create the commemorative painting of that major landmark in racing history when Frankie Dettori won all seven races at the Ascot Festival.

His first equestrian commission, uniquely, came from HRH Duke of Edinburgh in 1975 during a sitting with HRH for a portrait commissioned for the Welsh Guards. Prince Philip suggested the inclusion of a horse in the painting and then proposed an equestrian commission which, although his first, would put Barrie into the top echelon of this genre in one challenging step. This commission (30 x 46 ins), to paint Her Majesty's favourite mare and foals in 1976, was Prince Philip's Jubilee present to Her Majesty The Queen, resulting in further commissions from Prince Philip and from owners of top class horses.

Barrie Linklater is now an established international artist, his paintings are in America, Canada, Holland, Switzerland, Jersey and the Far East, Dubai and Australia. He now has thirteen paintings in the Royal Collection itself, with many watercolours and drawings in royal ownership.

His work has been exhibited at the National Portrait Gallery, The Royal Society of Portrait Painters, The Guildhall, the Patterson Gallery, Ackerman's, Spinks and Tooth's. He is a longstanding member of the Society of Equestrian Artists.

Barrie lives in rural Berkshire and works from the studio in the grounds of his 17th Century thatched cottage. He is well placed to study throughbreds at both Newbury and Ascot racecourses and trainer gallops nearby. He has a ready eye for the distinctive character of each horse, its beauty of form and movement, the light playing upon its coat, and he has the skills and sensitivity to express these many aspects in his paintings.

ELIZABETH McCRINDLE

Born in Ayrshire, Scotland, in the rural village of Knockentiber, where she still lives and paints from her home studio. A self-taught artist, once employed in the textile industry she now paints full-time.

Elizabeth has exhibited widely in numerous galleries including The Atholl Gallery, Dunkeld, The Torrance Gallery, Edinburgh, The Jerdan Gallery, Crail, The Red Rag Gallery, Stow-on-the-Wold, and many others. Paintings of animals feature greatly in her work and she has been particularly sucessful with her equine portraits, having been commissioned to paint many winning racehorses. her paintings of rural landscapes and woodlands are also very popular. Elizabeth paints in acrylic, pastel, oil and mixed media and her work hangs in many private collections throughout Britain, Northern Ireland, USA, Canada, Mexico, Zimbabwe, Hong Kong, New Zealand and Europe.

BOOTH MALONE

Georgia artist Booth Malone took up art professionally in 1985. An experienced painter of portraits, he now draws on all equestrian sports including racing, hunting, polo and three-day eventing, attending the meets to paint his subjects at first hand. His ability to capture the empathy between horse and rider go part of the way to mark him out as one of America's most unusal equestian artists today. But it is the angle he chooses–and his quickness in spotting a really strong image when it occurs–that sets him apart from his contemporaries. Depicting images of day-to-day life in the stable yard or the lilt of a lazy canter on the exercise track, his paintings combine his ability to capture a likeness whilst conveying the atmospheres of the day and the mood of the horse.

He has exhibited his work widely throughout the South-Eastern United States and in Saratoga Springs NY. His

paintings have been featured in many magazines and he has been official artist to a number of steeplechase meets. In 2002 he was artist-in-residence at the Kentucky Horse Park and he will complete a series of paintings commisioned for the United States Equestrian Team in 2003. Malone is a full member of the American Academy of Equine Art and has a considerable following in the United States. He is represented in the UK by Frost & Reed Ltd.

HARRY MATTHEWS

Harry Matthews was born on Merseyside, the son of a pre-war street corner bookie and is consequently a racing fanatic. A self-taught portrait painter and professional illustrator, his many qualifications include a fine art honours degree in printmaking and colour theory.

A prize-winning artist, he has exhibited at the Royal Academy, the Westminster Gallery and Mall Galleries, Goodwood House, Newmarket Racing Museum and many others worldwide. His work now hangs in the collections of royalty, well-known international celebrities and, most notably, other artists.

Acclaimed for his exceptional figure work, Harry has no set style but being a natural gambler will always seek to experiment. Commission prices on application.

ROY MILLER

SEA, AAEA, one of the world's foremost equestrian artists, has won awards with the society of Equestrian Artists, and the American Academy of Equine Art, and is a full member of both organisations.

A native of Manchester, Roy Miller began work as a commercial artist at the age of 14. In the evenings he studied at the Regional College of Art in Manchester. In 1959 he moved to London and worked as a freelance illustrator. Exhibited a racing picture in the Royal Academy summer exhibition 1961. Began specialising in equestrian painting about 1971, and has continued full time since 1974.

The Queen is among those who have a Miller in their private collection and he has painted for owners, trainers, jockeys and breeders worldwide. Was commissioned to paint the official pictures for the new racecourse at Sha Tin, Hong Kong and racehorses of year in Canada, Australia and Hong Kong. Has had one man exhibitions in USA, Canada, UK and Australia. He has also been commissioned to design and paint the originals for the Lester Piggott gates at Epsom racecourse. Roy Miller has also successfully published many limited edition prints. Please see our print section for further details. Commission prices on application.

GLYNIS MILLS

Her passion for art is equalled by her love of horses. Therefore combining the two was a natural progression. Over the years she has worked closely with several hunts (especially the Bramham), racing yards and owners, pony and riding clubs, BHS and horse trials as well as numerous top dressage trainers, publications and events. She is responsible for some of the best equestrian logos including Dressage at Hickstead, British Riding Clubs and Landrover's Men's Point-to-Point Championship.

Over the last twenty-five years commissions have formed the majority of her work and have included such prestigious animals as 'Kir', 'Dragon' (famous stud hound) and 'Uncle Pokey' and many less prestigious ones but just as important in their owner's eyes.

FILIP MINARIK

Filip Minarik (1979, Prague) studied at Prague artistic college SMSUD (painting). He works as a painter in pastels, oils, acrylics and watercolours, specialising in racing scenes–finding inspiration in the colour, movement and atmosphere of the races. Filip was riding as an amateur jockey in The Czech Republic. He is living in Ireland now–Filip was riding out for trainer W.P. Mullins for over a year. Then he was in the yard of dressage trainer Gisela Holstein as a working student. Filip is a full time artist now and he exhibits his works in the Redmond Gallery.

NICOLA MOORE - PIGSTY STUDIO

Nicola is an award-winning equestrian and animal artist who works from her studio in Lancashire. She has work hung in collections both in the UK and abroad and has undertaken many notable equestrian commissions from clients including the Royal Artillery Hunt, The King's Troop Royal Horse Artillery, and the British Horse Society. She won the painting prize at this year's AFAS exhibition at the Mall Galleries for her equestrian watercolour study Hosing Down RHA.

Pigsty Studio also produces illustrations for publications and cartoons under the name of Nik and also works in graphic art and book design.

Nicola is a qualified BHSAI and has worked with horses both abroad and in the UK. She established the studio in 2002 and exhibits throughout the UK. She will be exhibiting with the Society of Equestrian Artists at the Mall Gallery at the beginning of September and at the Palace House, Newmarket in October.

Her work can be viewed on the website _www.pigstystudio.co.uk_

KRISTINE NASON

Kristine Nason trained as a graphic designer before becoming involved with fine-art publishing—both as an artist and a company director. Prints of her work have been marketed all over the world through publishers in the UK, Europe and the USA.

For the past ten years Kristine has concentrated on equestrian art and portrait painting. Using watercolour, she has developed a style where attention to detail and anatomical accuracy are as important as the essence of character captured in her work.

Kristine has won several awards for her portraits, and her work as an equestrian artist has featured in the Master Painters UK Showcase section of International Artist magazine. Commission prices on application.

WILLIAM NEWTON

In 1987, following eight years as a professional National Hunt jockey, William Newton returned to his first passion of sculpture. Much of his work, and one of his greatest strengths, is in the portrait sculpture of animals, in particular horses.

Besides having taken part in numerous mixed exhibitions he has held successful one man shows at Jonathan Cooper's Park Walk Gallery, London SW.

He was responsible for sculpting the prestigious trophies for both the 1998 and 1999 Vodafone Derby and Oaks - Epsom Downs.

GILL PARKER

Gill cast her first bronzes in 1983. An early association with the Sladmore Gallery led to her first one woman exhibition in November 1984. Successful exhibitions around Britain and the United States followed, as have two more solo shows with the Sladmore Gallery. Since 1985 she has lived in the small village of Upper Chute, Wiltshire

A member of the Society of Equestrian Artists, Gill won the President's Medal at their annual show in 1993. Entirely self taught, she has kept horses for many years and has an appreciation and knowledge of all aspects of the equestrian world. Gill has completed commissions of some of the greatest horses in the racing and eventing world including Dancing Brave, Rainbow Quest and Mrs Moss. Limited edition bronzes are available, commission prices on application.

K G PARKER-BARRATT

This artist started drawing at a very early age. Fascinated by the movement of a horse, he always enjoyed drawing and painting horses. He had no formal art education and was completely self-taught. In his teens he started to take an interest in the life and works of Sir Alfred Munnings and has done extensive studies on this artist. Most of his work is done in acrylic and oils.

Two years ago he moved to Penzance, Cornwall. In the short time he has lived there he has taken an interest in the local race meetings and he is now in the process of completing two paintings of St Buryan races and the Penzance Mounts Bay race meetings.

LEIGH PARRY

London born Leigh Parry attended St Martins School of Art. He now works as an illustrator and painter in oils, watercolours and pastels, specialising in equestrian events. His experience includes hunting with the Fitzwilliam and the Burghley Hunts and six years as President of the Pastel Society.

Elected a full member of the Society of Equestrian artists in 1981, his work features in collections in the UK and Europe, Canada, North America and Australia. His many awards include the Cuneo medal and he has written and illustrated articles on drawing and painting horses.

KLAUS PHILIPP

After the war, Klaus Philipp returned to the farm from which he had been evacuated and spent the majority of his time looking after the horses and competing in many competitions successfully. He used to sketch the horses on the farm and paint commissions for friends to supplement his earnings.

Klaus later joined the mounted police where he became Captain in charge of a troop of 30 horses. He continued to paint and found that his love and feel for the horse helped him to portray the animal naturally. He left the police force in 1980 and became a full-time artist. His work is highly regarded and is found in many private collections worldwide. Commission prices on application.

PHILIPPA PORLEY

A competitive rider herself on the Showing Circuit, Philippa has been painting animals professionally since graduating from Hull University in 1995. Her first love is racing, and her most notable commissions include Cheltenham Gold Cup winner Cool Dawn, Grand National winner Red Marauder, the ill-fated but memorable French Holly and Channel Four Trophy winner, Flossy. Painting in all mediums, the artist loves the challenge of capturing all aspects of Equestrianism, and her trademark is achieving an excellent likeness. Commission prices on request.

MICHAEL ROBSON

Michael was born in Beverley in 1957, a stone's throw from the racecourse. He has been drawing and painting animals from an early age and has specialised in horses and racing scenes since turning professional in 1989. Michael spends a great deal of time working on commissions and will undertake any equestrian scene–prices on application.

DIANE SARGEANT

Diane Sargeant's interest in horses began at an early age. A great love and respect of the horse was developed whilst working with them. She carried this passion with her and now, as an entirely self-taught artist, gains inspiration for her paintings by attending race meetings and point-to-points.

Diane enjoys working in a variety of media and, although her love for the horse provides the main impetus for her work, she also portrays many other subjects, including wildlife, for which she has won awards.

Her work is exhibited regularly in and around Leicestershire, and is held in high regard by collectors both abroad and in the UK. Commission prices on request.

ELIZABETH SHARP

Since leaving Art College, Elizabeths' career has centred on commissions for private and corporate clients world-wide, and collectors range from the Prince of Wales and the Duke of Rutland, to the Royal Armouries and Melton Carnegie Museum, as well as many town councils, hunts, societies and private individuals. She also produces a few non-commissioned paintings annually which are exhibited locally, or in London Galleries such as the Mall, Tryon, Westminster and Christies.

An elected full member of the Society of Women Artists, and the Society of Equestrian Artists for many years, Elizabeth has served on both the Executive Committee, and the selection panel for the London exhibitions of the latter. She has also won several prestigious international art awards. A lifelong association with horses–her favourite subject–allows her to paint these difficult animals with some authority! However, she will tackle any subject, from Historic Royals to classic cars, in oils, acrylics or bronze!

Recently Elizabeth has turned to illustrating the books of International Military History publishers 'Osprey'. To date four books have been published, with another in progress. Elizabeths' paintings are available in print and card format, hopefully soon to be available directly from her website *www.stantongraphics.co.uk*

PETER SMITH

Peter Smith was born in 1949 and has always been fascinated by horses. Having studied at the Carlisle and Glasgow Colleges of Art, he now lives near Ayr racecourse where he makes the preliminary sketches on which he bases his paintings. Originally influenced by Stubbs and Munnings, Peter's work now has a strength and directness that is completely his own. His mastery of colour is combined with the unique ability to capture on canvas the speed and movement of steeplechase racing which is his hallmark.

Frost and Reed have exhibited Peter Smith's paintings for some years in the United States and, as a result, he has a large clientele there as well as in the United Kingdom. His sole agents are Frost & Reed.

KATY SODEAU

Katy is a self-taught artist in her thirties. She originally trained and worked in architecture but became hooked on painting horses when she lived in Newmarket in the 1980s. Katy is still fascinated by the challenge of portraying the speed and excitement of horseracing in her painting.

Katy has now been working as a professional artist since 1995. She has had successful solo shows in a variety of venues around East Anglia and has exhibited at the Society of Equestrian Artists in London and Newmarket. Katy has her own website at *www.equinepainting.co.uk*

BRIAN STANLEY

Brian Stanley is a self-taught artist specialising in painting horses. He has undertaken many commissions including the famous Lloyds black horse. He exhibits locally and also in London and the Cotswolds. His paintings have sold in North America and throughout Europe and the United Kingdom.

He has won two blue ribbon awards at the Three Spires Art Show in Truro and has exhibited at the Society of Equestrian Artists. Commissions undertaken.

JACQUELINE STANHOPE

Jacqueline Stanhope's love of horse racing began when, at the age of seven, she saw Nijinsky win the Derby and the mightiest son of Northern Dancer became an enormous source of inspiration for the horse-mad little girl. An only child, with time to kill, she would while away the hours drawing and painting and already in secondary school she began selling her work. Not surprisingly, Nijinsky was the subject of that very first sale.

Academically as well as artistically gifted, she horrified everyone when leaving school at 16 to paint professionally, eschewing a potential career in medicine in the process. "I would sell paintings and drawings for a pittance in order to scrape together enough money to go racing," she remembers.

Conservative and unpretentious, she regards herself as a simple recorder of anatomy. Her enduring fascination for the mechanics and texture of animals allows her

Artist: **Elizabeth Sharp WOODLAND EXERCISE** *Courtesy of:* **The Artist**

to bring accuracy and realism to her work. "Every painting is a tribute to the animal and it makes no difference whether it is Sadler's Wells or an unwanted greyhound."

The confidence that comes with success has enabled Jacqueline to tackle larger, more complicated portraits. It was a brave decision to paint Sadler's Wells standing in front of a mirror with his own reflection and that of a ballet dancer in the background. A most remarkable feature of Jacqueline's work is the quality of her human portraits. "There is no point in spending hours capturing a horse's likeness and then ruining the picture with a poor rendition of the jockey," she says.

Jacqueline has an international profile and stages an annual solo exhibition at Tattersalls December Sales, Park Paddocks, Newmarket. More information about Jacqueline and her work can be seen on her website at _www.jstanhope-fineart.co.uk_

Jacqueline's work can be seen throughout the Flat and National Hunt seasons at Newmarket, Ascot, Royal Ascot, York, Cheltenham, Sandown. At these venues she exhibits at the 'Conversation Pieces' gallery of David Fish (webiste _www.cvps.co.uk_).

HEATHER ST CLAIR DAVIS
1937-1999

Born in the Cotswold Hills, Heather was brought up amid horses and art and, after graduating from Art College in Cheltenham, she moved to the USA, where she lived with her family on a farm in Vermont. Over the years she established a distinguished reputation as a leading contemporary equine artist. Heather's outstanding ability as a painter of landscape and her professional knowledge

of horses were fundamental to her success. She returned to England for her subjects: hunting scenes, racehorses exercising, the excitement of steeplechasing or flat racing, horses hacking home after a morning ride or quietly grazing in a sweeping Gloucestershire landscape. Her work is inspired, original and rewarding to own. Heather was a founder member of the American Academy of Equine Artists. Her work is available through her former agents, Frost & Reed.

PHILIP TOON

An entirely self-taught artist who has been painting professionally for about seven years. His main interests lie with racehorses and racing scenes. He has exhibited his work at Newbury and Warwick racecourses and many galleries up and down the country. Philip undertakes many private commissions: mainly equine, but he also covers many other subjects. Commissions are undertaken and prices are available on request.

JONATHAN TROWELL

Was born in Durham in 1938. He studied at the Sunderland College of Art and won a scholarship to the Royal Academy Schools. He received the Landseer Silver Medal for Painting, the Bronze Medal for drawing and the Sir James Knott Travelling Scholarship which enabled him to work in Spain and North Africa.

He has exhibited at the Royal Academy Summer Exhibition, the Royal Society of Portrait Painters, Young Contemporaries and the Fine Art Society. His work features in many private and public collections including those of HRH The Prince of Wales,

Culham College, Oxford, Newnham College, Cambridge, The Royal College of Art, the Imperial College, The Bank of Japan, BP, de Beers and CIBA-Geigy.

DAVID TRUNDLEY

David Trundley, born in 1949, was bred in Cambridgeshire. He grew up a keen sportsman reaching county standard at football, cricket, squash and athletics. Later, he moved to Taunton from where he paints racehorses with a passion. Most of his spare time is spent at racecourses gathering material for his paintings and the result is a delightful enthusiasm shining through his charming pictures.

David paints mostly in acrylic and adopts a fresh, impressionistic approach to his work. He exhibits at the Tryon Gallery, London. Commission prices on application.

MARTIN WILLIAMS

After gaining a BA(Hons) degree in graphic design, Martin Williams worked in the creative departments of several major advertising agencies in London.

Since painting his first equestrian subject 'by pure chance', his fine art career developed rapidly. His work is now in the collections of many leading owners, trainers and jockeys around the world and he has been paid the ultimate compliment of having his work purchased by fellow artists and sculptors.

Martin's increasing reputation is based on an impressive use of colour and the ability to capture light, mood and atmosphere in a range of media. Although specialising in racing subjects, he is also an accomplished landscape and portrait painter.

Artist: **Peter Smith FIRST SNOW OF THE YEAR** _Courtesy of:_ **Frost & Reed**

Martin has recently exhibited in Tokyo but his work can be seen on a more regular basis at Equus in Newmarket and at the Osborne Studio Gallery in London. Commission prices on application.

ALISON RUTH WILSON

Alison studied Fine Art at the Slade School in London. She then spent several years working in London as a theatre scenic artist. She is committed to the survival of the practice of teaching formal Life Drawing to art students, and for some years she worked as a part-time specialist lecturer in the subject. Although she now paints full time, she still teaches the occasional life class.

Her work is predominantly in oils, but she also works in other media such as pencil, pastel, and silverpoint; a large proportion of her work involves horses. The precise structural drawing and exacting technical standards that characterise her work make her particularly in demand for portrait commissions.

SUE WINGATE

Sue Wingate is an established equestrian artist who has painted many outstanding racehorses during her career, the most recent being Persian Punch whose portrait was chosen for publication on the Injured Jockeys Fund Christmas Card for 2004.

Many well known racehorses feature in her portfolio, including One Man, Red Rum, Desert Orchid and Dancing Brave, but in fact the artist is possibly even better known for her scenes featuring horses in landscape –paintings of horses at stud or in recreation and early mornings on the gallops. She has also painted many wintry scenes which have featured on the Christmas cards produced by her own company, Field Galleries *(www.field-galleries.co.uk)*, and which have been sold all over the world to individuals and companies with an interest in the bloodstock industry. Field Galleries was formed in 1989 and exclusively reproduces the artist's work on its selection of greetings cards and limited edition prints.

Since the artist undertakes many private commissions she is only able to exhibit occasionally–most notably in 1990 when she had a 'one man' exhibition at the Doncaster Musuem of Arts and Sciences and in whose permanent collection her painting entitled "The Spirit of the St Leger" now hangs. In 1999 she had another large exhibition in Palace House, Newmarket (a former residence of Charles II) which provided a magnificent setting for this artist's work.

SIAN WYNN

Sian comes from Yorkshire but, after many moves, is now based in Cambridgeshire trying to work around her husband, 2 daughters, assorted horses (their own and other peoples!) 2 cats and a Border Collie. Saturday morning life classes at Leeds College of Art in the late 60s convinced her that she and they were diametrically opposed, so she went to Manchester University instead, graduating in History of Art. She has been largely self taught, but has benefited immensely from attending painting and life classes at Malvern Hills College and, latterly, from membership of the Newmarket Art Group. Sian has been a Friend of the Society of Equestrian Artists since 1993 and was made an Associate in 2001. She has exhibited work in London and Newmarket.

Sian learned to draw horses at a very early age. Her Grandfather and great uncles taught her to draw (around racing pictures in the Yorkshire Post!) and introduced her to most of the horses in the vicinity–hunters and point-to-pointers in the yard of her grandfather's friend, Gunner Welburn, hackneys and riding school ponies, not to mention Bluebell, the last working horse in the village. With this early indoctrination it is hardly surprising that Sian has always loved horses. An on and off riding career began at the age of 4, but she regrets that she has never been better than a mediocre rider–and a wimp (and wouldn't dare get up on either of her daughters' horses!). For many years horses dropped out of her life and she painted very little (blame small children!). Both loves were rekindled when she began to help with Disabled Riding. Sketching at lunchtime led to her first commissions, and a chance lunchtime ride began the rot which 3 years of living in America compounded! There she had shares in a couple of nice horses, and had a lovely mare on loan. Her husband learned stoically to be a 'Horse Show Dad' (hauling trailers, holding ponies and shelling out money!) as his daughters showed a friend's hunter pony on the Midwest circuit. The sketchbook went everywhere–horse shows, deserts, mountains, caves, etc! Throughout these years the occasional sketch for a friend developed into a steady flow of commissions on both sides of the Atlantic. She continues to paint for customers in the USA and has also sent work to Malaysia and Japan.

Sian works mainly in pastel, watercolour and pencil, but occasionally in oil or acrylic. She is happy to take commissions, and can be contacted via her website: *www.sianwynn.co.uk*

*Artist: **Sue Wingate** SPRINTING AWAY Courtesy of: **The Artist***

The Spirit of Cheltenham

Put together one of the greatest occasions in the sporting and social calendar with some of the sports most compelling writers and in Trevor Jones the sports most respected equine photographer then you have a book of distinction.

The Spirit of Cheltenham from the publishing stable of The Spirit of Racing and Travelling the Turf will be a celebration that reflects all the passion, grace and sheer excitement that is the National Hunt Festival.

Over 200 photographs and provocative essays will bring to lasting memory some of those unforgettable moments on and off the racecourse. Images of those memorable last strides of Gold Cup glory will mix with shots of champions relaxing or working at home.

The build up, the party, the history and behind the scenes pictures that can only be Cheltenham will make this a one off celebratory book that should adorn the home of all lovers of the most spectacular sport that is National Hunt racing.

List price £20

**Kensington West Productions Ltd, 5 Cattle Market, Hexham,
Northumberland NE46 1NJ
Tel: 01434 609933 Fax: 01434 600066
e-mail: kensingtonwest@btconnect.com**